Praise for

A GOOD AMERICAN FAMILY

"A winner of two Pulitzer Prizes in journalism and one of our most talented biographers and historians, Maraniss has used his prodigious research skills to produce a story that leaves one aching with its poignancy, its finely wrought sense of what was lost, both in his home and in our nation."

—*The New York Times*

"Clear-eyed and empathetic, Maraniss's engrossing portrait of a patriotic, baseball-loving red reveals the complex human motivations underneath the era's clashing dogmas."

—*Publishers Weekly*, starred review

"An absorbing history of American political and cultural life in the 1940s and '50s. . . . A clear-eyed, highly personal view of a dark chapter in American history."

—*Kirkus Reviews*

"[A] beautifully realized account of an ordinary family in extraordinary circumstances and of how easily 'normal' life can be disrupted by a powerful megalomaniac with a dangerous political agenda."

—*Booklist*

"Audiences interested in the domestic implications of the Cold War will be captivated by this journalist whose patriotism was measured by actions and not exaggerated by words. . . . [An] absorbing account of Elliot's life and the lives of his family. Readers will be fascinated by their successes, failures, and tragedies."

—*Library Journal*, starred review

"Fascinating . . . engrossing . . . absorbing."

—*Minneapolis Star Tribune*

"*A Good American Family* enriches our understanding of the era through vivid, humanizing portraits of individuals on both sides of the ideological divide. . . . A tale of resilience and redemption. . . . [An] elegant, emotional, and empathetic narrative."

—*Psychology Today*

"A thoughtful, poignant, and historically valuable story of the Red Scare of the 1950s."

—*The Wall Street Journal*

"In this moment of dueling political hysterias ('The fascists are at the gates!' 'The socialists are within the gates!'), it is reassuring to remember that America has quickly recovered from some previous plunges into overheated anxiety. David Maraniss understands this. . . . His readers will admire his emotional equilibrium, and can take comfort from this story of national equilibrium lost and restored."

—George Will, author of *The Conservative Sensibility*

ALSO BY DAVID MARANISS

Once in a Great City: A Detroit Story

Barack Obama: The Story

Into the Story: A Writer's Journey through Life, Politics, Sports and Loss

Rome 1960: The Summer Olympics That Stirred the World

Clemente: The Passion and Grace of Baseball's Last Hero

*They Marched into Sunlight: War and Peace,
Vietnam and America, October 1967*

When Pride Still Mattered: A Life of Vince Lombardi

*The Clinton Enigma: A Four-and-a-Half-Minute
Speech Reveals This President's Entire Life*

First in His Class: A Biography of Bill Clinton

The Prince of Tennessee: Al Gore Meets His Fate (with Ellen Nakashima)

"Tell Newt to Shut Up!" (with Michael Weisskopf)

The Red Scare
and My Father

A
Good
American
Family

David Maraniss

Simon & Schuster Paperbacks

NEW YORK   LONDON   TORONTO
SYDNEY   NEW DELHI

Simon & Schuster Paperbacks
An Imprint of Simon & Schuster Inc.
1230 Avenue of the Americas
New York, NY 10020

First Simon & Schuster trade paperback edition November 2020

SIMON & SCHUSTER PAPERBACKS and colophon are registered trademarks
of Simon & Schuster, Inc.

For information about special discounts for bulk purchases,
please contact Simon & Schuster Special Sales at 1-866-506-1949
or business@simonandschuster.com.

The Simon & Schuster Speakers Bureau can bring authors to your
live event. For more information or to book an event, contact
the Simon & Schuster Speakers Bureau at 1-866-248-3049
or visit our website at www.simonspeakers.com.

Interior design by Paul J. Dippolito

Manufactured in the United States of America

1   3   5   7   9   10   8   6   4   2

Library of Congress Cataloging-in-Publication Data is available.

ISBN 978-1-5011-7837-5
ISBN 978-1-5011-7839-9 (pbk)
ISBN 978-1-5011-7838-2 (ebook)

To my parents, Mary and Elliott Maraniss,
with eternal gratitude

Contents

Author's Note

Think of this story as a wheel.
The hearing in Room 740 is the
hub where all the spokes connect.

But the truth, the first truth, probably, is that we are all connected, watching one another. Even the trees.

—*Arthur Miller,* Timebends

— PART ONE —

Watching One Another

1

The Imperfect S

I WAS NOT YET THREE YEARS OLD AND HAVE NO MEMORY of anything that happened that day. It was March 12, 1952. My father, Elliott Maraniss, sat at the witness table in Room 740 of the Federal Building in Detroit, where he had been subpoenaed to testify before the House Committee on Un-American Activities. As the questioning neared the end, he asked whether he could read a statement. There were several points he wanted to make about his freedoms as an American citizen, as an army veteran who had commanded an all-black company during World War II, and as a newspaperman. John Stephens Wood of Georgia, chairman of the committee, rejected this request. "We don't permit statements," Wood said. "If you have one written there, we shall be glad to have it filed with the clerk."

The chairman's denial was arbitrary. If a witness was compliant, named names, repented, and humbly sought absolution, then a statement might be allowed. But my father was not compliant. He challenged the committee's definition of what it meant to be American and invoked the Fifth Amendment in refusing to answer questions about his political activities, so his statement was submitted—unread—to the committee clerk, and from there essentially buried and forgotten. No mention was made of it in newspaper accounts the next day, nor was it included as an addendum to the hearing transcript published by the U.S. Government Printing Office months later. It was just one more document entombed in history, eventually stored in the vast collections of the National Archives in downtown Washington, the same vaulted building that holds original copies of the Declaration of Independence, the U.S. Constitution, and the Bill of Rights—the foundation trinity of the American idea.

By the time I looked at the committee's old files, sixty-three years had passed since the hearing. My father was dead, as were Chairman Wood and all the other players in that long-ago drama. But the moment came alive to me as soon as I opened a folder in Series 3, Box 32, of the HUAC files and found the statement. Three pages. Typed and dated. When I began reading the first page, it was not the writing that struck me but the physical aspect of the words on the page, starting with the first letter of the first word of the first line:

Statement of Elliott Maraniss.

That was the line, though in the original, the capital *S* of "Statement" jumped up a half-space, as capital letters on manual typewriters some-times did. And in typing his first name, it looked as though my father twice hit the neighboring *r* key instead of the *t*, and rather than x-ing it out or starting over again he had just gone back and typed two *t*'s over the *r*'s.

The pages that followed were resonant with meaning. My father was trying to explain who he was, what he believed in, and the predicament in which he found himself. But it was the composition of that prosaic first line that hit me hardest, the imperfect *S*.

This seems to be how life often works; the smallest gestures and details can assume the most significance. Now I could place myself in 1952, sitting there in Detroit as my father composed his statement only days after being fired from his newspaper job in the wake of a subpoena and the testimony of an FBI informant who had identified him as a member, or former member, of the local Communist Party. I could see my dad at the typewriter, a place where I had watched him so often in later years. He was a hunt-and-peck typist, jabbing away at an old dusk-gray upright with his index fingers, a Pall Mall (and later Viceroy) burning beside him in a heavy glass ashtray strewn with half-smoked and twice-smoked cigarette butts. There was a certain violence and ve-locity, thrilling but harmless, to his typing. He was messy and noisy, accompanying his work with a low, vibrating hum, thinking wordlessly aloud. He punched so hard and fast that ribbons frayed and keys stuck. He slapped the carriage return with the confidence of an old-school newspaperman. He was always making typos and correcting them by x-ing them out or typing over them, like those *r*'s and *t*'s.

It is invariably thrilling to discover an illuminating document during the research process of writing a book, but in this case that sensation was overtaken by pangs of a son's regret. Looking at the typed statement, I started to absorb, finally, what I had never fully allowed myself to feel before: the pain and disorientation of what my father had endured. For decades I had desensitized myself to what it must have been like for him. I had always considered him in the moment, rarely if ever relating present circumstances to the context of his past. As much as I loved him, I had never tried to put myself in his place during those years when he was in the crucible, living through what must have been the most trying and transformative experience of his life. Until I saw the imperfect *S*.

THE RESEARCH VISITS to the National Archives came at the beginning of my long-overdue attempt to understand what had happened to my father and our family and the country during what has come to be known as the McCarthy era, named for the demagogic senator who emblemized the anticommunist Red Scare fury of the early 1950s. Joseph McCarthy himself enters this story only as a shadowy presence in the background. As far as I can tell, my father never encountered him, and McCarthy never uttered his name. Their connection was more poetic than literal. McCarthy came from Wisconsin and died in 1957. That is the same year my father emerged from five years of being blacklisted and our family's fortunes changed for the better when he was hired by the *Capital Times* in Wisconsin, a progressive Madison newspaper that made its name fighting McCarthy.

But even while McCarthy grabbed sensational headlines, the House Un-American Activities Committee, as it was commonly called (hence the acronym HUAC), was closer to the center of it all. Committee members and staff positioned themselves as arbiters, investigators, inquisitors, judges, juries, crusaders, patriots. In Washington and at hearings on the road like the one in Detroit, their intent was to root out and publicly shame people who had been affiliated with the Communist Party. *Are you now or have you ever been . . . ?* The assumption was that a party member was indisputably unpatriotically un-American.

Un-American—a bland word construction with explosive intent, and peculiarly American at that. To accuse a citizen of France of being un-French or a Brit of being un-British or a Swiss of being un-Swiss would mean—exactly what? The first impulse might be to conjure up some innocuous stereotype of each country: the un-French not liking food, the un-British disdaining flowers, the un-Swiss afraid of heights. But the un-American label came to connote something more sinister. To be labeled un-American by the committee meant that you were considered subversive, scary, alien, spineless, spiteful, and disdainful of wholesome American traditions. You probably hated apple pie and baseball, but also had no use for democracy and were intent on the violent overthrow of the government.

I knew my father as none of those things. By the time I reached political consciousness, he had survived, adjusted, and moved on, rarely looking back. That earlier period, as my older brother, Jim, once explained to me, "was like another life, one that didn't belong to him anymore at all, just a folly, and it was a dead letter to him, and should stay dead."

My father was born in Boston in 1918 and spent most of his childhood years in Brooklyn, but once he left the East Coast to attend college in Michigan he turned into a booster of the people, places, and sensibility of Middle America—of Big Ten universities and glacier lakes with swimming beaches and dairy farmers and black earth and corn on the cob and Tigers or Cubs or White Sox or Braves games on the radio. When we moved to Madison, he brought with him only a few exotic remnants from his past, including an appetite for bagels and onions and liverwurst and the delight he took in teaching us silly tunes from his New York childhood. *The Bowery, the Bowery, they say such things and they do strange things on the Bowery, the Bowery. I'll never go there anymore.* And another that ended *Go easy on the monkey wrench, your father was a nut.* But his tastes beyond that were decidedly Middle American. He would sit in front of the television set in his big chair in the living room and watch Red Skelton play the country bumpkin Clem Kadiddlehopper and laugh so hard that he'd start coughing. Every time we drove around the curve of Lake Michigan, traveling between Madison and Ann Arbor, he'd have us recite the same ditty: *Chicken in a car and the car can't go. That's how you spell Chi-ca-go.*

In politics and journalism, he taught me to be skeptical but not cynical, to root for underdogs, think for myself, be wary of rigid ideologies, and search for the messy truth wherever it took me. So many better-known figures of the Old Left had taken other paths, either toward neoconservatism and staunch anticommunism or toward bitterness and despair, but he had done neither. He emerged as a liberal but undogmatic optimist. There was no sourness or orthodoxy in him. His favorite essayist was George Orwell, whose leftist politics were accompanied by a clear-eyed assessment of the totalitarian horrors of the left as well as the right. He was a newspaperman first and foremost, with a keen appreciation for human foibles and failings. He was generous with money, affection, encouragement, and the benefit of the doubt. He seemed tolerant of almost everything but intolerance. Hate the action, not the person, he would say; racism, not the racist. "It could be worse" was his mantra, a phrase that represented his response to daily vicissitudes but carried a meaning deeper than I realized—as did most of his teachings. It is hard for me to overstate how much of a force for good he was not only in my life and those of my siblings, but also in the lives of scores of newspaper people, professional acquaintances, and friends of the family who were heartened and encouraged by his intuitive intelligence and positive nature over many decades.

But there was a time when Elliott Maraniss was a communist. I say this without hesitation, without shame or pride. There are aspects of his thinking during that period that I can't reconcile, and will never reconcile, as hard as I try to figure them out and as much of a trail as he left for me through his writings. I can appreciate his motivations, but I am confounded by his reasoning and his choices. He wanted the reality of American life to live up to the words of the Declaration of Independence and the belief that all men are created equal. He was driven by a quest for racial and economic equality, for the betterment of humankind, and believed that capitalism had benefited the rich at the expense of working people, of that I am certain. But among other indefensible positions, how could he buy the Soviet line after the 1939 Nonaggression Pact between the Soviet Union and Nazi Germany? It was a head-spinning turnabout; suddenly the world's most ardent antifascists were talking about the need for peace in Europe and denouncing capitalist warmongers almost as loudly as they denounced Hitler. In retrospect, it seems obvious that for an extended period of his young life he was naïvely in service to rigid ideology, to the God that failed, as the title of a powerful book of essays by former communists put it. Perhaps he was even blinded by love, though I find it inadequate to attribute his involvement with communism to an attempt to please my mother, Mary Cummins Maraniss, who with her older siblings was a young communist long before meeting him.

So he was not falsely accused of being a communist because, for a time, he was one. But didn't being a citizen of this country give him the freedom to affiliate with the politics of his choosing and to write and speak his mind, as long as he didn't betray his country as a foreign agent? Wasn't there an essential radical tradition in America that was propelled by a desire not to destroy but to realize something better and fairer? Was he un-American? What does that even mean? By whose standard? Un-American compared to whom and to what?

IN MY SEARCH for answers, it seemed important to study my father's experience within the larger context of the combustible mix of other isms that shaped the middle decades of the twentieth century, including capitalism, racism, and anti-Semitism, but especially fascism and communism, the diametrically opposite political reactions to problems of the modern world that both gave rise to totalitarian systems and murderous rulers. Fascists mythologized the past, demonized outliers, and glorified military strength and will over reason; communists idealized the notion of an inevitable egalitarian future while mutating into a controlling and paranoid elite. Although my father would be the central figure in this story, my intent was not to deal with him alone, but to situate him and our family's struggle within a larger, diverse group of people who encountered one another in Room 740 of the Federal Building in Detroit during the late winter of 1952. Witnesses, lawyers, informants, politicians. What brought each of them into that hearing room? How might their actions help me understand my father? What did their stories say not just about that frightful era but about what it means to be American or un-American? The answers were to be found outside the hearing room, along winding paths through the twentieth-century world.

The cast of Americans includes Chairman John Stephens Wood, a southern Democrat who in his youth had briefly belonged to the Ku Klux Klan, had another dark secret in his past, and during his tenure in Congress supported the poll tax and opposed all attempts to desegregate private and public institutions, including the military. Another member of the committee, Republican Charles E. Potter of Michigan, had lost both legs and one testicle to a German land mine during World War II; he returned from the war as an outspoken anticommunist but later regretted the excesses of the McCarthy era, which he called "days of shame." The committee counsel, Frank S. Tavenner Jr., was a lawyer from the Shenandoah Valley of Virginia who did most of the interrogating at the hearings; before joining HUAC he had been the acting chief U.S. counsel at the Tokyo War Crimes Tribunal.

Along with my father another of the witnesses at the Detroit hearings was my uncle, my mother's older brother, Robert Cummins, who after graduating from the University of Michigan in 1937 boarded a ship to France, climbed over the Pyrenees and down into Spain, where he and other Americans joined forces with Spanish Loyalists fighting Generalissimo Francisco Franco and the fascists in the Spanish Civil War. Instead of being thanked for their service, these men were hounded by the U.S. government for years, scorned for their leftist politics and dismissed as "premature anti-fascists." Another witness was Coleman Young, a civil rights and labor activist whose unrepentant testimony at those hearings propelled him into a political life that eventually took him into the Detroit mayor's office.

My father's defense lawyer, George W. Crockett Jr., an African American, was a civil liberties advocate who was a partner in one of the first integrated law firms in the country, and earlier had represented defendants in the Foley Square trial, the seminal legal battle concerning the rights of Communist Party leaders in the United States. These men were charged, tried, convicted, and imprisoned for nothing more than being leaders of the party. Crockett and the other defense lawyers were also eventually jailed for contempt of court.

The informant who named hundreds of names at the Detroit hearing, Bereniece Baldwin, was a grandmother who had been recruited by the FBI to infiltrate the Michigan Communist Party, a secret life she carried out for nine years.

IN HIS UNREAD statement, my father refuted the committee with his own definition of being American. In what followed that imperfect S, he said that he had been a loyal citizen of the United States all of his thirty-four years, through war and peace; that he had enlisted in the army one week after Pearl Harbor and served for more than four years, ending with the Okinawa campaign, after which he was discharged as a captain; that he was a homeowner and taxpayer, husband and father of two boys and a girl; that he was taught in school to defend the principles of the Constitution and to try to secure for all Americans the blessings of peace, freedom, and economic well-being; and that for doing no more than that and exercising his right of free speech he had been fired from his job and blacklisted.

Now, he wrote, "I must sell my home, uproot my family and upset the tranquility and security of my three small children in the happy, formative years of their childhood. But I would rather have my children miss a meal or two now than have them grow up in the gruesome, fear-ridden future for America projected by the members of the House Committee on Un-American Activities. I don't like to talk about these personal things. But my Americanism has been questioned and to properly measure a man's Americanism you must know the whole pattern of his life."

As a biographer and chronicler of social history, I've spent my career trying to understand the forces that shape America and to measure individuals by the whole pattern of their lives. Before now, I had always done this by researching the lives of strangers until they became familiar to me. I would do that with some people again this time, but with a twist. One of the figures was intimately familiar to me at the start. I wondered—and worried—whether by the end my father would be more of a stranger to me. But something else happened instead. I emerged with a clearer appreciation of the contradictions and imperfections of the American story—and with a better understanding of my father, of our family and its secrets, and of myself.

2

In from the Cold

UNTIL THE MOMENT BERENIECE BALDWIN TESTIFIED BE-fore the Subversive Activities Control Board in Washington on February 12, 1952, only a handful of people knew the secret life she had been living for the previous nine years. One former husband, Harvey Baldwin, knew, as did two of her adult children and one son-in-law and several special agents at the Federal Bureau of Investigation. But the world at large had not a clue. Why was this seemingly ordinary woman testifying against communists?

Bereniece Baldwin was forty-nine years old, a grandmother with gray hair and deep circles under her eyes. Born in 1902 in Mount Pleasant, in the dead center of Michigan, she had been a Detroiter most of her life. She had quit high school before graduating, and her various jobs since then had included restaurant manager, industrial diamond cutter, teletype operator, secretary at Michigan Central Depot, bookkeeper, and licensed practical nurse. Baldwin was her third surname. Her maiden name was Bamber. Husband number one was Burnett Ashley, with whom she had three children. Number two was Baldwin. Now twice divorced, she lived inconspicuously in a modest one-story brick bungalow at 16272 East State Fair Road on the working-class East Side between Seven Mile and Eight Mile. Her neighbors considered her unremarkable. She was described as pleasant, mild-mannered, plump, and matronly, standing barely five feet, with high cheekbones that relatives attributed to her maternal grandfather's side, where the heritage was French Canadian and Cree Indian. She liked to tend her garden and care for stray cats.

When she came in from the cold on that winter morning in the nation's capital, the realization of what she had been up to caused a sensation, especially back in her home state. Her main job for nearly a decade, it turned out, had been as a paid confidential government informant infiltrating the Detroit branch of the Communist Party USA.

The Subversive Activities Control Board was one front in a vast government effort to combat communism in America during the cold war. It had been established by the McCarran Internal Security Act of 1950, a variation of legislation first drafted by Richard Nixon in the House two years earlier, and its purpose was to identify what were known as communist action organizations or communist front organizations and require them to register as foreign agents with the Department of Justice.

Bereniece Baldwin was called as a witness for the government, considered an expert on the inner workings of the party in the middle of America. She told the board that members of the Communist Party USA were trained in Marxist dogma and were expected to know and recite the "right answers" to all major economic and political issues. They learned these answers, she said, from club discussions, party schools, a bookstore, and a series of pamphlets from the state and national organizations that even the lowest-echelon party members were required to read, including *Background of the Berlin Crisis* and *The World Significance of Events in China* and *A Discussion Outline of the Marxist Position toward War*. She testified that she had attended classes over the years at the Michigan School of Social Science in Detroit, an institution established by the party to teach Marxist-Leninist or Marxist-Stalinist social doctrine, and often visited the Detroit Book Store, which later changed its name to the Progressive Book Store, located across from the party headquarters on Grand River Avenue.

When Frank DeNunzio, the deputy attorney general, who served as the government's lawyer at the Washington hearing, asked her to establish her bona fides, Baldwin presented her party membership cards and records showing her dues payments. She also recited more than twenty-five names of key leaders in the CP in Detroit and said she had hundreds more in her files from her years as party bookkeeper and dues collector.

All of this was banner headline news in the Detroit papers.

REDS IN DETROIT NAMED BY NURSE

RED ACTIVITIES IN CITY BARED

FBI SPY DESCRIBES THOUGHT CONTROL

GRANDMA'S SPY ROLE AMAZES NEIGHBORS

For the press and public in Detroit and for people who belonged to or were connected to the Communist Party in Detroit, the revelation of Baldwin's secret life served as a foretaste of what was to come. Her Washington appearance was her public debut, but her starring role as the grandma commie informer was booked for two weeks later back home, when the House Committee on Un-American Activities would arrive for two weeks of hearings on the subject "communism in the Detroit area."

Depending on one's vantage point, the prospect of her testimony in Detroit was tantalizing, exciting, or chilling. One of the hundreds of names in Baldwin's files was the name of Elliott Maraniss, who then worked on the rewrite desk of the *Detroit Times*, a Hearst-owned newspaper known for its fervent anticommunism. One can only imagine the wave of adrenalized fear that he felt when the report of her testimony came across the teletype. I can picture him standing there, perhaps hearing a conversation among colleagues about how juicy the story would be when Baldwin started ratting out all the Reds in Detroit.

IT WAS HARVEY Baldwin, her fiancé at the time, who nudged Bereniece into the confidential informant business in late November 1942. What prompted him to direct his soon-to-be wife into that unlikely line of work has never been clear. By the time she talked about her past, he was long gone; they were divorced in 1950, and soon after that she lost track of him. Her children and grandchildren, all the products of her first marriage, knew little about Harvey. Two of her grandchildren said they had been told that Bereniece divorced him because he was an abusive alcoholic. What is known from her own testimony is that during the early years of World War II she was working at a restaurant in Detroit frequented by local left-wing activists with whom she had a superficial acquaintance. One day Harvey suggested to her that the government could use her, that she might be valuable because of her secretarial skills. He persuaded her to accompany him to the FBI's Detroit Field Office, where he introduced her to an agent. Not quite the usual date for a courting couple.

After a brief conversation, the agent told them to talk to him again after they got married. The wedding took place on February 13, 1943, and in April they paid another call. This time the agent broached the subject: the FBI wanted to place an informant inside the local Communist Party. Would she be interested? At the time, Bereniece did not know "exactly what the Communist Party was." The agent suggested that she attend the next party function so that both she and the FBI could get a sense of whether being an informant was something she could handle. On May 7 the agent called to say that later that week there would be a rally in Detroit for Earl Browder, general secretary of the Communist Party USA, who was traveling the country promoting cooperation between the Soviet Union and the United States.

The Baldwins attended the rally, and when it was over, they joined the party. Two weeks later, Bereniece received her membership card in the mail along with a notice of the next meeting of Section 3, Branch 157, at an address on Michigan Avenue. That marked the beginning of her nine-year involvement with the local CP, a journey that took her from group steward to city dues collector to out-state membership secretary, and eventually custodian of all Michigan membership lists and financial records. During that time, she dropped her old-fashioned first name and went by her preferred nickname, Toby.

Baldwin's role as a paid confidential informant differed from the world of informants who joined the party out of conviction or peer pressure and then, disillusioned, fearful, weak, or angry, decided to reveal to authorities the communist affiliations or pinko taints of former friends and associates. If there was a sense of duty in what Baldwin did, it was not prompted by ideological misgivings; hers was a predetermined assignment. She was working for money—$16,717, documents would later show. As Victor Navasky aptly described it in his book *Naming Names*, this was "less a matter of betraying a friend than doing a job— dirty work though it may have been." To perform her mission, Baldwin had to be trusted as a comrade and at times an intimate friend. The line between duty and human connection inevitably blurred. She later acknowledged that she liked many of the people she was spying on. She attended the baby shower for Stephanie Allan, wife of Billy Allan, editor of the local edition of the *Daily Worker*, at a club member's home on the West Side, and made the arrangements for a fellow member's wedding at the home of Saul Wellman, a local Communist Party leader who had served with the Abraham Lincoln battalion in the Spanish Civil War. At the ceremony, she kissed the bride, whose name she later reported to the FBI.

Toby Baldwin's name and face were familiar to most Michigan communists. She attended state party conventions, New Year's Eve parties, and testimonial dinners, and she picketed outside the Federal Building to protest the deportation of Nat Ganley, a local party leader. She had contacts in virtually every club and cell. Frederick Douglass Community Group, Nat Turner Club, Whitman Club, 14th Congressional Group, Ford Section, Briggs Section, Automobile Miscellaneous, Downtown Club, Midtown Club, Delray Club, Dave White Club, Ralph Neafus Club in Ann Arbor, Iron River Club in the Upper Peninsula, the bookstore, the Michigan office of the *Daily Worker*—Baldwin was familiar with the entire network, which in trying to avoid government harassment was constantly renaming, reforming, reshaping, submerging, resurfacing, and occasionally purging.

Membership in the Communist Party USA and in the Michigan district had dropped year by year since the end of the wartime U.S.-Soviet alliance and the onset of the cold war. In a population of about 6.4 million Michiganders, there were 1,332 dues-paying CP members by the late 1940s. They were a variegated collection of outcasts and outliers, hardline ideologues and naïve dreamers who believed that communism might succeed where capitalism had failed in securing economic and racial equality and world peace. They never posed a serious threat to the American capitalist system, yet they became the objects of fear and the cause of hysteria, tracked and prosecuted as dangerous revolutionaries. For their part, many still thought of themselves as members of a transformative political vanguard, leading to a mix of inflated self-importance and intermittent paranoia.

The more responsibility Baldwin was given, the more she was put to the party loyalty test. Before she was placed in charge of membership cards in 1948, a party official called and told her that a woman she had never met would be arriving at her home and staying for the night. It appeared that this austere stranger, who would not give her name, was a party functionary who also taught at a nearby college and was sent in to check on Baldwin's reliability. Later that same year, two men from the party burst into her house and demanded to see all the records. She directed them to a filing cabinet in her bedroom, hoping they would not discover papers detailing her contacts with the FBI that were hidden in a clothes bureau nearby. As Baldwin later remembered it, one of the men interrogated her about the luxuries in her home—how could she afford that television set?—while the other took some of the records to her basement and threw them into the furnace. "Gotta be careful about old records, ya know," she recalled his telling her before the men left.

In 1951 the organizational secretary for Detroit's East Side clubs, a man named Oscar Rhodes, pulled up outside her house with a large cardboard box in the backseat of his car. He told her that the box contained important CP material that was too sensitive to keep in his office. Did she have a safe place to store it? When she suggested the attic, he agreed and went out to his car to fetch the box. But he returned empty-handed, saying that two men in a black car drove by and he was certain he was being watched by the feds. More than he knew.

IN THE FIRST weeks of 1952, staff investigators for the House Committee on Un-American Activities, who had been in Detroit on and off for several months, began the final stage of preparations for the hearings. They set up shop first at the high-rise Whittier Hotel, overlooking Belle Isle and the Detroit River, and later at the Book-Cadillac Hotel downtown. W. J. (Jackson) Jones drove around the city serving subpoenas to friendly witnesses. One of his first trips was to East State Fair, where he delivered a subpoena to Bereniece Baldwin. His colleague, Donald T. Appell, conducted most of the prehearing interviews with Baldwin and other informants. Appell was a veteran at this, having recently spent several months doing legwork for the committee's headline-grabbing spectacle out in Hollywood looking for communist influence in the film industry. Hollywood was a particular HUAC obsession, as was Broadway to a lesser degree, not because leftist artists in either place presented a serious threat to national security, but because they offered an easy means of gaining publicity and intensifying public concern and fear over the Red Menace.

Detroit was another inviting target. Here was the city that had helped win World War II when its automotive industry was transformed into an airplane and armaments factory, "the Arsenal of Democracy," as it was called. Detroit was also the heart of the American labor movement, headquarters for the United Auto Workers. While Walter Reuther, the UAW president, was a liberal anticommunist, one wing of the UAW seemed notably pink and red: its massive Local 600, representing nearly sixty thousand workers at Ford Motor Company's River Rouge plant. It was the promise of exposing communists in Local 600 that brought the committee to Detroit. Whether this was intended to strengthen or weaken the American labor movement was open to legitimate debate, a variation of the debate that continued in the progressive wing of the Democratic Party between anticommunists and the double-negative-bearing *anti*-anticommunists. But there was no doubt that the committee was depending on Bereniece Baldwin and other informants to name names inside the Local, and that miscellaneous party members named as a result were essentially collateral damage. This other group included my father and uncle.

In looking for dope on Local 600, Appell turned not only to the informant network but also to the Ford hierarchy, especially company executive John S. Bugas, who before joining the automaker had run the FBI's Detroit Field Office. It might be assumed that someone with

Bugas's history would be eager to share with the committee the names, addresses, telephone numbers, and work schedules of suspect Ford employees. So it says something about HUAC—its tactics and problematic status within the anticommunist network—that Bugas and his colleagues were a hard sell, according to internal Ford documents.

Appell paid his first visit to Bugas at Ford headquarters in Dearborn on the Tuesday afternoon of January 22. The committee, he said, understood that Ford "possessed considerable information and records regarding subversive activities, particularly within Local 600 of the UAW," and was puzzled as to why the company was not fully cooperating with the congressional inquiry. The first part of that assessment was, if anything, an understatement. Since the days of founder Henry Ford and his union-busting goon squad, led by the notorious Harry Bennett, Ford Motors had compiled voluminous files on radical union members. But Bugas remained noncommittal. He wrote in a memorandum to the file that he was "very sympathetic with the HUAC objective" but thought the committee's hunger for publicity might be counterproductive. "To expose communists usually is to drive them and their plans and manipulations deeper under-cover," he suggested. "It is my strong feeling that it is much more desirable, particularly in this 'twilight' period, which is neither peace nor war, to assist the FBI in maintaining a close watch on such bad security risks than it is to assist HUAC in sensational exposures which will serve a publicity objective but not add to the long-range security of the Ford Motor Company and its properties."

For the rest of the week, Appell kept pushing. On Friday afternoon, before catching a flight back to Washington, he placed a call from his room at the Book-Cadillac to Ford's general counsel, Gordon Walker, and persuaded Walker to meet with him early that evening. When Walker reiterated what Bugas had been saying, "Appell indicated considerable irritation," Walker wrote in a memorandum. "He stated that he could not understand the policy which we have adopted, that we had 'dug deep' to 'come up' with such reasoning and that he was sure the committee, upon learning of our attitude, would 'keenly resent' our lack of cooperation and would construe our action as an insult to a congressional committee." The committee might go so far as to publicly condemn Ford and subpoena its records, Appell said. He urged Ford to consider the consequences of that threat.

By February 12, the day the secret informant came in from the cold to offer her sensational testimony to the Subversive Activities Control Board in Washington, Bugas had finally relented. The auto company, in the end, did not want to be embarrassed by the committee, and word had come down from director J. Edgar Hoover that the FBI was co-operating fully with the hearings. So Ford began providing committee staff with internal information. Appell was told that the U.S. Marshal's Office should contact Joe Patton, supervisor of security at the River Rouge plant, and he would let them in and help them locate anyone they wanted to question. Subpoenas for Ford workers and other Detroiters identified by informants were served in the following few days. The full effect of Bereniece Baldwin's secret life would soon be evident.

I CAN MUSTER no hard feelings toward the woman who would name my father to the committee two weeks later. I have no desire to call her a rat or stoolie or any other derogatory characterization. I've read the transcript of her testimony at the Detroit hearings over and over without anger or dismay. Maybe I'm channeling my father's attitude, though he never talked to me about her. He was a forgiving person, above all. He likely would have blamed the feverish times and the hypocritical politicians on the committee, especially the segregationists, and acknowledged his own mistakes and misjudgments before taking aim at a working-class grandmother who was caught up in the maelstrom of larger world events.

There is another reason I found myself drawn to her story more out of curiosity than anger. In living a secret life for nine years, she might have experienced many of the same feelings as my father did: anxiety, a sense of displacement, of doing something outside the normal lines, of being an outsider—the *other*—while at the same time wanting to belong, to enjoy a feeling of comfort and commonality. Those seem like competing emotions, yet I know they coexisted in my father, and perhaps they do in all of us.

3

Outside the Gate

MY FATHER GREW UP ON THE OUTSIDE LOOKING IN FROM the other side of the gate. This was in Brooklyn, on the western end of Coney Island. He and his parents, Joe and Ida, and his younger sister, Celia, lived on West 36th Street near Neptune Avenue. Less than a block away was Sea Gate, a middle-class enclave, not overly fancy but a step higher in status and protected from the teeming masses by security guards and fences and high iron bars with spear tips. Many decades later, whenever our family visited Coney Island, we heard stories about how young Elliott and his pals exchanged rocks and insults through the fence with the spoiled Sea Gate boys. Not that he was envious. He was on the side he preferred.

During the Depression years of his adolescence, Coney Island was a fantasyland, wondrous and grotesque. It was still known as the Nickel Empire, an escape valve of sand and sea and boardwalk, freak show and Wonder Wheel and Nathan's Famous frankfurter, only a five-cent subway ride from Manhattan and the other boroughs. But just as it reflected the carnival excesses of a yearning populace, Coney Island could also evoke a sense of despair, with streetscapes of boarded-up windows, vacancy signs, and unemployed young men loitering on the stoops. A visit there by Federico García Lorca, the Spanish poet, inspired a haunting poem he titled "Landscape of a Vomiting Multitude"—Coney Island as a symbol of American decay.

Although my father loved the nearby ocean, an affinity for bodies of water that he carried throughout his life, he found the summer tourist season as much burden as boon during those trying times. He brought in money for the family by working boardwalk concessions, while Joe ran a small printshop. Ida, often drained from allergies and lung problems, took in itinerant strangers, hoping to charge them room and board, though Joe often insisted that guests stay free.

The living quarters were crowded and tense. "I never cared much for those summers," my father recalled later in a letter to my mother. "Boarders, congestion, and endless work and worry for my mother." This kept him out of the house as much as possible. "I remember when I was a kid—a street urchin if you will—we used to change games every season with the precise regularity of the calendar. Our 'playing field' usually remained the same—the street on which we lived—but the games changed from baseball to stickball to touch football to roller-skate hockey back to baseball. When we had a regular game, or 'challenge' as we called it, we moved over to another all-purpose playground—the beach. Swimming, by the way, was the only sport that defied the seasons: we'd take our first dip in late March and we wouldn't quit until sometime in early October."

The Boy Scouts kept him busy when he reached his teens. Troop 162 held its meetings at P.S. 80, a four-story brick fortress near 19th and Mermaid, where a janitor nicknamed Slim opened the school at night and provided them with materials that were in short supply. The Coney Island boys excelled in seashore skills, especially knot-tying and semaphore flag signaling, defeating Troop 82 from Kings Bay and Troop 250 from Columbia Heights in borough contests.

It was a bustling troop that consisted mostly of Jewish and Italian kids from the neighborhood split into three patrols. My father belonged to the Silver Fox patrol and was "dogged"—initiated—into the Ronoh Fraternity—"honor" spelled backward. He was lean and tan, smart and handsome, with jet-black hair and deep eye sockets, and anything but suave; food always found a way to stain his clothes as well as sate his appetite. My dad never was much of a handyman, but the skills he learned as a Scout stayed with him. He was proud of the precise hitch knots he could tie to secure a tarpaulin covering the suitcases atop our Rambler station wagon for the annual summer trip from the Midwest to New York; once we reached the Coney Island beach, where he had first practiced semaphore, he would whip through the hand-movement lettering again for us.

I took these gestures as small signals of belonging, or trying to belong. To what, I could not say.

Boy Scout Troop 162 attended the Wali-Ca-Zhu (what an old-fashioned, fun thing to say) Scout gala at Ebbets Field in May, the Camp-O-Ral on Staten Island in June, and Camp Calabough up along the Hudson River during the Thanksgiving break. My father boxed and played baseball for the troop teams, a counterpuncher and lefty-hitting first baseman, and wrote for the troop newspaper, the *Barker*, launching a lifelong career in journalism (a word he never liked; he thought it sounded too snooty and preferred being called "reporter" or "newspaperman" to "journalist"). He and his friend Irving Schneider formed a Fourth Estate Club that took field trips to the newsrooms and pressrooms of the city's many newspapers, including the *Brooklyn Daily Eagle* and the *New York Times*. For my father and his troopmates, children of the Depression, many of them first-generation sons of Jewish immigrants from Russia and Eastern Europe, the Boy Scouts experience helped shape their idea of what it meant to be American.

WANTING TO BELONG and feeling apart. Our last name alone starts to take me down that contradictory path. Maraniss is thought to be a variation of Marrano, or derived from it. "Marrano" was a disparaging term applied to Sephardic Jews who converted to Christianity in an effort to survive during the Spanish Inquisition, while secretly trying to maintain their Jewish beliefs and practices. That is a simplification; there were many permutations and conflicting accounts of the lives and times of Marranos, but the essence of their existence is that they were caught between different worlds.

During a trip to Spain, I found myself absorbed by the accounts of Marranos at a small Sephardic museum in the ancient Jewish quarter of Seville, an Andalusian city that long ago was a vital center of Sephardic culture. "Long ago" in this case means seven centuries ago, back to 1391, when a series of devastating pogroms were incited by the anti-Semitic rants of the region's archdeacon, a fanatic who accused Seville's Jews of poisoning wells and causing the plague. This was a full century before all Jews were expelled from Spain or forced to convert. Of those who stayed and underwent conversions, the exhibit label explained, "torn between an imposed belief and an inherited one that would be forgotten, many of them turned indifferent to religion. They saw the origin of free thought as a refuge in which knowledge, liberty, and survival were the axis of existence."

After the expulsion, thousands of Marranos left the Iberian Peninsula, first from Spain and then from Portugal, spreading out to North Africa; Amsterdam and London; Ferrara, Venice, and Pisa in Italy; Salonika in what is now Greece; Aleppo in Syria; and Constantinople and several port cities along the Black Sea. This diaspora included booksellers, binders, scribes, poets, and politicians. Among their descendants were the philosopher Baruch Spinoza in Holland, the publisher Blanco White in England, the British prime minister Benjamin Disraeli, and the American jurist Benjamin Cardozo.

My family's branch of the Marranos apparently ended up at some point in Odessa, or near Odessa, since that is where my grandfather Joseph Maraniss was born in 1888, the oldest child of Esocher and Fanny Maraniss. Once a city known to be tolerant, Odessa had been changing since a violent pogrom took place there seven years before his birth, the first of many government-incited attacks against Jews that continued in parts of Russia for the next four decades, during which at least two million Jews fled the country. Some members of the Maraniss family, with variations on the surname's spelling, fled to Colombia, others to Canada, while Joseph and his parents came to the United States, arriving at the Port of Boston when he was two. Census documents later stated incorrectly that he was born in America, though his four younger siblings were born in Boston.

This was not a happy family in the New World, and unhappy in its own, Tolstoyan way. The father was said to be a religious zealot, and the mother struggled with a mental illness that led to her being institutionalized intermittently. The children—Joe, Celia, Hyman (or Herman), Louis, and Hilda—spent parts of their childhoods in an orphanage.

Celia (for whom my father's sister was named) was the rock of stability among the siblings during those difficult years and maintained that role later, after she worked her way through Radcliffe College and eventually married a wealthy Bostonian who owned a chain of theaters. Herman showed academic brilliance as well, was accepted into Harvard at age fifteen, and had a successful career in the sound and music industry, ending up as an executive at the Victor Talking Machine Company and then RCA Victor. Joe was the black sheep. He did not attend college and married Ida Balin, an impoverished young immigrant who had arrived on a boat from Latvia as a teenager. Among other things, politics separated Joe and Herman. Herman grew conservative with success as he worked in the songwriting world of Tin Pan Alley in Manhattan and then the nascent Hollywood music scene in Los Angeles. Joe was a socialist, once a member of the Wobblies (Industrial Workers of the World), and went through several jobs, including as a circus advance man, before moving his family to Coney Island in the late 1920s and opening a printshop. The family story goes that Ida prompted the move, saying the sea breezes and salt air of Coney Island would be healthier for her and the children.

My grandfather died before I turned ten, and I have only vague memories of him. I remember that we called him Poppy (and our grandmother Bubby) and that he would tell funny stories and teach us New York ditties when we visited. He was slight compared to my father and reminded me of Jimmy Durante. I also remember that he pronounced our last name differently, with the accent on the second syllable, Muh-RAN-iss, which sounded more ethnic than accenting the first syllable, the way my father did. I think that pronunciation change was another small sign of my father's desire to mix in and belong, to Americanize. He also dropped his middle name, Spergol, the maiden name of his grandmother, Joe's troubled mother, sometimes telling us that he did not have a middle name and sometimes that, like Harry S. Truman, the S stood for nothing.

Long after Joe was gone, my father received a letter from Irving Schneider, his Boy Scout friend, who recalled how the two would occasionally perform odd jobs at the printshop, including once sorting

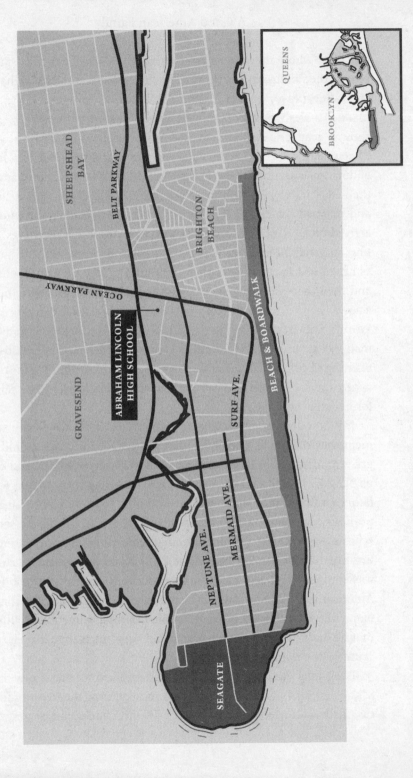

and stacking hundreds of masks of comic book characters that needed lettering on the back, meant to be premiums awarded for cereal box tops. "Your father was very kind to me," Schneider wrote. "He seemed to enjoy my interest in typography and graphic arts, and generously gave me a book he had gotten through an acquaintance in an advertising agency. It was a limited-edition, expensively made-up book."

ABRAHAM LINCOLN HIGH School was born of hope and necessity in a time of American despair. It opened its doors on Ocean Parkway less than a year after the 1929 stock market crash, when the foundation of the nation's economic system seemed to collapse. New York was undergoing a public high school building boom just then, as the sons and daughters of the city's immigrant population inundated the system. Samuel J. Tilden High in East Flatbush and John Adams High in Queens joined Lincoln as a trio of new schools in 1930, with Bayside and Grover Cleveland soon to follow, all relying on the same basic construction blueprint. In its first year Abraham Lincoln alone took in 3,500 students from Coney Island, Brighton Beach, Manhattan Beach, and up to Midwood; the demand was so great that two cohorts were formed for each class, one graduating in January, the other in June.

At the school's first assembly, Gabriel R. Mason, the principal, offered up a dreamlike, ideal vision of his new school, almost daring the Depression to darken his mood. "I would like our school to be an interesting school where not only lessons will be taught and examinations given but where dozens of extracurricular clubs will carry on their specialties in that contagiously invigorating atmosphere that prevails when interested students gather around an enthusiastic leader of personality," Mason declared. "I would like our school to be a beautiful school. I would like our school to be a democratic school. I would like our school to be a happy school where a spirit of joy and an atmosphere of good cheer will prevail."

But American life then could not be that cheery. Among Mason's first students at Abraham Lincoln was an indifferent scholar named Arthur Miller, the son of a wealthy manufacturer who had hit hard times after the stock market crash. Once, young Miller had been chauffeured to school in Manhattan in the back of a dark sedan; now he was out in Brooklyn walking from Avenue M and 3rd down to Lincoln, past drifting crowds of jobless young men. Miller thought of himself as "neither bright nor especially well read," more interested in baseball and football (a 125-pound end until he wrecked his knee) than books. But he was then and always keenly observant. Decades later, after he had emerged as a playwright, Miller reflected on the "dusting of guilt" that he saw fall upon so many failed fathers who were traumatized by the Depression and suffered "an endless death in life down to the end"—a bleak theme that would weave through many of his plays. It was only the American tendency for people to blame themselves rather than the system, Miller thought, that kept the United States from revolution during that era.

Principal Mason was a liberal thinker who belonged to the Socialist Party, but he was far from a revolutionary. He tried to use his optimism and belief in the essential goodness of humankind to overcome the turbulence of the times. He was deeply invested in the American idea as conveyed by Ralph Waldo Emerson, whom he called "the great American liberal of the nineteenth century." Roaming the marble floors of his high school, Mason carried an annotated edition of Emerson's essays in his pocket, inspired by what he called the "courageous, pioneering, upstanding Americanism that seeped into several generations of our citizens from Emerson," with his "heart-stirring, untraditional, iconoclastic words about initiative, conformity, consistency, truthtelling, prayer, and independence." To Mason, Emerson's ideas on slavery, women's suffrage, and the righteousness of the school's namesake, Abraham Lincoln, seemed as relevant in the 1930s as when they were written, as was his belief that the state was not superior to the citizen, a concept, Mason said, that "both Fascists and Communists should note."

Emerson was the first among many liberal thinkers in Mason's pantheon, which also included Lincoln, Thomas Jefferson, Henry David Thoreau, Walt Whitman, Oliver Wendell Holmes, Albert Einstein, and two men who happened to be Marranos. One was Benjamin Disraeli, the nineteenth-century British prime minister who was a Tory and liberal only in the classical sense, and the other was Baruch Spinoza, the seventeenth-century Dutch rationalist philosopher. More than the others, even more than Emerson, Spinoza was Mason's intellectual inspiration. He had come across Spinoza's writings as a senior at the City College of New York and was so taken by him that he made Spinoza the subject of his PhD thesis at New York University.

Before dying at age forty-four of a lung ailment perhaps caused by his work grinding glass lenses, Spinoza had been excommunicated from the Jewish synagogue in Amsterdam for rejecting the notion of a material God and replacing it with one rooted in nature and science. This philosophical love of a pantheist's God appealed to Mason, the son of Russian immigrants, and many other liberal Jewish intellectuals of his generation who thought of themselves as free thinkers and had become disillusioned with the Jewish orthodoxy of their parents. In 1933, when Elliott Maraniss was a sophomore at Abraham Lincoln, Mason wrote a poem about the philosopher that was published in the *Spinoza Quarterly*. "Impious wretch, vile atheist," the poem began.

> *Why hast thou forsaken the faith of the fathers?*
> *Busily grinding his lenses*
> *He heard these imprecations*
> *But he heeded them not.*
> *His thoughts were with the One,*
> *The all-absorbing, the all-inclusive God,*
> *The infinite, the eternal, the ineffable.*

The fact that a Spinoza scholar would be running a high school in New York was not unusual in that era. With both overt and covert quotas keeping many Jewish academics from attaining positions they deserved in higher education, high schools like Abraham Lincoln were staffed with scores of overqualified teachers and administrators. They also tended to be socially conscious liberals. Bertrand R. Burger, an English teacher who was an expert on Willa Cather and taught a special course in journalism, was a favorite of Irving Schneider and Elliott. Burger died before Elliott graduated, but by then the teacher had inspired him to take the step up from the *Barker* newspaper of the Boy

Scouts to the school paper, the *Lincoln Log*, where he eventually became sports editor. The notice in the *Landmark* yearbook of Burger's early death called him "an assiduous student of a society whose inadequacies he deplored and strove to perfect" and "a student of art, and life, and literature, which he approached with a zest nothing short of contagious."

The student body was as impressive as the faculty. Arthur Miller's brilliance would only become evident later, rewarding him with world fame and a Pulitzer Prize for *Death of a Salesman*. Walking Abraham Lincoln's halls during his years were two science whizzes who went on to win Nobel Prizes, Jerome Karle in chemistry and Arthur Kornberg in medicine. Teenagers share certain interests in all eras, in dating, sports, music, gossip, clothes, status, and friends, but it was difficult for the students at Abraham Lincoln in the mid-1930s to ignore the larger forces shaping their lives: the Depression, the rise of fascism and Nazism in Italy and Germany, the lingering disorienting effects of World War I, the greed and false frivolity of the Roaring Twenties, the yearning for world peace. These sobering themes were passed down to them from their teachers and principal year after year. Nearly two decades later, when Elliott's Americanism was questioned, he wrote that he was taught in school to do his part in securing peace and economic well-being for the American people. Here was the early context to that statement.

"I rejoice that you do not go out into the world in those mad days we knew five or six years ago," one of the activist teachers, Florence K. Weisberg, declared to the students in 1934, when Elliott was a sophomore. The excesses of capitalism, the worship of money, she said, had led the nation in the wrong direction. "For all the world knows now, as some knew then, that the things men strove for then were valueless; that the gilt and glamor, the tawdry trifles for which they paid so dearly, often sacrificing love and loyalty and honor, are not everlasting. . . . Bitterly disappointed in the last generation, the gods pin their faith on you."

The next year, Elliott and his schoolmates heard a bleaker message from Principal Mason. Drawing on his Emersonian ethos, he told them it would take more to right the world situation than President Franklin D. Roosevelt and his New Deal, whose reach had extended by then into the halls of the school, with its vibrant murals commissioned by the Works Progress Administration. "Our body politic is sick," Mason asserted. "We are suffering from the contagion of war, we are victims of the germs of jealousy, the bacteria of misunderstanding, the convulsions of cutthroat competition. Our little earth is seriously ill and foully diseased. To remedy the situation, we need not a few super-intellectual brain-trusters, but an alert, intelligent, socially-minded, idealistic citizenry. Such I sincerely hope you will all be, for your own good and for the honor of Lincoln."

Three years into the New Deal, the national unemployment rate still hovered near 20 percent, even higher in Brooklyn. An essential section of the school's yearbook amounted to a list of various professions that might offer graduates hope of being hired. But what Mason called "the contagion of war" seemed to weigh more heavily on their minds. Even as Hitler and Mussolini militarized the European continent, there was a strong peace movement developing in America, led by the "war babies" born during the first worldwide war who did not want to die in a second one.

This is why, as Robbie Cohen writes in his illuminating book *When the Old Left Was Young*, "during a time when economic issues were primary for most of Depression America, peace emerged as the hottest issue among college students." In New York and a few other cities, the movement also filtered down to the high schools. Elliott was a member of the Railsplitters baseball team, sports editor of the *Lincoln Log*, and a stringer for the *New York Times* (earning a salary of five dollars a week) in the spring of 1935, when the National Student League and the Student League for Industrial Democracy organized a massive student strike for peace, a walkout that drew about 175,000 participants nationwide, including 26,000 from New York City colleges and high schools, among them Abraham Lincoln.

The strike started at eleven that morning in the East and spread across the nation hour by hour, to North Carolina and Ohio State and Oberlin and Michigan and Wisconsin and Chicago and Northwestern and Minnesota and Texas and Berkeley and Stanford and UCLA and dozens of other schools. Students from several New York schools gathered near Brooklyn College, where young people marched behind large peace banners and carried signs declaring "Schools Not Battleships," "We Fight War and Fascism," "Our Lives Are at Stake," "War Funds or Schools?" Someone carried an American flag with swastikas replacing the stars.

At the high schools, the largest walkout strikes were at New Utrecht and Lincoln. The *Brooklyn Daily Eagle* reported that student demonstrators at Lincoln, joined by a few dozen mothers, marched up and down the sidewalk outside the main entrance "chanting antiwar slogans and singing strike songs loud enough to disturb classroom work." Some faculty members were supportive, especially Martha K. Feingold, who was later described in the *Landmark* yearbook as "an ardent exponent of the antiwar movement, in school and out of it." But Principal Mason, even though he was fiercely opposed to war, thought the strike was a breach of law and propriety and came out harshly against the action, which was not endorsed by the city school system. This was not the "happy school" he had envisioned. When some mothers tried to enter the building to present a resolution to Mason, he declined to see them and dispatched a detail of police, led by Capt. Henry Bauer, to block their way. In an oral history, Morton Jackson, a Lincoln student who participated in the strike, said he was stunned that Mason, a former conscientious objector to war, "took the lead in repressive actions." To Mason, it was a matter of following the rules.

This reflected a familiar split between liberals and radicals: caution versus urgency, a general liberal philosophy that relied on civic decency and goodwill versus a well-defined ideology that was more deterministic and structural. It also marked the beginning of a period of misdirection and contradiction involving the American left and the world. With noble intentions, the student peace movement was shaped by lessons from the past that were becoming increasingly irrelevant with every passing year of Hitler's rise. The movement was born from a desire not to repeat the mistakes of the Great War, a horrifically deadly international dispute involving competing capitalist factions fighting over turf and power and resources, not simply the great struggle to make the world safe for democracy that President Woodrow Wilson declared it to be. With an exception carved out for the Spanish Civil War, the argument that war benefited only capitalist profiteers dominated rhetoric on the left for the next six years and influenced the thinking of Elliott, whose attachment to the peace movement and disillusionment with the course of American capitalism began at Abraham Lincoln High and intensified in college. The thinking was that while fascism and Nazism were unspeakable evils, another worldwide war was not in the interests of the people. Until, ultimately, it was.

THE COMMENCEMENT CEREMONIES for Elliott's class were held in January 1936 at the Brooklyn Academy of Music. He finished 75th in a class of 567 midyear graduates. With excellent scores on the Regents Exam—92 in English, 91 in History, 88 in Algebra—his academic standing was good enough to get him into the University of Michigan, following a well-worn path of Jewish students from the East Coast out to the land grant universities of the Midwest, especially Michigan and Wisconsin. Arthur Miller, three years older, reached Ann Arbor before him, though Miller's grades were so mediocre that he had to sit out a year and then persuade a dean to take a chance on him. Two pleading letters finally did the trick.

Among other enticements, both Miller and Elliott were drawn to Michigan by the reputation of the *Michigan Daily*, the student paper, as well as a highly regarded English Department and the possibility that they might win an esteemed Hopwood Prize for writing that would help with tuition. Joe and Ida had no savings or disposable income to put toward their son's schooling, so the family turned to the rich relatives, Joe's brother Herman and sister Celia, to see if they might help. The most Herman would do was buy Elliott a new suit. Celia not only provided some financial assistance; she started a warm letter exchange with her nephew that would continue for his first three years at Michigan.

The final words to the Lincoln graduates came from their principal. It was a plea for liberal moderation and reverence for the American system, despite its failings. "Dear Graduates," Gabriel Mason wrote them, "because of the havoc, chaos and injustice brought on by the Depression, it is popular today to find fault with our statesmanship and our democratic system of government. To be sure, our democracy is far from perfect, but we are all mindful of the barriers, the obstacles, and the pitfalls that have bestrewn the path of progress of democracy in the age-long and incessant struggle for its ideals. If we regard our democracy as a social institution that is in the process of growth and that will have its fullest efflorescence sometime in the future, only then do our country, our constitution, and our form of government gain added significance, and only then are they entitled to our renewed loyalty and increased devotion."

It was with a belief in a better future that Elliott left Coney Island behind.

4

Red Menace

THE TRAVELING ROAD SHOW OF THE HOUSE COMMITTEE on Un-American Activities swept into Detroit on the very weekend that Elliott celebrated his thirty-fourth birthday. This was the Saturday and Sunday of February 23 and 24, 1952. The committee's hearings on communism in the Detroit region were set to begin on Monday in Judge Arthur A. Koscinski's borrowed courtroom on the seventh floor of the Federal Building. The hearings would have the trappings of a trial, with committee members posing as judge and jury and the committee counsel in the role of lead prosecuting attorney, but without most of the rights the judicial system provides the accused. No cross-examination, no pretrial discovery, no right to mount a defense. Witnesses could refuse to answer questions citing the Fifth Amendment, but the committee made sure that was interpreted as a confession of guilt.

The purpose of the hearings was to expose people whose political beliefs made them guilty of being un-American. The committee already knew who these people were. The FBI and Detroit Police Department's "Red Squad," using surveillance and a network of informants, had been chronicling their activities for years. Dossiers were kept on each of the suspected political outliers. Where they lived, the names and ages of family members, what car they drove, where they worked, what buildings they entered, what parties and functions they attended, with whom they were seen, what they wrote and said—all of it was in the files. As Charles E. Potter, the Republican congressman from northern Michigan, acknowledged, the committee knew everything, "but this will be the public's first knowledge of what is going on." It was hoped and expected, Potter said, that public exposure would "break the back" of the local Communist Party.

The House committee had not held hearings in Detroit before, although the presence of communists in their midst would not come as a surprise to the city's residents. The internal threat of the Red Menace dominated recent headlines, ever since Bereniece Baldwin's testimony in Washington two weeks earlier, and had been a sensational local story for years. In 1948 the *Detroit News* ran a series for twenty-nine straight days entitled "Communist Plot Exposed" whose plotline was that "a Communist Fifth Column was at work in the U.S. as part of Russia's vast plan for world domination." The following year, a prominent black attorney from Detroit, George Crockett, my father's lawyer, gained notice by serving on the defense team representing the eleven top leaders of the Communist Party USA, including Carl Winter of Detroit. That tumultuous 1949 trial at the Foley Square federal courthouse in Manhattan was covered day after day for months in the Detroit papers, and appeals in the case were still being heard.

Most Michiganders, like most other Americans, would have a hard time naming their congressman, but they were likely to pay attention when the press reported on communist influence among movie stars. The committee had just completed its second round of attempts to expose communists and communist sympathizers in Hollywood. Its first investigation in 1947 involved the Hollywood Ten, a group of screenwriters who gained national notice by refusing to answer the committee's questions, citing their First Amendment right to freedom of speech and assembly. For that they were charged and convicted of contempt of Congress and sent to prison. If nothing else, Detroiters could hear all about it from Hedda Hopper, the famed Red-hunting Hollywood gossip whose columns were featured several times a week in the *Free Press*. The committee's most recent report, released on February 16, focused on its second Hollywood investigation in late 1951, and also warned that the television industry and universities were vulnerable to "large-scale" communist infiltration.

All of this occurred in the larger context of cold war alarm, real and imagined. The Soviets had the atomic bomb. Julius and Ethel Rosenberg had been convicted of conspiracy to commit espionage in connection with that daunting development and were facing the death penalty. U.S. troops had been in Korea for two years fighting the communist armies of North Korea and Red China in a brutal land war. Several sensational trials revealed that some Americans had in fact worked as Soviet agents. And along came Senator Joseph McCarthy of Wisconsin as the town crier of communist infiltration of the U.S. government. An insecure publicity hound posing as the ultimate patriot, McCarthy began his campaign of reckless charges based on flimsy evidence with a relatively obscure but soon-to-be-notorious speech on February 9, 1950, in Wheeling, West Virginia. It was there that he told the Ohio County Women's Republican Club that he had "here in my hand" a list of 205 people in the State Department who were known to be in a Soviet spy ring. McCarthy had no such list in his hand, but when the press played up the story, "McCarthyism" was born.

Was America winning the cold war? That question seemed urgent when the committee arrived in Detroit to launch its hearings. Eddy Gilmore, the Associated Press correspondent in Moscow, filed a dispatch that weekend asserting that the Soviet press was answering the question with a resounding *nyet.* "There has hardly been a time when Russia's newspapers and their leading writers seemed more sure that time is on the side of the U.S.S.R. and the nations allied with her," Gilmore wrote. The Soviets were taking note of inflation and corruption in the U.S., cracks in the NATO alliance, and the independence movements in Africa, Indochina, Iraq, Iran, Malaysia, and Burma as encouraging signs for world communism.

There was also a complex political context to the anticommunist intensity of that moment. While few Democrats or Republicans wanted to be considered soft on communism, many liberals believed the right wing was using the issue as a means of dismantling the New Deal and two decades of Democratic policymaking through the administrations of FDR and Truman. And this was just the beginning. For the next half-century, Republican politicians would master the political art of appearing more patriotic than their opponents, portraying liberals as leftists and communist sympathizers if not outright Reds. Truman and the Democratic leadership found themselves on the defensive, trying to maneuver the fine line between civil liberties and political survival.

The first dispute in Detroit, as it turned out, involved not the committee and its targets but Democrats and Republicans. As soon as Chairman Wood arrived from Washington, he announced that the hearings would not be televised. He said he was acting at the direction of Sam Rayburn, Democratic speaker of the House, who had found an obscure House rule to block TV cameras from the courtroom. This came as a surprise to the national networks and disappointed the three local television stations—WWJ, WXYZ, and WJBK—who had been planning on airing the proceedings live to their three million local viewers. It enraged Republicans, who thought Rayburn's decision was a political calculation, a way to limit the publicity value the hearings would have for Potter, the Michigan Republican who was on his way to becoming his party's nominee for the open U.S. Senate seat that year.

Television was still a new medium in 1952. The networks had gone to full prime-time schedules only four years earlier, there was a paucity of daytime content, and more than half the homes in the U.S. were without sets. But Congress had already provided some of the best live entertainment around with the Kefauver hearings on organized crime, a televised real-life drama featuring Mafioso characters like Lucky Luciano and Frank Costello, revelations of crime syndicates from Manhattan to Chicago and Las Vegas. The protagonist in this drama was Estes Kefauver, a coonskin-cap-wearing Democratic senator from Tennessee, who, as David Halberstam later wrote, came across as a southern version of the actor Jimmy Stewart.

Republicans fought the Rayburn ruling vociferously. The hearings were scheduled to open at 10:30 Monday morning, but at that hour the five committee members in Detroit and their staff were huddled down the hall in the offices of Homer Ferguson, the state's Republican senator. Behind closed doors, Donald Jackson, a Republican congressman from California, pushed a resolution stating that the committee should not convene until Rayburn proved that shutting down the television coverage was within his powers. Wood, a conservative southern Democrat, not as progressive as Rayburn but still beholden to him, over-

ruled the Jackson motion. The situation was so politically sensitive that
Democrat Blair Moody, who was holding the Michigan Senate seat as a
temporary appointment by the Democratic governor since the death of
longtime Republican senator Arthur Vandenberg, placed a call to Rayburn and urged him to relent. Here again was a dilemma for Democrats.
Which would be worse: allowing Potter to get all that air time or being
portrayed as soft on communism for keeping the full story from the
widest public audience? At 11:00 a.m. Frank Tavenner, the committee
counsel, emerged from the contentious private huddle and announced
to the press that the hearing would not start until 1:30 that afternoon.
Crews from the three Detroit stations were there, waiting, with all their
equipment ready to go. More debate, more calls to Washington, and in
the end, Rayburn prevailed, as usual. He said nothing in the House rules
permitted the recording of committee sessions and that his decision
would stand unless the House changed its rules: there would be no live
coverage.

THE FBI SENT advance word to the committee that protesters would
picket outside the Federal Building and try to disrupt the proceedings inside Room 740 by packing the courtroom. The bureau knew this because
one of its informants attended a Saturday meeting of forty subpoenaed
witnesses and supporters where the protest plan was hatched. In response,
to bolster the usual retinue of federal court bailiffs, the Detroit Police Department sent over a seventeen-man detail led by Inspector Cornelius
Boyle to patrol the sidewalks and interior corridors. And to ensure that
protesters did not snag too many of the seventy-five seats available in
Judge Koscinski's courtroom, committee officials decided that most of
those seats would be reserved for government officials and lawmen.

The line for public seats began forming in the seventh-floor corridor
at eight that morning and had grown to two hundred by the time Counsel Tavenner came out to announce the delay. It was then that a guard
finally opened the courtroom door, but he allowed only fifteen spectators inside; already the benches were full. Outside on the Lafayette Street
side of the building, the first protesters were arriving and organizing

their picket line under the leadership of Arthur McPhaul, who was executive director of the Michigan chapter of the Civil Rights Congress and
a witness subpoenaed to appear later in the week. The Red Squad police
were also there, snapping photos and writing down names. "There were
approximately thirty-nine or forty persons in this picket line, which was
carried on in an orderly manner," the police noted in their after-action
report. "The following persons were recognized"—and then they listed
the names of all the protesters they could identify. In a reflection of the
times, the list had one minor annotation: "* Denotes Negro."

Elliott was not among the names on the list. He was working that
day at his newspaper job on the rewrite desk.

Two women among the orderly picketers handed out leaflets calling
the committee "most un-American of all" and urging it to get out of
town. One picketer wore the white robes and hood of the Ku Klux Klan
and carried a cardboard puppet in the likeness of Chairman Wood.
McPhaul and another man carried a large banner that outlined their
version of the "glorious history of [the] un-American committee":

1st chairman Martin Dies—Texas poll taxer
2nd chairman John Rankin—Mississippi poll taxer
3rd chairman J. Parnell Thomas—convicted New Jersey embezzler
4th chairman John Wood—Georgia Dixiecrat

The banner was provocative but mostly factual. Dies was the first
chairman of the committee, starting in 1938, when it was in fact known
as the Dies Committee. He not only supported the poll tax and other
discriminatory measures but dismissed a call for the committee to investigate the Ku Klux Klan, which he called "an old American institution." Rankin, from Mississippi, never chaired the committee but was for
many years its most bigoted member. He not only supported the poll tax
but consistently spoke disparagingly of blacks and Jews, publicly calling
them "niggers" and "kikes," along with almost all foreigners. Thomas,
a Republican from New Jersey, took over the committee in 1947 and
launched the first investigation of communist influence in the film industry. Soon thereafter he was convicted on charges of salary fraud and

kickbacks in the conduct of his House office and ended up serving an eighteen-month term at the federal prison in Connecticut. In an instance of life as burlesque, among his fellow prisoners was Ring Lardner Jr., one of the Hollywood Ten whom Thomas had helped send away.

Up and down the sidewalk picketers marched, carrying signs that were variations on the theme of the large banner.

EVERYONE IN LOCAL 600 CAN VOTE:
HOW ABOUT IN GEORGIA?

WOOD VOTED FOR POLL TAX

NEGRO-WHITE UNITY IS NOT SUBVERSIVE

WHY DON'T YOU SPEND OUR MONEY
INVESTIGATING LYNCHINGS IN FLORIDA?

When the hearing opened that afternoon, Chairman Wood read a long statement that was aggressive and defensive. He talked about how the committee once had investigated fascism and Nazism and was interested in all forms of "totalitarian 'isms' designed to overthrow by force and violence the constitutional form of government under which we live." He denied accusations that the committee was out to injure the labor movement, saying its only intent was to help certain unions rid themselves of communist domination. And then the Georgian came to the issue of race. He was a southern segregationist. Along with leftist union leaders, many of the targeted witnesses in Detroit were black activists. "You will also be told by the communists and their fellow travelers that this committee is motivated by a desire to raise racial issues," he said. "This typical propaganda effort on the part of the communists has been worn threadbare." He and his committee, Wood asserted, believed in "the basic integrity, character, and loyalty of all Americans, regardless of race and creed." For his defense, he turned to a scene involving Jackie Robinson, the great athlete who broke the color line in Major League Baseball.

In 1949 Wood and the committee had called Robinson to testify as a means of refuting the words of another prominent African American, Paul Robeson, the formidable, deep-voiced American singer, athlete, actor, and outspoken leftist partisan who never tried to hide his communist sympathies. Robeson had rejected America's position in the cold war and spoke admiringly of the Soviet Union, seeing there a hope for world peace and a contrast to the painful struggle for equality in his home country.

Jackie Robinson, in an appearance before HUAC on July 18, 1949, took issue with Robeson, and used a disparaging allusion that Chairman Wood now recited verbatim in Detroit: "I and other Americans of many races and faiths have too much invested in our country's welfare for any of us to throw it away because of a siren song sung in bass. I am a religious man. Therefore, I cherish America where I am free to worship as I please, a privilege which some countries do not give. And I suspect that nine-hundred and ninety-nine out of any thousand colored Americans you meet will tell you the same thing."

Robeson, who had been an ardent supporter of Robinson, felt betrayed by those words. The sporting and political press of America, on the other hand, wrote glowingly about Robinson, some with more support than they gave him during his brave and lonely fight to integrate baseball. Lost in the coverage, as the writer Gilbert King later pointed out, was another part of Robinson's testimony, in which he said, "The fact that because it is a communist who denounces injustice in the courts, police brutality and lynching, when it happens, doesn't change the truth of his charges." Discrimination, the racial pioneer said, was a reality, not a figment of the communist imagination.

Wood omitted that section of Robinson's testimony from his opening statement in Detroit. Considering the chairman's history, that was no surprise.

5

Wheelman Wood

AT THE TIME OF THE DETROIT HEARINGS, JOHN STEPHENS Wood was nearly twice as old as Elliott Maraniss and came from a very different place. He was born in 1885 on a farm near the hamlet of Ball Ground in the hills of north Georgia. In his region of America, the founding ideal of life, liberty, and the pursuit of happiness depended entirely upon the color of one's skin. From the year of his birth to 1930, when Wood first left Georgia to serve in Congress, at least 458 black citizens were lynched in the state. That was second only to Mississippi.

For black Georgians, the reality of inequality reached down to every level of their lives. Not only were they required by law to attend separate schools, drink from separate water fountains, ride in the back of the bus, and sit in separate areas in theaters, restaurants, and waiting rooms, but their mental patients could not be treated in the same hospitals as whites, their barbers could not cut the hair of white women, their children could not play in parks designed for white kids, and their dead could not be buried in graveyards intended for the bones of dead white people. If a birth certificate showed one parent was white and the other "colored," the State Board of Health had to report this to the state attorney general, who was required to open criminal proceedings against the offending couple. To accuse a white woman of having sexual intercourse with a black man was grounds for slander.

Blacks were kept out of the democratic process through poll taxes and ad hoc oral exams imposed on Election Day. In what essentially was a one-party state, the dominant Democratic Party maintained a segregated process called a White Primary, prohibiting black participation

altogether in the choosing of party nominees. This most blatant disen-
franchisement of African Americans was in place for most of Wood's
elections in Georgia and was not abandoned until after World War II.
All this was tolerated, accepted, enforced. None of it was considered
un-American activity.

Wood did not think of himself as privileged. He was one of fourteen children of Jesse and Sarah Holcomb Wood, who worked a small
corn and cotton farm in Cherokee County near the Etowah River. It
was only fifty-one miles due north of Atlanta, but that made it remote
enough in those days. Wood's rise out of that desolation seemed like the
mythic American success story of a politician emerging from nowhere.
From the farm, he went to live with relatives so that he could attend
public schools in Dahlonega and then go to North Georgia Agricultural College there. He was handsome and athletic and a sharp enough
student to get into law school at Mercer College in Macon. In 1910 he
was admitted to the Georgia Bar and began practicing law, first in Jas-
per, the county seat of sparsely populated Pickens County, and then
in Canton, the business hub of Cherokee County. It was there that he
connected with Newton Augustus Morris, the circuit-rider judge for
the Blue Ridge Circuit in north Georgia. Morris was a generation older
than Wood, and it seems that he became the young lawyer's mentor, or
at least at times had Wood serve as his junior wheelman, driving the
judge from town to town. That is where the story gets interesting, and
at times murky. It involves a lynching, one of the most publicized in
American history, which says something both about the incident and
about race, class, and geography in America. The man lynched in this
case was Jewish, not black, relatively wealthy, not poor, and came from
the North.

NEWT MORRIS ALSO came out of rural Cherokee County and was a
man of influence in the legal, political, and financial circles of Georgia
by the time Wood fell into his orbit. From his home base on Sugar Hill
near the town square of Marietta, twenty miles northwest of Atlanta,
Judge Newt, as he was called, launched a career in the state legislature

in 1897. He swiftly rose to leadership positions as Speaker pro tem and then Speaker of the House, where he wielded a mahogany gavel crafted from a stair rail taken from the historic Heard House, where Jefferson Davis had conducted the final meeting of the Confederate cabinet. When he left the Georgia State Capitol for the Blue Ridge judgeship in 1909, Morris was a wealthy man, a developer and construction company owner, boss of the town. People respected him or feared him or both. "A fourteen-carat son of a bitch with spare parts," one Marietta lawyer said of him.

On April 26, 1913, a murder occurred in Atlanta that stirred the passions and prejudices of Georgians like few before or since. The victim was from Marietta and her name was Mary Phagan. Although not yet fourteen, she was already holding down a job in the city, riding the streetcar to the National Pencil Company plant on South Forsyth Street to fit tiny erasers into the metal socket on pencils. On the day of her death, she had gone into the factory to pick up a paycheck. Her body was found near an incinerator in the basement. Her boss, the superintendent at the pencil factory, was Leo Frank, twenty-nine, married, Jewish, a transplant from Brooklyn, and said to be the last person in the building known to see her alive. He was charged with her murder and convicted, a finding based largely on the testimony of Jim Conley, the factory's janitor, who was also in the building that day. Conley happened to be black. The fact that a white man would be convicted on the word of a black man was highly improbable in racist Georgia, but only one of many improbable aspects to this sensational case.

Stories about the murder of Mary Phagan, the trial and conviction of Leo Frank, and Frank's many unsuccessful appeals, dominated the front pages of newspapers not only in Atlanta but in most of the South and North month after month. The *Atlanta Constitution* believed Frank guilty from the start, and its daily accounts fueled a mob mentality. The fact that so many reporters and columnists from New York and Chicago and other northern cities descended on Atlanta and questioned Frank's prosecution only heightened the animosity of the local populace. In her hometown of Marietta, and elsewhere in Georgia, Mary Phagan became the martyred symbol of white female vulnerability and innocence, a sentiment always present in southern culture but intensified in this instance by the victim's tender age. There was also a complicated mix of class friction and populism at work. Before her murder, she had already been victimized by a system that encouraged child labor, low pay, unregulated working conditions, and long workweeks. From the perspective of Frank's supporters, he was the victim of a rush to judgment fueled by a convergence of this economic resentment and anti-Semitism. The South was changing, losing some of its distinct agrarian culture, its leading cities becoming more industrialized and complicated, and a Jewish industrialist was unfairly paying the price for being a symbol of unwanted and disorienting change.

Newton Augustus Morris and John Stephens Wood had little to do with the case up to this point, other than paying attention to it like everyone else in Georgia. The trial, conviction, and sentence of capital punishment for Leo Frank played out with Judge Newt and his wheel-man on the periphery. But during the long appeals process and eventual commutation hearing, as Frank's defense team began uncovering more and more evidence showing his likely innocence and that the perpetrator was probably the prosecution's prime witness, Jim Conley, the presence of Morris started to be felt. When word spread that a private detective from the North was nosing around looking for information, a local mob in Marietta chased him down and cornered him until Judge Newt, the most powerful man in town, came upon the scene and brokered a deal. If the investigator promised to leave Marietta and never return, he could get out unharmed.

Most historians have determined that Frank was innocent and that Conley was the perpetrator. The evidence was circumstantial, and more of that circumstantial evidence pointed toward Conley than Frank. That conclusion was reinforced generations later, in 1982, when two reporters for the *Tennessean* in Nashville, Jerry Thompson and Robert Sherborne, interviewed a local man named Alonzo Mann, who seven decades earlier had worked as Frank's young office boy. Mann had testified briefly at the trial but had never been asked directly about what he had seen, and he talked about it later only with relatives, until the two reporters approached him. He told them that on that long ago April day at the pencil factory he stumbled upon Jim Conley holding the limp body of a young white girl who seemed dead. Startled that someone had caught sight of him, Conley told the office boy, "If you ever mention this, I'll kill you," Mann recalled. The *Tennessean* reporters asked Mann to take a lie detector test and psychological examination and reported that he "passed both impressively."

But whether Frank was wrongly convicted and Conley was the murderer is only tangentially relevant to the later involvement of Morris and Wood. The governor of Georgia, John Slaton, was persuaded by the defense evidence presented during the commutation process and, in an act of political courage, decided to commute Frank's death sentence. The commutation created a furor in Georgia, riling the anti-Frank mobs into action. A group was formed in Marietta calling itself the Knights of Mary Phagan, a precursor to the second coming of the Klan. The rage was fueled by the rhetoric of Tom Watson, Georgia's most well-known populist politician-journalist, who had remained relatively quiet during the trial but now was so outraged that he began campaigning for the people to take the law into their own hands. "Lynch law is a good sign," he wrote in *Watson's Magazine*. "It shows that a sense of justice lives among the people." Many of the men of Marietta agreed.

As reconstructed with meticulous detail in Steve Oney's groundbreaking book *And the Dead Shall Rise*, the plot to lynch Leo Frank was conceived and carried out by a gang of righteous hooligans orchestrated behind the scenes by some of the most powerful people in Marietta and throughout Georgia. After his death sentence was commuted, Frank was held at the state prison in Milledgeville. The lynching plotters worked it out so that everything was fixed to ease the way for the henchmen to kidnap him and hang him from a tree. In the logistics of getting the lynching party of twenty-five men and eight cars to the prison, into the prison, out of the prison, and back to Marietta, nothing was left to chance. Oney wrote, "During the past weeks, the band of 25 had made a trial run between Marietta and Milledgeville, learning which roads were passable while greasing the palms of various sheriffs. Cars were gassed, guns loaded, alibis (something about a fishing trip) were concocted and resolves firmed."

Late on the night of August 16, 1915, with the complicity of prison officials, Frank was snatched from the prison by the lynching party and thrown into the back of a car. This was the early era of automobiles. It had taken the men seven hours to drive about 120 miles from Marietta to Milledgeville, and it would take another seven hours back. News that Frank had been kidnapped spread across the state quickly as the caravan rumbled through the darkness down dusty roads on a circuitous route past one sleepy small town after another. By the time the caravan neared its destination, a large crowd had amassed in a grove at Frey's Gin on the outskirts of Marietta, and more citizens were heading there by car and horse and foot from all directions. The tree, the noose, the hanging table—all had been set up and were ready and waiting. Oney described what happened next: "With soft morning sunlight dappling down through the late-summer foliage, the vigilantes blindfolded Frank, bound his feet together, cinched a khaki cloth around his exposed lower torso, lifted him onto the table and placed the noose over his head. . . . A man identified in most reports as simply 'the leader' pronounced the court's sentence and kicked over the table. The time was 7:04." Frank fought against the suffocating of the hangman's rope so much that it took him several minutes to die, his shirt bloodied by the frantic jerking that broke open flesh on his neck. He remained there, dangling from the tree, as the grove at Frey's Gin filled with onlookers, eventually numbering over a thousand, the mob drugged with an adrenaline-fueled concoction of primal vengeance and ghoulish curiosity. To one rabble-rouser in the riotous mob, a man named Howell, Frank's hanging was insufficient. He wanted to cut the body into pieces. The mob appeared ready to partake in the mutilation.

It so happened that Judge Newt was there, with Wood at his side. He stepped from the crowd to take command with these words: "Whoever did this thing did a thorough job. Whoever did this thing left nothing more for us to do. Little Mary Phagan is vindicated. Her foul murder is avenged. Now I ask you, I appeal to you, as citizens of Cobb County in the good name of our county, not to do more. I appeal to you to let the undertaker take it."

Frank's body was cut from the tree; there were a few final kicks and shouts before it found its way to the undertaker's basket and was loaded up for the drive to the mortuary in Atlanta. It ended up in the backseat of the Model T driven by Judge Newt's wheelman, John Stephens Wood. In the car were Morris, Wood, and Rogers Winter, a reporter for the *Atlanta Journal*, which had editorialized in favor of a new trial for Frank. Winter had the firsthand scoop:

Opening wide his throttle, Wood poured his motor everything it would hold.

By his side, with drawn face and gleaming eyes, Judge Morris strained forward, peering through the dust, waving his arms and shouting for automobiles to make way.

Crosswise of the tonneau [open rear passenger compartment], the end of it projecting a foot or more on each side of the car, jostled and swayed the undertaker's long basket with the dead body inside.

Down the road toward Atlanta sped the car, and up the road toward Marietta sped automobiles loaded with men going like mad to see the body.

The car with the body gave the cars with the sightseers just enough room for the end of the basket to miss a collision, and the cars with the sightseers gave equally as little room for the car with the dead man.

Low over the road hung an endless roll of dust, and through this dust the three men in the death car would dimly see cars coming one after another, a procession of them, all speeding like racers; and the death car would swerve a little to the right to pass them, which made the basket jostle and sway and rattle, while the sightseers flashing past would wave their hands and shout hoarse shouts as they raced northward to Marietta hoping to see the body hanging in the grove.

A logical impression at this point is that the judge and his wheelman acted with noble intentions. Morris calmed the mob, averted the mutilation of Frank's body, and Wood drove fearlessly to deliver the body to the undertaker for proper burial. But then a question arises: What were Morris and Wood doing at the lynching field in the first place?

The answer had always been that they learned of it by happenstance and acted out of probity and concern. As the two men, judge and protégé, told the story to associates, they happened to be staying overnight in the town of Alpharetta on Sunday, August 16, so that Judge Morris could hear cases there the next morning, a Monday. In researching his book nearly eight decades after the event, Oney interviewed a lawyer named Herman Spence, who in Wood's later years served as his law partner. As Spence told Oney, according to notes of the interview in the files of the Georgia Historical Society, Wood explained that he had gone out for a walk early the next morning and happened to see some cars on the road to Marietta, and it appeared that "there was a sheeted figure in the middle of one." Convinced that this figure must be Leo Frank, Wood went back to the hotel and alerted Judge Newt, who said they should follow the lynching party to its destination, so they hopped in Wood's Model T.

Wood's grandson, John Gollner, offered another recollection that differs in some details but follows the same general outline. Long after Wood had retired from Congress and was living in Canton, Gollner heard a story about the Frank lynching and was so alarmed that he called his grandfather. "I called him up from Atlanta, got the maid, and told her I needed to speak to my grandfather. She said, 'You know he tries to nap in the afternoon,' and I said, 'I don't care, I need to talk to him,' and she finally drags the phone far enough to his room so he can answer it, and I say, 'Grandpa, someone just told me that you were there when Leo Frank was lynched. Is that true?' He was real quiet for a second, then he started laughing, and I was like, 'I don't think it's funny,' and he said, 'I'll see if I've got a copy of the newspaper article around here, but whoever told you that didn't read the whole story. And the judge and I were in court and heard that they had broken out and lynched him, which was what we were afraid would happen, and typically when they lynched someone they would mutilate the body, and I didn't really believe he was guilty, and neither did the judge, and we went down and cut him down and carried him down to the funeral home.'"

Milledgeville was southeast of Marietta, while Alpharetta, where Morris and Wood were preparing for court, was northeast, so it was a roundabout route that the kidnap caravan took on the way to the lynching. Oney determined that they did that on purpose, driving north to Eatonton and Lawrenceville and then turning west in Alpharetta and from there down into Marietta. This was done to avoid Atlanta and any police in the state capital who were under orders to protect Frank. And it made it appear the lynching party was just a group of men heading home from a fishing weekend in the north Georgia mountain streams. But there was another reason: so that Judge Newt could accompany them on the final leg. He was not as removed from the lynching as he wanted people to believe.

The timing of events that morning punches a few holes in the Wood-Morris version of events. Frank was lynched at 7:04. The caravan on its long and roundabout haul from Milledgeville was traveling at about eighteen miles an hour. It was about nineteen miles from Alpharetta to Frey's Gin. Wood and Morris arrived at the lynching field at the tail end of the caravan, well before Frank was hanged. If you add that time with the time it took Wood earlier to get back to the hotel and put the judge into the Model T, that places Wood going out for his morning walk well before six in the morning. In that part of Georgia in mid-August, the sun rose at seven. This means Wood was walking in darkness.

Possible, if problematic. But there is far more to it. Through documents and interviews Oney uncovered the hidden figures who were the brains and influence behind the lynching drama. Several relatives passed on information that had been kept secret while the participants were still alive. One descendant kept a Bible that had a handwritten list of the lynching plotters inside. The mayor of Marietta was in on it, a former governor was in on it, a sheriff was part of the plan, legislators and several of the business leaders in Marietta helped execute it, and at the center of it all was Newton Augustus Morris. He did not just stumble upon the lynching scene; he was essential to its planning. He had been involved in the key meetings beforehand. The lynching party did not drive by Alpharetta by accident, but to pick up the mastermind.

"It was, in its way, an extraordinary group," Oney wrote. "Yet had it not been for Judge Newt Morris, it would have been lacking in the raw nerve essential to the task under consideration. Where [others] were drunk with the idea of lynching Frank and would attempt to intoxicate both their fellow Cobb Countians and the officials in Milledgeville with the same wine, Morris was coldly sober." Some in the group, Oney wrote, thought they were doing their duty as citizens or refighting the Civil War or wreaking revenge against political opponents, but Morris was "amassing capital for future use."

Most of Marietta wanted Frank dead, and all of those who were part of the secret mission would from then on owe allegiance to Judge Newt. His final act of refusing to allow Frank's lynched body to be mutilated reflects the limits of his allowable behavior, but it also helped establish the larger alibi.

And his wheelman, his young disciple, was John Stephens Wood, the man who had the authority to question whether Elliott Maraniss was sufficiently American.

ONE YEAR AFTER he drove the Model T carrying Leo Frank's lynched body down the highway toward an Atlanta mortuary, Wood won a seat in the Georgia legislature representing Cherokee County. He ran as a populist in the Tom Watson mold, promising free schoolbooks for children and raises for teachers (white children and teachers, that is), and took office in 1917, only to resign a year later to go off to war. "With the resignation comes a vigorous expression of patriotism that is refreshing even in this day when the spirit of loyalty is sweeping the country as never before," wrote James A. Hollomon in the *Atlanta Constitution*. Hollomon quoted from Wood's letter of resignation to the governor, in which the freshman legislator said that he had hoped to get a leave from Camp Dick in Dallas, where he was a member of the 8th Cadet Flying Squadron, but was unable to unless he resigned from the service altogether, forcing him to choose. "Although I keenly appreciate the importance of the work to be done in the legislature at this time," Wood wrote, "I feel that in the present crisis every citizen should serve in the capacity that will render the maximum of benefit to the government regardless of the sacrifice on the part of the citizen."

Wood was already thirty-three when he enlisted. The army sent him from Camp Dick up to the military aeronautics school at the University of Illinois, but he never reached the battlefields overseas. When the war ended, he went home to Canton, resumed his law practice, and became what he called "sort of a joiner." He joined the Masons and the American Legion and the Great Council of the Improved Order of Red Men, the oldest secret organization in America, going back to the Tea Party in Boston—that is, oldest depending on how one defines America. Despite its name, the Order of Red Men wanted nothing to do with Native Americans; it was a white-males-only group that in the twentieth century became known for its opposition to welfare and communism. Since the murder in the pencil factory and the lynching at Frey's Gin and the emergence of the Knights of Mary Phagan, another likeminded civic group was rising in Georgia when Wood got home, one that all the leading men in Georgia were joining. So the joiner joined, writing out a check for fifteen dollars to attend an initiation meeting of the Ku Klux Klan.

By Wood's later account, that was his one and only Klan meeting. When an organizer said that he would have to wear a hood and administer punishment to anyone the KKK deemed undesirable, he left and did not return. The Klan kept his fifteen bucks, he said.

In the forgiving spirit of my father, I'd like to give Wood the benefit of the doubt. There are no records, the people are all dead, the truth hard to discern. But there is a context to consider, both what Wood would do and say later and what he already had said and done, starting with the fact that for the rest of his life he would maintain a cover story to conceal his aiding-and-abetting role with Judge Newt in the lynching of Leo Frank.

WHEN WOOD WAS first elected to the U.S. House of Representatives in 1930, the *New York Times* characterized his congressional district as perhaps the most isolated in the nation. His territory encompassed the mountains and hollows of north Georgia. Of the nineteen counties in his district, two lacked telephones, two others had no newspapers, and seven were so remote they could not be reached by railroad. From his base in Canton, Wood knew how to negotiate the winding backcountry roads all the way up to Rabun Bald Mountain near the North Carolina border, having traversed them as a solicitor and then judge on the Blue Ridge Circuit. His victory over incumbent Thomas M. Bell, who had served in Congress for a quarter-century, was attributed to the fact that he "went out among the hillbillies."

By the time of his rise to Washington, Wood was far from being the Ball Ground corn and cotton farm boy of his youth. After a failed first marriage, the second time around he had married Louise Coggins Jones, and in so doing joined the first family of Canton. Louise was the third child of the second marriage of Robert Tyre Jones Sr., known as R.T., who had eleven children by his first wife and four by his second. R.T. founded the Jones Mercantile Company, offering goods to Cherokee County farmers in exchange for cotton, then started the Canton Cotton Mill, a textile plant that served as the major employer for generations of Canton's working-class families, and from there established the Bank of Canton, known informally as "the Jones bank." He also served as councilman and mayor and had a stake in the Hotel Canton and the local newspaper. In every respect, the Jones family ran the town.

Two years after their marriage in 1926, Wood and his wife moved into a redbrick Colonial Revival nestled on an expansive estate high above the Etowah River on the edge of Canton. The home had been in the Jones family, and the deed was registered to Louise. Wood was a circuit judge then, and people in Canton referred to him as Judge Wood. Many of them spoke glowingly of his courtroom skills as lawyer and jurist, but his affiliation with the Jones family is what burnished his reputation and gave him great cachet. Among Louise's many half-brothers was Robert Permedus Jones, an Atlanta lawyer whose son was one of the most famous athletes during the Golden Age of American sports, the brilliant amateur golfer Robert Tyre Jones Jr., known to the world as Bobby Jones.

Wood also had strong connections in Marietta, a city halfway between Canton and Atlanta that was not in his congressional district but had been part of his judicial circuit and the longtime domain of his mentor, Judge Newt. Before Wood left for Washington, Marietta's legal establishment honored him at a luncheon with a luggage set for his trip north. He went to Capitol Hill as a conventional southern white politician of that era, unwavering in his opposition to desegregation and civil rights, rationalizing Jim Crow society as an expression of states' rights. He was closely allied with Richard B. Russell Jr., Georgia's new governor and a former ally in the Georgia House, who within two years would join Wood in Washington and launch a Senate career making him one of the nation's most powerful legislators.

When Russell was governor, he and his father, Richard B. Russell Sr., then chief justice of the Georgia Supreme Court, were honored along with Wood at a ceremony by the United Daughters of the Confederacy. Old man Russell was awarded the Cross of Honor, while Russell Jr. and Wood each received the Cross of Service. At the time, the United Daughters of the Confederacy was instrumental in perpetuating the myth of southern innocence, its leaders playing key roles in determining how the antebellum South and Civil War were portrayed in Georgia's textbooks: slaves were well treated, cheerful, and prosperous; slavery was not the cause of the war; Robert E. Lee was the hero, not Abraham Lincoln.

During the time when Wood had the power to deem who and what was un-American, he sought to put the best face on racism. He was unlike two of his predecessors in that respect. Former chairman Martin Dies of Texas and influential member John Rankin of Mississippi were open about their bigotry even as they chaired the committee. Wood was more genteel and defensive. Aside from asserting that he had been involved with the Klan for only one meeting and had joined only because he was a joiner, he often tried to emphasize his impartiality by citing a case he brought against alleged Klan members in Marietta when he was solicitor general on the Blue Ridge Circuit.

This was the *Hasty* case, in which the defendants were a local celebrity named Keller Hasty, a major league pitcher for the Philadelphia Athletics; two of Hasty's brothers, Arthur and Frank; and Tom Black,

Joe Bramlett, and Parks G. Cook. The six men were charged with donning Klan hoods one night in 1923 and heading out to the highway near Smyrna in search of Mrs. Bertha Holcombe and a companion, S. H. Norton of Atlanta, whom they proceeded to "whip, flog, wound and ill-treat almost into insensibility." When Wood declared in court that he intended to "prosecute this flogging case to the full extent of the law, regardless of the affiliation of any of the parties concerned," he earned the editorial praise of the *Atlanta Journal*, which hailed him for "protecting community and commonwealth against inroads of lawlessness." Wood and his allies used this editorial as Exhibit A of his strong character decades later, when his sentiments about the Klan came into question.

It is a low bar to gain credit for bringing a flogging case to court, but in that time and place it was rare for any cases to be brought against Klansmen, so credit where credit is due, however minimal the expectations. But there is a coda to the *Hasty* case that Wood and his supporters failed to mention. The first defendant, Parks G. Cook, claimed that he was at home in bed when the floggings occurred at 8:30 that night and denied that he ever wore a mask or was a member of the Klan. Bertha Holcombe clearly identified him, but the jury did not believe her and voted for acquittal. When that happened, Solicitor Wood made a motion to dismiss all charges against the others, including the ballplayer, and the judge agreed, instructing the jury to return with verdicts of not guilty. The courthouse, according to newspaper accounts, rang with applause as the verdict was announced.

THERE WERE SECRETS in the life of Chairman Wood, as in all lives. One was the role he played as the wheelman for Newt Morris in the lynching of Leo Frank. Another was less damning but interested me just as much in a different way, revealing an odd contradiction. This was a secret that involved his relationship with his second wife, Louise Jones Wood. It was a secret known to the family, including John Gollner, one of their grandsons. Gollner had problems with his grandmother Louise. He said she was a proper southern lady who was also an alcoholic who "stayed buzzed most of the time." He thought she was a racist who never saw a need to pay her black maid and driver as long as they were provided food and shelter and who became agitated when her daughter Bobbie, John's mother, "began to express her beliefs that blacks were treated unfairly." Beyond all that, John noticed the way she treated her husband, his grandfather. It was a cold relationship, he thought. They seemed to lead separate lives, even as they stayed married.

Once, as a boy, John asked his grandfather, "Why aren't you and Grandma close?"

As he recalled, his grandfather responded, "She found out about my background and didn't like it."

What she found out about his background was that his mother was mostly Cherokee Indian. "I got the impression that he was very happy with their marriage until she found out that he had Indian blood, and she was very upset. She told him she'd never have married him had she known that and was angry at him for not telling her. In her eyes, he had shamed her in front of her friends and her family."

The chairman of the House Committee on Un-American Activities apparently was not American enough for his own wife. Or he was the wrong kind of American.

"Negro, Not Niggra"

ON THE FOURTH DAY OF TESTIMONY, THE HEARINGS IN Room 740 took a dramatic turn. What started that Monday as an investigation into communism in the Detroit area, with a focus mostly on radicals inside Local 600 of the United Auto Workers union, had turned into a profound debate about race in America. The committee itself, through its lineup of witnesses, seemed to choose this course, perhaps seeking to mitigate the fact that Jim Crow segregation in the South and inequality in all aspects of American life revealed a glaring weakness in the nation's cold war claim as the beacon of liberty.

As a northern city with a vibrant black population in the middle of America, Detroit seemed like the right place to take on this subject in 1952. With the calm, relentless questioning of Chief Counsel Tavenner, the patriotic summations from Representatives Potter and Jackson, and the powerful anticommunist testimony of the first witness in this debate, Edward N. Turner, it seemed that the committee's rhetoric and logic might prevail. By day four, after the testimony of Coleman Young, that prospect was less certain. The HUAC hearings had been turned upside down.

Turner was brought in to testify in the manner of Jackie Robinson a few years earlier, as a respected figure in the black community who had broken barriers and believed in the American system, despite all its flaws. His credentials were impeccable: undergraduate degree from Michigan, law degree from the Detroit College of Law, president of the state and local branches of the NAACP, and membership on the Mayor's Interracial Committee for the City of Detroit. He came to the hearing without a lawyer, as a friendly witness, and was permitted to say whatever he pleased, since the staff had already interviewed him and knew his message. Tavenner, who throughout the hearings served as chief inquisitor, felt obliged to go through the ritual of allegiance, asking Turner whether he was then or ever had been a member of the Communist Party. No and never, Turner responded, and with that he began his story.

Democracy in America was a work in progress, and a slow one at that, he said, noting that in Detroit, far from the Jim Crow South, blacks faced job and housing discrimination, inadequate medical and hospital services, de facto segregation in the schools, and "flagrant denial of service" in public accommodations. "I would say, frankly, that this is not a pretty picture, and it certainly does not speak well for democracy," Turner testified. "These are the unsavory parts of the American scene with which we must live daily. Mind you, they are the unfinished business—they constitute the unfinished business of democracy in this country, and they should be corrected, not just because the communists seize upon these situations to exploit them, but they should be corrected because they are morally wrong."

Then, following a script laid out for him by the committee's questions, Turner made the turn, pointing out what was right about America and wrong with communism. He testified that groups like the NAACP, along with the Urban League, Catholic Interracial Council, Jewish Community Council, Michigan Committee on Civil Rights, and Council of Churches, were able to agitate for change within the democratic system in the United States. He asserted that elected officials and the courts in response were slowly but surely advancing the cause of racial equality. And he dismissed American communists as ineffective, manipulative, and only feigning interest in the problems of minority groups, making them able to attract "only a very insignificant number of Negroes" to their cause. "It would seem to me that to associate or even to attempt to associate communism with the struggle for civil rights in America is the most dangerous mistake that could be made."

Representative Potter agreed. The only objective of the Communist Party, he said, was "to gain their ultimate objective, namely, gaining large groups for an effort to eventually overthrow our Government."

Representative Jackson concluded his questioning with a powerful statement juxtaposing the differing paths toward freedom being followed by the United States and the Soviet Union. Jackson was a former marine and public relations man who had replaced fellow Californian Richard Nixon on the committee after Nixon rose to the Senate. Progress in America might be slow, he said, "but I think that anyone who stops to realize that within the memory of living man, slaves were sold from the auction block of this country, will realize that we are moving away from the auction block, and that the Soviet Union is moving toward it. The latest figures on total camp population, penal camp population of the Soviet Union, is set between three million and perhaps as high as fifteen million. Those are men and women who have lost their liberties and lost them forever. I would certainly recommend to you, if you have not seen this, Mr. Turner, 'Slave Labor in the Soviet World' published by the free trade committee of the American Federation of Labor. It should be read, I think, by every American who wants to know what goes on behind the barbed wire."

The AFL document citied by Jackson was published in 1951 and became one of the most compelling and publicized informational weapons in the cold war struggle with the Soviet Union. In cartographic detail, it located 175 forced labor camps in the vast Soviet Gulag network and accompanied the maps with photographs and depictions of the repression in the camps. ("Gulag" is an acronym in Russian for Chief Administration of Corrective Labor Camps.) The work of the free trade committee prefigured more gruesome revelations to come, year after year, though it would be another twenty-one years before the publication of Soviet dissident writer Aleksandr Solzhenitsyn's *The Gulag Archipelago*, a dark and depressing trilogy that chronicled the daily sufferings of those consigned to Soviet labor camps.

Chairman Wood dismissed the friendly witness with a brief expression of gratitude: "The committee feels a very deep appreciation for your taking your time to come here and give us your expression of your views, and the benefit of your observations in this area." During his career, Wood had supported every form of racial segregation that Edward Turner and the NAACP condemned.

THE COMMITTEE'S INTERACTION with the first witness the next morning was decidedly less friendly. The Rev. Charles A. Hill did not appear voluntarily in Room 740, and he came accompanied by my dad's lawyer, George W. Crockett Jr. Hill was among Detroit's most renowned black preachers, a pastor in the city for thirty-five years, now leading the flock at the thousand-member Hartford Memorial Baptist Church. His story reflected the complicated nature of the American melting pot. His mother was a German American immigrant, and his father was African American, a dentist who left the family to practice in Chicago. Much of Hill's youth was spent in orphanages as his mother was unable to support him. In his early days as a preacher, he was an assistant at the famed Second Baptist Church in downtown Detroit, but he left there for political reasons, disturbed that the church had a cozy relationship with the Ford Motor Company that encouraged the hiring of black citizens as nonunion scabs. This marked the beginning of Hill's affiliation with labor and civil rights causes.

The Detroit Police Department's Red Squad and the FBI had been following Hill for years, keeping track of his activities, and though they had no proof that he belonged to the Communist Party, no document showing his party number, they had accumulated reams of evidence that he had worked on causes with known communists and communist front organizations. The goal on the morning of February 28 was to try to shame him into acknowledging his missteps and naming names. Hill was not inclined to do so, and he had the bulldog Crockett at his side to put the committee on the defensive.

Crockett started by pointing out that Turner, the previous day's friendly witness, was permitted to consult note cards in providing his testimony. This in effect meant that the committee had granted Turner the right to deliver a statement, so Hill should be afforded the same privilege, the attorney asserted. Wood shut him down, declaring that statements were not allowed. When Tavenner then asked the "Are you now or have you ever been" question, Crockett tried to argue that the question was immaterial since the committee had acknowledged that it had no evidence of Hill's belonging to the Communist Party. Again, Wood cut him short, stating that Crockett could consult privately with his client but was not allowed to make direct arguments to the committee. Eventually Hill declined to answer the question, citing his Fifth Amendment privileges.

"I am rather disappointed that that is your position. It was my purpose—" Tavenner responded. He got only that far into the sentence when Crockett interrupted. If he was prevented from making political statements as counsel to the witness, why wasn't Tavenner, as the committee's counsel, held to the same standard?

Chairman Wood had had enough. Crockett had a well-known history of disputatious behavior in responding to authorities he believed were trying to silence him or who were questioning the Americanism of his clients. At the very time of the Detroit hearings, remember, Crockett was facing the prospect of going to prison for contempt of court in another case in which he had defended communists.

"One more address from you to this committee will result in your expulsion from the committee room," Wood admonished. "This committee will not have its rules constantly violated in this flagrant manner, as you are undertaking to do."

Exhibit No. 1 in Tavenner's case that Hill associated with communists was the program for a testimonial dinner in Detroit honoring two top party officials. The back of the program listed Hill as a sponsor of the event.

"I have before me the program, the printed program," Tavenner said to Hill. "I hand it to you and ask you if you will identify it."

The official transcript of the hearing, published later by the U.S. Government Printing Office, notes in brackets, "[Whereupon, Mr. Crockett attempted to take the exhibit]." Reporter Fred Tew, covering the session for the *Free Press*, offered a more colorful description: "At one point in the testimony, a committee aide and Hill's attorney, George Crockett, nearly came to blows. Each held one corner of an exhibit that was being handed to Hill. They glared at each other as Chairman Wood rapped his gavel time and again for order."

For the next hour Tavenner continued his effort to connect Hill to one Communist Party activity after another while acknowledging that Hill himself was not a party member. He got nowhere, as Hill consistently and tersely refused to answer each carefully laid out question on Fifth Amendment grounds.

Near the end, it was left to Representative Jackson to denounce Hill while making the case for why a churchman should choose American democracy over communism. "Men who have the high calling of the ministry, men who are dedicated to God and to his works are today rotting in prison cells in every country in the communist orbit," Jackson said. "Their Bibles are rotting beside them. It is bad enough in these days when we are waging a war against communism, when men are dying by the thousands, that any man can commit the treason of membership in the Communist Party or of lending aid, or comfort or assistance to the Communist Party. To do so stamps them as enemies of the United States of America. For a minister, a man of the cloth, to aid and comfort or endorse or lend his assistance to communists or the Communist Party, is to compound the offense by including God Almighty in his treason."

Hill remained calm in response to this assault on his faith and loyalty. "If I might say, Mr. Chairman: What I have done, if I have violated any law, then I am willing to go into any court, meet my accuser, and be cross-examined. I have been interested in primarily one thing, and that is discrimination, segregation, the second-class citizenship that my people suffer, and as long as I live, until it is eradicated from this American society, I will accept the cooperation of anybody who wants to make America the land of the free and the home of the brave."

Mr. Jackson: I would suggest that you accept the help and
   assistance of some good, loyal Americans for a change. You
   will have a chance to meet your greatest accuser on some other
   plane.
Mr. Hill: I do it all the time.

IN HIS TOWN Crier column on Thursday morning, *Free Press* writer Mark Beltaire confessed that he had a difficult time understanding

something: "Whenever folks talk about the Communist hearings, the
same note of puzzlement comes up: 'How does a person born in America get to be a Communist? He must be nuts!' Inelegant perhaps, but
not so far off the beam. Not as far, anyway, as the person who thinks he
prefers Russia's way of life to ours. A psychiatrist who prefers anonymity diagnosed the underlying factor as 'rebellion against the parental figure.' In this case the Government. That's oversimplification, of course,
but there's a sickening quirk, a hidden frustration among most of these
characters that makes them dangerous."

Coleman Young was subpoenaed to testify that day and proved to
be the most rebellious witness of all. He brought Crockett as his lawyer,
just as Hill had, but never needed him. Twenty-two years later Young
would be elected mayor of Detroit, the first African American to run the
city, and it could be said that the reputation he carried into the mayor's
office, as a fearless fighter against the white power structure, was ignited
on the morning of February 28, 1952, inside Room 740.

Young was not quite thirty-four then, born the same year as my father. He arrived in Detroit from Alabama at age two, his family part
of the great migration of southern blacks seeking to escape Jim Crow
segregation and find work in the industrial cities of the North. As a
teenager, he was tutored in Marxist politics by his neighborhood barber, Heywood Mayben. After high school he worked a variety of jobs: at
Ford Motor Company, the post office, a dry-cleaning plant. He was fired
from Ford's, as the auto company was known in Detroit, for coldcock-
ing a company thug with an iron pipe. He was fired from the post office
for leading an organizing drive. He had served as a Negro officer in the
Army Air Corps during World War II, where he bristled at the military's
discriminatory policies and wrote articles criticizing army segregation
under the pen name "Captain Midnight." At war's end Young went to
work as an organizer in Detroit for the Congress of Industrial Organizations and by 1952 had become executive secretary of the National
Negro Labor Council.

Just as he did with Reverend Hill, Tavenner felt obliged at the start to
say that the committee's investigators had not uncovered evidence that
Young was a member of the Communist Party. Nonetheless he had to

ask, and that is when Young made it clear he was not going to follow an accommodating script.

"I refuse to answer that question, relying upon my rights under the Fifth Amendment, and, in light of the fact that an answer to such a question, before such a committee, would be in my opinion a violation of my rights under the First Amendment, which provides for freedom of speech, sanctity and privacy of political beliefs and associates," Young asserted. "And further, since I have no purpose of being here as a stool pigeon, I am not prepared to give any information on any of my associates or political thoughts."

Tavenner persisted. The committee counsel was known for being direct and hard to fluster. He came from the Shenandoah Valley of Virginia, from the segregated South, and spoke with a southern drawl. The next exchange resounded in Detroit's African American community for years and decades thereafter:

> Mr. Tavenner: You told us you were the executive secretary of the National Negro Congress . . .
> Mr. Young: That word is Negro, not Niggra.
> Mr. Tavenner: I said Negro. I think you are mistaken.
> Mr. Young: I hope I am. Speak more clearly.
> Mr. Wood: I will appreciate it if you will not argue with counsel.
> Mr. Young: It isn't my purpose to argue. As a Negro, I resent the slurring of the name of my race.
> Mr. Wood: You are here for the purpose of answering questions.
> Mr. Young: In some sections of the country, they slur . . .
> Mr. Tavenner: I am sorry. I did not mean to slur it.

From then on, the committee was mostly on the defensive, Young on the offensive. He said that HUAC, or at least its former chairman, John Rankin, had once declared the NAACP to be a subversive group and that in his opinion the committee itself was un-American. Pressed to answer whether he knew of any Communist Party activities in Detroit, he turned the question into a heated dispute over stool pigeons with Potter, Michigan's usually temperate congressman.

Mr. Young: You have me mixed up with a stool pigeon.

Mr. Potter: I have never heard of anybody stooling in the Boy Scouts.

Mr. Young: I was a member of the organization.

Mr. Potter: I don't think they are proud of it today.

Mr. Young: I will let the Scouts decide that.

Not long after that, Young took on Wood, again over a southerner saying "Niggra," this time as a way to probe deeper into the Jim Crow legacy of the chairman and his home state. The exchange began when Wood asked Young to differentiate between the National Negro Labor Council and the National Negro Congress.

Mr. Young: I would inform you, also, the word is Negro.

Mr. Wood: I am sorry. If I made a different pronouncement of it, it is due to my inability to use the language any better than I do. I am trying to use it properly.

Mr. Young: It may be due to your southern background.

Mr. Wood: I am not ashamed of my southern background. For your information, out of the 112 Negro votes cast in the last election in the little village from which I come, I got 112 of them. That ought to be a complete answer of that. Now, will you answer the question?

Mr. Young: You are through it now, is that it?

Mr. Wood: I don't know.

Mr. Young: I happen to know, in Georgia, Negro people are prevented from voting by virtue of terror, intimidation, and lynchings. It is my contention you would not be in Congress today if it were not for the legal restrictions on voting on the part of my people.

When the discussion turned to fascism and Nazism and whether Young would defend the country against foreign enemies, Potter took the lead again. By his own history, he had the most authenticity in the room. He was sitting there with prosthetic legs. But even here, Young held his own.

Mr. Potter: Mr. Young, I believe in your statement that you said
that you were in the service fighting fascism during the last
war.

Mr. Young: That is right.

Mr. Potter: Then it is proper to assume that you are opposed to
totalitarianism in any form, as I am.

Mr. Young: I fought and I was in the last war, Congressman, that
is correct, as a Negro officer in the Air Corps. I was arrested
and placed under house arrest and held in quarters for three
days in your country because I sought to get a cup of coffee
in a United States Officers Club that was restricted for white
officers only. That is my experience in the United States Army.

Mr. Potter: Let me say this, I have the highest admiration, yes, the
highest admiration for the service that was performed by
Negro soldiers during the last war. They performed brilliantly.

Mr. Young: I am sure the Negro soldiers appreciate your
admiration, Mr. Potter.

Mr. Potter: At the same time, while I am just as much opposed
to Nazism and fascism as you are, I am opposed to
totalitarianism in any form. As you well know the Communist
International as dictated from Soviet Russia is probably the
most stringent form of totalitarian government in the world
today. In case, and God forbid that it ever happens, but in
case the Soviet Union should attack the United States, would
you serve as readily to defend our country in case of such
eventuality as you did during the last war?

Mr. Young: As I told you, Congressman, nobody has had to
question the patriotism, the military valor, of the Negro
people. We have fought in every war.

Mr. Potter: I am not talking about the Negro people. I am talking
about you.

Mr. Young: I am coming to me. I am part of the Negro people. I
fought in the last war and I would unhesitatingly take up arms
against anybody that attacks this country. In the same manner,
I am now in the process of fighting against what I consider to

be attacks and discrimination against my people. I am fighting against un-American activities such as lynchings and denial of the vote. I am dedicated to that fight and I don't think I must apologize or explain it to anybody, my position on that.

When his testimony was finished, Young rose from the witness table and strode toward the rear of the chamber, surrounded by supporters and other witnesses who reached out to shake his hand and offer words of praise. He had bucked the committee in a way no one else had, and the effect was electric. Reporters were stunned and asked Tavenner and the congressmen how and why Young got such leeway to spar with his inquisitors. "It just happened," a reporter for the *Free Press* was told. The paper's story about the confrontation in Room 740 ran under the headline "Committee Loosens Reins, Defiant Witness Runs Wild." The subhead: "Fight over Terminology Bitterest of Hearing."

For days thereafter, as Coleman Young moved through the streets of Black Bottom and Paradise Valley and all the black neighborhoods in town, he was hailed as a hero. "I felt like Joe Louis home from a fight," he said later in an interview with Studs Terkel, the oral historian, in reference to the heavyweight champ who lived in Detroit. "People called out my name as I walked down the street and small crowds gathered when I stopped. Guys patted me on the back in the barber shop. That single incident endeared me to the hearts of black people. Fightin' back, saying what they wanted to say all their lives to a southern white."

THERE WERE SIX other witnesses called before the committee that day, but only one drew much press attention. "A bespectacled veteran of the Spanish Civil War and World War II defied efforts of the House un-American Activities Committee to link him with Red youth movements," the page 7 article on this witness began. "Robert Cummins, 35, of 3026 Pingree, hid behind the Constitution to evade answering questions. Cummins, jobless paint salesman and graduate of the University of Michigan in 1937, jousted frequently with Frank S. Tavenner, committee counsel. The committee learned nothing from Cummins that it had not known before he took the stand."

Michigan graduate, veteran of the Spanish Civil War; Robert Adair Cummins was my mother's older brother.

7

A New World Coming

THE LATE-NIGHT HANGOUT FOR STUDENTS WHO WORKED at the *Michigan Daily* in the 1930s was a dark and dank basement joint called Hagen's Recess Tavern on Ashley Street between Liberty and Washington. "Enjoy your beer in atmosphere," was the Ann Arbor bar's slogan, and it was advice the young journalists heeded, especially on Friday nights after the week's run of papers was done. Once a year, on a Friday evening in early May, there was a ritual at Hagen's during which the *Daily* crowd drank and partied with even more intensity. That was the night appointments for the next year were being decided: who would get reporting and subediting slots and who would make the masthead as managing editor, city editor, and editorial director. Everyone came to this annual event, from freshmen tryouts to graduating seniors, bringing individual anxieties about their futures. By the end of the night, the prodigious consumption of beer was intended to ease all concern.

At the 1937 gathering, the freshmen tryouts included Stanley M. Swinton, and among the soon-to-depart seniors was Bob Cummins, my uncle. Swinton would go on to become city editor of the *Daily* three years later, and from there launch a distinguished life in journalism. He viewed Mussolini's corpse in Italy, interviewed Ho Chi Minh in Hanoi ("Nobody will bring freedom to you, you must fight for it," Ho told him), and ended his career in New York City as vice president of the Associated Press. But before all that, in the second semester of his first year at the University of Michigan, he observed the raucous appointments night in the basement tavern. It was an evening he would not forget, largely because of one townie who had enrolled at Michigan at the bottom of the Depression four years earlier and was about to step into a wider world that seemed on the brink of frightful collapse.

The seniors were wistful about leaving a fraternal newspaper sub-culture that had defined their college existence, Swinton later wrote. And within that cohort "the picture of one is focused more sharply on my memory than any other—Bob Cummins. Brown-haired, short [five eight], alive with a strange, amusing personality he exhibited only after too much beer, the Bob of that night was a memorable person. He would leap to his feet and roar the words of 'Solidarity Forever' [the anthem of the labor movement] in a voice tremendous for one so small. And after he was finished, a slightly sodden onlooker would giggle a request for the 'Viennese Bon-Bon' and Bob would hide under the table or scuttle across the room in a feverish, intoxicated attempt to escape from view before others took up the cry. We had all had enough to drink so that it seemed tremendously funny. In a minute, Bob would peek through a crack in the door or stick his head out from under a table and, reassured that he was no longer the center of attention, rejoin us."

When the drink fest broke up at two in the morning, after "the last quarter-barrel of beer had been emptied and the manager wisely re-fused us another on credit," the raggedy *Daily* platoon staggered back to the Publications Building on Maynard Street. Lagging far to the rear were Bob and a fellow senior, Joe Mattes, the managing editor, who had stopped at Capitol Market to buy one last six-pack, and they were making their way through the dark streets belting out more verses of "Solidarity Forever."

> *Is there aught we hold in common with the greedy parasite*
> *Who would lash us into serfdom and would crush us with his might?*
> *Is there anything left to us but to organize and fight?*
> *For the union makes us strong.*

It was not just because of the things Bob did that night that Swinton remembered it so vividly. It was also because of the seriousness of what he undertook next. Within five weeks, as soon as he graduated, Bob left

Ann Arbor to fight against fascists in Spain. That part of his story was rooted in American geography and belief and then nurtured by an idealistic habit of mind on the Michigan campus.

THE CUMMINS FAMILY arose from the middle of America. This was not the setting of pastoral heartland mythology but a hard land of hard times. My grandfather, Andrew Adair Cummins, was born in a slanting one-room dugout cut into the slope of a hillside amid the wheat fields south of Cawker City in north-central Kansas. If Kansas was a prairie state, it was not a monotonous plain. The country near Cawker City had rolling hills and valleys and was "windswept, open and free," as he later described it. The year was 1887. Buffalo had roamed there only a few decades earlier, and so had the Pawnee. His parents arrived in that spot after traipsing from place to place in the aftermath of a grasshopper plague in 1874 that had driven them off a farm near Great Bend, a hundred miles to the south. Grasshoppers by the millions, vast swarms that blackened the sky to the horizon and descended like violent thunderstorms pounding the Plains.

In the Cummins lineage, that plague was not necessarily the worst horror. Andrew's father's father was said to be a plague all to himself, an irascible man out of Indiana whom "Jesus Christ himself couldn't get along with," as a family friend once lamented. This Cummins was so ornery he was likely to coldcock anyone nearby when the mood struck, and once for no reason he clobbered Andrew's father over the head with a pitchfork.

Grasshopper infestations and rugged living conditions were all part of life on the Plains. Six people lived in that one-room dugout near Cawker City: my grandfather, his three older brothers, and their parents. It was their home for a few years, until they found a rickety farmhouse where they stayed until the second of two wheat crop failures drove them off the land for good. In 1895 they bundled all their belongings into a covered wagon, tied a cow and a pony named Flora to the back, and left Cawker City for the big city of Wichita. They slept on the side of the sticky clay roads and cooked at campfires in the rain. The

180-mile trip took ten days and changed Andrew's life for the better. He excelled at school in Wichita and as an athlete, and eventually went on to the University of Kansas, where he competed as a two-miler on the track team (his nickname was "Little Cummins") and took physical education courses from James Naismith, the inventor of basketball.

He had to leave college when he ran out of money, returned for a while, and then, as a broke upperclassman, withdrew for good before graduation, but by then he had learned enough at Kansas to develop skills for his life's profession as a civil engineer. He met a diminutive blond-haired farm girl named Grace Dever, my grandmother, at one of his first jobs, at the Coleman Lamp Company in Wichita. Grace was from the Leon area in Butler County, east of Wichita and between Augusta and El Dorado, the communities where Barack Obama's maternal ancestors, the Paynes and Dunhams, lived. Her family left the state for a stretch, when her father participated in one of the Oklahoma land rushes that allowed stake claims on "unassigned" territory snatched from relocated Indians, but eventually they returned to the more familiar turf of Kansas.

After Andrew and Grace were married, the pattern of their existence evoked a variation of what came before, repeating on a larger scale the nomadic early life of Andrew's parents. With five children along the way—Bob and his twin sister, Barbara, born in 1916; a younger brother, Phil, two years later; then my mother, Mary; and the baby, Jean—they embarked on a decade-and-a-half-long journey around the Plains and Midwest. My grandfather referred to himself professionally as A. A. Cummins, civil engineer, in his constant search for work at dams and other major construction projects. At times he left the family temporarily behind; at other times his wife and children came along with him to Wisconsin, Nebraska, Ohio, Indiana, or Michigan. As a young girl, my mother accompanied him on one summer job; she remembered sleeping in a trailer in the woods near a construction site.

The Depression had cost A.A. a place to work and, by 1931, his life's savings. It also "changed his opinion about the benevolence of business, and his political orientation," my mother recalled. He transformed from a Country Club Republican into a Democrat who would vote for Roosevelt in the next presidential election. In defiance of the bleak economic conditions, he borrowed enough money from a contractor associate and an insurance policy to start his own engineering firm with partner Hawley Barnard. Cummins & Barnard specialized in the modernization of manufacturing plants with cost-effective heating and cooling systems. He and Grace chose to locate the business and their family in Ann Arbor precisely so their five children, all bright students, could attend the excellent schools there, including the university.

In one of their many stops before that, when the family lived in Evansville along the Ohio River, three of the Cummins children, led by Bob, gained recognition as Best Citizens at Campbell Elementary School, demonstrating self-control, fair play, helpfulness, industry, courtesy, cheerfulness, loyalty, kindness, reliability, and cleanliness. The Cummins clan had tempered considerably since the days of that old man who cracked the head of his son with a pitchfork. These school honors were an unprecedented achievement that brought the parents a letter of praise from John O. Chewning, the superintendent of Evansville schools. "Dear Mr. and Mrs. Cummins, Your children, Robert, Barbara and Phillip, have brought extraordinary honor to your household," Chewning wrote. Other families had produced two Best Citizens, but the Cummins family stood alone with three. "This is a remarkable testimonial to the fine influence of your home." That was in 1928. Within a decade, all three of those Best Citizens would be young radicals.

Baseball was Bob's first love. When his father was on the road, young Bob wrote him long letters that meticulously detailed the latest news in the American League and recounted ball games he had listened to on the radio. "How is the Philco radio?" he asked his dad in one letter. "Ours is slightly better, I think, since I changed the tubes around a bit. Washington comes to Detroit tomorrow. The Tigers are hitting and pitching, and I look for them to take three out of four. They are only ½ game from seventh place and 10 or 11 from the first division." On the back side of that letter, Bob, like a budding sportswriter, presented a full report on the game of the night before under the penciled all-caps headline "TIGER BATS DEFEAT RED SOX. HEAVY HITTING ENABLES TIGERS TO WIN, 9–6. BOSTON RALLY CUT SHORT."

THAT PASSION FOR the national pastime would never wane, and once Bob reached the University of Michigan he continued writing about it as a cub reporter for the *Daily*. With upperclassmen taking loftier assignments, his first bylines during his freshman year were in the sports section. He reported that more college graduates were going into the major leagues, thus raising the average age and education of ballplayers. He declared Whitey Wistert's one-hit, sixteen-strikeout game against Ohio State at Ferry Field the outstanding Wolverine sports achievement of 1934. He correctly predicted that the Detroit Tigers and St. Louis Cardinals would meet in the World Series, then turned to football for stories about the hundred-man crew that cleared snow from the seats and aisles of Michigan Stadium and spread a tarpaulin across the field before bad weather games, and how the offense was going to be led by a pint-sized 140-pound quarterback. Back to baseball the next spring, with an American League preview and a piece about Casey Stengel's Brooklyn Dodgers, a team, he concluded, that "will still be daffy and still be trying."

The *Daily* came out five mornings a week, with an after-midnight press run of 3,500 copies, written by and for Michigan students. Yet to call it a campus newspaper seems wholly inadequate. Reading through old issues from the 1930s, I was struck by the depth and breadth of its coverage, which surpassed all but a select few American newspapers. Bob's early musings on big league baseball were merely entertaining footnotes in the information-laden publication. It subscribed to the wire services and ran lengthy national and world dispatches, then supplemented those accounts with analyses from professors, scientists, and public officials. There was an earnestness to the paper's interests that reflected the seriousness of the era. Here were multipart series on the decline of southern agriculture and the menace of Hitler's Germany and the importance of federal support of theater; essays on the writers Thomas Wolfe and Richard Wright, and reviews of James T. Farrell's

Studs Lonigan trilogy. And there was uncommon talent on the staff, men—and a few women—who were future top editors of magazines, newspapers, and wire services, as well as poets, novelists, and playwrights, the most famous being Arthur Miller, who had arrived in Ann Arbor from Brooklyn a year after my uncle and joined him on the *Daily* staff, one of their many connections.

Their habitat was the second floor of the Publications Building, a redbrick and white stone structure that opened in 1932, which in the long tradition of newspaper offices almost immediately devolved into a raucous mess of stray paper, inkpots, broken chairs, cigarette butts, clacking typewriters, clanging phones, throbbing teletype machines, stale food, discarded clothes, and constant arguments. Most of the disputes were some combination of personal and political, Miller recalled. "In the thirties the building was home to every disputatious radical splinter group, along with the liberals and conservatives shouting back at them, since all political groups inevitably wanted to dominate *Daily* editorial policy on the issues of the day." Those on the left usually prevailed, but there was a communal bond among them despite ideological differences, a sense that they were all partaking in something exhilarating and important.

Life in America seemed to be changing day by day, new ideas and possibilities emerging. It was a time, Miller remembered, "when the nation, like its soil, was being blown by crazy winds." Not long before, the Michigan campus had seemed preoccupied with fraternity parties and winning football teams. "Instead, my generation thirsted for another kind of action." Labor organizing, peace actions, experimental theater, civil rights. "We . . . saw a new world coming every third morning, and some of the old residents thought we had gone stark raving mad."

For Miller, the Michigan experience had begun in the fall of 1934, when he reached Ann Arbor by bus, wobbly from the long ride from New York yet feeling reborn. He had been out of Abraham Lincoln High for more than a year, his college career delayed until he could persuade the dean of students at Michigan to let him in despite mediocre grades and an inability to pass algebra. By then he had moved beyond a teenage preoccupation with sports to other interests, mostly literature, a transition inspired during the post–high school interregnum when he lived at home and commuted by subway to a dreary warehouse job, one hand clinging to the pole, the other holding an open copy of *War and Peace*. His escape to Ann Arbor was liberating. He found the college town beautiful and comforting, just as Elliott would when he followed that same path from Abraham Lincoln High to Michigan a few years later.

To help with tuition, Miller held various jobs at school, including one that understandably haunted him. The assignment: late in the afternoon, trudge out to the ice-cube-shaped Laboratory of Vertebrate Genetics on the far edge of campus, where university scientists housed a jittering colony of mice stacked in cages up to the ceiling, and feed them rotten vegetables. What for many might already be a squeamish task was made even more unsettling, Miller later wrote, by the Pavlovian response of the tiny creatures. "Wired to each cage was an identification tag, and when the thousands of mice heard us entering the silent, tree-shrouded building, they would rush around, and the jangling of the cages would send chills up my spine." For that he was paid fifteen dollars a month.

Another job, a more typical form of college drudgery, was to wash dishes three times a day in the kitchen of the Wolverine, the cooperative restaurant for students. One of the exotic things about Miller's life in Michigan, he admitted, was that he encountered types of Americans he had not met during his youth in New York. One of his new friends came from a potato farm in the Upper Peninsula. Another was the son of an Arkansas banker. And then there was Ralph Neafus, a forestry student and varsity wrestler who grew up on a ranch near Newkirk, New Mexico, and was now standing next to Miller day after day in the Wolverine kitchen, washing dishes. Earnest and soft-spoken, wearing octagonal glasses atop a snub nose, his hair combed with a middle part, Neafus presented what Miller thought of as "a rather stolid Dutch look." He was also a budding young communist, and another link, in addition to their work at the *Daily*, between Miller and Bob Cummins.

With every passing month, these young men were turning more toward politics as themes emerged that would shape their careers:

UNIVERSITY
OF MICHIGAN
MID-CAMPUS

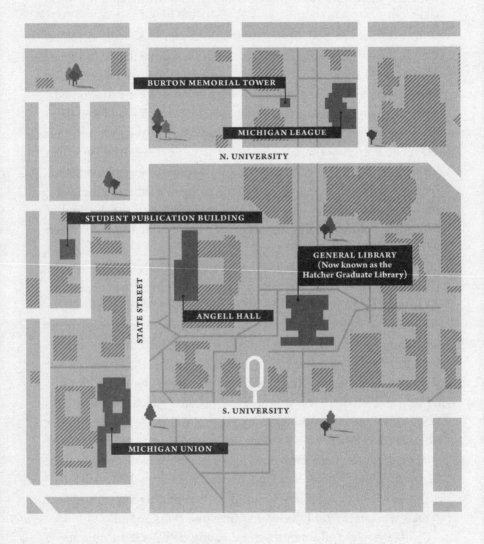

dissent, patriotism, fear, loyalty, equality, repression, and what it meant to be American. For several days in April 1935, the *Daily* editors sent Miller to the state capitol in Lansing to write about measures that would keep the Communist Party off the ballot in Michigan and make it a felony to advocate "in any way" the overthrow of the government. Similar bills were being considered around the nation and were seen by civil liberties advocates as a way for authorities to intimidate and arrest communists, student radicals, and labor organizers, depriving them of their First Amendment rights. The United Auto Workers at the time was organizing the car industry, centered in Detroit, and conservative politicians and corporate executives were fighting against unionization and trying to label the movement socialist, communist, and unpatriotic. Miller sat in the gallery among hundreds of protesters when the Michigan House debated the measures. He described how the assemblage fell silent as one opponent called the legislation "un-American" and warned that "when you suppress, you condense, and like gasoline, when it is condensed, it explodes." Miller also observed that the daily gaggle of American Legion delegates was absent from the balcony that day—a sure sign their side had the votes.

Bob Cummins had become a prominent figure in the student activist ranks by then. His father was much more moderate politically, yet stories Bob had heard about Andrew's early experiences in Kansas and around the Midwest influenced his thinking even as he rebelled against him on campus. Bob saw virtue in the working-class people of America, farmers and plant workers and small businessmen, that the system frustrated and repressed. His leftist political sentiments had emerged late in his freshman year, when he joined the Michigan Vanguard Club, composed mostly of young Marxists. The club believed that students should self-govern, that all wars were economic and should be condemned, and that "the present politico-economic system being inadequate to prevent the decline of civilization, planned worker-societies are necessary in which the real producer of goods shall be returned the real value of the goods produced."

Over the next year his grades deteriorated from A's and B's to mostly C's. He was consumed by other things as night editor at the *Daily*, a new recruit in the Young Communist League, and a leader of the Vanguard Club. That group, which later morphed into the Progressive Club, was a local affiliate of the American Student Union, the same student league that on a national level organized the Peace Day school walkout that included protesters at Abraham Lincoln High in Brooklyn, awakening students like Elliott Maraniss. On the Michigan campus, among Bob's close allies in that movement were an anthropology student named Elman Service, the Michigan-bred son of a classical violinist, and Arthur Miller's dishwashing compatriot, Ralph Neafus. They were quiet, determined young men impassioned by calls to action all around them, local and global, involving labor and peace and antifascism, a cause that soon bonded them forever.

During the summer of 1936, between Bob's junior and senior years, his attention turned to Spain, where on July 17 a band of right-wing generals led by Francisco Franco began a rebellion to overthrow the democratically elected left-leaning Republican government. The civil war that ensued drew lines that delineated the politics of the midcentury world. On Franco's Nationalist side were Mussolini's fascist Italy and Hitler's Nazi Germany, along with most of Spain's upper class and Catholic Church hierarchy. On the Republican side, the Loyalists were an uneasy coalition of government bureaucrats, peasants, workers, liberals, anarchists, and communists, bolstered by support from the Soviet Union and a diverse international brigade of young leftists. Three powerful democratic nations—France, England, and the United States—could have sided against Franco and the fascists but instead adhered to a Neutrality Pact that Germany and Italy ignored.

Arthur Miller, Bob Cummins, Ralph Neafus, Elman Service, and many of their like-minded friends were among the Michigan students who felt deeply that Franco had to be stopped. "We had been certain that if Franco could only be defeated a new world war might be averted," Miller wrote, "since a democratic Spain on Hitler's flank would act as a brake upon him, while a fascist ally would surely bring on a general European war." By that fall, with the start of the new school year, the *Daily* was running reports on Spain on its front page nearly every issue, though Miller recalled that for one brilliant Marxist student named Joe

Feldman, their coverage was inadequate. Wearing a fine tweed jacket over his pajama top, the bushy-haired Feldman stormed into the *Daily* offices one night, clambered onto a tabletop, and implored the young journalists to quit hiding behind what he called false objectivity. "What is this about planes *allegedly* flying for Franco? Are you trying to become the *New York Times* for Christ's sake?" Feldman bellowed, according to Miller's recollection. "Do we not have photographs with Nazi Germany identification on the engines? Rouse yourself from this pro-Fascist funk you're in, stop playing with yourself, and turn this into a newspaper!"

Closer to their Ann Arbor environment, in the first days of 1937 the union representing autoworkers, seeking to standardize contracts and working conditions around the country, orchestrated an ingenious sit-down strike at the General Motors Fisher Body Plant No. 2 in Flint. Two thousand workers refused to leave the factory, establishing an internal government that set down rules of behavior and made sure the strikers were fed and entertained and kept in contact with friends and supporters on the outside. The sit-down tactic, in place of outside-the-plant picketing, was conceived as a means of preventing management from bringing in strikebreakers to continue car production. Instead of scabs, on January 11 the authorities sent in the police, who, despite using tear gas and bullets, were thwarted by workers fighting back with volleys of bottles and stray car parts in what they called "the Battle of the Running Bulls." There were a few dozen injuries but no deaths, and the strike ended after forty-four days when the owners finally granted the United Auto Workers legitimacy as the exclusive bargaining agent for all General Motors plants.

During that period, Miller was getting ready to stage his first student play, *They Too Arise*, a Hopwood Prize–winning work that evoked the trying experiences of a Jewish family in New York. The father runs a small cloak factory where the workers go on strike. Professor Kenneth T. Rowe, one of the Hopwood judges, said the play had a dramatic power that went beyond its politics, revealing "a marked depth of character creation and development, particularly in the mature characters, which is unusual in the drama of so young a writer." Miller later called it the most autobiographical of his plays. As *They Too Arise* was being produced on campus, Miller was writing another play, *Honors at Dawn*, that was not produced. It was about students who organized workers in a factory and faced expulsion by the university administration, a drama that drew material from the labor organizing in Michigan and featured a character loosely resembling Ralph Neafus.

ELLIOTT WAS IN Ann Arbor by then. He had arrived for the start of the fall semester in 1936, following Miller's path from Brooklyn, though not before hitchhiking from Coney Island across the continent and halfway back. He found quarters at Wilma Nye's rooming house on Thompson Street, within easy walking distance of classes he would take at Angell Hall. Like Miller, he felt liberated by the college atmosphere. He thought he might play baseball at Michigan, but one glance at a bona fide varsity Big Ten athlete, Elmer Gedeon, who would have a brief major league career before being killed in World War II, dissuaded him, and he moved on to the more serious pursuits of journalism and politics. Along with Stan Swinton, he was among the freshmen tryouts in the basement of Hagen's on that Friday night during their second semester on campus when Bob Cummins and his comrades belted out "Solidarity Forever," their brotherly warbling no doubt inspired by the events in Flint and faraway Spain. Elliott knew of Bob as a respected old-timer on the *Daily* but was closer with his younger brother, Phil Cummins, who was the same age and in a few of the same classes.

In the days after the Flint sit-down strike, Phil joined his older brother and Neafus in the cause of establishing worker rights for Michigan students who were employed by restaurants and other establishments in town or who had found jobs through the New Deal's National Youth Administration. Neafus had recently returned to Ann Arbor after working briefly as a foreman at a Civilian Conservation Corps camp in the Nicolet National Forest in northern Wisconsin. They formed a Student Workers Federation and elected Neafus to serve as its chairman, the Cummins brothers helping with publicity. The federation started with 150 members but hoped to represent some three thousand working students in Ann Arbor. They set up a strike fund and launched their first project, a test case of sorts, involving a strike by the pin boys who worked at the Ann Arbor Recreation Center, a bowling alley on Huron Street. The pin setters were paid sixteen cents an hour and claimed that management broke an agreement to pay them four cents more.

The drama that followed took up most of a month that spring semester. When the strikers and their supporters set up a picket line outside the rec center, the police came to break it up and arrested Neafus on disorderly conduct charges. Their first justification was that demonstrators were blocking the sidewalk, making it impassable. Several witnesses, including Phil Cummins, testified in court to refute this claim, insisting that pedestrians were walking past with no trouble. The officers then said Neafus had been arrested because he did not have a permit to speak and he was drawing an unruly crowd. A six-man jury deliberated only twelve minutes before finding Neafus guilty. He was sent off to spend the night in jail. An editorial in the *Daily* the next day took note of what it characterized as the "magniloquent" closing address by the city attorney, who had argued that in the halcyon days when he was on campus, they "used to give vent to their enthusiasm by overturning trolley cars. Now instead they hold mass meetings and make all this disturbance."

Neafus was not long for Ann Arbor in any case. Nor were Bob Cummins and Elman Service. They felt an unstoppable impulse to go to Spain. While serving as Michigan delegates to the Eighth National Conference of the Young Communist League in New York that May, Bob and Neafus were recruited by two acquaintances, George Watt of Brooklyn and Danny Cohen of Trenton, New Jersey, to join the International Brigade in the fight against Franco. Service, who had been active in supporting the Spanish cause on campus, decided to join them. "It was the discovery of fascism, the discovery that freedom and democracy might be a fragile thing," Service explained later. "People just didn't believe that World War II was coming and Hitler was likely to win it. A lot of people woke up at that time. I didn't know what I was getting into."

Bob and Elman left together for New York by bus. Elman still had a year to go in school; Bob missed his own graduation. He told friends at the *Daily* what he was doing but asked them not to report it because he had told his mother that he was taking a pleasure trip to France and England. What they were doing was not only dangerous; it was against the law. The United States had not joined the fight, and Americans were banned from taking up arms if not for their country. As Stan Swinton watched Bob leave, he thought back to that evening in the basement when he had listened to the inebriated senior belt out the verses of "Solidarity Forever." It made sense now; Bob must have known what was coming next.

"There was much for Bob to leave behind. His family, friends, work in Ann Arbor's radical societies and labor movement, journalistic ambitions: these were important yet at the same time insignificant once he had seen his way," Swinton later wrote in an essay for a history class at Michigan. "Perhaps it was easier because four years of *The Daily* were over and those lusty companionships so close to his heart would have soon been terminated. That only Bob knows. A great decision must be made, one that necessitated rational thinking when rational thinking was extremely difficult. I do not know to what degree external factors affected Bob's conclusion. I do know that idealism was victorious. . . . Youth, royally bold despite its insecurity of mind, finds no jewel more intriguing than the diamond of idealism. Its gleam makes sacrifice less difficult."

Arthur Miller considered joining his pal Neafus but could not abide the idea of "not living to write a great play." He was also afraid of telling his mother in Brooklyn that he was going off to die. It never occurred to him, he acknowledged later, that he might survive. Nor did it occur to him that Neafus would leave Spain alive. Miller ended up as a driver instead, taking Neafus from Ann Arbor to catch the ship in New York that would carry him across the Atlantic. They rumbled through Ohio and New York State in Miller's cramped 1927 Model T coupe, two suitcases tied to the running board on the passenger side. The entire way, Miller was haunted by a sensation that the friend next to him, the New Mexican with the eight-sided glasses and middle-parted hair and laconic demeanor, was a dead man. At one point, on Route 17 near Buffalo, the rain was so unforgiving that Miller stopped the car by the side of the road. He decided to ask Neafus a few logistical questions. Neafus replied that he had an address to report to in the city, that the Communist Party would give him papers, and that he was pretty good with a rifle.

When they reached New York, Neafus stayed with the Millers for three days, waiting for his ship to leave. On the fourth morning, the two young men walked three blocks to the Culver Line station, where Neafus would take the subway to his meeting point. "At the turnstile Ralph glanced back and gave me a dry, silent wave and was gone into the rickety train, his heavy valise packed with all he owned in the world banging against his leg," Miller wrote. "So wrapped up in his mission was he that I wondered for that instant if he would mind dying." When Neafus disappeared, Miller turned and sprinted home, his heart pounding wildly.

Elman and Bob were waiting for Neafus at the dock. The RMS *Aquitania*, an old ship from the Cunard Line, would take them to France, sailing out of New York Harbor on June 16, 1937. Her nickname was "Ship Beautiful." Robert Adair Cummins, age twenty, carried an American passport in his pocket. It was Number 433504 and was stamped "Not Valid in Spain."

A Brief Spanish Inquisition

FRANK TAVENNER, THE CHIEF INQUISITOR IN ROOM 740, was portrayed in the local press as an unassuming protagonist in the unfolding drama. A tall, heavyset, bespectacled lawyer of fifty-seven who spoke with the soft drawl of a southern gentleman, Tavenner was a World War I veteran and former prosecutor from the western district of Virginia who pursued Appalachian bootleggers and Hollywood communists with equal persistence. He had followed his father into the law profession and the family apple business, operating orchards in the Shenandoah Valley "on soil he hopes to keep American," as one enraptured journalist wrote. Since 1949, when Tavenner took the committee counsel position, HUAC had held more than one hundred hearings, published nearly forty volumes of testimony, and issued a dozen reports under his supervision, including *Guide to Subversive Organizations and Publications.*

His style was understated and professional, in contrast to the bombast and recklessness that so often defined the committee in its earlier years. He never raised his voice but tried to maintain a deadpan demeanor even when under attack from a recalcitrant witness. To a reporter for the *Detroit News,* the way to read Tavenner was by watching his manipulation of his glasses. "He peers over the top of his glasses in showing skepticism," wrote William W. Lutz. "He takes them off and folds them slowly in showing a willingness to listen to a witness's explanation. He quickly puts them on to show he is tired of a harangue and anxious to continue the questioning."

When Bob Cummins was subpoenaed to testify before the committee, Tavenner conducted the interrogation. Bob testified that he was born in Chippewa Falls, Wisconsin, on July 28, 1916, that he graduated from the University of Michigan in 1937, and that by the time of the hearing he had lived in Detroit for ten or eleven years. He said his last job had been selling paint at Montgomery Ward & Co. during the Christmas season.

Then Tavenner went through the routine with his glasses as he began asking Bob about his time in Spain.

Mr. Tavenner: Mr. Cummins, I show you an application for a passport which was issued on June 4, 1937. It is a photostatic copy of a passport. Would you examine it please and state whether or not you executed it?

Mr. Cummins: I invoke my privilege under the Fifth Amendment and decline to answer that question.

Mr. Tavenner: Will you examine the passport and read what it says as to the country in which travel was sought to be engaged? Now will you read what it says?

Mr. Cummins: I think it is your job to read the document into the record.

Mr. Tavenner: I will read it for you then. At the top of the second page of the application there appears the following language: "I intend to visit the following countries for the purposes indicated: Great Britain, study and travel."

Did you travel to Great Britain in 1937?

Mr. Cummins: I invoke my privilege under the Fifth Amendment and decline to answer that question.

Mr. Tavenner: You stated earlier that you were at the University of Michigan in 1937, correct?

Mr. Cummins: That is right.

Mr. Tavenner: When did you leave that institution?

Mr. Cummins: I graduated in June 1937.

Mr. Tavenner: This application bears the date of June 4, 1937. Will you examine the photograph appearing on the application and state whether or not it is a photograph of you?

Mr. Cummins: I invoke my privilege under the Fifth Amendment and decline to answer that question.

Mr. Tavenner: Isn't it a fact, Mr. Cummins, that you did not intend to go to Great Britain for the purpose of study and travel, but you actually intended to go to Spain to fight as a member of the Abraham Lincoln Brigade?

Mr. Cummins: I invoke my privilege under the Fifth Amendment and decline to answer that question.

Mr. Tavenner: If you are concerned about any possible criminal prosecution for the preparation of a false application for passport, the statute of limitations would have long since elapsed and if that is true on the ground as far as a false application is concerned, it has been held many times that the provision of the Fifth Amendment would afford no immunity.

You may consult with counsel and obtain his advice on that subject if you desire. So far as any danger of criminal prosecution from the making of a false application for a passport is concerned, there could be no fear of criminal prosecution as the statute of limitations has run. So I would like to ask you again whether or not you did state in your application to travel to Great Britain that the trip was for the purpose of study and travel whereas in fact you desired to travel to Spain to fight as a member of the Abraham Lincoln Brigade in the Spanish War?

Mr. Cummins: I invoke my privilege under the Fifth Amendment and decline to answer that question.

Mr. Tavenner: Did anyone solicit your participation in the fighting in Spain?

Mr. Cummins: I invoke my privilege under the Fifth Amendment and decline to answer that question.

Mr. Tavenner: Do you know of any person at the University of Michigan other than yourself who made an application for passport to go to Spain for the purpose of fighting in the Abraham Lincoln Brigade?

Mr. Cummins: I invoke my privilege under the Fifth Amendment and decline to answer that question.

Mr. Tavenner: Did you go to Spain for the purpose of fighting in the Abraham Lincoln Brigade?

Mr. Cummins: I invoke my privilege under the Fifth Amendment and decline to answer that question.

Mr. Tavenner: Will you inform the committee how persons who accepted the enlistment for fighting in Spain received their transportation or the money for their transportation abroad and who made the arrangements for the transportation, if you know?

Mr. Cummins: I invoke my privilege under the Fifth Amendment and decline to answer that question.

Mr. Tavenner: Do you recall the exact date of your graduation from the University of Michigan?

Mr. Cummins: I do not.

Mr. Tavenner: Was it about the date of June 4 or later of the year 1937? Would it have been a day later than June 4, 1937?

Mr. Cummins: I don't know.

Mr. Tavenner: Was there in existence on the campus of the University of Michigan at the end of the term year of 1937 and during the term a Young Communist League chapter?

Mr. Cummins: I invoke my privilege under the Fifth Amendment and decline to answer that question.

Mr. Tavenner: I desire to offer a photostatic copy of the passport in evidence, Mr. Chairman, and ask that it be marked "Cummins Exhibit No. 1."

And that was that when it came to Spain. Tavenner never asked my uncle why he chose to fight—what he was fighting for and what he was fighting against. If he had been interested in those questions, he might have kept his glasses off, listening, for quite some time.

9

The Runner

AFTER SEVEN DAYS AT SEA IN MID-JUNE 1937, THE RMS *Aquitania* reached Cherbourg, where Bob Cummins and his two Michigan comrades disembarked and were met by a representative of the U.S. consul's office. Their intentions were apparent, and ostensibly against American law, but no effort was made to detain them. The usual routine in dealing with young men obviously bound for Spain was to record their names and ages and urge them to go no farther, a warning invariably ignored. Soon they were on the train to Paris, and from there aboard another train for the overnight journey south to Perpignan, near the Mediterranean coast. That was the easy part; making their way into Spain was more daunting. The border was sealed by French patrols enforcing the nation's nonintervention policy.

Foreigners who wanted to join the fight had two choices, both dangerous. They could enter by sea, but that route had proved deadly only weeks before, on May 30, when the *Ciudad de Barcelona*, a merchant ship carrying Scottish, English, and Canadian volunteers from the port in Marseilles, had been sunk by torpedoes from one of Mussolini's submarines, with at least sixty-five anti-Franco recruits among the dead. Earlier that year a band of volunteer stowaways aboard the *Sans Pareil*, a small fishing craft that failed to live up to its name, had been discovered and seized by a French patrol in the Gulf of Lion. Eighteen Americans and Canadians, clothes spattered with bilge muck and oil, were arrested and returned to Perpignan, jailed, tried, and convicted on charges of breaking the nonintervention act.

The other option, more arduous but more commonly used, was to hike up and over the Pyrenees, and that is what the three young Michigan men did. They joined a group of fifty volunteers who were taken through the mountains by guide-smugglers known as *passeurs*. There were three passes through the Pyrenees, all equally demanding and seemingly unending, trudging up six thousand feet and short-stepping down the other side, day into night, hauling heavy valises and packs, knees growing sore, dodging border patrols, until finally there were no more ridges, just Spain at last in its sun-splashed ocher vastness, the sky high and dazzling, a deeper shade of blue than the Americans had ever seen. The route from there was well-worn: from the old fort at Figueras to Barcelona and then onward via train and truck to the training base in the impoverished village of Tarazona de la Mancha, one hundred miles inland from Valencia and twenty miles north of Albacete.

Ralph Neafus was twenty-three, Elman Service twenty-one, and Bob Cummins still a month shy of his twenty-first birthday. They were not mercenaries; their pay, never certain to be forthcoming, would be thirty pesetas a month. They were not drafted; their country was not at war, not being invaded. No one forced them to put their lives in danger. As the historian Peter Carroll wrote about the American soldiers in that civil war, "They went to Spain as political people. Very few admitted any other interest." Whatever else they were, they were uncommonly brave just to go. Neafus, from America's western ranchlands, had some experience with guns, but Service and Cummins were much more comfortable in the classroom than on the range. They knew nothing of war beyond what they read in books and newspapers. The *Daily Worker*, journal of the Communist Party, was full of glorified accounts that made it seem that Franco was soon to lose and the people prevail. Reports from the *Michigan Daily* and *New York Times* made the prospects seem less clear. Without armaments or other aid from the U.S., Great Britain, and France, the Spanish government might be outmatched by Franco and his fascist benefactors.

What could be more ominous than the fate of Guernica, a market town in Spain's Basque Country that had been bombed into oblivion that April by Hitler's Condor Legion, a wing of the Luftwaffe? Soon to be memorialized forever in Picasso's haunting mural, what had happened at Guernica was a war crime that accomplished two purposes at once: it tested Germany's devastating airpower for future use while also demonstrating that Franco's side held an overwhelming advantage in firepower. But after a year of fighting, Madrid had held; Spain's two other largest cities, Barcelona and Valencia, remained strongholds of the Republic; and optimistic young international fighters still washed into Tarazona in recurring waves.

There was no typical American among the more than three thousand who came to Spain, but statistical studies later showed some tendencies. The volunteers were from every state except Delaware and Wyoming. The preponderance, about 80 percent, were from America's largest cities. The youngest were eighteen, the oldest sixty, and two-thirds were under thirty. Few were married. About a third were Jewish and two-thirds had some affiliation with the Communist Party, which paid the way to Spain for many of them. Few had connections to the nation's political elite, but among the exceptions was David McKelvy White, the son of George White, a former Ohio governor. (When I saw that name, it resonated from the larger story of Room 740. At the meeting of the Detroit Communist Party attended by FBI informant Bereniece Baldwin when she was deciding whether to take the undercover assignment, the first person she encountered, at a table outside the assembly hall, was this same David McKelvy White.) Most of the volunteers, unlike the Michigan trio, did not have a college education and came from the working class, but there were also PhDs, novelists, screenwriters, and journalists in the mix.

The common assumption is that these Americans came to join the Abraham Lincoln Brigade, but that is a romanticized simplification. There was no Abraham Lincoln *brigade*, ever, though a support group called Friends of the Abraham Lincoln Brigade had been set up during the war, and returning veterans preferred that appellation after the fact. The Americans belonged to the International Brigade, numerically the XV Brigade. Within that, there was an Abraham Lincoln battalion and a George Washington battalion, which merged into the Lincoln after both were thinned by casualties at the battles of Jarama and Brunete on the eastern and western rims of Madrid. Then came a third battalion composed of Americans and Canadians called the Mackenzie-Papineau battalion, so named because a thousand-plus Canadians fighting in Spain felt neglected and wanted their own heroes recognized. William Lyon Mackenzie and Louis-Joseph Papineau were nineteenth-century leaders of Canada's independence movement.

This battalion of about five hundred men was just being formed when my uncle and his two Michigan comrades arrived in Tarazona in early July, and it was to the Mac-Paps, as the unit was known, that they were assigned. They slept in cramped barracks with stone floors in a village of peasants, donkeys, dry olives, rationed food, spookily blacked-out nights, and narrow streets of packed dirt bustling in daylight with children who trailed the soldiers begging for bread. Alvah Bessie, an American writer who had trained there, could never forget the faces of these children. He called them "singularly beautiful." The trainees spent their days studying map reading, fortifications, first aid, Spanish history, and political indoctrination. With little ammunition to spare, they had no grenade practice and scant work on the firing range. Most of their rifles were dregs from the Soviet Union's aging stockpile. They learned to march in formation, a drill of no use to them later.

The two top officers of the Mac-Paps during their training period in Tarazona were both Americans—college educated, married, around thirty years old, with divergent reputations. Robert Hale Merriman, their first military commander, had ventured into Spain in the first days of 1937 from Moscow, where he had been living after finishing his graduate work in economics at Berkeley. He already had fought with the Lincoln battalion in February at Jarama, where he was wounded, and was now spending the summer preparing to get back into the action. Merriman was tall, charismatic, admired by his men, and well known to the international correspondents who covered the war, including Ernest Hemingway, who by most accounts drew on him as the prototype for Robert Jordan, the tragic hero of *For Whom the Bell Tolls*.

The political commissar was Joe Dallet, a graduate of Dartmouth from a conservative upper-class background who abandoned that life to work as a labor organizer in Chicago and in Youngstown, Ohio, and was now affecting a persona that seemed some combination of steelworker ruffian and strutting big shot. Dallet had been the leader of the group of foreigners arrested aboard the *Sans Pareil*. He had made a demonstrative name for himself during the trial, and after serving a brief time in jail arrived in Spain through the Pyrenees with a sense of destiny. The all-for-one, one-for-all brotherhood and sisterhood cherished by the most idealistic of the antifascists, especially anarchists centered in Barcelona, was not Dallet's way. He was more comfortable with the unsparing, unsentimental discipline of the Soviet apparatchik, a style he embraced at the Soviet-run officer training school in nearby Pozorrubio. He strapped a Belgian Browning 9mm semiautomatic handgun to his belt, smoked a Stalin pipe, and insisted that officers eat and sleep apart from their men. His troops, according to historian Cecil Eby, responded with "a daily chorus" of complaints against him, calling him "cocksure, dictatorial, megalomaniac, boy-scoutish—and no end of unprintable."

Dallet showed a more paternalistic side in letters to his wife, Kitty, during that summer training period. "The battalion gets better every day (I guess I sound like a proud father)," he wrote to her on July 9, a week after Cummins, Neafus, and Service arrived. "I am sure they will conduct themselves well at the front."

Two weeks later he expounded on how he trained the Mac-Paps. "Training a battalion is very much like training a football team in some ways. You know you have a certain minimum period in which to prepare the men. Into that period, if you have worked as we have, you are set to go, and what is more, the boys are set to go. That period ended with the ending of our four-day maneuver. Now the boys are set, they are waiting for the word, and the danger exists that, lacking the word, with the suspense naturally accumulating, they will go stale. We are alert to the danger, and taking a whole series of steps to avoid it." He and Merriman cut back on heavy work under the midday sun and drilled the battalion in the early morning and at night. They also started tournaments in volleyball, softball, and soccer and staged a picnic near a swimming hole. "Spain is a funny place," Dallet wrote. "Some of the best people at home crack up badly here and some of the least significant ones from home come through with flying colors. You can see men changing before your eyes."

Letters from Tarazona could not be sent by civilian mail. They were routed through the International Brigade post office in Albacete, examined by the censor department, then shipped in pouches to an office at 1 Cité de Paradis in Paris, where French stamps were attached and the letters forwarded to addresses in the States. My uncle's first letter to Ann Arbor arrived in August. He sent it to friends at the *Daily*. "The staff planned to publish it and then remembered that Mrs. Cummins did not know of Bob's true whereabouts," Stan Swinton recalled. "The story was immediately killed." Bob's mother remained in the dark, and the Mac-Paps remained in Tarazona. They were at camp all through the relentless heat of August, when in preparation for combat their ranks were bolstered by an infusion of young Spanish recruits.

Bob Cummins, son of the Jayhawk two-miler "Little Cummins," was assigned as a runner. His job would be to carry battlefield messages between brigade and battalion and between battalion command and its companies. Many of the other Mac-Paps runners were Spaniards who knew the countryside. Bob was not familiar with the land, but he had stamina and excellent orienting skills. During his childhood, his father had taught him how to navigate by the stars at night.

Service was assigned to drive a truck, and Neafus was attached to the headquarters staff as a scout. In a buoyant letter to a friend, Neafus asserted that this army now "compares with any in the world." A miner was his immediate supervisor, and a college professor above that, reflecting the diversity of the unit. "There are labor organizers, students, workers of all kinds, a farmer or two, a few lumberjacks, sailors, several teachers, and as far as nationalities go—every kind. Our battalion has Americans and Canadians with a Finnish section of thirty men in addition, and half the outfit is Spanish in conformity with the government's policy."

THE MAC-PAPS WERE deployed at last in the second week of September, moving by train from Tarazona to Valencia and northwest toward Hijar on the edge of the Aragon front, where they were held in reserve after other elements of the International Brigade had prevailed, though suffering heavy casualties, at Quinto and Belchite. The battalion rotated in circular fashion from Albalate del Arzobispo to Senés de Alcubierre to Quinto before being sent into battle at Fuentes de Ebro, a village along the Ebro River south of Zaragoza, the capital of Aragon province.

It was October 13. The well-trained but untested Mac-Paps advanced against blistering gunfire, and their leaders fell one by one. Commissar Dallet did not last his first day in battle. He was shot in the groin and was crawling back to shelter when his body was shredded by machine-gun bullets. One of his company commanders was also killed and two more badly wounded. The Michigan boys survived. Neafus described his experience in a letter afterward: "The baptism is over. It took! I'm still on two feet, but there are a goodly number of the boys who are not. We went over the top for the first time on the 13th. At the present time we have a nice cross-fire that makes us keep down during the day. Today a bath for the first time in three weeks. During that time, I have washed my hands twice. There is only water to drink. We are a dirty, unshaven lot—dead tired but still very much anti-fascist." Not a word about losing Dallet or the other brass.

My uncle, describing that period in an essay he wrote later, made it sound almost carefree. Perhaps it was an expression of survivor's relief, but it reflected a public attitude of optimism from which he rarely wavered, even when free of the censor's pen. All wars are brutal, and this one was far from an exception, with horrors all around. Mass executions, desertions, prison camps, fright, stench, chaos, destruction, bombardment—all there, but little of that evoked in Bob's writings. "When we came out of the lines at Fuentes we knew we were going into rest. We were back at Quinto and waiting for transportation. Those were very happy times for most of us. The recruits had come through their first action successfully. It made us feel good to see our Fifth Army Corps posters on the walls of all the Aragon villages, showing a menacing soldier with fixed bayonet and the simple legend 'Fifth Army Corps,' and down the sides the names of its victories: Jarama, Guadalajara, Villanueva de la Canada, Brunete, Estacion de Pina, Quinto, Villamayor, Code, Belchite."

In the aftermath of battle, Quinto felt like a war museum to the Mac-Paps. "We loafed there for a week," Bob wrote, "walking around seeing where the machine gun nests had been and what streets the tanks had come down two months before, reading the fantastic accounts of the war in old copies of the fascist *Heraldo de Aragón* that we found lying around. We could buy small, bright colored bottles of crème de menthe, rum, and cacao for two pesetas. There was lots to eat." After seven days in Quinto, word came in the middle of the night that they were to pack up and prepare to leave for another holding station near Madrid.

"It took three trains to move the whole brigade. We traveled in box cars, the most comfortable way, and we brigade runners had one box car to ourselves although there were but fourteen of us. Of the fourteen, seven were English-speaking and seven were Spanish." They rode from Quinto to Tarragona on the Mediterranean coast, then down to Valencia and inland again across the country to Toledo province south of Madrid. So glorious was this journey that Bob said three days was not enough; he wished it had taken a week. "Every day was a beautiful Indian summer day. We could slide the doors wide open on each side and sit, our legs dangling out, with the sun warming us and the woods rolling by, bright red and yellow in the autumn. At all the stations there were crowds, partly just to see the brigade and partly in the hope of seeing a son, husband, or brother. We had brilliant posters plastered on the sides of the box cars telling who we were and there was lots of singing and cheering because Spanish trains stop at every station."

Among the Spaniards, a runner named Rafael became Bob's best friend. They bonded during that sunny autumn train ride by talking about their siblings. Bob had one brother and three sisters, including my mother, Mary, then a junior at Ann Arbor High School. Rafael told him that he now had only sisters; all his brothers had been killed by the fascists in Granada in July 1936, forcing his parents and sisters to flee to a section of Córdoba province still held by the government. He took out a photograph of the family. It struck Bob that they were "posed stiffly, in an old-fashioned way." After his brothers were killed, Rafael enlisted in the Republican army. He was slightly older than Bob, twenty-three, and not a college man but a self-taught scholar who learned to read at age sixteen and now loved to study the history and geography of Spain. He taught Bob about all the provinces and seemed to have "very nearly memorized the first geography book he had read" so that he could tell the American "to the meter how high were the greater mountains in Spain."

The thirteen other runners voted unanimously to make Rafael their *responsable,* the comrade in charge of dividing up food, acquiring new clothes and shoes, and making out the duty schedules. Proud of his hard-earned literacy, he drew up "elaborate tabulations and charts" to keep track of their assignments. "In the daily political periods when events were discussed and analyzed, it was always Rafael who read the newspapers aloud." Bob came to think that Rafael was fighting for his right to education. "Fascist Spain would deny him that right as surely as monarchist Spain had done for the first sixteen years of his life."

Another Spanish runner was Llorens, a bank clerk and Catalan nationalist who volunteered when he turned eighteen and who impressed Bob by singing most of the Cole Porter songs from *Top Hat,* the 1935 Ginger Rogers–Fred Astaire musical. "He sang them in English and once came to me asking the meaning to the words in 'Night and Day,'" Bob recalled. *Like the drip, drip, drip of the raindrops / when the summer shower is through / So a voice within me keeps repeating—you, you, you.* There was also a Valencian fishmonger nicknamed Captain Fish, who had the best singing voice in the battalion, and the poet Genaro and the firebrand Antonio, who came out of an anarchist trade union, and Luis, a working-class kid who lied about his age so he could enlist and was dead within a few months, before he had turned seventeen, killed by the concussion of a bomb that never touched him. Some American soldiers spoke disparagingly of the Spaniards on their side, portraying them inaccurately as feckless, but from my uncle's perspective they were the noble reason to be there.

Their destination near Madrid was an expansive villa with a paper mill on the estate in the village of Ambite, fifty kilometers east of the capital. It was a luxurious resting spot for soldiers of the International Brigade, who set up an encampment there and in the nearby village of Mondéjar. The villa itself was a frequent stopping place for sympathetic visitors. There are photographs of Hemingway standing outside the main building with a group of soldiers and officials, and Clement Attlee, the British Labour Party leader, paid a visit while the Mac-Paps were there. It has been said that he was greeted first by Segundo, the village dwarf.

Late in November, Bob wrote a letter to Ed Magdol, a former *Daily* colleague, that described that time near the mill in Ambite. The mid-summer heat of Tarazona de la Mancha seemed distant. "We have had lots of rain this month and now it is getting colder," he wrote. "I am reluctant to warm myself before the kitchen fires for fear I won't be able to take it the rest of the day and days to come. But I really have become used to living continuously in a temperature never better than 50 degrees. Movies and books on war themes seem the most popular in Spain today—at least I have encountered them in unusual proportions. That is natural."

Bob then recalled the scene from that first day of battle at Fuentes de Ebro in October, a sight vivid in his memory, his rendering one of fearlessness. "It was the long line of men of the brigade, unrenowned, moving up, just before dusk of a cloudy afternoon, through our communication trenches, paying no attention to shells falling about them; them taking up positions for the attack, then attacking superbly. That was a sample of the people's army that is growing in numbers and experience every day. It was an unforgettable sight. Because that long line knew that many among them were living the last 15 minutes of their lives, but there was none who did not subordinate that thought to his determination to save his people from fascism."

The reality was that some soldiers, as in any war, withered at the approach of battle, and some drifted away. Camp Lukács, an International Brigade prison camp near Albacete, was filling with a few thousand deserters, along with anarchists, socialists, and others who, though committed to the anti-Franco cause, had in various ways run afoul of the brutally unscrupulous and controlling Soviet advisers and communist hardliners who dominated the leadership. Many at Camp Lukács were "re-educated" and sent back to battalions; some deserters were executed.

During that rest period at Ambite, Bob was granted a brief leave and escaped to Madrid, where he stayed at the Hotel Alfonso near the Gran Via. "It was well run by the trade unions—the chief fault was that there was no glass in the windows. Also, there was no place to hang the laundry but in the corridors." Those minor inconveniences were nothing compared to the field; the besieged city seemed vibrant to Bob. "The city was everywhere decorated in honor of the year of its successful defense and the 20th birthday of the Soviet Union. Although artillery, and in the still early morning hours, machine guns can be heard, the streets hum and there is a gay café and theatre life, of which I drank deep until sugar candy mixed with Spanish cognac forced me to a bed of pain my last night."

With Christmas and the new year came new battles. The Mac-Paps were sent to Teruel, a contested city due east of Madrid and halfway back to the coast. For several months, one side and then the other had held Teruel. In a surprise offensive, the Republican army had retaken the city in December, and in January 1938 Franco's troops were mounting a fierce counteroffensive. The Mac-Paps came in to help hold it. Known for its Moorish, or Mudéjar, architecture, Teruel sat high on the hills above the confluence of the Turia and Alfambra rivers. The Mac-Paps were assigned a dangerous position west of town. The winter there had been unforgiving. Snow remaining from a four-day blizzard made maneuvering slow and treacherous. The men had to survive below-freezing temperatures, wholly inadequate clothing, hundreds of cases of frostbite, and Hitler's Condor Legion, whose planes had been grounded during the worst weather but eventually resumed a relentless air attack. A peak known as La Muela, or "the Tooth," rose above the Mac-Paps on one side, and to their backs was a seventy-foot cliff. Virtually trapped and freezing, they endured an unceasing barrage and suffered heavy casualties during five weeks of fighting, with at least 150 wounded or dead.

When the brigade finally withdrew in February, lines were still disputed, both sides claiming victory. But the damage on the road toward Valencia when the Mac-Paps moved out was frightful. "As far as the eye could see there were wrecked, blackened tanks, strafed trucks, demolished staff cars and piles of house rubble," historian Eby wrote of the scene. Adam Hochschild, in his evocative history *Spain in Our Hearts*, quoted an ambulance driver watching a battalion moving toward him. They "came up the road in the moonlight. Too tired to swear, the men were wordless. The torn blankets over heads and shoulders and tied like skirts around the waist, the shoes wrapped with rags, the rifles on their shoulders gave them the appearance of a battalion of beggars. Ranks of stretcher-bearers with eight-foot spear-like poles added to the Biblical quality of the scene."

Bob was among the walking wounded, nipped in the ear by shrapnel. Back in Ann Arbor, his mother had learned the truth. Her son was not on some grand tour of France and Great Britain, but fighting in Spain. At least he was alive.

ON MARCH 14 correspondent William P. Carney of the *New York Times* marched into the town of Alcañiz in the protective pocket of Nationalist troops who now were executing a devastating maneuver designed to slice apart the Loyalist lines from Aragon and western Catalonia all the way to the Mediterranean. Carney was known as Franco's man on the *Times*. He was granted friendly access to the generalissimo's men and wrote sympathetically about the right-wing rebels. His dispatches on the course of the war contrasted sharply with those of another *Times* reporter, Herbert L. Matthews, who covered the antifascist side. But on March 14 Carney's embedding with Franco's troops led to a disquieting revelation. It came in a story he wrote that night and sent by courier to Zaragoza, where it was transmitted by wireless to the offices in Manhattan.

Carney reported that more than 1,500 prisoners had been seized by the Nationalists near Alcañiz in recent days, including an entire unit that was surprised and rounded up the previous night in nearby Calanda without a shot being fired. (Calanda was known as the hometown of Luis Buñuel, the avant-garde director who was in Paris and Geneva during that period, supporting the antifascist cause by making pro-Republican propaganda films.) The commanding general in the unit

Carney accompanied gave him permission to interview some Americans who had been captured that day and were being detained along
with scores of other prisoners inside Alcañiz's Iglesia del Carmen, an
imposing cathedral high on the hill. "I saw the beautiful entrance of the
church bordered by chiseled marble—the work of a seventeenth century craftsman—still intact except the head had been hacked away from
a sculptured life size figure of the Virgin above the doorway," Carney
wrote. "The interior had undergone the same change as the cathedral,"
with all sacred images stripped from the walls and altar. "We found four
Americans, two Englishmen and two English-speaking Scandinavians
in a group by themselves in a corner." The Americans told him they
had been on the run since Belchite fell and that they had been captured
separately on the roads between Belchite and Alcañiz. "They explained
that each seemed to have become separated from his outfit. With their
limited knowledge of Spanish and their unfamiliarity with Aragon's
geography, they were completely lost." Then Carney named the four.
He described one as a schoolteacher, another as a shoe salesman, and a
third as hailing from Oklahoma.

The fourth was Ralph Neafus.

The dispatch was printed in a late edition of the *Times* on Wednesday, March 16, and went unnoticed in Ann Arbor until a few days later,
when students who had been trying to send the three University of
Michigan volunteers packages of chocolate and cigarettes through the
Friends of the Abraham Lincoln Brigade in New York were told about
the Carney story. "A hectic search through several editions of Wednesday's *Times* brought no results until the Late City edition was uncovered," the *Daily* reported. "It is known that two other Michigan students
were also attached to the Mackenzie-Papineau battalion. Cummins was
a runner and Service a truck driver. Since they were not mentioned as
being among the four Americans captured, conjectures are that they
either were not at the front at the time or else escaped during the march
into Alcañiz."

News of Neafus's capture consumed the Michigan campus, "temporarily replacing sex and the coaching situation" in student bull sessions,
as the *Daily* put it. Arthur Miller was haunted by the memory of driv-

ing Neafus from Ann Arbor to New York the previous June, when he could not shake the feeling that he was taking his pal to his imminent death. Now Miller was about to graduate, and Neafus was in grave danger. Was he somehow responsible for what happened? Could he have prevented it?

There were larger, less personal questions to be answered. What would the Roosevelt administration do about the captured Americans? Would there be a diplomatic effort to free them, or at least protect them from being killed? Leaders at the *Daily* and student organizations supporting the Spanish Republic sent a telegram to Cordell Hull, the secretary of state, urging help for Neafus. The twenty-one signers included the *Daily's* lead night editor, Elliott Maraniss. On the night of March 22, the day the telegram was sent, more than 150 students gathered in the Michigan Union ballroom to "protest the failure of the State Department to recognize any diplomatic responsibility toward Neafus and to protest the neutrality policy of the administration toward the Spanish war."

More telegrams were sent, one intended to reach Franco himself, along with letters to Congress, the White House, and the Department of State. Michael Evanoff, a young lawyer in Flint, wrote to Prentiss M. Brown, a U.S. senator from Michigan, "A few days ago, I learned that a very close friend of mine, my best pal in college days, Ralph Neafus, had been captured by fascist troops in Spain. His life, if not already lost, is in grave danger. This boy comes from New Mexico, has lived in Michigan many years, and is an American if there ever was one. He went to Spain to fight in the ranks of the Republican army because of his intense love of democracy and the belief that by helping to keep democracy alive in Spain he would be helping to preserve liberty in America."

The issue was taken up by the Michigan Student Senate, where Phil Cummins, Bob's younger brother, argued that the student government should go on record asking Secretary Hull for help, but the measure was defeated by one vote, 14–13. The position against supporting Neafus was articulated by students William B. Otto and Chas D. Johnson, who called student supporters of the Loyalist cause "a small and blindly prejudiced minority" and said the idea that Neafus was fighting for democratic principles was a "gross misrepresentation."

This line of thinking is what compelled Stan Swinton to write an essay for his history class, the paper that opened with his memories of Bob Cummins in the basement of Hagen's Recess Tavern five weeks before he left for Spain. Swinton called Otto and Johnson "two gentlemen whose dogmas seem to have been little modified by contact with a supposedly intellectual community." What separated Neafus and Cummins from so many contemporaries, he asserted, was the courage to follow their convictions. He quoted what a Toledo newspaperman had told him a few days earlier—"If I had any guts I'd be over there myself"— and said that was a sentiment he and many of his classmates shared. Neafus and Cummins "were good friends, enlisted at the same time, fought for the same reasons. Both Ralph and Bob rather thought they were communists. Neither was sure. But their adherence to the great American bogey was a minor matter in influencing their decision. They were fighting for democracy."

In search of more influential voices, the Michigan students turned to Henry Wallace, FDR's progressive secretary of agriculture, and persuaded him to write Hull, his cabinet colleague. Wallace told Hull that Neafus had worked as a young forester in his department—the U.S. Forest Service is in the Ag Department's domain—and lamented, "It would be sincerely regretted if so promising a life should be lost without an effort." The reply was blunt. Neafus went to Spain under false pretenses, a Hull deputy told Wallace. In his passport application, he said he intended to visit England, Germany, Sweden, and France for travel and study. He signed an affidavit stating that he would not use the passport to travel to Spain. The passport was stamped that it was not valid for travel to Spain. The conclusion: "This department cannot intervene."

Soldiers from the International Brigade captured by Franco's troops were usually held at San Pedro de Cardeña, a former monastery transformed into a concentration camp near Burgos. Was Neafus there? The American consulate in Seville was asked to find out and eventually filed a dispatch to Washington. With reference to the capture of Neafus and the three other Americans named in Carney's article, the dispatch writer noted, "I have the honor to inform the Department that ... General Queipo de Llano informs me that, according to a letter received by him from the Inspector of Concentration Camp of Prisoners, none of the persons named are included among prisoners." Some honor. This was not good news, and it was soon followed by worse, when Carney in a follow-up article reported that "from unofficial but usually well-informed sources he had heard that some Americans with whom he had already talked had been shot without trial shortly after having been captured."

NEAFUS'S SISTERS AND mother would continue to hold out hope for months, writing one heartbroken letter after another, pleading with U.S. officials to secure Ralph's release or check on rumors that he might be in a hospital in Barcelona and so badly wounded that he could not write them. The truth was he was dead. As Carney suspected, Neafus and the other American prisoners detained at the church in Alcañiz were executed by Moorish troops under Franco's command, their bullet-riddled bodies dumped into an irrigation ditch.

"This was one of the debts I would carry in my heart, an invisible force," Arthur Miller later wrote of the moment he received the news.

Nearly eighty years later, my wife and I visited Alcañiz. Our guide, Alan Warren, an expert on the Spanish Civil War, rode with us up the serpentine streets to the Iglesia del Carmen, a religious bulwark at the top of the city, its beige cut-stone front encrusted in centuries of dirt. It was 4:30 in the afternoon. As we approached the front entrance, a stork swooped overhead and roosted atop the bell tower. Life or death. Then a watchman scampered up the steps carrying oversized keys. He opened the giant medieval doors and led us inside. The darkened chamber, cold, damp, and musty, evoked the interwoven history of violence and Catholicism in Spain, especially during the Spanish Civil War. I felt overtaken by the past as we walked down a dimly lit aisle, votive candles flickering in the distance, and thought back to Ralph Neafus's final hours in this silent cathedral that once had been used not for worship but as a gloomy dungeon of death.

IN THE DAYS just after Neafus disappeared, another piece of alarming news reached Ann Arbor. A sister of Grace Cummins, Bob's aunt Lucia, who lived in Spokane, Washington, saw a photo in the Spokane *Spokesman-Review* that was taken on March 20 and showed twenty Loyalist prisoners being paraded through a town near Belchite, where another round of fighting was taking place. She clipped the page and mailed it to Bob's parents. The picture was blurry, but Lucia thought one of the soldiers looked like Bob. Grace and Andrew had not heard from their son since February, just before the battle of Teruel, when Grace first learned that he was fighting in Spain. Now this. The fact that one of the other Michigan students had been captured raised the likelihood that Bob had also. Looking at the photo, his family thought it might be him. Phil brought the clipping to the *Daily* offices, and they ran a story about it under the headline "Michigan Grad Feared Captured." The night editor, my father, called World Wide Photos in New York and asked for the original print. When the print came in at the end of March, the family was relieved. They said that Bob's resemblance to the prisoner in the photo was "very slight." But there was still cause for concern. No one had heard from him in more than a month.

Friends back in Michigan had also lost touch with Elman Service. He had become ill with dysentery earlier that year and, after his release from a hospital, returned to the front lines as an ambulance driver. The International Brigade was in full retreat and disarray by then. Franco's troops and a unit of Italians had driven them down from Belchite and Alcañiz. The town of Gandesa was taken and the Mac-Paps and the Lincolns were cut off on the wrong side of the Ebro River in western Catalonia. Robert Merriman, who had left the Mac-Paps to return to his original Lincoln battalion, was dead, probably surrounded and killed while taking cover in a furrow off the road to Corbera, though his body was never found. Neafus was gone, and now gone as well were the two top officers who had trained the Michigan men at Tarazona de la Mancha the previous summer.

As the companies were riven and officers lost, any sense of command dissolved. Men were left to fend for themselves and scramble as best they could to the safer side of the Ebro. They were hunted, hungry, and desperate, eating grass and roots and sleeping in prickly gorse. In his account of the retreat, Eby mentioned my uncle, the runner. "Robert Cummins wandered alone and was completely lost when he spotted a Moorish cavalry patrol regarding him from a hilltop. He knew it would be death to run. He had lost his army cap in the melee and with a blanket over his shoulders, poncho-style, he prayed that the Moors would mistake him for a local campesino. When he covered enough distance to look back, the Moors had disappeared."

In a letter he wrote long after the retreat, Bob did not mention seeing the Moors. He said only that he was surrounded and managed to escape, but he was more descriptive in relaying news about how his friend Service survived those chaotic hours: "Elman marched along with a fascist column for three or four kilometers. He set his pace for the most part a little faster or slower than the column so he wouldn't have to speak with them. One insisted on talking and Elman said he was a German technician to explain his inadequate Spanish. He was believed. I met him on the road later. We were very glad to see each other."

Bob and Elman were among the Mac-Paps who regrouped near the river town of Móra la Nova. Alvah Bessie, who was also there, later wrote that the area was "jammed with ragged and demoralized men, wandering idly about in the utmost confusion." On the second morning, as Bessie looked toward distant Gandesa, he saw "great clouds of smoke rising from a valley between the hills." Then he noticed a car approaching from the other direction. Three men emerged from the car: Herbert L. Matthews of the *New York Times*, Sefton Delmer of London's *Daily Express*, and Ernest Hemingway. "They had rushed down from Barcelona after hearing that the XVth Brigade had been annihilated," Bessie recalled in his battlefield memoir, *Men in Battle*. "Concluding their interview, Hemingway, who had a penchant for histrionics, shook his fist at the far shore and shouted, 'You fascist bastards haven't won yet. We'll show you!'"

Bob wrote three letters to his family later in April, but they would not reach Ann Arbor until mid-May. His parents in the intervening weeks grew increasingly worried that he had been captured or killed. A. A. Cummins sent letters to the Department of State in Washington and the

Friends of the Abraham Lincoln Brigade on West 45th Street in Manhattan seeking any information on his son's whereabouts. State said it had nothing to tell him, but assured him, "Inquiries will be continued and upon the receipt of any report you will be informed." New York came back with a similar report, prompting A.A. to write another letter saying that Bob should be sent home, where he would be more valuable spreading the story of the antifascist effort and its need for American support. On Friends of the Abraham Lincoln Brigade stationery came this reply:

> Mr. and Mrs. A. A. Cummins
> c/o Cummins and Barnard
> Wolverine Building
> Ann Arbor, Michigan

My dear Mr. and Mrs. Cummins:

Though I very well understand your desire to have your son, Robert, back and though I do not doubt his value in the States as one who can very successfully bring the cause of the Loyalist Spain before the eyes of the American people, I regret that I can do nothing at all for you in this direction.

It is only natural that no organization in this country should have jurisdiction over the question of repatriation in Spain. We in this country can have no contact with the rapidly shifting circumstances surrounding each man which must determine this question. The question of the return of a man is taken up by the individual himself and his application is considered by the Brigade. Therefore, I suggest that you write to your son telling him of your desire to have him back and your reasons.

I am sorry that there is nothing positive we are able to do for you and ask you to write us again if there is any other information we are able to give you.

Very sincerely yours,
David McKelvy White
National Chairman

The name reverberates through this story: David McKelvy White had gone to fight in Spain, after graduating from Princeton and teaching at Brooklyn College. He was in the war for six months, serving as a stretcher-bearer for a machine-gun company in the George Washington battalion, and returned to the U.S. in September 1937, just as Bob was moving to the Fuentes de Ebro front with the Mac-Paps. Back in the States, White took up the Spanish cause with the Friends, the precise path that A. A. Cummins hoped his son would follow. The coda to White's story shifts it into tragedy. When he died in July 1945, the fascists of the world had been defeated. First reports said that White succumbed to a heart attack. Later it was determined that he committed suicide when members of the Communist Party threatened to expose him as a homosexual.

The Mac-Paps and the rest of the International Brigade spent most of May, June, and July regrouping, retraining, repairing. Their encampments were in and around Marçà, a Catalonian village on the safe side of the Ebro, seventeen kilometers to the northwest of the river. Situated on hills, with narrow streets and old stone and cement houses, Marçà was the quintessential Spanish village. The soldiers mingled with townspeople for festivals and concerts. They played soccer in a field next to an old theater where they staged intense political meetings at night. The Mac-Paps slept in a rolling field near a swimming hole surrounded by smooth boulders, the officers quartered in an old stone-and-plaster command building a hundred yards away. The building, long since abandoned, was still there when we visited this remote site in 2017. One of the haunting aspects of a Spanish Civil War tour is seeing how many ruins have been left untouched.

The Mac-Paps trained by day and took turns on guard duty at night. Bob wrote several letters home from Marçà. He said he had borrowed a pencil from his fellow runner, Captain Fish, the fishmonger from Alicante, to let them know he was safe. But he had another message. If the Loyalists were to prevail, they needed help, especially from the U.S. government. He was writing, he said, "on the assumption that a plea would be made for Spain. But you already know how much the lifting of the embargo would help, I think."

Elman Service was encamped nearby with the Lincoln battalion, where he became close friends with Jim Lardner, the second of four sons of Ring Lardner, the American humorist. Lardner, then a twenty-three-year-old reporter in the Paris Bureau of the *New York Herald Tribune*, had arrived in Spain in the company of Ernest Hemingway and the *Tribune*'s top foreign correspondent, Vincent Sheean. The trio shared a compartment on the long ride down from Paris's Gare D'Orsay, and once in Barcelona took rooms at the Majestic Hotel. After ten days there, Lardner announced that he felt compelled not to write but to fight. "What's the good of that?" Sheean asked him, amazed. "It's pretty late to do that." Lardner responded that he was tired of "pounding a typewriter" and that if he had any choice in the matter he would join the Lincolns, which he soon did. He met them in Marçà in May.

His politics were leftist; he believed that capitalism was doomed and some form of communism was the future. During officer training there, he and Service were both promoted to squad leader in the same platoon, an event they celebrated by downing two bottles of Spanish champagne and crashing a party for officers. They were such pals that they slept side by side, sharing blankets and talking into the night, even hatching plans to start a newsmagazine after the war that they would name *TRUTH*. They read each other's mail, shared the same birthday, May 18, and on that day decided that each would write a letter to the other's mother. Service lost his before he could mail it. Unlike Bob Cummins, Lardner did not keep what he had done from his own mother. In an early letter home after joining the Lincolns, he instructed her not to say that she wanted him to come home. "I know you do, and always will, but it is liable to get letters stopped if you write it. You asked me how long I enlisted for. There is only one way of enlisting: for the duration of the war. . . . I don't mean to be cruel. But it is better that you should resign yourself to my being in Spain indefinitely. A good soldier is hard to hit and I am going to be a good soldier."

It was through his friendship with Lardner that Service met Sheean and Hemingway. He came to think that there were two Hemingways: "I saw both. He was a very appealing person with a dark reddish complexion. He seemed kind of shy. He always deferred to others. You'd see him

SPANISH
CIVIL WAR

SPAIN 1936–1939

FRANCE

PYRENEES

EBRO RIVER

• LEÓN

FUENTES DE EBRO — QUINTO

BARCELONA

AMBITE — BELCHITE

PORTUGAL

MADRID ◉ — MARÇÀ

ALCAÑIZ

SPAIN

TERUEL

VALENCIA •

LISBON

TARAZONA DE LA MANCHA

• SEVILLE

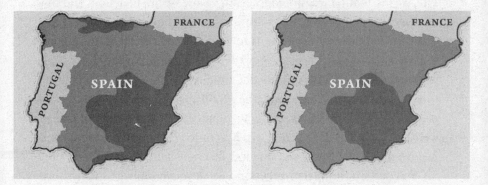

FRANCE

PORTUGAL

SPAIN

FRANCE

PORTUGAL

SPAIN

NOVEMBER 1936   **FEBRUARY 1939**

NATIONALIST-CONTROLLED TERRITORY

REPUBLICAN-CONTROLLED TERRITORY

looking and listening. He was not drunk until late in the day. Then I never saw anybody change so much. He was a drunken bombastic braggart and fool. He had what he called the fiesta concept of life. I think he was a very shy man and was anxious to overcome it."

In the last week of July, the Loyalist forces, restored and replenished, left Marçà and launched a major offensive. Bob's unit crossed the Ebro, 150 yards from shore to shore, near Vinebre, just south of Ascó, using boats and pontoon bridges. The brigade headquarters was established high on a hill above La Fatarella, with an expansive view down toward the valley and the river and thirty kilometers to the horizon. The Moorish tower in Ascó, the village of Flix, the mountains, the pines, the fog of the river, all within sight. When my wife and I visited the site eight decades later, the remnants of the officers' bunkers were still there, and the scene was the same except for a nuclear power plant now rising near Ascó. When my wife mentioned the scent of wild rosemary, our guide said that veterans of the Spanish Civil War could not eat pork roast spiced with rosemary because it reminded them of the smell of battle.

As a runner, Bob carried messages between headquarters and Cota 403 and Cota 705, hills where the Mac-Paps were situated during the early days of the offensive. On his first night across the river, he wrote a letter to his father. Only a few days earlier, he had written to his brother, Phil, saying that he was bored to death. "Now we are in action, and the bombers have been over three times in the last hour. We went into action last night. Everything seems to be going well, although of course the operation has been in progress only a few hours. Everyone seems to be feeling good and optimistic." One reason for the optimism: in their first outing that morning, the Mac-Paps had taken twenty-seven prisoners. Bob was struck by how young they looked. Enemy planes were overhead but did not concern him much. "The bombers that have just been over have bothered me less than any since Fuentes [de Ebro, his first battle]. Bombers really don't do so much damage to anything except morale. I think the reason I don't mind these bombers is that we have good anti-aircraft batteries here, and lots of anti-aircraft guns make so much noise that they drown out the bombs' noise. They've dropped three loads in this vicinity, but the nearest they got to me was a few hundred meters."

They were in the hot season, Bob told his father. The sun beat down on them from nine in the morning to six at night. "On top of that, the kitchen had to serve hot rice for dinner this noon." He'd been able to bum a few cigarettes, but none had been issued for several days. They received iron rations just before heading out, but he had already consumed his chocolate and a can of sardines. And he hadn't seen any American newspapers in several days. "I noticed that the National League beat the American in the all-star game and that Menow beat War Admiral at Suffolk. Please send me sport and racing pages when you write. My ear is healing up all right."

A few days later, Service and Lardner were in a group leading a company of captured Nationalist soldiers back across the river to a detention camp. As they moved through an apple orchard, Lardner was wounded. So much for the naïve boast that good soldiers don't get hit. One piece of shrapnel hit him in the inside of his thigh, another in his lower back. In a letter informing Lardner's mother of the incident, Vincent Sheean softened the news: "If you are going to get shrapnel, these are good, harmless places. It has the further advantage (from your point of view, not his) that it removes him from the front lines, where the fighting just now is pretty terrific, with constant bombardments from the air." Lardner was taken to the hospital at Villafranca. The next day, during a dawn skirmish in a vineyard near Gandesa, Service was shot through the left lung. He was stuck on the battlefield for hours, bleeding, drifting in and out of consciousness, weakened by the blinding sun. His wound was bound with paper, no bandages being available, until finally he too was carted off on a stretcher and taken to the hospital, where he would remain for several months.

STAN SWINTON, NOW a rising junior at Michigan, spent much of that summer of 1938 in Europe. When he sailed across the Atlantic on the SS *Roosevelt*, the *Queen Mary* passed in the night going the other way, huge and brilliantly lit. As much as Swinton admired Cummins,

Neafus, and Service, he did not intend to fight in Spain or try to visit the country. But he felt the reverberations of the Spanish war all around as he and a few college friends traveled through France, Switzerland, Germany, Italy, the Netherlands, and England. In Geneva he visited the headquarters of the League of Nations and was struck by the diversity of the woodwork and stonework in the new building. "Here is Swiss oak, Danish walnut, South African stinkwood," he said in a letter to his parents. "Best of all, though, the council room with tremendous paintings on its walls which represent humanity's tremendous progress. They are surrounded by gilt and ironically enough, were presented by the Spanish government."

In France, much of the talk Swinton heard was about Spain and the prospects of a larger war. "Europe knows war is coming, knows it and is resigned," he wrote. But still the mood could be summarized in two words: *not yet.* "Sentiment in France favors the Loyalists—but it's a different sentiment than found in the States. The last war is not forgotten. The people know they will have to fight again, but they will not hasten the day. Support is verbal or limited to buying the Standard Packets on sale in Paris or Marseilles. These cost 30, 40, or 70 francs and include such staples as sugar, soap, corned beef, and condensed milk. Rumors, too, of wounds bound in newspapers and the absence of hospital facilities discourage volunteers. The French are too near, they see and hear too much of what distance keeps from America, to volunteer. They sympathize—rarely do they do more."

ON SEPTEMBER 21, as the battle of the Ebro wore on, Juan Negrín, the prime minister of the Spanish Republic, announced to the League of Nations in Geneva that his government would unilaterally withdraw all foreign volunteers from the battlefield. The naïve hope was that this move would compel Germany and Italy to withdraw from the war as well. The Mac-Paps and Lincolns and all the other international fighters were going to be sent home. Jim Lardner was out of the hospital by then and back with the Lincolns. The day after Negrín's announcement he went on patrol to the rear of his battalion in the Sierra de Pándols, the contested mountains west of the Ebro and south of Gandesa. There was heavy enemy fire, and Lardner did not return. His body was never recovered; on the battlefield later, searchers found only his press credentials. He had left a suitcase of belongings back at the Majestic Hotel in Barcelona, and Vincent Sheean instructed the hotel manager to open it. Inside were clothes (later distributed to Jim's friends in the battalion), letters to his mother, a telegram from one of his brothers, Ring Lardner Jr., several telegrams from the *Herald Tribune*'s Paris office, tickets for the Berlitz school where he had studied Spanish, a notebook of his observations on the war, and three passport photographs.

Elman Service was still in the hospital when he learned of his friend's death. "I'll not try to tell you in this letter how I personally felt about Jim's loss, or how sorry I am for you," Service wrote to Lardner's mother. "I am writing this only to introduce myself and to tell you I am coming to see you."

Bob Cummins had just returned from the front lines when he heard all the news, good and bad. "We just came out of two months in action," he wrote to his father. "And in action you don't feel much like writing, nor do you for a few days afterwards, so I've fallen behind. I suppose you've read about Negrin's speech at Geneva, so I'll be coming home."

It took Bob and Elman and their American compatriots longer to withdraw from Spain than they expected. The logistics of leaving were complicated by the Soviets, who had taken most of the passports and wanted to evaluate all departing soldiers for their future value to the Communist Party. The Mac-Paps and Lincolns reestablished the camp near Marçà and stayed there for several weeks, with one trip up to Barcelona for a grand farewell parade, where hundreds of thousands of people cheered as the foreign units, proud if beleaguered, marched through the streets. It had all the markings of a victory parade, yet many who marched and many who watched knew that it was probably the opposite. From there the departing troops went up to Ripoll, in the mountains near the French border, which would be their point of embarkation. Service was still in the hospital, but walked out on his own and made his way to Ripoll when he heard his comrades were about to leave. He did not want to be left behind.

He and Bob were among the 327 Americans who left Ripoll on November 23. They were seen off by a saluting crowd, fists pushed high into the air. One Spanish officer had tears in his eyes. The trip to the French border was short and harrowing. They had to reach France before German Junkers spotted them from the sky. "The train was chugging along, and I was thinking, God, let me get there," Service recalled. They did, barely, crossing into France just as bombs from five Junkers demolished the tracks behind them. At Latour-de-Carol station on the French side of the border, as Eby described the scene, the Americans "trooped through the station whooping like school boys on holiday. They gorged on a simple meal of butter, bread and ham (too rich, many threw up). They chain smoked through packs of French cigarettes. The Republic gave each a cheap pinstriped suit, but no overcoats, so they shivered in the chill."

They rode through France in sealed compartments, tired and crowded but proud of what they had done and happy that they had survived it, singing and drinking through the night, greeted at each stop by Frenchmen saluting with clenched fists. When they finally reached their destination, the port of Le Havre, they were met by police and shipping officials who bore bad news: the seamen were on strike. The Americans did not want to break the strike, and the strikers were sympathetic to the Americans; they thought of one another as brothers of the left. But the situation was delicate and took two weeks to resolve. Finally, the troops were shipped by train over to Cherbourg, where their conveyance home, the SS *Paris*, was ready to depart. The *Paris* was a luxury liner, with a sleek Art Deco interior design, none of which mattered to the returning soldiers. Nor did the stormy weather that followed them across the Atlantic. There is a photograph of seventeen men below-decks, with Bob and Elman on the left side, back row, smiling. Bob is wearing a beret and an overcoat that appears to be several sizes too big.

"LOYALIST VETERANS GET WELCOME HERE" was the headline in the *New York Times* on December 16. "149 Who Return on Paris Are Hailed by 1200 in Ceremony in Madison Square Park. Group Parades from Pier. 200 Police There to Hold Crowd Back—Wreath Is Placed Near the Eternal Light."

That was part of the story. After the SS *Paris* docked at the French Line pier at West 48th Street and 12th Avenue, the Spanish war veterans were held aboard ship until all other passengers were ashore. Officials made them prove their citizenship. They were fingerprinted and interrogated. Finally, they marched down the plank and past a large welcoming party to the accompaniment of patriotic music played by the Brighton Beach Community Center Drum and Bugle Corp. With flagbearers leading the way—carrying the American flag, the Spanish Republic flag, and the banner of the Lincoln battalion—the returning vets marched east on 48th to 8th Avenue, turned south to 24th Street and east to Madison Square. There were shouts of "Lift, lift the embargo on Spain!" along the way, and once they reached the park there were speeches and a wreath was laid, though not at the base of the Eternal Light flagstaff honoring soldiers and sailors of World War I. The police prevented that, saying the marchers did not have the proper permit. Then Taps, and it was over.

On that same day and night, the Statue of Liberty reopened after twenty months of repair work. President Roosevelt led groundbreaking ceremonies at the Jefferson Memorial in Washington. A German Exposition and Christmas Market was held at Grand Central Terminal, where anti-Semitic literature was on display along with bicycles and beer. And six thousand people attended a rally at the Manhattan Center protesting radio stations for banning the anti-Semitic rantings of Father Charles E. Coughlin, the Catholic priest hatemonger from Detroit.

THREE WEEKS LATER in Ann Arbor, as a new semester in the new year of 1939 began on the Michigan campus, Robert Cummins and Elman Service were greeted as returning heroes. They spoke to a crowd of six hundred on January 6 and were honored at a banquet at the student union two nights later. Among those in attendance were Bob's little sister, Mary Cummins, and Elliott Maraniss, who was covering the events for the *Daily*. And that is how my parents met.

10

Named

IT WAS LEAP DAY, FEBRUARY 29, 1952. A FRIDAY. THE FIFTH day of testimony at the Communism in the Detroit Area hearings of the House Committee on Un-American Activities. There was only one witness all day, "the committee's clean-up hitter," as the press described her. Bereniece Baldwin entered Room 740 with a protective cordon of bodyguards, ready to recite all the names she had compiled during nine years inside the local Communist Party.

The hearing convened at 10:45, and for the next two hours, until the committee took an hour-and-a-half recess for lunch, Baldwin and Frank Tavenner engaged in a carefully scripted dialogue as he took her step-by-step through the chronology of her involvement with the party and the names of people she encountered along the way. Chairman Wood and Representatives Potter and Jackson were also there, but spoke little.

Wood interrupted once to ask, "How do you spell that?" As it happens, his spelling question came at the mention of a communist club in Ann Arbor named in honor of Ralph Neafus, the Michigan graduate who fought and died in the Spanish Civil War. "R-a-l-p-h N-e-a-f-u-s," Baldwin responded.

Potter perked up when Baldwin cited a communist club in the Upper Peninsula, part of his congressional district. He asked her to name the leaders there.

An hour into the session, Jackson sought to be recognized with a polite "May I ask a question at that point, Mr. Chairman?" When Wood acknowledged him, Jackson asked Baldwin, "To what extent does a communist fear exposure, if at all?"

Mrs. Baldwin: Well, I am glad you added that [*if at all*]. They don't
fear exposure as long as they are working in the open. But they
would fear exposure underground.

Mr. Jackson: If they had been up to that time concealed?

Mrs. Baldwin: That is correct.

Mr. Jackson: He is no longer useful, once exposed?

Mrs. Baldwin: That is correct.

Potter joined the conversation to sum up: "So by that statement,
Mrs. Baldwin, we will say in Detroit there are many persons who have
never been identified as members of the party, but once the identity has
been made, the Communist Party has lost a useful worker for them; is
that true?

Mrs. Baldwin: That is too true.

By 12:45, when Chairman Wood called for a lunch recess, Baldwin
had cited seventy Communist Party clubs in Michigan and named
eighty people. During the break, she strolled over to the press table and
pulled up a chair.

"You know you are sitting in Billy Allan's chair," said Kenneth McCor-
mick of the *Free Press*. Allan covered the hearings for the *Daily Worker*.
Baldwin had known Billy and his wife, Stephanie, for years. Until recently
they had thought of her as a friend and comrade. She had attended a
baby shower for Stephanie.

"Yes, I know it is," Baldwin responded. "Where is Billy?"

Allan was not at the press table that day, perhaps because he knew
that Baldwin would name him. Her "Where is Billy?" is telling on a few
levels. It reveals Baldwin's familiarity with many of the people on whom
she was informing. It makes apparent the contradictions inherent in a
job whose purpose was to deceive and then expose supposed friends.
And it shows the comfort level she had reached in undertaking this difficult mission. What motivated her to do this? Most likely it was not one
thing but a combination of factors. This was a job, to be sure. The FBI
had been paying her for her work. And it seems from her testimony that

she found some thrills in the cloak-and-dagger life. Finally, there was the patriotic impulse. "People will ask why my mother went into this dangerous work," said her daughter. "I can only answer that she was one hundred percent American, through and through."

Courtroom observers were struck by how tiny Baldwin was, barely five feet tall. She wore no makeup, and her face was pale, with "deep, dark hollows around her eyes." E. A. Batchelor Jr., covering the hearings for the *Detroit Times*, was particularly taken by those eyes. "They are dark and flashing and they meet one squarely," he wrote. "They bored right into chief counsel Frank Tavenner as Mrs. Baldwin unfolded her amazing evidence. Her eyes recalled the statement of a neighbor woman when Mrs. Baldwin's role was first revealed. The neighbor had said, 'You would think she was just a run of the [mill] person until you took a second look at her eyes. They seemed to go right through you.'" With her penetrating eyes and confident manner, Batchelor added, "Mrs. Baldwin cast something of a spell over the courtroom."

THE *DETROIT TIMES* was an evening newspaper. Early editions hit the newsstands in midafternoon and late city editions were delivered by paperboys in time to be read before supper. Evening papers were on the decline by the early 1950s, with the rise of television, but they still had some advantages, one being that they could publish stories on the same day as the events they were covering instead of the next morning. With tight deadlines, reporters in the field often dictated rough drafts or scribbles from their notebooks back to the newsroom, where rewrite men—in that era they were almost always men—turned them into polished stories.

One of the top rewrite men on the copydesk at the *Times* was Elliott Maraniss, who was at work on the day Bereniece Baldwin testified in Room 740. At 1:20 that afternoon, during the lunch recess of the hearings, W. Jackson Jones, a HUAC investigator, walked into the *Times* newsroom in the Times Square Building at 1370 Cass Avenue with a subpoena that had been signed earlier in the day by Chairman Wood. Jones said he was looking for Maraniss. I presume that Jones conferred with the editors, explaining the purpose of his visit. I can only presume because all the journalists are dead, there are no records aside from the subpoena, and my father never talked about it. The only detail documented is the result: as soon as the subpoena was served, my father was fired. He told my brother later that his boss on the copydesk did not want to fire him, but the brass insisted.

I came across the original subpoena in Series 3, Box 32, of the HUAC files at the National Archives, the same folder where I first saw the imperfect *S* in my father's unread statement to the committee. Holding the subpoena in my hands had a similar effect. It put me in the moment and made me sense—with remorse for my previous obliviousness— the fear and anguish my father might have felt at that difficult time. The language of the subpoena was archaic and intimidating. He was ordered to appear at the Federal Building at 10:00 a.m. on March 12. "Then and there to testify touching matters of inquiry committed to said Committee; and he is not to depart without leave of said Committee." Jones, the server, was instructed, "Herein fail not, and make return of this summons."

ABOUT A HALF hour into the afternoon testimony, the reason for the subpoena became public. Tavenner was asking Baldwin about certain names in a section of the local party that included members of the intelligentsia who had not been exposed.

Mr. Tavenner: Are you acquainted with a person by the name of Eliot Marioniss?

Based on the official transcript, Tavenner must have used a visual aid in his presentation, because Baldwin told him the name was spelled wrong.

Mr. Tavenner: Is that an improper spelling?
Mrs. Baldwin: Yes.
Mr. Tavenner: What is the proper spelling?

Mrs. Baldwin: M-a-r-a-n-i-s-s.

Mr. Tavenner: Were you acquainted with him?

Mrs. Baldwin: I was.

Mr. Tavenner: Will you state the circumstances?

Mrs. Baldwin: I was very well acquainted with him when the
Michigan Herald, a publication of the Communist Party,
printed in Detroit, began their subscription drive the latter
part of 1946. I was assigned as secretary of that paper. The
building that we occupied was at 1310 Broadway. Elliott
Maraniss, I understand, worked for the *Times* paper.

Mr. Tavenner: What do you mean the *Times* paper?

Mrs. Baldwin: The *Detroit Times*. And he did not wish his identity
to be known. He gave me and others in there strict orders not
to call him by his name, either given or last, but to use the
name "Ace."

Baldwin said my father was active at the *Herald* from the time it was
launched until it was dissolved and folded into the *Michigan Worker*.
She said she saw him there as late as April or May 1950.

Then the counsel brought up my mother, but used a name I had
never heard.

Mr. Tavenner: Did you become acquainted with Mary Morrison?

Mrs. Baldwin: Mary Morrison Maraniss—Mary Morrison is Elliott
Maraniss' wife. Prior to her marriage she was an officer of
the YCL. That would be approximately 1944, 1945. They had
an office on Broadway near Grand Circus Park. I made it my
business to go there. I wanted to make a direct connection
between the YCL and the CP.

Mr. Tavenner: By "YCL" you are referring to the Young Communist
League?

Mrs. Baldwin: I am. At that time, Bridget Polson and Mary
Morrison were in charge of the office. I purchased a YCL bond
from them and upon questioning and inquiries they denied
any connection with the Communist Party. However, within a

short period, when I was working in the district office, Bridget Polson put in an appearance and then embarrassedly tried to explain her situation. She shortly thereafter made a trip to Europe, to England, and has not returned to my knowledge.

Morrison was not my mother's middle name, nor her maiden name. It could have been an alias, since my father wanted to keep a low profile and have people refer to him only as "Ace." Why Baldwin thought my mother was single until 1944 or 1945 I have no idea. My parents met at the University of Michigan in January 1939, and by Christmas of that year they were married.

Baldwin continued naming names, dates, and places for another hour, and near the end, before the committee finished its work for the day and wrapped up the week, not to start up again until March 10, the congressmen bathed their star witness in praise, one by one.

Representative Potter said that men in combat received decorations for gallant service, and he could think of no person "more worthy of a decoration for gallantry than you, Mrs. Baldwin." Representative Jackson noted that in joining the Communist Party as an informant, she had been shut off from friends and associates for years. "The American people have no way of expressing directly to you their thanks," he said. "You will receive abuse and vilification from those who are part and parcel of the international conspiracy. I should like to say, as one representative of the American people, that I feel you have rendered a tremendous service to human freedom and to our country." Chairman Wood thanked her for her contribution "to the cause of democratic government everywhere throughout the world." He also thanked the state police, the federal judges, the Detroit Police Department, the Detroit Loyalty Board, and all Detroit citizens "who have evidenced such widespread interest in the work of the committee, and who have contributed so warmly and generously to the pleasure of our stay here."

By the time Wood gaveled the day's proceedings to an end at 4:30, my father had straggled back to the family, which had gathered at our aunt's house on Pingree Street. "Well, I got fired," he announced.

11

Ace and Mary

ANOTHER MEMORABLE EVENING TOOK PLACE AT HAGEN'S Recess Tavern, this one exactly two years after Stan Swinton, as a freshman, watched Bob Cummins, a senior, drink and sing wistfully with his *Daily* colleagues in the lead-up to his leaving Ann Arbor to fight in the Spanish Civil War. Swinton now was nearing the end of his junior year. He and my father had risen in the college newspaper's ranks semester by semester, and this marked the culmination of their efforts. Late on that May night, word reached their basement hangout that the *Daily* board had selected the top editors for the 1939–40 school year. Elliott Maraniss was named editorial director, Stan Swinton city editor, Carl Petersen managing editor, and Mel Fineberg sports editor. Recalling the scene years later, Swinton wrote about the night "when Carl Petersen and Ace Maraniss and I celebrated the board verdict by drinking flagons of beer and walking Ann Arbor streets until dawn in excited discussion of our plans." Their mission, they decided, was to dedicate the paper to "the objective pursuit of truth."

The news of Elliott's ascension to the paper's lead editorial position was announced in his hometown *Brooklyn Daily Eagle* along with the Detroit papers and the *Daily*. Ace Maraniss was the quintessential big man on campus. He wrote and edited for the *Daily* and *Perspectives*, its current events supplement; organized and cochaired the American Culture panel at the Spring Parley; had been inducted into Sphinx, a junior honor society, and Quadrangle, a literary club; and was about to be initiated into Michigamua, a prestigious society of senior men whose past members included Gerald Ford, athletic legends Fritz Crisler and

Fielding Yost, university president Alexander Ruthven, and Roosevelt's attorney general Frank Murphy. A lanky left-hander with thick black hair and penetrating brown eyes, he patrolled the environs around the school's central Diag with a bounce in his step, zigzagging from one gathering to the next, from Angell Hall to Hill Auditorium, the Michigan Union, and on to the Publications Building.

Ace had known Mary Cummins for a few months by then, and they were already attracted to each other. Mary thought Ace had "a certain magic" unlike any young man she had known before. He was from the East Coast, already an adult at twenty-one, a confident and outspoken upperclassman. Mary was only seventeen and in her first year at Michigan, a thoroughly midwestern townie, intelligent and socially minded yet introverted and introspective. Standing barely five two, with strawberry-blond hair, a smooth-soft complexion, and rosy cheeks, she was the fourth Cummins sibling at the university, retracing the steps of her older brothers, Bob and Phil, and Bob's twin sister, Barbara.

She had followed them not only to Michigan but also into leftist politics. By her second semester on campus, Mary was running for student senate as a member of the American Student Union, the only woman on the ticket. The party platform included setting up courses on Negro culture and problems of war and racism, exposing groups on campus that fomented anti-Semitism, and recognizing that fascist aggression was "the real war danger today and that appeasement and isolation meant selling out to the fascists." At the time of the student vote on March 31, 1939, the world seemed at its most vulnerable. Her brother's cause defending the Spanish Republic had been lost irretrievably three days earlier, when Franco's troops marched into Madrid. In three years of civil war, at least a half million people had been killed in Spain, a countrywide internecine slaughter in which most of the victims were civilians, along with 110,000 Loyalist and 90,000 Nationalist troops. And the bloodletting was not over; many thousands more now faced Franco's murderous retribution even as the new pope, Pius XII, and the U.S. government moved to recognize the generalissimo's ascension. Nationalist police had already begun rounding up Franco opponents whose names were listed on voluminous index card files.

Two weeks earlier, Nazi troops had thundered into Prague as Hitler declared that Czechoslovakia no longer existed, an aggression obliterating the Munich Pact that Western powers had signed with Germany months earlier. In an article in the *Daily*, Ace took note of Hitler's alarming moves toward world domination: "Hitler had already merged most of the old empires of the Hohenzollerns and Hapsburgs, acquired three times the territory lost at Versailles, and commanded an empire which comprised 269,000 square miles with a total population of 88 million. The German dream of political and economic sovereignty over Central and Eastern Europe, a dream characterized by the German term Mitteleuropa, is now an inescapable reality."

After a day of voting on the 31st, the university ballot counting began at 7:00 p.m. in the Publications Building and dragged on late into the night. It was a convoluted election process in which students could vote 1 for their first choice, 2 for their second, and on down as many slots as they wished. A candidate needed to reach a certain threshold to be declared a winner, and lagging candidates could transfer their votes to others after each count. Ace was among the *Daily* journalists observing the process; Mary was there with the other candidates. She made it through fourteen rounds before giving up and transferring her votes to Joseph Gies, another ASU candidate and a friend of Ace's from the paper. The loss did not deter her. She would run again in the next election, risking herself in front of her peers in a way that seemed unlikely given her sensitivity.

Throughout her early life, Mary customarily had been the youngest person in her group. She jumped a grade in elementary school because of her facility with reading and writing and from then on was at least a year younger than most of her classmates. At home and in the neighborhood, she tried to tag along with her older siblings. She was self-conscious about being called "Four Eyes" because of her glasses and "Carrot Top" because of her hair. She yearned for more affection. Looking back on her childhood in a self-reflective psychological history, she described a "need for that early fondling, kissing, emotion, talking, hugging, sentiment that was not part of Scots-Irish families." She bristled at traditional gender roles set by her Kansas-bred parents, finding it "demeaning to be expected to wait on the males, do the dishes, make the beds, while the boys did the yard work. The old farm division of labor."

Her perspective on life was shaped by anxious images of growing up in Middle America. *Evansville, Indiana*: the drowsy ennui of a summer Sunday and church. "Boredom, strangers, sun, dust, dryness of unwashed streets on the way, an empty afternoon." *Newago, Michigan*: living near the Hardy Dam as her engineer father helped with its construction; workers falling to their deaths, her father diving in to save a man from drowning; young Mary being spooked by the evangelist tent and the traveling wrestling shows attended by "men who had been lucky enough to latch onto this job after the depression hit." *Ann Arbor*: the pocket notebook in which her father jotted down all household expenses in the neat block lettering of a draftsman; her mother's careful shopping "and simple lunches like milk toast—buttered toast broken up with warm milk poured over it and an extra dab of butter"—and dinners of stuffed beef heart and veal stew made from the cheapest cuts.

Her older brother left for Spain while she was at Ann Arbor High School. Unlike her mother, who was kept in the dark for months, Mary seemed to know from the start where he had gone, and why. One of Bob's friends, Bill Rohr, had been like another big brother to her from the time the family moved to Ann Arbor. Rohr eventually fell in love with her, and though the romantic attraction was not reciprocated (she had a high school boyfriend named Eddie Weinstein), she enjoyed hanging around with Rohr. Decades later she wrote about being drawn into "some of his left-wing contacts, creative, arty, bohemian people on the fringes of the university that he was involved with as a socialist and active supporter of the Loyalists." Mary thought of Rohr as "a Pete Seeger" type. As she followed him on rounds for the cause, going door-to-door in Ann Arbor collecting food and clothing for the Spanish Republic, one image stuck in her memory: visiting "an eccentric donor to good causes, an old woman, secluded in a smelly old frame house on the edge of town, with fifteen or twenty cats."

In her final year in high school, Mary belonged to a current events group that met near campus in the parlor of the Unitarian Church at the corner of State and Huron. She felt comfortable there, with "a group of high school kids who were not 'in' and were interested in what was happening in the world." They played pool and talked about Spain and the labor movement and the New Deal and other issues of the day, their conversations encouraged by the minister, Rev. Harold Marley. Although the church was bleeding financially, its congregation down to a mere seventy-nine members by 1937, and the old stone Romanesque church building was falling into disrepair, Marley remained a significant liberal figure in Ann Arbor. He was an ACLU member, a peace and labor activist who gave physical and spiritual support to the United Auto Workers during their sit-down strike in Flint, helped organize the local Committee to Aid Spanish Democracy, and opened his meetinghouse doors to radical groups at the university, including the American Student Union. An editorial in the *Daily* called Marley's church "a center of activity in behalf of true democracy—and a genuine force in our social thinking."

The activist minister was a connection between Mary and Ace when they first met, and he would connect them officially a year later.

WHEN I FIRST thought about writing this book, my brother, Jim, challenged me with two essential and related questions: How could I ever presume to know what our parents were thinking? How could I do more than scratch the surface? Jim is five years older than me. He went to Harvard and got a PhD at Princeton and spent his career teaching Spanish and Spanish literature at Amherst. When HUAC came to Detroit in 1952, he was a precocious six-year-old, soon to turn seven, and he knew what was going on, unlike me, who at age two had no idea. We loved our father equally but approached the family history from unavoidably different perspectives. What happened in Room 740 affected him immediately and directly. To me it was a dim and distant shadow.

Jim's questions had a personal resonance, but they also raised a larger issue that I had faced many times as a biographer: How can you presume to know what any other human being is thinking? The only answer: most of the time you can't. Most of the thoughts that go through our heads remain there, never expressed, not in what we say out loud, not even necessarily in letters or journals or anything else we write. I accept that I will never know my father's internal thoughts during that period of his life. I can only work with what he left behind. Since he talked very little about it, what he left behind consists of what he wrote. That does not explain everything, certainly, but in reading his articles, essays, editorials, and letters, I often felt that he was lighting a path for me to follow below the surface.

Anyone who read the *Daily* between 1937 and 1940 became familiar with Ace Maraniss's rhetorical style. He had been writing editorials, book reviews, and news analysis pieces since his sophomore year, more than 150 pieces in all. While his politics evolved during that time, or devolved, his motivations seemed not to change. Distraught over the injustices and horrors of the twentieth-century world, he reached for a systematic explanation of what happened and the best way to create something better. He wrote with confidence, in a voice ranging from sardonic to scholarly to didactic, his approach alternating between a newspaperman's keen realism and a romantic idealist's yearning for perfection. Yet at the core, always, was a deep belief in America and an American ideal.

Even when propounding ideas in the newspaper that followed the party line or had "the tinct of popular front dogma," as my brother once described it, my father did not shut out arguments with which he disagreed. He had diverse tastes, and an affinity for literature and newspapering and baseball that seemed as essential to his self-identity as his political beliefs. His favorite teacher, he later wrote, was a young English instructor named Fred Cassidy, who infused in him a deep appreciation of language. "I loved listening to his soft, melodious voice, with its Jamaican rhythms, its Elizabethan cadences, and the underlying, unmistakable, infectious love for the English language in all its glorious variations, accents, dialects and literature."

Cassidy, who would have an illustrious career as creator and editor of *The Dictionary of American Regional English*, was one of many professors Ace admired at Michigan because of their intellectual gravitas more than their politics. "Michigan then was in one of its own golden periods. Its faculty roster was crowded with the names of great scholars, all of whom also taught undergraduates," he recalled. "It didn't seem unusual at the time that among my teachers were Marckwardt, Seager, Williams and Davis in English; Dumond, Slosson, and Boak in history; Shepard in psychology, White in anthropology, Haber in economics, and Henle in philosophy." To take just one example from that list: Preston W. Slosson, who taught popular survey courses on European history, was constantly warning the young student radicals about totalitarianism from the left as well as the right.

The first front-page story Ace wrote for the *Daily* was an interview with Ford Madox Ford, the British novelist. In the fall semester of 1937, Ford was teaching a comparative literature course at nearby Olivet College, and he came to Ann Arbor on November 9 to attend a concert by the Cleveland Symphony Orchestra. In an interview with Ace beforehand, Ford was dismissive of most young American writers. He admired Hemingway but had little good to say about the rest. To write a decent novel, he said, one must have "experienced danger, despair, anxiety, hunger, and bankruptcy." Ace's first editorial, appearing two days later, looked a few years ahead toward potential Republican candidates for president in 1940, with kind words for Thomas E. Dewey, the governor of New York, as "a man who will not resort to extremist methods to accomplish his ends." He ended that month with a series on the Tennessee Valley Authority, presenting arguments for and against the New Deal project and concluding that it would be left to the Supreme Court and the electorate to decide "how far the government may compete with and replace private enterprise."

By the spring semester of his sophomore year, Ace's name was on the masthead as night editor, a job that did not curtail his writing. His political perspective was on the left side of the New Deal, which was common among *Daily* editorialists. The paper had conducted an internal analysis and found that of 195 editorials written in the previous year, "135, or about two thirds, have been written by a group of editors who align themselves with leftist or so-called liberal points of view on campus." One of Ace's early editorials examined New Deal accomplishments and frustrations and the changing American psyche: "When Franklin Delano Roosevelt took his inauguration on March 4, 1933, imminent catastrophe seemed about to overwhelm the entire American economic and social structure. Unemployment and its inevitable concomitants—destitution, frustration, and decadence—swept over the land, a modern Black Plague, leaving a permanent army of 15 million victims in the ranks of the disinherited. The inexorable concentration of wealth and power threatened to annihilate the small business unit and the farm, and together with them the political structure of democracy, the constitutional safeguards of liberty and justice, and the Jeffersonian principle of 'men enjoying in ease and security the fruits of their own industry.' Although Americans still felt psychologically and politically classless, economic discontent was for the first time in the country's history taking on the European class aspect."

In assessing how the Roosevelt administration responded to this crisis, Ace believed that while New Deal policies successfully averted a complete economic collapse, the administration's efforts to rein in corporate monopoly through regulation were doomed to fail because they prevented "the evolution of modern capitalism from taking its natural course." Here he was making a Marxist argument. Monopoly, he said, could not be regulated out of existence. "If Mr. Roosevelt could by some magic halt the process of monopoly, if he could roll back the wheels of history, his efforts to restore freedom of competition would have profound significance. But with large scale production units, concentration, and monopoly forming the most dominant factors in present day society, his efforts to return to the economy of an earlier day" were outmoded. "The problem is not one of bigness, but of control."

People tend to see what they want to see and not see what they don't want to see. One of the lessons I learned from my father decades later, after he had put the trauma and mistakes of his earlier life behind him, was to try to look beyond my own biases and be open to evidence that contradicted my assumptions. And so, more than his essay on monopoly, there was another story in the *Daily* that same week in March 1938 that left me wondering what he was thinking. It was an Associated Press dispatch from Moscow reporting on the summation of a show trial in the Soviet Union, a chilling demonstration of one of many ways Stalin ruled as a lethal despot, using trumped-up charges to execute former comrades deemed threats to his control.

"Death for 19 of the 21 defendants in Russia's greatest blood purge trial was demanded today by Prosecutor Andrei Y. Vishinsky at the climax of a furious summation of treason and murder charges," the AP article began. "For five and a half hours, in the glare of floodlights, the prosecutor packed in details of the prisoners' confessed plots, calling them human scum and unscrupulous tools of foreign intelligence services. . . . Most of Vishinsky's fury was heaped on Nikolai Bukharin, chronicler of the Red revolution, on whom fell most of the blame for the confessed Rightist-Trotskyist plots. He also demanded the head of Genrikh G. Yagoda, once the chief of the secret police and the most feared man in Russia, whom he compared to Al Capone. 'We cannot leave such people alive,' he said. 'They can do so in America with Al Capones who kill and kidnap people they want to get out of the way. But Russia, thank God, is not America.'"

The story was impossible to ignore, and my father undoubtedly read it and talked about it. I have a hard time imagining how he could absorb the facts and still ascribe positive intentions to the Soviet version of communism. I know he admired the playwright George Bernard Shaw, but I struggle with the notion that his reasoning could have followed along the lines of Shaw, who once wrote that the evils of the show trials had been exaggerated and that some old revolutionists had no idea how to administrate and had to be "pushed off the ladder with a rope around their necks." Such cold-blooded thinking was utterly unlike my father as I understood him, at least the "push off the ladder" part. Decades later he broached the subject of his mind-set during that period without being specific, describing himself at Michigan as "stubborn in my ignorance and aggressive in my prejudices." An honest yet gentle self-appraisal.

One of his favorite subjects was how words were manipulated for political purposes. The fact that he did not apply this to the Soviet Union shows an inconsistency in his thinking but does not fully negate the strength of his argument. In one essay, he discussed how the word "tolerance" was being misused as a subterfuge for the repression of other virtues and an excuse for inaction.

What seemed most pressing on his mind was the U.S. government's neutrality in the Spanish Civil War. At the time of this essay, the three Michigan students who had left Ann Arbor to join the International Brigade in Spain—Cummins, Service, and Neafus—were engaged in brutal fighting near Teruel. "The Spanish people may be fighting for the same principles that have animated mankind in all ages," my father wrote, "but to be truly tolerant we must haughtily proclaim that the Spanish people have a right to work out their own destiny, without the intrusion of foreigners. We may protest in our individual consciences, but it must never become concerted or official. It is this last provision which exposes these ardent exponents of tolerance as mere opportunists who have pounced upon what is in essence a fine practice and transformed it into a diplomatic and political expedient. . . . A true interpretation of tolerance is one that links it inextricably with freedom, liberty and other natural rights of man which supersede government and politics. And for us who sit in comparative freedom to openly refuse to uphold the cause of those who suffer is to betray our heritage and our hope for the future."

Spain was the dominant issue on campus in 1938 and became all-consuming during the weeks when the fate of Neafus was uncertain beyond reports that he had been seen captive inside the dank cathedral in Alcañiz. My father helped organize the letters and telegrams to officials in Washington seeking to secure Neafus's release, all to no avail. His position then, which would lurch back and forth over the next two years, was that standing up forcefully, and even militarily, to the totalitarians in Germany, Italy, and Spain was vital, overtaking the left's earlier peace movement. On May 17, after Neafus was presumed dead and as Cummins and Service were regrouping on the safe side of the Ebro River, my father wrote an editorial decrying Western complacency: "While the democracies of the world were continuing in their futile attempts to fashion realistic foreign policies by watchful waiting, non-intervention and power politics, Mussolini took occasion in the course of a speech Saturday in Genoa to remind them, with all the subtlety of a battleship, that the totalitarian states will present a united international front in case of a world crisis. Now there is no doubt that the American people feel only distaste and disgust for the fascist dictatorships, but there is no indication that they are consciously preparing for a war against the totalitarian heresy. Individual citizens are ready to fight the fascists on ideological grounds."

BETWEEN HIS SOPHOMORE and junior years, Elliott remained in Ann Arbor. He took a room at a boardinghouse on Division Street and kept writing. His landlady, Mrs. A. C. Miller, thought he was quiet and bright, but she was suspicious of him. "Mrs. Miller was of the opinion that subject was Jewish," a government intelligence report stated years later, "because he was always with a group of about eight or ten Jewish boys, his appearance was decidedly Jewish, and his people frequently sent him some hard tack (Matzos) from home." This report, revealing in its latent prejudice, was not entirely accurate. His orbit did include several Jewish classmates, including Harvey Swados, who went on to become a novelist, and Mel Fineberg, who covered sports for the *Daily* and was later killed in World War II. But another of Elliott's close friends was Dennis Flanagan, a classmate and *Daily* colleague who later would run *Scientific American* for four decades. Another was John Malcolm Brinnin, a poet in the class a year behind him, who worked at a bookstore Elliott frequented and who accompanied Dylan Thomas, the Welsh poet, on a tour of America. Carl Petersen was of Finnish heritage; Phil Cummins was Scots-Irish. Perhaps my father liked matzo in college; by the time I knew his eating habits he preferred saltines.

According to university records, Elliott's father was incapacitated by illness at this time and on a two-year hiatus from the printshop. Elliott paid his tuition and room and board through a forty-cents-an-hour National Youth Administration job doing clerical work at the university registrar's office, and also received continued financial assistance from his aunt Celia, with whom he regularly corresponded. "For an aunt and nephew who saw each other rarely, and knew each other mainly through letters, we were pretty close," he recalled years later in a letter to Mary. "I've always had an instinctive liking for her; and she in turn treated me like an adult and wrote me frankly about herself and family. For a time, I felt, although there was nothing but impressions to substantiate the feeling, that she was grateful for the opportunity to confide in me—anybody, in fact, even a young nephew who lived in another world."

Aunt Celia's world was one of wealth. Elliott later compared her situation to the dissatisfied characters in *H. M. Pulham Esq.*, a novel about the confining conventions of Boston high society. She and her husband, Nat, whom Elliott called "so rich he could not be ignored," had penetrated the social and business inner circles of Boston's Back Bay, at least on the surface, overcoming a prevalent upper-class prejudice against Jews. They had residences in West Newton, Bretton Woods, and Florida and sent their daughters to Vassar. In letters to her nephew, Celia wrote in a way that led the young Elliott to believe that she felt trapped, having chosen material comfort over an earlier commitment to social activism. "Aunt Celia was a sensitive and intelligent and ambitious young woman. She worked her way through Radcliffe on scholarships. She was a tireless social worker in the Boston slums. She then became an executive in the Massachusetts State Department of Welfare. Then she was the personal secretary of the governor. Then she met and married Uncle Nat. You know the rest."

It was during that summer that Elliott became preoccupied with the meaning of America and his generation's role in the American story. This was captured first in a long essay he wrote on July 3 published in the *Daily* under the headline "Need Seen for Spiritual Renewal of Declaration of Independence." The piece had an earnestness of purpose that seemed more revealing than whatever political theory lay behind it. The language was dense and at times overwrought, nothing unusual for a college student. He wanted to speak for his generation: what it had learned, what it had endured, what it had rejected, and what it would do.

"Pessimism could very easily take hold of us as it did the generation preceding," he wrote. "We could, with easy justification, indulge in the same low-grade rationalizations of the F. Scott Fitzgeraldian youths who condemned the earth and man as insatiably malicious demons incapable of anything but bestiality, helplessness and greed, then proceeded to drink themselves merrily to hell." But his generation, coming of age during the Depression, was different, he insisted. "However much the provocation, ours is not the neurotic revolt of the 'lost generation' of the twenties. No generation is ever lost; it loses itself. Ours is, on the contrary, a powerful desire to affirm once more the intrinsic majesty of man, to refuse to shrink away in disgust and despair from the realities, confusion, and squalor of the contemporary scene, to probe it, diagnose it, until we find the principles that are essential in the realization of the most humanly ethical ideal; the full development of the capacities of the individual."

Elliott did not want his generation to reject the past but to draw inspiration from the best and most optimistic poets of American promise. Here it was clear that he had been influenced by the philosophy of his principal at Abraham Lincoln High in Coney Island, Gabriel Mason, who carried an edition of Emerson in his back pocket as he strolled the hallways. "Emerson, Whitman, Thoreau, the trumpeters of the Golden Day, were all possessed of the vision of a spiritually beautiful and materially secure America and, if for no other reason, they are the men to whom democratic America is now turning for the literary manifestation of its own dream. It is of course impossible to return to the past, even to Whitman and Emerson. But they are essential links; from them and from the entire epic through the last two centuries, we can make our own departure. The American scene is still as much of a challenge as it was in 1776. Thoreau's dream of what it is to live a full life, and Emerson's vision of a society that shall be oriented completely towards life, must still be our philosophical guides."

At Lincoln High and again at Michigan, Elliott and his classmates constantly heard the refrain from their elders that they carried the hopes of the nation. He embraced that expectation without irony or sarcasm: "We believe and intend to fulfill that admonition. There are many factors in the America of today that we cherish and would like to see perpetuated. America is still the land of opportunity, but those opportunities must be open to all, not confined to a few lucky individuals."

WHAT DOES IT mean to love America? Elliott asked that question again and again in various ways from different angles. In a review of *My*

America, a book by Louis Adamic, a leftist Slovenian immigrant writer, he praised the author for appreciating the country's complexity. "His mind is still fluid enough to refuse to put America into a nutshell, to squeeze America into a tight definition, to hang America on some 'ism,' to tie America to some program. America is a continent, a thing in process, elemental, ever changing, calling for further exploration."

During his junior year, Elliott continued his own exploration of the meaning of America in essays he wrote after the death of the author Thomas Wolfe and the retirement five months later of Justice Louis Brandeis from the U.S. Supreme Court. He identified with Wolfe for his evocation of America's youthful aspirations and admired Brandeis for his strengthening of American liberalism.

In a long appreciation published in *Perspectives*, the *Daily*'s current events supplement, Elliott wrote that Wolfe's death at age thirty-seven signified more than the loss of a major literary figure. He saw Wolfe's hunger as his generation's hunger. "He stood for us, spoke for us. . . . He was the bard of our democratic aspirations. Through him our values, our yearnings and our attempts at comprehension were embodied in imperishable words. America's first Gargantua since Whitman, he stalked through the land like a modern Quixote, searching for manifestations of the democratic spirit, and when he found them he raised his voice in loud and long songs so that we who also searched could rejoice with him. . . . Deeply conscious of the vastness of America, he was in turn disturbed and exalted by it."

When Brandeis, the first Jewish member of the Supreme Court, retired at age eighty-two, Elliott praised him as a believer in "the living law" who committed his legal career to social betterment and represented the spirit of America. Born in Louisville, the son of Czech immigrants, Brandeis was trained at Harvard and gained prominence in Boston as "the people's lawyer." He challenged the railroad monopolies and public corruption; helped shape the legal concept of a right to privacy; pushed for workers' rights, including a minimum wage; and popularized the idea of pro bono legal work, refusing to be paid when it was for a cause he thought important. "Brandeis is the pioneer in the development of a jurisprudence built about social change," Elliott wrote. "His method of adjusting a body of legal rules to the changing needs of changing conditions and social experiences, and the humanitarian and ethical motivation of his judgments place him in the front ranks of the body of men who have contributed to the preservation and extension of American democracy."

The Brandeis essay was popular on campus. Erich Walter, a dean and professor of English, thought so highly of it that he considered it for his well-regarded *Essay Annual*, featuring the work of a who's who of American letters, including E. B. White, James Thurber, Pearl Buck, Malcolm Cowley, and Ida Tarbell. But Elliott Maraniss got cut from the table of contents before Scott, Foresman and Co. published the book. He did break out of the college market once, when an essay on American agriculture was reprinted in the *St. Louis Post-Dispatch*.

ELLIOTT SPENT ANOTHER summer in Michigan before his senior year. He worked as a research supervisor at the Michigan Historical Records Survey, a New Deal initiative sponsored by the Works Progress Administration that served two purposes at once. It gathered unpublished government documents down to the county level, classified them, and made them available for public access. Equally important, it provided Depression-era jobs for unemployed white-collar workers. Before the start of classes, Elliott moved into the Wolverine Co-op at 209 State Street, in the same building where Arthur Miller and Ralph Neafus had washed dishes side by side. It was adjacent to the State Theatre and three blocks from the Publications Building. His roommates were two *Daily* colleagues, Mel Fineberg and Morton Linder. By then he was dating Mary Cummins.

Autumn was his favorite season, going back to his teenage years on Coney Island, but especially in Ann Arbor, and especially that autumn of 1939. Mary lived at home with her parents and younger sister, and at the end of many days, Elliott walked with her down State and turned left at Packard and south twelve blocks to the Cummins house at 1402 Henry Street. From there, on Saturday afternoons, they would head west on Stadium Boulevard to watch the Wolverines, led by All-American

halfback Tom Harmon and quarterback Forest Evashevski. It was such a
gentle scene, Elliott later recalled. He and Mary "loved the big trees and
the green lawns and the flowers and the neat, well-built houses, especially a little blue house on Stadium Boulevard" they thought was just
the sort they would want to live in someday.

It was the American Dream, shared by a member of the Young
Communist League and her leftist reporter boyfriend, who also shared
the socialist dream, what Malcolm Cowley later called the "Dream of
the Golden Mountains." That was Mary and Ace that fall, a reminder
of the universality of basic hopes and desires and frustrations. They
loved the promise of America, were disoriented by the economic collapse of the U.S. economy during the Depression, were seeking answers
to the chaos of the world, and at the same time wanted to believe in a
virtuous, peace-seeking, equality-minded Soviet Union. They thought
they were working toward a true and open American democracy even
as they were rationalizing the actions of what was in fact a ruthlessly
totalitarian foreign power. Two opposing ideas, one noble, the other
false and naïve, coexisted in their minds.

Late that summer, before the new school year began, the geopolitical
map flipped again, and with it the opinions of some American leftists
like Elliott and Mary. On August 23 the Soviet Union and Nazi Germany shifted from bitter ideological foes who seemed headed toward
military confrontation to conspiring partners of convenience. This
happened with the signing of what was called the Nazi-Soviet Pact, or
the German-Soviet Non-Aggression Pact, or the Molotov-Ribbentrop
Pact, so named because of the foreign ministers who worked it out,
Vyacheslav Molotov for the Soviet Union and Joachim von Ribbentrop
for Germany. The pact was not only a commitment to neutrality between the two nations; it also secretly allowed them to divide territory
in Poland, Romania, and the Baltic nations into German and Soviet
spheres of influence. Within two weeks of the agreement, both countries
had invaded Poland, the Nazis from the west, the Soviets from the east.
Hitler's invasion broke the Munich Agreement and drew Great Britain
and France into war with Germany. The Gestapo and the NKVD, the
Soviet secret police, began sharing intelligence, leading to the capture

and execution of scores of German and Austrian antifascists betrayed by the manipulative Soviets. The two nations also exchanged goods, minerals, and armaments that one had and the other needed.

It was a stunning turn of events, difficult for many Western leftists to comprehend and explain. For some it was a breaking point; for all it was a dividing line. There were those who could not accept Stalin's embrace of Hitler and turned away from communism in bitter despair. This group included many hundreds of Jewish members of the CPUSA and some of the "premature anti-fascists" who had risked their lives and seen comrades die in the fight against Franco, Mussolini, and Hitler in Spain. "Bitter mutual recriminations erupted between those who left and those who stayed; sometimes men who had fought together in Spain stopped speaking to each other," wrote Adam Hochschild in *Spain in Our Hearts*. Those who stayed, asserting that there were sound reasons for the unholy alliance, ranged from singer-activist Paul Robeson to British historian Eric Hobsbawm. By the end of September, a series of explanations and rationalizations were passed along through the Comintern, the international arm of Soviet communism: the pact was necessary for the defense of the Soviet Union; the rallying cry was no longer "Kill the fascists"; war served only imperialists and greedy corporations. For Elliott and Mary, "peace" became the watchword again, just as it had been before the outbreak of the Spanish Civil War.

So much for Mary's earlier campaign platform stating that "isolation meant selling out to the fascists" and Elliott's earlier assessment that the West had to prepare for war against the "totalitarian heresy." In a front-page editorial Elliott cowrote with managing editor Carl Petersen on September 26, the *Daily* officially took the side of neutrality and a form of isolationism. The "sands of peace ran out in Europe" when Hitler invaded Poland, drawing Great Britain and France into war, they said. "The editors of the *Michigan Daily*, like the great majority of Americans, are of the opinion that there is no more urgent problem confronting the people of this country than that of devising effective methods of keeping the United States out of war." They were in full accord "with the contention of the English and French that for decent, democratic folk there is no living on this earth with the barbaric credo of Nazism," but maintained that this particular war was not the answer. Instead they called the current situation "a clash of rival imperialisms" propelled by an effort by "certain groups to . . . protect the profits they derive" from world conflict.

The *Daily* soon started receiving angry letters, many from students and professors who ranged from conservative to liberal to leftist, none fond of this iteration of the peace argument. Robert Rosa, a PhD candidate and leading member of the American Student Union at Michigan, noted with astonishment that Maraniss and Petersen seemed to outdo the reactionary America First movement. "Not even such influential supporters as Henry Ford, Lindbergh and the Bund have dared propose complete non-intercourse (as the editors did)." Rosa's comments marked a split in the ASU between communists and noncommunists that would widen over the coming months and lead to the student movement's eventual rupture and collapse. The strongest voice on Rosa's side was Joseph P. Lash, the national ASU's executive secretary, who considered the Nazi-Soviet Pact a sellout to Hitler, causing him to lose all faith in the Communist Party as an ally in the fight against fascism.

Another letter lambasting the editorial arrived from Professor Slosson of the History Department, who knew Elliott from class. Slosson said it was contradictory for Maraniss and Petersen to say they hated and feared fascism and yet argue that the U.S. should not align with the nations fighting fascism. Isolationism would not lead to peace because it divided the world rather than uniting it, the professor warned. And he labeled it hypocritical and "dishonorable" for the editors to condemn Neville Chamberlain for abandoning Spain and then Czechoslovakia, but then turn around and claim indifference to the fates of England, France, and Poland.

Elliott gave Slosson's letter prominent display, then wrote in response, "This is not a war against fascism, it is not a people's war and does not attack the vital causes of war." He concluded, "We absolutely abhor the idea of a Europe controlled by Hitler and fascism. But we also doubt very sincerely the value of supporting a war that will not, as a matter of fact could not, do anything to prevent another Hitler from arising." As Elliott once said in retrospect, he was stubborn in his ignorance.

Time magazine ran an item in its press section shortly after that, citing the views of various student newspapers on the issue of the war and American neutrality. The newspapers of Dartmouth, Yale, Harvard, Vassar, North Carolina, Louisiana State University, Texas, Wisconsin, Northwestern, Illinois, and Southern Cal were all mentioned, but not the *Michigan Daily*. The feeling at the *Daily* was they had been snubbed because *Time* did not like their position. "*Time* has apparently forgotten that the *Daily* has been rated the outstanding collegiate publication in the nation [winner of the Pacemaker Award] for the past four years straight," wrote associate editor Morton Linder in his "Morty Q." column. "The fact that *Time* didn't even mention the *Daily*'s firm stand on neutrality as expressed in the front-page editorial makes it seem as if they purposely passed them up—possibly because they may have objected to the side the *Daily* took." Linder stood up for his roommate. "Speaking of brilliant or astute editors, Mr. Q. will stack Elliott Maraniss against any collegiate analyst in the country."

That same week the university's chapter of the American Student Union held its annual membership meeting at the Michigan Union. The gathering opened with the singing of the ASU's national song, "Academic Epidemic," followed by a reading of poems from *Dead Reckoning* by Kenneth Fearing, who was known as "the proletarian poet" of the 1930s. Robert Rosa was elected president, and Mary Cummins was chosen as recording secretary, reflecting the divergence of opinions within the organization.

The debate over the Nazi-Soviet Pact and the proper response to Hitler's aggression dominated the political discussion on the Michigan campus and in the pages of the *Daily* throughout the fall semester. In his editorials, Elliott argued that the Soviet goal was to buy time to construct "a great defensive barrier from the Baltic to the Black Sea" that would hold off Nazi aggression. He called the European conflict "a robber's war" that America should avoid. He decried the existence of a new congressional committee, chaired by Martin Dies of Texas, that had started to investigate peace activists on the American left as subversives for exercising their constitutional right to free speech. And he kept publishing letters from students and professors who thought he was utterly wrong. Robert Anderson, a graduate student, wrote a long letter asking whether "Mr. Maraniss was acting as an American intent on defending the rights of Americans to enjoy the Bill of Rights or as a communist following the party line."

"My motives in this regard," Elliott responded, "are actuated only by a conviction that America must remain at peace, that the American people have nothing to gain from entrance into a bloody conflict in Europe. My motives, my interests, and my allegiances are entirely American."

ELLIOTT AND MARY were married on December 16, 1939. He was twenty-one, she eighteen. It was a small wedding, officiated by Reverend Marley and witnessed by Mary's family and many of Elliott's colleagues at the *Daily*. Mary later said that they asked Marley to perform the ceremony mostly as a way to "pass some money to a needy cause," the cause being the minister and his threadbare church. Elliott called him "a campus hero." Harvey Swados stood up as best man, and the couple's most cherished wedding gift was a volume of William Blake signed by the poet John Malcolm Brinnin, who brought it from the bookshop where he worked. His inscription read:

> *For Elliott and Mary*
> *Not pyramids nor carillons with bells*
> *May say your special wisdom to the earth*
> *Who are its fabulous inheritors.*

"Swados and Brinnin were just two of an unusually talented group of writers at Michigan in our years there, attracted by the Hopwood cash awards for creative writing and an outstanding English department," Elliott wrote later. "Among them were Arthur Miller, whose first play was produced on campus, Maritta Wolff, whose first novel was also published while she was a student [*Whistle Stop*, later turned into a movie starring Ava Gardner and George Raft], and the poets John Ciardi, Kiman Friar, Chad Walsh, and Ed Burrows, all of whose work already was gaining critical attention. My colleagues on the *Daily* included Dennis Flanagan, Stan Swinton, Harry L. Sonneborn, Norm Schorr, Morty Linder, and Carl Petersen and Mel Fineberg. . . . Almost all of them knew Mary, the youngest among us. Most of them attended our modest, austere wedding, and lined up to kiss the bride, but had to go somewhere else for their beer."

Not long after the wedding, at the semester break, Elliott and Mary headed off for their honeymoon, a national convention of the American Student Union at the University of Wisconsin. Mary was a delegate from Michigan; Elliott covered it for the *Daily*. They hitchhiked in freezing weather down to Chicago and around Lake Michigan and up to Madison. "Hitch-hiking was our only mode of transportation for two or three years," Elliott recalled. "If I was a poor stand-in for Clark Gable, Mary certainly filled in for Claudette Colbert. We never had to wait long for a ride, although most of the drivers grumbled about having to take me along." (In the movie *It Happened One Night*, Gable plays a newspaper reporter and Colbert shows off a shapely leg to get cars to stop when they hitchhike together.)

The rift within the ASU was deeper than ever by the time Elliott and Mary reached Madison. An internal dispute that began with the Nazi-Soviet Pact in late summer intensified after November 30, when the Soviet Union invaded Finland, its democratic neighbor, and started what became known as the Winter War. In that 105-day conflict, the greatly outnumbered Finns, fighting fearlessly on skis against Soviet tanks, battled the invaders to a near draw. The Soviets argued that they had been trying for months to reach an accommodation with Finland that would provide a protective barrier from German attack into Petrograd and sent in its million-man army only in self-defense after diplomatic efforts failed. The League of Nations considered this a sham and expelled the Soviets from the organization. Sentiment in the United States was overwhelmingly in favor of the underdog Finns. The young communists and Soviet sympathizers in the ASU now had two problematic issues to explain and defend.

But Joseph Lash and his liberal allies within the organization were vastly outnumbered in Madison. In the decisive vote, a resolution opposing the Soviet invasion of Finland was defeated 322 to 49, and an effort to send the issue to a membership-wide referendum was also rejected. Lash was out as executive secretary, replaced by a leader of the Young Communist League, Bert Witt. Delegate Mary Cummins voted with the dominant bloc on all these issues, a winning side that was careening toward a larger defeat. As the Old Left historian Robert Cohen explained, "Though the communists won all the key votes in Madison, this quickly proved to be a hollow victory. The convention's refusal to criticize the invasion of Finland did irreparable harm to the ASU's reputation. Former admirers now felt that the organization had been converted into a puppet of the Communist Party. The *Nation* termed the ASU vote on Finland 'a precious gift to Martin Dies.' The *New Republic* fretted: "What has happened to the American Student Union?" The headline in Madison's *Capital Times*, the progressive paper where my father would find salvation seventeen years later, the paper that in many ways saved our family, was "THE STUDENT UNION SIMPLY A COMMUNIST ALIAS."

Honeymoon over, Elliott and Mary hitchhiked back to Ann Arbor and began married life in a one-room basement apartment they rented on East Washington across the street from the new Rackham auditorium. Mary took part-time work as a nurse's aide at the university hospitals, a job that had the bonus of allowing them to eat lunch in the hospital cafeteria for twenty-five cents. They spoke at meetings at the Unitarian Church and Michigan Union to explain their version of what happened in Madison. As the global situation grew more perilous, Elliott's editorials in the *Daily* did not waver from the argument that peace and national prosperity were more important than participation in what he called "the second imperialist war in Europe."

In February, Elliott hitchhiked to Washington, DC, to cover the annual convention of the American Youth Congress, a broad-based coalition of leftist and liberal college students. The platform discussed at the gathering called for strict neutrality in the European war, the formation of a peace commission, full employment and education for American youth, and protection of civil liberties. First Lady Eleanor Roosevelt expressed sympathy for the group, which recently had come under attack as a communist front, some of its leaders subpoenaed to testify before the Red-hunting Dies Committee. Her husband was less accommodating. Speaking from the South Portico to an assembly on the White House lawn, FDR urged the youth delegates to reject dictatorships of the left and right and called their position on the Soviet invasion of Finland "unadulterated twaddle." The comment elicited some boos from the crowd.

From his editorial perch at the *Daily*, Elliott took issue with Roosevelt. "If the President thinks we are capable of nothing but 'unadulterated twaddle' he has greatly misjudged the sentiments and capabilities of American youth," he wrote at the end of an essay describing what was "deep in the hearts and minds" of the delegates.

As usual, Elliott devoted much of the space on his page to those who disagreed with him. Louis P. Nadeau wrote in a letter to the editor, "It is nothing less than an insult to the young people of this country to say that their aspirations are identical with the selfish purposes for which the American Youth Congress was assembled. Most of us hate and fear war and want to retain our civil liberties and increase prospects for a life of greater opportunity and security. All this is true. But we do not allow our dislike of war to stifle our sympathy with the Finnish people in their struggle against the world's most despicable tyranny. Nor do we desire a permanent NYA [National Youth Administration] to continue its paternalistic subsidization of American higher education."

Elliott had been a B or B-plus student during his first three years at Michigan, but during the final semester of his senior year he was so preoccupied with the newspaper, politics, and married life that his grades plummeted. He remained deeply immersed in the intellectual life of the campus, if not the classroom. In April he wrote an essay for *Perspectives* on *Native Son*, the bold new novel by Richard Wright: "The best way to indicate the importance of this book is to compare it to *The Grapes of Wrath*. What Steinbeck did for the Okies, Wright does for the Negroes in America. Both men deal with a dislocation of life so vast as to stagger the imagination. Both deal with impulses, emotions, and attitudes of plain people. Both have a revolutionary insight into the realities of the problems that affect nearly two-thirds of the nation. And both books are sweeping men and women toward a new conception of the way things are and the way they ought to be. Yet *Native Son* is more than a first novel; it is also the first work in American fiction to deal intelligently and profoundly with the life, mind and emotions of the American Negro in action under the stress of unrelenting economic, racial, and social and spiritual oppression."

In its spring 1940 edition, published at the end of the school year, *Gargoyle*, the student literary magazine, published an illustration of all the *Daily* editors in various satiric poses. The caption for the illustration is "PREPOSTEROUS PERSONS." Elliott, with his brush of black hair, is in the upper right corner holding a bomb with a lit fuse, papers scattered across his desk. "The swarthy, bomb-slinging gent on the right is YCL's Maraniss. He's been affiliated with every liberal organization on campus since Samuel Gompers was a little boy. He smells the bourgeois motive in anything he finds distasteful."

The 1940 *Michigansian* yearbook features photos and verses about the Big People on Campus. They include Fielding Yost, the athletic director; Tom Harmon, the football star; and Elliott Maraniss:

> *For the title of "Most*
> *Misunderstood Man"*
> *We nominate Elliott M.*
> *The Ace has been roast*
> *Ed and put on the pan*
> *For more things than we can remem*
> *Ber. Some say that he gets*
> *His pay check direct*
> *From Moscow, all signed in red ink,*
> *And some would lay bets*
> *That the rumor's correct*
> *That the Ace is the true missing link.*

SOMETHING ODD HAPPENED at the *Daily* offices one afternoon that semester that was described by Elliott's former roommate, Morton Linder, in his "Morty Q." column: "The outside editorial office was fairly busy getting the editorial material ready and the page laid out. Typewriters were clicking and voices were buzzing. . . . In barges some red-faced guy with a tripod and a camera which he proceeds to set up. He looks around the room and wants to know where is Petersen or Maraniss? I'm Maraniss, says the Ace coming out from behind his hair in the corner. The photo-flub looks at him with that watcha-trying-to-hand-me look and says: Gowan, you ain't Maraniss. Whereupon he is assured by those in the room that if it isn't Maraniss it's a damn good imitation. But the guy is sure. So he gathers his stuff and barges out, sneering that he knows Maraniss when he sees him."

Was it a ruse? A joke? The FBI? The answer is lost to history. But the phrase "he knows Maraniss when he sees him" is what jumped out at me. Did I know this young Maraniss when I saw him? Did I recognize my father when I studied his actions and writings during that period long before I was born, when he was young and brilliant and searching for meaning?

Sometimes, yes—in his idealism and his evocation of Emerson and Whitman, Thomas Wolfe, Louis Brandeis, and Richard Wright and the yearning for a better America. At other times, I found myself muttering, like the mysterious photo-flub, "Go on!"

12

Fear and Loathing

AS THE ACE OF THE COPYDESK, MY FATHER EXCELLED AT rewriting a lead, or lede, as the word came to be spelled in the newspaper business. Now, after Bereniece Baldwin named him at the HUAC hearing, he became not the rewriter of a lede but the subject of one. "The House un-American Activities Committee has left town, but reverberations are still being felt," began a story in the *Detroit Free Press*. "Latest to feel the sting of investigations into Communist activities in Detroit was Elliott Maraniss, a copyreader, who was fired by the *Detroit Times*." The story included a photograph of him, a tiny headshot that appeared in all three city papers over the weekend.

At the time this happened, we lived in a brick bungalow at 7735 Beaverland, out near Rouge Park. I was only two and had no idea about my father's firing. My sister Jean, who was five, does not remember being affected by it. But Jim, the oldest sibling, knew what was going on. He was almost seven and attended Ann Arbor Trail elementary school. "I remember being told by a kid down the block on Beaverland that my dad was a communist," Jim recalled. "He could scarcely have been accused of anything worse, I knew that. The atmosphere was replete with fear and loathing of communism. When I went home, whimpering, and Dad asked me what the matter was, I replied that someone said my father was a communist. Dad told me he wasn't. Then he asked me if it would matter if he were. I said no. (What was I going to say?) From that moment, or before that, I felt emotionally allied with my 'subversive' parents."

I cannot say for certain why our father responded that way to Jim. Did he tell the fib out of shame, or anger, or because he did not want to frighten or alarm his precocious and vulnerable oldest child, whom he loved dearly? Most likely some combination of the three. In any case, I understand it. Every family has secrets, subjects that are difficult to confront head-on, and this was ours. It would reverberate in different ways from then on for all of us.

THERE WAS MORE to come, in ten days, when the committee would return for another round of hearings from March 10 to 12, including the day when Elliott was scheduled to testify. The story of "Reds on Doorstep," as one headline put it, dominated local news. The only event drawing comparable attention was an upcoming boxing match at Detroit Olympia between Gene Hairston and Jake (Raging Bull) LaMotta, former middleweight champion of the world, a local fan favorite who fought more than twenty times in Detroit over the years, including two bouts against his archrival, Sugar Ray Robinson. The press was clamoring for another knockout against the commies—and lobbying for a wider audience. Front-page editorials accompanied petitions that readers were instructed to cut out and send to Congress urging them to "televise the Red hearings!" "Public hearings of committees of Congress are the business of all the public. The people of Detroit are deeply and understandably concerned over the presence of Communists in their midst," a Detroit News editorial asserted. "They want to know who the accused Communists are and what they are doing. They want to hear and see these persons for themselves."

Elliott was not the only witness who had been identified and punished, if not seen on television. Ten Detroiters named by Baldwin or other informants had been summarily fired already. The Detroit Housing Commission served eviction notices on two tenants identified as communists, including Billy Allan, the Detroit correspondent for the Daily Worker, whose family was uprooted from Herman Gardens, a public housing project where they had lived in a forty-six-dollars-a-month two-bedroom apartment. A young stenographer in the city purchasing department was fired after being named, and a doctor was dropped from a referral list for injured city workers. There seemed to be no love lost between blue-collar factory workers and their Red proletarian colleagues. Refusing to work on the assembly line with communists, workers staged walkouts at Dodge Main, Zenith Carburetor, and Midland Steel.

Editorials and letters to the editor bemoaned the fact that witnesses at the hearings could cite their Fifth Amendment right and decline to answer the committee's questions. "Most Detroiters were indignant that witnesses suspected of subversive affiliation could get away with this so blithely," lamented the *Detroit Times*. At the Michigan State Capitol in Lansing, lawmakers drafted legislation calling for mandatory two-year prison terms for communists who failed to register their affiliation with the state police, and another bill that would kick the party off the state election ballot. In Ann Arbor, University of Michigan officials banned a scheduled appearance before the campus civil liberties committee by Arthur McPhaul, who was described as an "uncooperative witness at last week's communist probe in Detroit." It was only the third time in university history that a speaker had been banned.

Barnes Constable, a reporter at Elliott's collegiate newspaper, the *Michigan Daily*, had traveled to Detroit to cover the hearings, and wrote a nuanced summation during the break under the headline "Double Hysteria." Constable thought the witnesses and groups under attack had utilized tactics similar to the committee itself, "perpetuating hysteria" by using "emotional clichés" in describing the hearings as a smear and a witch hunt. But he concluded, "It takes no emotion to point out that the committee has proved nothing worthwhile to date; that it has, inevitably, failed to corroborate by testimony data compiled by the FBI; that it has provided sensational copy for the slanted accounts of Motor City newspapers; that it has exiled its subpoenaed witnesses from a secure existence; that it has virtually outlawed the Communist Party with no statutory basis. These are the facts. A fair-minded journalist is obliged to point them out—again and again. The average American is not so stupid that he can't recognize them—unless he is hemmed in by hysterical rantings on both sides of the fence."

There was another political angle to the Detroit hearings, a more familiar party dispute between Democrats and Republicans. Michigan's governor G. Mennen (Soapy) Williams tried to walk a fine line, saying the committee's exposure of communists was "of great value to the cause of Americanism." But he was critical of one committee member, Republican Charles Potter, who was hunting down un-Americans at the same time that he was preparing to run for Michigan's open U.S. Senate seat. According to Williams, Potter was engaging in "political mud-slinging" and "attempting to make political capital for himself out of the work of the committee." There was no doubt about that latter assessment. Radio stations in Potter's constituency in northern Michigan carried his weekly broadcast. His reports aired on WMBN in Petoskey on Thursdays and then could be heard in Soo, Escanaba, Alpena, Marinette, Rogers City, and Gaylor at various times over the weekend. In the week between committee sessions, his broadcast was all about the hearings in Detroit.

Potter said he was "appalled to discover that the communist set up" in Michigan was one of the most extensive HUAC had uncovered. "It is natural to assume that the Communist Party will do everything possible to infiltrate and intensify their efforts in Michigan, Michigan being the arsenal of democracy," he said. "But even knowing that Michigan was a great prize for the Communist Party, we never realized that they had been as successful as they have been. For example, so far in the investigation we have discovered there are eighty-six communist groups in Michigan. Most of these are in the Detroit area. The groups vary in size, but normally will average around 150 per group. As you can well imagine, their main effort was to infiltrate the defense industry, and most of their activity has been with various labor unions. However, we have also discovered that they have eleven professional groups, made up of editors, lawyers, doctors, and white-collared workers."

ON THE DAY the hearings resumed, word came from Washington that the U.S. Supreme Court, after three years of appeals through the federal courts, had upheld the convictions on contempt charges of the lawyers who represented the eleven imprisoned Communist Party leaders at the 1949 Foley Square trial. This was unwelcome news for George

Crockett. The Supreme Court ruling meant that Elliott's lawyer soon would be serving time in a federal penitentiary.

That night, two women arrived in Detroit from Washington to lend moral support to John Stephens Wood. A photograph of them appeared in the *Detroit News* the next day under the cutline "THE FAMILY OF RED INQUIRY CHAIRMAN. Chatting with Rep. Wood, chairman of the House Un-American Activities Committee, are his wife and his daughter, Mrs. Bobbie Gollner, of Salisbury, Md. Mrs. Gollner, mother of a 10-month old son, was widowed when Navy Lieut. Joseph H. Gollner was shot down over Korea. The women were visitors at the committee hearing in the Federal Building Tuesday."

Joe Gollner was twenty-four when he died. His son would never know him, and his wife and in-laws barely did. He and Bobbie Wood had met at a dance at the Naval Academy, where he was a member of the class of 1949 and she was among a group of women visiting from the Delta Delta Delta sorority at the University of Maryland. Joe was a dashing young midshipman known to fraternity mates at Sigma Chi as "the Count." He competed on the water polo team, loved music and parties, and "could play the drums like Krupa." He graduated from Annapolis in 1949 and went off to flight school in Pensacola, where he and Bobbie became engaged. They were married in her hometown of Canton, Georgia, on November 11, Armistice Day, and soon he was gone to another war overseas. He flew with the VF-54 fighter squadron based on the USS *Essex* aircraft carrier plying the waters off Korea's northeast coast. Another aviator running missions off the Essex then was Neil Armstrong, the future astronaut who eighteen years later would become the first man on the moon. Also aboard for a time was James Michener, gathering string for what would become his Korean war novel, *The Bridges at Toko-Ri*.

At 12:35 on the afternoon of January 11, 1951, Gollner roared off the *Essex* for the last time. Takeoff seemed normal. Everything after that was not. According to an after-action report, he "jettisoned 1 one-thousand bomb then climbed abruptly to about 900 ft., made three shallow turns to the right, the last turn steepened into a nose down diving spiral. The plane sank immediately after striking the water. Two helicopters conducted a fruitless search for the pilot. No radio transmissions were received from the pilot at any time. Cause unknown."

Fourteen months later, his widow came to Detroit and posed with her mother for a *Detroit News* photographer outside Room 740. Wood is wearing a suit and white shirt, a floral tie settling over his protruding belly. He is saying something to his wife, in the middle of the picture, who seems to be holding an unlit cigarette in her right hand. Bobbie, a striking young woman with dark hair and high cheekbones, stands to the side, staring at her father.

There is nothing extraordinary about the scene, a moment captured and soon forgotten, yet it had a deeper meaning to me when I came across it more than six decades later. The untold story of the couple in that photo is that Wood's wife was there mostly for show, that she never thought her husband, chairman of the committee hunting for un-Americans, was American enough after she found out about his Cherokee blood. It was Bobbie Gollner's infant son who many decades later would share the story of his grandparents' chilly relationship, an estrangement they hid from the rest of the world. The photo became another artifact for me, like the imperfect *S* in my father's written statement to the committee, taking me back to an anxious time and place. It provoked a swirl of emotions about lives intersecting in the stream of American history, about family and security and fragility and patriotism and war—and my older brother, Jim, coming home quivering because a kid down the block called our dad a communist.

PART TWO

In a Time of War

13

Something in the Wind

ELLIOTT WAS STATIONED AT A MILITARY BASE IN THE British West Indies when he wrote a letter home to Mary on June 4, 1942, describing the peculiar meteorological patterns of the Caribbean: "Once again the sun is shining brightly—a hot, brilliant, directly overhead sun. How long it will last is another matter. One thing about the rain here that is different from anyplace else: you can see it coming. It starts over in the mountains, which suddenly become gray and dark, then it moves along the ground and sky, kicking up the dust, until it reaches the spot where you are standing."

Although Elliott was not aiming for metaphor, the weather report fit his life. Rainstorms distant, but all seemed sunny overhead. Just that week a cherished gift arrived in a letter from Mary: a lock of her strawberry-blond hair. "It was almost as if my sweet Mary herself had fallen out of that envelope," he wrote. "Right into my lap."

He had enlisted in the army two weeks after Pearl Harbor, in December 1941, leaving behind his young wife and a job on the copydesk at the *Detroit Times*. Service number 0-1585810. After basic training at Jefferson Barracks in Missouri, he was shipped to Trinidad, a tropical island off the Venezuelan coast, and assigned to base operations at Edinburgh Field, a bustling new air base handling the overflow of Air Transport Command aircraft headed for nearby Waller Field. He was a private doing the work of a sergeant, learning air traffic regulations and procedures and acquiring a "thorough knowledge of types of aircraft of all nations." The two sergeants in his unit were on furlough, leaving Elliott on call day and night. "I like the work a great deal and I am continually learning more about it, but it's a big responsibility and I have to be on the ball all the time," he confided to Mary. "Perhaps this month another rating will come through. I'm not worried, though, and if the Operations officer thinks I can handle the work, even though I'm only a Pfc, and the job calls for a master sergeant, then it's OK with me."

One of his friends from their days at the University of Michigan, George Mutnick, was also stationed at the Edinburgh base. They had made the sea voyage together, sailing to Trinidad in February from New Orleans, where they had been seen off by their wives, the double-M girls, Mary Maraniss and Margie Mutnick, who shared an apartment on Gladstone Street on Detroit's West Side. This allowed the husbands to swap letters from home to get more news about their wives. "It is a great comfort to know that I have an additional source of information about you," Elliott wrote. "Margie wrote Geo to tell me that you look very beautiful in your new haircut and that you are wearing short skirts that show off your beautiful legs. She says that you are all making an effort to look especially nice, although it seems to me it isn't very much of an effort for girls like you and Margie to look beautiful. You must spend half your time chasing all the boys away. Just out of curiosity, how do you spend your spare time, anyway?"

Elliott and George spent what spare time they had wandering over to nearby Port of Spain, the island's principal city. One night in town they went to the movie house and saw *The Invaders*. Elliott's review: "A dandy picture about the adventures of six members of a crew of a U-Boat who land in Canada and try to make their way into the United States. It was a very good portrayal of the psychology of the Nazis, and all-in-all it was very well acted, directed, and written. It had some re-markable shots of the Canadian Arctic, the Northwest, the wheatlands, farmers, soldiers etc." On the way to and from the cinema, Elliott took note of the ambiance of Port of Spain, reinforcing his affinity for what he called salt-of-the-earth people. "It is a dirty, dingy town, as you might have expected. Like all other tropical cities, the streets are filled with vendors and beggars. The people are very poor. As far as I can de-termine they feel no resentment against American troops. In fact, they credit the arrival of Americans as the cause of some slight increases in their standard of living recently. They are a keen-witted, social-minded people."

Elliott occasionally found time to play baseball, his favorite sport, with a fellow soldier he identified only as Ed in letters home. "Ed and I hauled out a couple of gloves and a baseball and let fly at each other with all our speed from fifteen feet. I get a lot of fun out of that, as does Ed, and we stand there for hours trying to knock each other down. Ed was a crackerjack semi-pro ball player in Chicago, who like me, was out of shape when he joined the army. Some afternoons when we are both off we get a bat and ball and hit long flies to each other. The only trouble is that we both would rather hit than field."

This was Elliott's trinity of life: Mary, baseball, and writing. Politics came in fourth, though it was connected to the others in various ways and at times overwhelmed all else. He loved to write, and Mary urged him to keep a journal of his army life, but he said his letters to her would have to suffice. "I will try to make my letters to you take the place of keeping a journal, because I won't be able to do both. I feel that my strongest inclination and talent are for reportage, essays, criticism, and historical writing. And you simply don't knock those out in five minutes, or every time you get a couple of minutes." Yet he started writing letters to her every day, sometimes twice a day, a practice he would maintain whenever they were apart for the next three and a half years; they were part romance, part journal, part reportage, part essay, part criticism, and part history. In them, he evinced the practiced sarcasm and wise-to-the-world attitude of a soldier, yet rarely lost his native idealism and optimism.

"I don't know exactly what kind of place America is going to be after the war," he wrote in one letter that June. "But I do know, in general, that it's going to be a healthier, happier, and more secure country, because the threat of external aggression, which now bears down so heavily, will be removed and it will be free to pursue the labors of peace. I look forward, with unmitigated delight to our reunion and our labors after the war. For two high-spirited and zestful young people like us, postwar America should provide a great many opportunities to lead constructive and joyful lives."

AS A MICHIGAN man in the army, a zestful young Elliott had ambitions beyond his status as private first class. He wanted to be an officer, maybe in the Signal Corps, drawing on the semaphore skills he had acquired as a Boy Scout in Coney Island, or go to cadet school and become an aviator. By early June he had filled out his application for Officers Candidate School. The orderly room would finish off the paperwork, he told Mary, "then it will go to my squadron commander, Captain Kates, who has informed me that he will approve it. Then it goes to the base commander for his approval, then to the board who will examine it and call me in for a verbal interview when they have another session. Still a long way to go yet, as you can see, but at least they are beginning to move."

Elliott sensed that "something was in the wind," and he had every reason to be optimistic. In his initial assignment at Edinburgh Field, he had achieved the highest score in the radio detachment on an aptitude test involving sending and receiving coded messages on the wireless radio, getting 77 out of 78 units correct. No sooner had he started that job than the Base Operations officer pulled him from the squadron to work with him on a sensitive assignment providing pilots with information for their flights through analytical work on "the radio, telephone, maps, charts, geographical and political documents." Along with good efficiency reports, he bolstered his OCS and cadet school applications with letters of recommendation from former teachers and bosses. Stuart Portner, supervisor of the Michigan Historical Records Survey, where Elliott worked as a Michigan upperclassman, wrote that "his efforts merited high praise in many quarters and his writings—cogent, profound, and brilliantly phrased—were reproduced widely." Harold M. J. George, chief copy editor at the *Detroit Times*, called Elliott a credit to his staff and said his old job awaited him upon his return. "Mr. Maraniss' character is above reproach and his habits exemplary. It is a great pleasure to me to recommend him for any consideration his superior officers might give him." And Carlton F. Wells, professor of English at Michigan, said that he knew Elliott from class and extracurricular activities and "regarded him as a young man of exceptional ability, intense purposiveness, and a steadfast devotion to his convictions." If Elliott wanted to be an aviator, Wells added, his convictions "will make him a better combat flier for the fact that, in this war, he had long seen (long before the average American realized it) the far-reaching, inescapable conflict represented by ruthless Nazism."

(Yes, but with a caveat, I thought to myself as I read this last statement in the FBI files. My father had seen the threat early, supporting Bob Cummins and the other young American leftists who fought against the fascists in the Spanish Civil War, but he rationalized the threat later, during the period of the Nazi-Soviet Pact, and returned to his original position on the inevitability of conflict only after Germany launched Operation Barbarossa in June 1941, attacking Soviet-held territories on the Eastern Front and drawing Russia into the war. It was then that he readied himself to volunteer as soon as the U.S. entered the war. Yet that too can lead to a misrepresentation. It was not that my father felt more strongly about the Soviet Union than his own country. In all of his previous writings, he showed a deep belief in America and the American promise. He was a patriot in his own way.)

As it turned out, something else was also in the wind during my father's balmy days in Trinidad. The Military Intelligence Division of the War Department had launched an investigation into his background. The documents from that investigation were later sent to the Federal Bureau of Investigation, and I eventually acquired them through a Freedom of Information Act request in a supplementary bundle of documents that were part of his FBI file. The military intelligence investigation was launched in late July 1942 and went on through late November. *Case B201-Maraniss* was conducted by agents from the Sixth Service Command headquarters in Chicago. Special Agent W. F. Maranda was dispatched to Ann Arbor and Detroit, assisted occasionally by Special Agent Anthony Cuomo.

Agent Cuomo checked records at the University of Michigan and found that Elliott had maintained a B average until the final semester of his senior year, the semester after he had married, when he received three C's, two D's, and an Incomplete. Cuomo also checked the National Youth Administration records at Michigan, which showed Elliott was paid forty cents an hour in 1937 for doing clerical work for the university bursar. Agent Maranda obtained Elliott's employment records at the *Detroit Times* and reported that he started work there on June 25, 1941, that he belonged to the American Newspaper Guild, and that before that he had worked at the *New York Post* from June 1940 to June 1941 as aide to the executive editor at a salary of thirty dollars a week. Cuomo and Maranda checked with police departments and credit bureaus in both cities and found no blemishes on the records of either Elliott or Mary.

Then Maranda began conducting interviews. He talked to Elliott's colleagues at the *Detroit Times*. According to his report, copy editor S. R. McGuire said "SUBJECT'S honesty, character and integrity were above reproach. He described SUBJECT as quiet and retiring. SUBJECT was very liberal in his views and admitted being a communist to Informant. He kept company with a couple of boys from the University of Michigan who went to Spain with the Abraham Lincoln Brigade. In spite of this, SUBJECT never made any remarks against this government, and tried very hard to get into active service. McGuire did not think that SUBJECT'S viewpoints were so deeply imbedded that they would sway his loyalty to this country."

Another copy editor, Guy M. Whipple, said he had worked with Elliott at the *Michigan Daily*, where they both were into radical politics, although Whipple said his own political views had "cooled off" since his university days. He told Maranda that he had helped Elliott land a job on the Detroit paper's copydesk after he left the *New York Post* "in their big economy purge." He described Elliott as "a smart fellow, well above average intelligence. He became too much interested in the *Michigan Daily* and let his school work 'ride to hell' after he became editorial director." "In conclusion," Maranda wrote, "Whipple stated that SUBJECT was an amiable fellow, easy to get along with and not the hot-tempered type. He was honest and above-board, and never made any derogatory remarks against this government. SUBJECT'S chief attraction was baseball."

George Weiswasser, another *Times* colleague, remembered Elliott expressing his liberal political and economic views a few times when he was handling stories. He told Maranda, "SUBJECT displayed his real loyalty to the United States on the first day of the war; the minute he heard of the attack on Pearl Harbor, he tried to enlist in any of the branches of the service and even took days off from work to accomplish his purpose. Although the Navy rejected him because of his eyesight, the Army accepted him." Colleague Clyde Davis told Maranda that Elliott "possessed no communistic tendencies, never made any remarks against this government, and could be classified as a 100% American. He tried to get into the army and from the tone of several letters he had written to the boys in the office, he is trying hard for advancement." While Whipple said Elliott's main interest was baseball, Davis, according to Maranda's report, remembered that "SUBJECT'S favorite pastime was playing poker."

Maranda concluded the newspaper interviews by talking to Elliott's supervisor, Harold George, who had already recommended him as an OCS candidate. George repeated his previous comment, that Elliott had a job waiting for him when the war was over. He told the investigator that Elliott never discussed his political views in front of him, and he "would not say that Maraniss was a communist because the latter never said or did anything that would indicate that."

Pursuing the investigation in Ann Arbor, Maranda heard a different story. He interviewed Edson Sunderland, a distinguished law professor and longtime supervisor of the *Michigan Daily* board, who had "very distinct" recollections of Elliott—all negative. He said Elliott came to Michigan "primarily for the purpose of getting a key position on the *Michigan Daily* and succeeded in his purpose." According to Sunderland, "he was thoroughly imbued with the Russian ideas and he thoroughly thought that the Russian experiment was the best thing in the world. He stood blindly for everything that was Russian." Elliott's tolerance of the American government, Sunderland told Maranda, was temporary, "pending our helping Russia." He said Elliott was "always interested in radical things such as labor, strikes etc." and that he was "kind of fanatic, controlled by emotions rather than by intellect." He married a girl just like him, Mary Jane Cummins, and "went to pieces in his school grades after he married that girl." He believed that Elliott "despised our government, the President, the administration, and anything that meant order and even looked upon the faculty of the school as a necessary evil." Sunderland concluded that Elliott was not to be trusted in the U.S. Army, "even as a private."

At the *Daily* offices, Maranda interviewed the student who now held Elliott's old position as editorial director. His name was Morton Mintz. As I leafed through the FBI file and came across the document of Mintz's interview, it affected me in a different way from the other records. I knew Mintz from my own career in journalism. After Michigan he eventually worked as an investigative reporter at the *Washington Post* and was a legend by the time I arrived at the newspaper in 1977. He had done groundbreaking reporting on the dangers of several drugs, including the sedative thalidomide, which led to birth deformities when taken by pregnant women. For a few years, when I was the deputy investigative editor, Mintz was on the team of reporters I edited. He was fiery, fearless, and stubborn, and we got along well. I remember hearing from my parents during that time that they knew Mort from the old days, that he not only worked at the *Daily* a few years after my father but had been a classmate of my mother at Ann Arbor High. But there was more to the connection than I imagined.

Maranda visited the *Daily* offices in the Publications Building on October 14, 1942. "Mintz gave the following picture of SUBJECT," Maranda's report began. "He was one of those who, before Russia was in the war, was a strong critic of President Roosevelt and his policies. He was very cynical about Roosevelt, the administration, and the fate of humanity but would fight like a dog for what he thought was right. He was extremely dogmatic and intolerant of any view but his own. Maraniss was very prominent in the American Student Union, dominated it, and used it to his own ends. He strongly supported the Russian invasion of Finland and never deviated one iota from the Communist Party line in his ideas and principles. His views dominated the editorial columns of the *Daily* for a long time, and did the paper more harm than good. Maraniss was a very skillful writer but very unsympathetic."

Mintz also told the agent that he had heard rumors that Elliott's father had been killed in a strike and that he came from a very poor family, therefore he was "down on everybody." His wife was also a "Red," but the naïve type that was "taken in."

All of this led to Mintz's conclusion that "he would not want Maraniss in any responsible position in his army."

This document was a lot for me to process. I understood Mintz's dismay concerning the ideology my father expressed in his *Daily* editorials, positions that looked more errant from the perspective of 1942 than 1939–40. America was in the war now, "the good war" against the evil Axis powers, and my father's old arguments that the conflict was "a clash of rival imperialisms" seemed at best stale and irrelevant. Mintz's observation that my father seemed to change course in parallel with the Soviet line was undeniable. But in my reading of all of Dad's editorials in the *Daily*, I disagreed with Mintz's opinion that he was intolerant of any view but his own or that he was cynical about the fate of humanity. And I had no idea where he heard the rumors that my grandfather, Joe Maraniss, was killed in a strike, which was false. But most of all I wondered why Mintz, the journalist I knew to be skeptical of authority, a righteous antiestablishment maverick, decided to talk to military intelligence agents, in a sense joining the ranks of informants.

I did not have to imagine an answer to that question. Mintz was still alive, at age ninety-five, when I first reached him by email in August 2017. I wrote that I had an uncomfortable matter to discuss with him but knew that his lifelong devotion to truth and clarity would make it easier. After providing him with Agent Maranda's account of their conversation, I added, "I know it's a difficult question, but I am wondering how you decided to talk to the agents about my father, whether you had a debate with yourself about doing it, and how you felt about it afterwards."

His reply came the next morning: "Dear David, It's a very painful question. I can't recall the details, but my best recollection is I was so troubled by Elliott's views and conduct in that terrible time that I reported him to the authorities, believing, yes, that it was my duty to do so. I look back on what I did with shame."

That last sentence shook me again. My intention was not to shame

Morton Mintz, far from it, but when I saw his response I realized that I had not fully considered how he would feel. In studying Victor Navasky's seminal work, *Naming Names*, I had read many accounts of informants who felt righteous at the time but later suffered severe doubts and pangs of guilt about what they had done during the Red Scare. I had read this, but not internalized it until now. Just as I had failed to appreciate my father's situation until I saw the imperfect *S* in his statement to HUAC, I had failed to put myself in his informants' shoes. Perhaps it was presumptuous of me to try to absolve Mintz, but I felt I should let him know that I was not an aggrieved son and had no hostile intentions. "Dear Mort," I wrote back. "Thanks for your honest answer. Please, please forgive yourself. My father came out of that trauma a better person and was very forgiving."

On February 21, 2018, I went to see Mintz at his apartment in the Foggy Bottom neighborhood of Washington. He was ninety-six by then, and still in good health, though his memory was uneven. He could not remember anything about his discussion with military intelligence and again expressed dismay over it. "I am ashamed that I did it," he said, shaking his head. "Never done anything like it before or since." He did have one memory that provided context. His mother's sister, he said, was "a dedicated communist" who lived in Detroit and worked for Amtorg, a trading company that conducted international business for the Soviet government. Whenever that sister visited the Mintz family in Ann Arbor, Mort recalled, his father would not speak to her or even recognize her presence in the house. Mort's parents both came from Lithuania and were "very liberal" but anticommunist.

THE MILITARY INTELLIGENCE investigators conducted ten more interviews, two negative, the others positive or neutral. They also analyzed scores of editorials Elliott had written at the *Daily*, deducing that he was a liberal, a radical, and possibly a communist. In his final report, Maranda gave extra weight to the derogatory information provided by Edson Sunderland, noting that he was a highly esteemed law professor. Maranda concluded that Elliott was "communistic" and that his "toleration" of the U.S. government appeared to be temporary. The recommendation: "This Agent recommends that MARANISS should not be given employment in confidential work in the U.S. Army, but that he should be watched to determine the extent of his activities at the present time."

FOUR DAYS BEFORE Christmas 1942, the commanding general of the Trinidad Base Command received a memo from the Military Intelligence Service calling for Elliott's transfer in grade to a safe assignment in the medical detachment at Camp Claiborne, Louisiana, where agents could more easily keep an eye on him. The transfer never happened. In fact the directive came far too late. Elliott's work at Edinburgh Field had impressed his superiors enough that they had already approved him for officer training, though not for the Signal Corps or aviator school. "Soldier is no longer in this command, having been transferred to QMC, OCS," Air Corps Capt. Howard A. W. Kates informed Washington. The initials stood for the Quartermaster Officers Candidate School at Camp Lee, Virginia. Elliott had been studying at the sprawling camp near Petersburg since October 5, long before Agent Maranda completed the military intelligence investigation. Captain Kates had paved the way for his acceptance with an endorsement that said he "demonstrated good qualifications of leadership," scored well above the required level on the Army General Classification Test, and exhibited excellent character.

The Quartermaster Corps served as provisioners of the army, vital but unglamorous, feeding, clothing, and supplying the troops and repairing their equipment. Its training school was booming in 1942. More than ten thousand men were commissioned as second lieutenants, with eight separate thirteen-week class groups that year, each with between six hundred and twelve hundred soldiers. About two-thirds were college graduates, and a number of them, like Elliott, had histories or characteristics that precluded them from certain assignments. Elliott's was the final class, commissioned on December 23, two days after military intelligence belatedly had tried to hold him down to a private and transfer him to Louisiana. He executed the oath of office upon his appointment, solemnly swearing "to support and defend the Constitution of the United States against all enemies, foreign and domestic."

His first assignment after graduating was close to home, at Romulus Army Air Field on the outskirts of Detroit. At the start of 1943, he began work as assistant base quartermaster for the Ferrying Division, Air Transport Command, where he was personnel officer for the Quartermaster Section and in charge of base public relations, including putting out the base newspaper. Elliott enjoyed editing and layout as much as writing, and it did not take long for his superiors to notice the quality of his work. On February 5, Carlyle L. Nelson, commanding colonel of the Air Corps, fired off a memo of praise: "To: Lt. Elliott Maraniss. 1. I desire to convey my compliments to you and your staff on the merits of No. 2 edition of 'Wings over Wayne.' 2. Especially impressive is the cover design. It is clever and meaningful. Best wishes for the continued success of this publication are extended to you and your co-workers."

But military intelligence was determined to move him. They had been plotting his transfer even before he was praised for the quality of the base newspaper. In a January 28 special order issued by the director of military intelligence, Room 1804 of the War Department in Washington, the Military Personnel Division was instructed to transfer 2nd Lt. Elliott Maraniss "to an isolated post"—in this case Fort D. A. Russell, out in Marfa in west Texas. The reassignment was "per Capt. Munez, G-2, and concurred in by Headquarters of Army Air Forces and 8th Service Command." Again the military seemed at odds with itself. Elliott's immediate superiors thought well of him, and his personnel record was excellent. Col. E. S. Hetzel, chief of the Military Personnel Division for the Air Corps, noted that there was no record that the commanding general concurred with the reassignment and requested that Elliott be allowed to continue his activities at Romulus. This time, however, the G-2 prevailed, and Elliott was shipped off to Marfa, far from the action in Europe and the Pacific.

He was at Fort D. A. Russell from February through August 1943, serving as assistant sales officer, bakery officer, and athletic officer. It is easy to imagine my father organizing sports activities; he had obvious leadership and coaching skills, traits I saw later. But baking? They sent him to the Cooks and Bakers School at Ft. Sam Houston for a few weeks, but still it is hard to picture him making bread or pastry; the only cooking skill he demonstrated later in life involved timing a soft-boiled egg. The one story about his time there that we children later heard about was when my mother traveled from Detroit by train and bus to visit him all the way out in west Texas, boiling hot in the high desert of the Trans-Pecos.

ONE OF THE stops Agent Maranda made during his military intelligence investigation had been at an apartment complex at 2747 Gladstone Street in Detroit. He set up an appointment to interview the superintendent there, a man identified in the report as Mr. C. Lang, and on the way to that meeting he took note of the names that appeared on the mailbox for apartment B1: R. A. Cummins, Goodman, Beiswenger, Mariness, Mutnick, Campbell. The names were familiar to me. R. A. Cummins was my uncle Bob, who was overseas with the Army Air Corps in England. The Goodmans were Bob's wife, Susan, and her sister, Peggy. Beiswenger was Hugo Beiswenger, a Detroit communist who was also in the military and gone from Detroit. Campbell was the maiden name of his wife, who had moved to New York. At the time Maranda came spying there were four young women living there: my mother, whose name was misspelled on the mailbox, her friend Margie Mutnick, and the Goodman sisters.

Bob had met Susan Goodman in New York two years after returning from the Spanish Civil War. She was thin and striking, a dark-haired art student studying at the Art Students League of New York on West 57th, while he had a clerical job at a Manhattan bank and an apartment on East 53rd. They were both active in radical politics, which is how they met. Elliott and Mary were also in New York for part of that time. Mary had dropped out of Michigan after her sophomore year, escaping east with Elliott when he landed a job at the *New York Post*, and the young couples moved in the same political circles. But Mary and Elliott had left for Detroit and Elliott's copydesk job at the *Times* by the time Bob and Susan were married at City Hall on the morning of August 30, 1941.

It was while Elliott and Mary were still in New York that horrific news arrived in a letter from Ann Arbor. Phil Cummins, Mary and Bob's brother, had suffered a mental breakdown. He had been hospitalized with depression and irrational behavior that would be diagnosed as schizoaffective disorder. Among other, more problematic behaviors, he exhibited what was called "inappropriate laughter" and liked to wear a beret and pretend he was Lenin. By the time the war started and Bob and Elliott were in the army, Phil was at a sanitarium in the hills of western North Carolina. His mental collapse took a toll on the entire Cummins family. One son and brother had survived the calamity of the Spanish Civil War; now another had become a casualty of mental collapse. His father, Andrew, had struggled with depression off and on, and so had Mary, to a lesser degree. She was particularly empathetic when it came to people who appeared down and out, depressed, or somehow vulnerable or out of the mainstream—a characteristic, along with idealism and naïveté, that motivated her politics, and she ached deeply in sympathy with her brother.

All four roommates at the Gladstone apartment found jobs in Detroit's defense industry, doing their part in the Arsenal of Democracy, while continuing their leftist activism, especially on issues of race. Susan and her sister, Peggy, even sent off a telegram to Kenesaw Mountain Landis, commissioner of Major League Baseball, urging him to abolish Jim Crow segregation in the game "in the interest of national unity for winning the war and good baseball." Mary worked at a Briggs auto manufacturing plant that had been converted to war production. She was the quintessential Rosie the Riveter, working on a team that inserted rivets in the trailing edge of the wing tip of B-17 bombers. She was only twenty-one and appeared even younger, with her rosy cheeks and soft voice, but she was active in union affairs and the United Auto Workers shop committee appointed her a floor steward, charged with settling spot grievances.

One of the myths of the home front during the war was that Americans were working in unison and harmony for the same cause. In truth, there were many ugly divisions, none more than those involving race relations, and nowhere was that more intense than in Detroit. With tens of thousands of men and women, black and white, migrating to the city from Appalachia and the Deep South to work in the defense plants, tensions grew month by month, fueled by racism. Many white workers reacted forcefully and at times violently to efforts to bring more black workers into the plants and provide public housing for them, especially in areas bordering white neighborhoods. More than twenty thousand white workers had walked off the job at a Packard plant to protest the promotion of three blacks to work alongside them on an assembly line. Mary was an outspoken activist in the campaign to open up more and better jobs for African Americans at the Briggs plant and elsewhere, and for that felt the wrath of some coworkers. "That bothered her and saddened her," Elliott said later. "But it didn't stop her."

The racial tensions in Detroit exploded into a violent three-day riot in 1943, during which thirty-four people were killed, twenty-five of them black, and more than four hundred wounded, the preponderance again black. Most of the casualties came at the hands of police and federal troops. The bloodletting had begun with a confrontation between bands of young whites and blacks on the bridge leading out to Belle Isle on the boiling Sunday night of June 20. The riot spread through swaths of the city and continued into Tuesday, the 22nd. In between, on Monday, Mary had taken a streetcar from her apartment on Gladstone to the Briggs plant, and her route took her through a predominantly black section of the city's East Side.

Something happened that day that became the stuff of legend in our family, told in various ways, no doubt with various amounts of accuracy but always the same moral conclusion: we would be on the right side of racial justice, as my mother was that day, an aura she somehow conveyed on her way to work. My father's version went like this: It was "almost as if a guardian angel were looking after her. . . . Although passengers were being attacked and hauled out of some of the streetcars, Mary, sitting there with a kerchief on her head, a lunch bucket on her lap, and a union button on her blouse, a blonde-blue-eyed picture of white womanhood, was never touched."

AFTER THE VIOLENCE in Detroit and another race riot that summer at the shipbuilding yards in Beaumont, Texas, Langston Hughes captured in verse the dilemma African Americans faced during the war. His poem "Beaumont to Detroit: 1943" begins:

> *Looky here, America*
> *What you done done—*
> *Let things drift*
> *Until the riots come*

And ends:

> *Yet you say we're fighting*
> *For democracy.*
> *Then why don't democracy*
> *Include me?*
> *I ask this question*
> *Cause I want to know*
> *How long I got to fight*
> *BOTH HITLER—AND JIM CROW.*

FROM THE ISOLATION of west Texas, Elliott was next assigned to Borden General Hospital in Chickasha, Oklahoma, where he spent most of 1944. While there he was promoted to first lieutenant as he oversaw procurement and salvage at the 1,400-bed army hospital. He was eager to join the fight overseas but was held back because of his politics. Finally, on August 18, he received orders to return to Camp Lee. On the way east, he stopped in Ann Arbor for ten days with Mary. As she reported in a letter to her brother Phil at the sanitarium, she and Elliott slept ten to twelve hours a night, "ate Mother's delicious cooking," played Michigan rummy and cribbage, and went to see Donald O'Connor in *This Is the Life*.

Something was in the wind. Elliott's new army life would be spent organizing and training a salvage and repair unit in the Quartermaster Corps in preparation for taking his men to a battlefront overseas. In what was still a segregated American military, the army found a place where they could use him. His temperament, his worldview, and his leadership skills would all be of great value as the commander of what was then called an all-Negro company.

14

Legless

OF THE MORE THAN SIXTEEN MILLION AMERICANS WHO served in the military during the Second World War, about one million saw infantry combat. Charles Edward Potter, the future congressman and member of the House Committee on Un-American Activities, faced more than his share of enemy fire and suffered more than most soldiers who survived. He was operations officer in the 1st Battalion, 109th Regiment, of the U.S. Army's 28th Division as it moved across France and Belgium and into Germany in late 1944 and early 1945. "Bloody Bucket," the 28th was called, and though the nickname was inspired by a bucket-shaped red insignia, it was reinforced by all the bloody battles the division endured, from the Hürtgen Forest to the Colmar Pocket.

Potter was twenty-six when he enlisted in May 1942. He left from Cheboygan, a town nestled on Lake Huron on the northern tip of Michigan's Lower Peninsula, where he had secured a job as administrator of social aid for the county, helping down-on-their-luck rural families. Chuck, as he was known, had grown up a four-hour drive south of Cheboygan, on a farm near Lapeer in Michigan's thumb. He left the rural life to attend Eastern Michigan University in Ypsilanti with sixty dollars in his pocket and worked his way through college with jobs in a sawmill, a cannery, and on the graveyard shift at a Pontiac plant polishing pinion gear collars from eleven at night to seven in the morning. He had planned to go to law school but never made it, instead marrying the "charming, attractive" daughter of a prominent Cheboygan businessman, as reporters later described her.

His unit crossed the English Channel a month after D-Day and fought its way through the countryside hedgerows all summer from Saint-Lô to Paris, where the 28th joined the American contingent that marched triumphantly down the Champs-Élysées on August 29 to celebrate the liberation of France's capital. The elation of that moment was followed by some of the most brutal fighting of the war. First came the Battle of Hürtgen Forest along the West Wall, known as the Siegfried Line of defense, near Germany's border with Belgium. The forest was only eleven miles long and five miles wide, with perfectly aligned rows of fir trees interrupted by sloping creek beds and ravines wild with underbrush. The woods were so thick in places that one could see no more than thirty yards in any direction.

By the time Potter's battalion went into battle at nine on the morning of November 2, this contested territory had become an obstacle course of death. The Germans had planted thousands of land mines and could fire unseen from well-protected bunkers they had dug at effective angles. As if rain, mist, cold, and thick trees were not enough to haunt the battleground, the woods were also strewn with the rotting corpses of American soldiers from the 9th Division who had failed in an earlier attempt to push through the forest. Beyond those difficulties was what most military historians would judge as the bloody folly of a needless battle, poorly planned and fought in the wrong way in the wrong place. In retrospect, most of the blame would fall on Lt. Gen. Courtney H. Hodges, the cautious yet belligerent commander of the U.S. First Army, who failed to see that it would be better to circumvent the forest, seal it off from the side, and focus instead on controlling two crucial dams nearby on the Roer River.

The soldiers of Brig. Gen. Norman "Dutch" Cota's 28th Division paid the heaviest price for that mistake. Along a 170-mile front near the West Wall, they were the only ones sent to pierce it, and to do so through the woods. It was slow going for the three regiments on the attack, when there was any going at all. The 109th moved in from the left and advanced barely three hundred yards in the first day and a half. For every advance, there came a counterattack by the Germans, who proved more efficient with cannon fire, calibrating their fuses so that shells exploded at treetop level, raining deadly piercing tree shards onto the men below. American machine-gunners proved more effective at close range during the counterattacks, often waiting until the Germans were within six yards before firing. One lightweight .30 caliber machine gun, accurate only at close range, took down so many charging Germans that the gunners had to move the pile out of the way to keep firing. But American losses were enormous. Over seven days of fighting, with little accomplished, the division set up a defensive perimeter of land mines and made its way out, but by that time several battalions were shredded by casualties.

Potter got out unharmed, and a few weeks later he was interviewed by an army historian, Lt. Harry G. Jackson. Potter recounted the action day by day. He described capturing one hundred Germans on the second day, but not without the loss of some men to tree bursts, "the worst thing we had to contend with." He said German patrols made it behind the American lines at several points, and it was impossible to tell where they would pop up to attack supply routes. On the morning of November 6, he was at an observation post when they saw that a German patrol had outflanked them and was only fifty yards away. Potter called the battalion commander and said he and a few others were going to "try and make a break and get away." They succeeded, but about fifteen men at the observation post were soon captured, including the forward observer. On the afternoon of November 7, the commander of Potter's battalion, Maj. Robert Ford, was killed during a reconnaissance mission into the town of Vossenack, and Potter said he briefly took over until a lieutenant colonel was sent down from regimental headquarters. For a week after the division had withdrawn, they were still rounding up bunches of stragglers from companies that had been separated and lost during the fighting. By the time other elements of the 28th came to relieve them on November 18 and the 1st Battalion was able to pull out, its companies "had only about fifty men each," and A Company was the only one left with a commanding officer.

AFTER RECOVERING AND reorganizing at a camp along the Our River, replenished with more than three thousand new troops, the 28th soon found itself in a fight far more trying than the Hürtgen Forest. What became known as the Battle of the Bulge was the war's largest engagement on the Western Front, and Hitler's last major offensive, fought in unforgiving winter weather and again on dense and difficult ground.

The battle began on the morning of December 16, when a massive Nazi force comprising some 200,000 troops and one thousand Panzer armored tanks began moving through the Ardennes Forest determined to split four American divisions and drive across Belgium to the coast. A key highway in the German offensive was St. Vith, known to the Americans as Skyline Drive, which cut through land held by the 28th. One of its regiments, the 110th, took the brunt of the early assault, with shelling so intense and unrelenting that it knocked out all communication lines. Potter's 109th Regiment was then attacked by two German Panzer divisions rumbling along a nearby road. His 1st Battalion was stationed in front, serving as a holding force as a column of Panzers approached. It was during an attack on the tanks that Potter suffered his first combat wound; a shell fragment gashed his mouth, requiring stitches but resulting in no lost teeth. Holding and then retreating and holding again, the 28th was part of the effort that slowed the German offensive until Gen. George S. Patton's Third Army reached the Ardennes from the southern flank and took up the fight.

By the time the 109th Regiment left the field at the end of December, it was down to 111 officers from the 145 it had started with, and 1,976 men, out of the original 2,817. But for the operations officer of the 1st Battalion, the worst was ahead.

What came to be known as the Colmar Pocket was a compressed half-circle of territory held stubbornly by German forces in the central Alsace region of France. The topography was flat and unprotected, the winter weather frostbite Siberian, with deep snow on the ground, when the 28th Division arrived there to bolster an offensive led by the French First Army and two other American divisions at the start of 1945. Potter was wounded almost immediately upon entering the battle when shrapnel sliced into his left shoulder. His army records indicated there was "no nerve or artery involvement," and he was patched up and sent back into action.

Three days later, on the outskirts of the city of Colmar, Potter walked at the front of two advancing companies from the 1st Battalion, trying to find a machine gun that was slowing the battalion's advance. After spotting the gun hidden behind a five-foot-high dike along the Rhine, he organized a patrol of six men under the cover of early-morning darkness. It was about three on the morning of January 31 when he fell on a land mine while moving toward the machine-gun placement. The blast blew Potter high into the air; when he landed, still conscious, he could see that his left leg had been blown off and his right leg was a mangled mess. His men managed to drag him back to their perimeter, and from there he was taken by ambulance to an army hospital at Saint-Dié-des-Vosges, where doctors operated on him for sixteen hours, amputating his right leg above the ankle and his left leg at the hip.

For Chuck Potter, the war was over. Two months later, in a Texas hospital, he was awarded a Silver Star for his "gallant and courageous action." A long, difficult recovery had begun. He came out honored, alive, and legless.

Elliott Maraniss, my father, was intimately familiar to me, but I wondered whether he would seem like a stranger by the end of my research. Instead, I emerged with a clearer appreciation of the imperfections of the American story—and with a better understanding of my father, our family, and its secrets.

2

By the time Bereniece Baldwin testified before the House Un-American Activities Committee in Detroit in 1952, she had been a longtime FBI informant inside the Michigan branch of the Communist Party USA. The hundreds of names she provided the committee included Elliott Maraniss.

3

Baldwin (*right on couch*) was called "the grandmother spy" in the Detroit newspapers. Her neighbors considered her unremarkable—pleasant, mild-mannered, and matronly, standing barely five feet, with high cheekbones, gray hair, and deep circles under her eyes.

The HUAC chairman in 1952 was John Stephens Wood of Georgia. A southern Democrat who supported Jim Crow segregation, briefly joined the Ku Klux Klan as a young man, and had another dark secret in his past, Wood ran the congressional panel that decided who and what was un-American.

Wood's mentor was Judge Newt Morris, the behind-the-scenes mastermind of the lynching of Jewish industrialist Leo Frank, who had been falsely accused of murdering a young woman at his Atlanta factory. Wood drove the car that carried Frank's body from the lynching grounds.

Ace Maraniss, as he was known, was editorial director of the *Michigan Daily* at the time he married townie Mary Cummins on December 16, 1939. He was twenty-one, she was eighteen. They hitchhiked from Ann Arbor to Madison on their honeymoon to attend a heated convention of the leftist American Student Union.

Elliott (*third from left, top row*) enlisted in the army after Pearl Harbor. He was highly regarded by superiors even as he was investigated by military intelligence for his radical past. The army isolated him at remote posts in the southwest before finally giving him a chance to show leadership skills beyond the Quartermaster Corps and baseball diamond.

Elliott on home leave in Ann Arbor with Mary in 1944 before heading to Camp Lee, Virginia, to command an all-black salvage and repair unit in the still-segregated U.S. Army.

"The men are beginning to develop a group spirit that could come only from deep conviction that they are getting a square shake," Elliott wrote to Mary soon before his unit embarked for Okinawa. At the war's end, he was honorably discharged at the rank of captain.

UNIVERSITY OF MICHIGAN
IDENTIFICATION CARD
1935-1936
(Good for current college year only)

Robert Cummins
SIGNATURE IN FULL
1321 Minerva Rd. *1-3918*
ANN ARBOR ADDRESS   TEL. NO.
Same
HOME ADDRESS
is enrolled as a student in the University of Michigan.

Joseph A. Bursley.

No. _____   DEAN OF STUDENTS

ROBERT A. CUMMINS

Bob Cummins, Mary's older brother, was at the University of Michigan three years ahead of Elliott. The week he graduated, he and classmates Elman Service and Ralph Neafus left for Europe to fight with the Loyalists against Franco in the Spanish Civil War.

Bob and his Michigan compatriots took a ship to France, then climbed over the Pyrenees into Spain to join the fight. They trained with the McKenzie-Papineau battalion of the International Brigade and carried red passports issued by the Spanish communists.

12

Neafus, who was also a close college friend of the playwright Arthur Miller, was captured by Franco's troops and imprisoned at a cathedral in Alcañiz, where he and others were executed. When I visited the church eighty years later, it still felt like a gloomy dungeon of death.

13

Cummins (*second from left, top row*) and Service (*to Cummins's left*) survived the war and returned to the U.S. on the *S.S. Paris* in December 1939. When they reached Ann Arbor, hundreds of students filled the Michigan Union to honor them. Mary was there to see her older brother; Elliott covered the event for the *Daily*. That is where my parents met.

The good American family in 1950, a few days into the new year, assembled at the house of Andrew and Grace Cummins. Elliott stands upper left, the southpaw cradling infant David. Mary is center stage, warmed in fur. Jim and Jeannie Maraniss are in the scrum of kids up front, Jim with his mouth open, Jeannie looking with concern as Grandmother comforts a distraught cousin.

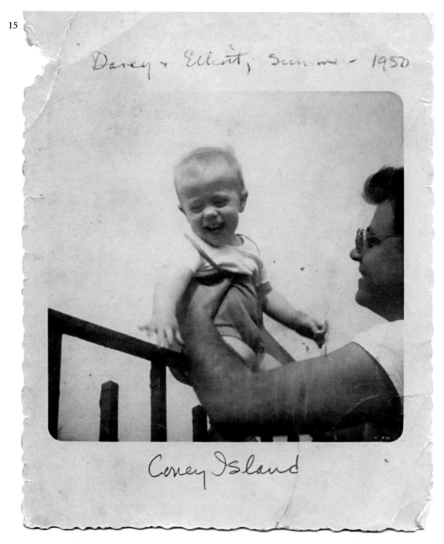

Davey + Elliot; Summer - 1950

Coney Island

Ace Maraniss was a busy man after the war, working on the copydesk of the *Detroit Times* and as an editor of the *Michigan Herald*, the Detroit affiliate of the *Daily Worker*, where among other things he ghostwrote a sports column for Olympic dash champion Eddie Tolan.

FREEDOM
IS
Everybody's Job!

The Crime of the Government
Against the Negro People

Summation in the Trial of
the 11 Communist leaders

BY

GEORGE
W.
CROCKETT, Jr.

10¢

George W. Crockett Jr. represented Elliott at the hearings in Room 740. Earlier he had served as a defense lawyer in the Foley Square trial of eleven leading American communists who were tried and convicted solely because of their politics. The judge in that trial cited Crockett for contempt of court, and he served a six-month prison term shortly after the Detroit hearings.

Frank S. Tavenner Jr. led the questioning of Elliott and others at the HUAC hearings in Room 740 of the Federal Building in Detroit. A lawyer and apple grower who came out of the Byrd political machine in Virginia's Shenandoah Valley, Tavenner served as committee counsel under Chairman Wood.

Charles E. Potter lost both legs and a testicle leading troops into battle in the Colmar Pocket during WWII, then returned to Michigan for a life in politics. He built his reputation as a strong anticommunist while serving on HUAC but came to regret the excesses of the McCarthy era, writing a book titled *Days of Shame*.

Summer '52

The Maraniss family on a ferry near the Statue of Liberty in the summer of 1952 after Elliott was fired from the *Detroit Times* when he was named by an informant at the HUAC hearings in Detroit. The first refuge was Elliott's parents' house on Coney Island.

The family had returned to Detroit, with Elliott working at a party supplies store, when Wendy was born in 1955, the youngest of four children. Elliott thought of her as the family's good luck charm. She was far more than that, but it was one way for him to sustain his optimism through his ordeals.

MI 100-13146

and the informant said that MARANISS in this series, as well as in his other stories, appeared to be a competent reporter, who was objective and fair-minded in his attitude. The informant understood that Mrs. MARANISS was a housewife and was not employed in any other capacity.

T-1 said that the MARANISS couple came from a town in Iowa to Madison, ELLIOTT MARANISS having been one of the managing editors of a labor newspaper in Iowa, which, despite MARANISS'S efforts, did not survive because of lack of support amongst its labor leaders. Prior to their stay in Iowa, ELLIOTT MARANISS has stated that he worked in Detroit newspaper circles but, aside from these past employments, the informant said that little was known concerning the background of Mr. and Mrs. MARANISS in Madison. T-1 advised, however, that no question had arisen concerning the loyalty of Mr. and Mrs. MARANISS since their arrival in Madison, and they appeared to be well regarded in the neighborhood in which they had lived until September of 1958.

On October 3, 1958 T-2 advised that ELLIOTT MARANISS, his wife MARY JANE and their children moved from 1443 Chandler Street to 1619 Regent Street in Madison about September 15, 1958.

COMMUNIST AND COMMUNIST FRONT ACTIVITIES

On October 2, 1958 T-1 advised that there had been no indications of Communist or pro-Communist sentiments or activities on the part of Subject ELLIOTT MARANISS since his arrival in Madison, Wisconsin in so far as the area of Subject's activity with which the informant was connected was concerned.

On September 28, 1958 and October 2, 1958 other confidential informants acquainted with Communist and pro-Communist activities in the Madison area were contacted concerning Subject. None of these informants knew ELLIOTT MARANISS, and none had any information concerning him.

- P* -

- 2 -

The *Capital Times* in Madison, staunch foe of Joe McCarthy, hired Elliott in 1957, righting his career and saving the family after five years of wandering. The FBI followed Elliott to Madison, but his file was soon closed, and he rose to eventually become executive editor of the paper. This is the last report of his thick FBI file.

Elliott was a natural editor with an electric presence in the newsroom. He taught me to be skeptical but not cynical, to root for underdogs but be wary of rigid ideologies of any sort, to search for the messy truth wherever it took me.

Mary and Elliott in winter. They emerged from hard times bonded by love and open to the world.

15

Know Your Men

FIRST LT. ELLIOTT MARANISS WAS WORKING LATE IN HIS office at Camp Lee, Virginia, on the night of February 1, 1945, the day after Charles Potter had suffered his debilitating injury. Elliott was commander of his own company, the 4482nd, a salvage and repair unit in the Quartermaster Corps. His men were being trained for battle, learning to march and shoot, but their primary mission involved work in trailers behind the lines. They were cobblers, tailors, sewing machine operators, electricians, textile workers, metalworkers, repairmen. From boots to canteens, whatever soldiers broke, the salvagers would repair. Aside from Elliott and two other officers, the men of the company had one characteristic in common: they were black. They had joined the great fight for liberty and democracy in a military—and for a nation—that segregated them and treated them as second-class citizens.

This discrimination had been reaffirmed as government policy on the eve of the war, after civil rights leaders failed to persuade President Roosevelt that it was time to integrate the military. A few concessions were won regarding racial equity in the defense industry, but in the military itself the separation of the races remained: "The policy of the War Department is not to intermingle colored and white enlisted personnel in the same regimental organizations. This policy has been proven satisfactory over a long period of years and to make changes would produce situations destructive to morale and detrimental to the preparations of our national defense." In keeping with that same racist logic, most black units were to be commanded by white officers, who were believed to be superior leaders.

At Camp Lee it had been clear from the start that many white Virginians did not want to host black soldiers. Before the post opened in 1940, a local congressman had pleaded with the War Department that "no Negro troops be stationed at Camp Lee." That request was rejected, and by early 1945 more than 3,500 black soldiers were in Unit Training Groups there, constituting about one-fifth of the camp's population. But reminders of the slaveholding Confederacy were everywhere, along with daily impositions of racial discrimination. The base was named in honor of Robert E. Lee, commanding general of the Confederate army, and the camp newspaper was the *Traveller*, named for Lee's horse. The barracks for black troops were isolated at the far end of the camp; the troops essentially marched and trained out of sight. Athletic teams were segregated; many of the best athletes were black, but the official Camp Lee basketball and baseball teams were all white. When soldiers went on leave to nearby Petersburg or Richmond, they were funneled into separate movie houses and USO clubs.

Camp Lee was "the most segregated, the most prejudiced camp in the United States," in the opinion of Jesse Johnson, who trained there as a private and went on to a successful army career as a lieutenant colonel. Johnson had spent his childhood in Mississippi and early adult years in Detroit and had endured both Jim Crow and de facto segregation, but the racism at Camp Lee struck him as among the worst he had seen. "In general, it was southerners, and most of the officers were southerners. They hand-picked them, especially with black troops. They were supposed to 'understand blacks better.' But they were going to segregate them more and mistreat them more and keep them discouraged."

Whether Camp Lee was worse than other southern military camps and forts could be argued. There were problems and periodic black rebellions against racism at many of the bases, but purposely selecting southern white officers for black units was in fact policy. In his seminal work, *The Employment of Negro Troops*, military historian Ulysses Lee said the War Department believed that white officers chosen to lead black troops "should have some acquaintance with Negroes." With that in mind, Lee wrote, "it was assumed that, since few individuals from other parts of the country had come into frequent contact with Negroes, they should be Southerners." There was one significant exception: officers who were political radicals or liberals. Many white officers considered an assignment to lead a black unit a dead end, but leftist officers who had been scrapping to get into the action since the war started saw it as an opportunity to serve two noble ideas at once: fighting against fascism and against racism. That group included my father.

On that winter night one month into 1945, Elliott was preparing to lead his men on their first company maneuver outside the boundaries of the camp. They were about to caravan seventy-two miles up the road to "the Hill," as it was known, the vast grounds of the A. P. Hill Military Reservation near Fredericksburg, for two weeks of extended field operations under bivouac conditions. This was to be an important test of the unit's readiness to join the fight overseas, and Elliott believed he and his men were making great progress. Racial justice was one of the ideas that shaped his politics, and he was eager to help this group of black soldiers demonstrate their merit in a system rigged against them from the day they were born. He was also focused on building the confidence and competence of a cadre of black noncommissioned officers, most of whom came out of the Jim Crow South and had been held back by economic inequity and educational neglect.

"They are learning things fast," Elliott wrote in a letter home that night to Mary, who was in the final trimester of a pregnancy and had moved from Detroit to Ann Arbor to stay with her parents at their house on Henry Street. "You have no idea what a great source of pride it is to me to see a man like Joe Brooks, for example, who eight months ago was an unschooled farm laborer in South Carolina, teaching a group of men a class on the use of the lensatic compass, and doing a right smart job, too, following all the rules of 'methods of instruction' that we discuss in our cadre classes. Naturally, I work very closely with a man like that. I spent from 7 o'clock to 11 last night helping him prepare for his 45-minute class. It was well worth every minute of it. I have a man now who knows how to go about educating himself, using his small, elementary education to full advantage; he knows how to use training aids, how to organize his material, how to get and hold the attention of the men. He has a great desire to learn and to live up to the three stripes he has earned. He started with native intelligence and a natural ability to lead men. Now that he's started there is no telling how far he will go, or along what lines his interests will develop. There are many others of whom I want to write you some time: Branch, who was a tailor in Harlem; Joyner, a farmer from Alabama and now a shoe-repair foreman; Clyburn and Dale Hall, who were former pro fighters, and many others."

THE 4482ND HAD been activated at Camp Lee six weeks earlier, on December 16, a day that happened to be the fifth anniversary of Elliott and Mary's wedding in Ann Arbor. From that first day Elliott seemed to push himself relentlessly, planning, organizing, and strategizing to create a successful company. "The days are full of work, worry, interest," he told Mary in one of his first letters. "Never have I been so grudging and demanding of every single minute of the day, and a good part of the night." He had devised a system that he hoped would make the best use of his time, setting a series of what he called "daily concentration points." One day he would meet with his supply sergeant to work out problems in that area, then choose another specific area to deal with each of the following days: the mess hall, administrative records, the training schedule, training aids, and inspections, all meant to help the company function better as a whole. At the same time he had to deal with the nonstop problems of personnel and supervision of the military and mechanical training.

At night he spent several hours in the orderly room doing company business, listening to CBS reporter Bob Trout's summary of war news on the radio, and consulting with a steady flow of soldiers who "want to see the company commander personally." They came between 1800 and 2000 hours, from six to eight. "One man wants me to help him fill out his income tax return. Another wants to know where he can get some legal advice. He is legally married to two women at the same time. It seems his first wife refuses to give him a divorce—and thus continues to get his allotment. I'm going to send him to the Legal Assistance Officer on Monday. Another man wants me to write a letter for him—three of those already tonight as a matter of fact. One man who was a shoe repairman for seven years in civilian life—and was sent to us as a truck driver—wants to be transferred to the shoe repair section. That didn't take much time! And so it goes. Not that I'm complaining, mind you. I'm glad of the opportunity to help the men and speak to them personally about their problems, because that is the best way for me to get to know them as individuals."

Tuesday nights were reserved for cadre school, where noncommissioned officers were tutored in methods of instruction, the best ways to teach the men under them. This is the school where Elliott had helped Joe Brooks, the South Carolina farmhand, learn how to teach a class on the use of the lensatic compass. For each class, two noncoms were assigned to teach two subjects of their own choosing for twenty minutes as if they were teaching their men. That was followed by a twenty-minute critique of each man's presentation, stressing the use of training aids, clear and forceful expression, logical arrangement of materials, and how to eliminate or minimize nervous mannerisms that detract from the class. From Elliott's perspective, these cadre schools served dual purposes, helping both the soldiers and the officers. One unintended benefit, he thought, had to do with race.

He wrote in a letter home, "Somewhere in some lecture I heard or manual I read, I remember the advice that was given to officers: Know your men, and you will not only solve a lot of problems, but you'll eliminate them. How true! I still don't know all of them as well as I'd like. But I know a great many, and all of my non-coms. It is surprising how true that maxim is, and how profound its ramifications. I've met some officers here who were appalled when they first were assigned to Negro troops. But they were serious men who were intent on doing a good job. So they went about their business and in the process of getting to know and work with the men, they gradually began to lose self-consciousness and some prejudices, and gradually came to look upon their men as soldiers, and not as Negro soldiers. Many of these officers, even a great many from the South, have turned out to be good officers, proud of their units and proud of their men. It only stands to reason, I think, that if a man makes a sincere effort to know and understand his men, his attitude is bound to change."

On the surface, Elliott's assessment here seems to contrast sharply with the disparaging impressions that Jesse Johnson, his fellow Detroiter, held about Camp Lee and its officer corps. One is the perspective of a white officer, the other of a black enlisted man. But there is more to it than that. The camp's handling of racial matters had improved by the time Elliott arrived in late 1944, more than a year after Johnson had left. And Elliott was positive by nature. His natural tendency was to try to see the best in others and to search for ways to improve human understanding. He believed that, given the right conditions, men and women could overcome the obstacles of race and class, education and geography and bias. At Camp Lee, as he had been before and would be for the rest of his life, he was driven by a sense of American optimism.

One southern officer who responded positively to working in proximity to black soldiers was Brig. Gen. George A. Horkan, the camp's commander, a West Point graduate and veteran of World War I who was born in Georgia and shaped by the racial mores of his native South. By the time Horkan took command at Camp Lee in 1944, he was white-haired and nearly fifty, a stickler for army discipline who coined the phrase "If it moves, salute it. If it doesn't move, pick it up. If you can't pick it up, paint it green and white." Beyond that, he gained notice for improving the treatment of black soldiers at the camp and was praised for resolving a festering problem involving segregation and transportation.

At the time Horkan assumed command, black enlisted men were required by Jim Crow laws to sit in the back of buses carrying off-duty soldiers to and from nearby Petersburg. If there was no room in the back but empty seats in front, the black soldiers still had to stand, stay behind for the next bus, or walk several miles to Petersburg. Jesse Johnson recalled a day when he and other black soldiers on the bus to Petersburg were forced to stand even though there were empty seats in the white section. When one exasperated black soldier decided to take an empty seat, a white captain snapped, "Soldier! You're not supposed to sit there." The black soldier got up, but "made a violent remark" to the officer, and a brawl was barely averted. The bus, Johnson said, was a place where "white soldiers were the aggressors towards us, racially."

It would be another dozen years before Rosa Parks changed America by refusing to leave her seat near the front of a bus in Montgomery, Alabama, but travel discrimination of the sort Johnson recounted was a frequent source of friction at Camp Lee, and General Horkan realized that it was wrong and weakening morale. Soon after he took over, he worked out a plan to get around the Jim Crow laws by reaching an agreement with the Petersburg–Camp Lee bus company to operate a certain number of buses exclusively for soldiers, with no separation of the races, where soldiers were seated on a first-come, first-serve basis, and with a military-only depot in downtown Petersburg where black and white soldiers would sit together in the waiting room. Orrin C. Evans, a black journalist at the *Philadelphia Record* who was investigating racial inequities in the military, praised Horkan for his innovations at Camp Lee, which eventually forced other southern camps to follow his lead. "Any Negro soldier who is in town can always get a bus back with no Jim Crowism and no more than ordinary delay, such as happens on buses elsewhere," Evans reported. This change, he wrote, was a major reason black soldiers at Camp Lee now appeared to be "high in morale, proud, and snappy."

The men in Elliott's company provided more than their share of talent for the entire camp. In one week in January alone, the soldiers enjoyed a boxing match at the Unit Training Group gym, where the 4482nd's Dale Hall, the Service Command heavyweight champ, defeated a Golden Gloves star from California, and then, a few nights later, Willie Reeves, another of the men in Elliott's unit, led a quintet of singers who "brought the house down" at a musical revue. The group's impresario was 1st Sgt. Walton Plinton, a noncom in the salvage company who had discovered their harmonic talents while training them.

One of the repeated themes in Elliott's letters home to Mary was belief in his company. "I wish you were here to share in some of our ceremonies," he wrote on the night of January 20, recounting that afternoon's events. "We were presented with our unit colors and standards and flags by the CO of the Unit Training Group. I accepted them for Col. Hunter in the name of the company, then turned them over to the First Sergeant, who in turn handed them to the color guard. All very military,

with salutes, snappy facings and bugles and three-shot volleys from the
ceremonial guard. Then, in front of the whole company, I made the
presentation of the warrants of the first group of non-commissioned
officers to be promoted since we activated. Then, to the music of the
First Training Group band, we marched in our first dress parade before
the inspecting party headed by Colonel Hunter. It was really very colorful, and smart, and I believe, unifying. I must say we really looked good.
I was very proud. Then we dismissed them at 4 p.m., one hour earlier
than usual. And if you think one hour doesn't mean anything to them
when it comes to taking off for the weekend, then you don't know the
American soldier."

That is not to say that everyone in his unit was gung-ho about the
military. Elliott had to deal with malcontents in the enlisted ranks. He
estimated there were ten to twelve in his company who did not want to
work and were looking for ways to prevent being sent overseas. "Without attempting to give an analysis of the motives and reasons for their
actions, I'll tell you what they are doing," he wrote. "They feign illness,
disregard the orders of their non-coms, taunt the other men who are
doing their jobs properly as 'suckers' etc." Elliott understood America's difficult racial history and the many subversive ways that African
Americans, from slavery onward, thwarted the intentions of powerful
whites as a means of protest. But he felt he could not allow the discontent to infect his unit.

"Of course, the really bad characters are screened from units before
they ship. But men whose only ailment—real or imagined—is gang-
plank fever, well, the army and my unit simply cannot operate on the
theory that overseas service is a sort of punishment that is handed out
in return for faithful service. It is a duty and obligation of every man
who is physically and technically qualified." His approach to dealing
with the problem, he told Mary, was twofold. "First, I am striving to in-
culcate in the company as a whole, a feeling of technical proficiency—
confidence in themselves and their ability to perform their job, that is
the backbone of morale. Also, without too obvious 'lecturing,' I'm trying to instill a desire to serve overseas, pointing out that our services
are needed to help bring victory and thus an end to the war. That is not

an easy task, but I think that we are definitely making progress. All my non-coms have that attitude now, and they are getting it down to the men. Concurrently, I'm trying to work on them individually, trying to find out exactly what they think and why, and thus make a start toward straightening them out."

AT SEVEN ON the morning of February 5, the company left by motor convoy for the A. P. Hill Military Reservation. By day's end, Elliott was at the company command post, working by the light of a kerosene lamp. He noted that he was stationed "at the very spot General Grant bivouacked in the last stages of his campaign to end the Civil War." He felt fortunate that his company had arrived without incident and was now bedded down for the night. That comfort did not last long, however. They were awakened at three the next morning with orders to move the entire company and its equipment to an area twenty miles away.

"I had been expecting that they would throw the book at us—and I guess they will all right," he wrote later. "'Shake down' move is what they call this business of packing up and moving the very first night that you hit a bivouac area. Well, we made it all right, with a lot of work and sweat and cold toes and noses. The only mishap was a busted window in one trailer. It was a shuttle march in which they had six trucks move the men, they load up and carry that group to an area and the rest march to meet them, then load up another group. Got the orders at 3 a.m. and got everyone to the new quarters by 10 a.m. They ate C rations for breakfast and then dug foxholes and camouflaged the trailers and tents." The feeling of satisfaction was disrupted the next day when two men turned up with spinal meningitis and were taken to a hospital in Fredericksburg. Doctors came out to the field to examine the other men in the company and slapped a three-day quarantine on the unit. "You can imagine how I feel," Elliott wrote. "This matter of having the safety and health and well-being of 200 men on one's hands is a tremendous responsibility. I hope I can meet it."

Once the quarantine was lifted, the place was "crawling with inspectors of all kinds and all ranks," including "a visit by General Horkan himself, who incidentally was taken prisoner by one of our sentries since he didn't know our password. He looked around and . . . I imagine he felt we were getting along ok. At any rate he didn't say anything that would indicate otherwise." Soon after the general left, the company was attacked by "Nazi" tanks and responded by raising "quite a furor." One of Elliott's men succeeded in putting an approaching tank out of commission by strategically placing logs in its track. After a week in the field, his troops were starting to act like seasoned soldiers. "They can balance mess kits on one knee, shave with cold water out of a steel helmet, wash their feet every night, fix their pup tents in the dark, dig a foxhole deep and fast, clean their rifles in the dark, use a compass at night." It was enough to draw compliments from a high-ranking officer in the Quartermaster Corps who visited the 4482nd in the field, Elliott boasted: "He paid us a very high compliment: He said we were far ahead of other salvage repair companies that activated the same day. Naturally, I was pleased, and passed the compliment on to the men, with the admonition that we still had a long and hard road ahead."

At the end of the two-week exercise, as the company was loading up the trucks from their final bivouac area, it started to rain, then snow and sleet. "The ground became soggy and wet; the temperature took a sharp drop. The ride back was cold and freezing and damp, but our spirits were pretty high and the weather didn't affect us much," Elliott recalled. "The men sang most of the way back. The current favorites in this company, I would judge, are 'Accentuate the Positive,' 'Into Each Life Some Rain Must Fall,' 'Till Then,' and 'Rum and Coca-Cola.'"

MARY WAS EIGHT months pregnant. Unlike Elliott, she did not write every day, but only when she felt she had something to say. And Elliott was not her only correspondent. She also received letters from her brother Phil, who was writing from Highland Hospital in Asheville, North Carolina. Mary and her siblings knew that Phil was brilliant; his IQ was 150. But mental illness separated him from the world. Dr. Otto Billig, chief psychiatrist at Highland, told Phil that he saw improvement after four years of treatment, but Phil wrote to his family that he felt the opposite. "I just feel that I am doomed to gradual incapacitation of a more or less general nature, being regarded as something of a sub-human species halfway between a gorilla and a man. For I am pretty much all by myself in the world, have difficulty in making friends and adjusting myself with no ideas practically, nothing to say and getting no enjoyment or satisfaction out of anything I do. I am also tired most of the time, worried, apprehensive, and very unhappy. It's downright torture, that's all it is."

On February 28, Mary wrote back to her brother. She offered sympathy and advice, venturing into delicate territory. "I admire you tremendously for the fight you've put up against that suffering and the way you've come out of it. I think that (despite Mother's teachings) if you do feel terrible, better to say it than try to fool yourself or others. As Sue [brother Bob's wife] said once, even for a person who hasn't been ill with schizophrenia, for a person who has only suffered from an acute case of shyness, inferiority, lack of confidence, or something of that sort, it's a very hard fight to abolish the constant worry about how one fits into the things that other people seem to be fitting into so easily—work, friends, recreation, avocations, etc. Am I right in presuming that that is one of the things on your mind that seems so darn pressing? Sue (although she didn't say so) was speaking from personal experience, and as a matter of fact, I agreed with her from personal experience. I've become convinced that President Roosevelt's slogan of 'You've nothing to fear but fear itself' is the best one to work by that I've ever heard. Whenever I start worrying about things I've done in the past that I haven't been satisfied with, or whether I'll be able to do something in the future, I make an effort to realize that the greatest impediment I'll ever have is simply the fear and worry I carry along."

Mary told Phil that she had just returned from Detroit, where a group of friends—including her sister, Barbara, sister-in-law Sue, Margie Mutnick, and Anabel and Gladys Purdy—hosted a baby shower. Anabel Purdy was the young widow of Harry Purdy, a friend from University of Michigan days when he and Phil and Mary had been active together in the Young Communist League. Purdy and his younger brother, Robert, left college early to work as labor organizers in the auto-related tool-

and-die industry in Detroit. They both enlisted after Pearl Harbor and joined the Army Air Corps. Harry was flying a B-24 on June 20, 1944, on his way to bomb an oil refinery near Pölitz, Germany, when his plane was shot down. According to military records, he parachuted behind enemy lines and apparently was captured and killed by civilians, who destroyed his dog tags. Gladys Purdy was the wife of Harry's brother, Bob, who at the time Harry died was being held in a German prison camp, where he would remain until the end of the war. He had been captured after his B-24 was shot down over Vicenza, Italy. Two Americans, brothers and leftists—one killed, the other imprisoned, fighting for their country.

Bob Cummins had already fought fascism once, in Spain, and when he enlisted with the army after Pearl Harbor his ambition was to be on a bomber crew, like his friends the Purdy brothers. But the military had kept close watch on him, just as they had on Elliott, and rejected his requests to fly combat missions or be transferred to the infantry. Instead he spent the final two years of the war at an air base in England as a mechanic with the 713 Bomb Squadron, 448 Bomb Group. That is where he was when his wife helped host the baby shower for his sister. The English winter, he reported in letters home, had been "damp and gloomy," but he saw signs that spring would be "worth its name." On a two-day pass, he had gone to nearby Leicester, attended a football match between Leicester City and Sheffield, and met a fellow named Derek Bircumshaw, who invited him to stay the night with his family. Back at the base, Bob studied hydraulics by day and in his spare time at night taught himself how to speak and read Russian. "They are really coming along fine," he said of his Russian studies. "I should be able to read newspapers, say, by next fall and after that it would only be necessary to extend my vocabulary."

The U.S. military's wartime handling of radicals, suspected communists, and Americans who fought with the International Brigade in Spain was uneven. Many of them were subjected to military intelligence investigations, like Elliott, or kept from combat, like Bob. Peter N. Carroll, in his book *The Odyssey of the Abraham Lincoln Brigade*, reports that many Lincoln veterans spent much of the war in the Aleutian Islands or were segregated in a company of suspected subversives at Camp Ripley in Minnesota. But their treatment was unpredictable, like most personnel matters handled by the wartime army bureaucracy. Along with the Purdy brothers, another young radical who was able to fly combat missions in Europe was George Watt, the Lincoln veteran who at a Young Communist League meeting in New York in early 1937 had recruited Bob Cummins and Ralph Neafus to fight in Spain. Six years later, on November 5, 1943, his birthday, Watt was a gunner aboard a B-17 Flying Fortress on a bombing mission from the Knettishall Airfield in England to Germany's Ruhr Valley. As the plane flew over Belgium, it was attacked and hit by a German Focke-Wulf 190. "It was not the first time I had known such fear," Watt wrote later. "In my first action at Fuentes del Ebro in Spain, six years earlier, we had been dive-bombed by German Stukas. I lay shivering with fright in a shallow communications trench as the near misses exploded all around us. Now I felt that same kind of terror again." The cliché was true: his life flashed before his eyes as the plane headed down. He kept saying to himself two words: "No regrets." No regrets about fighting fascism in Spain and flying in the war against Hitler. Then he parachuted out, landing in an open field near a river.

What happened after that was retold by Watt in his book, *The Comet Connection*, detailing the bravery of a network of villagers and underground fighters who helped him make a harrowing escape through enemy territory in Belgium and France. His final walk to safety had a poetic symmetry. He climbed over the Pyrenees, again, just as he and Bob Cummins had done six years earlier as Lincoln volunteers, an act of commitment and courage that prompted the U.S. government to label them "premature anti-fascists." Spain was neutral territory now, a free zone between the Axis and Allied powers, but still it could not seem like friendly ground to Watt, not with his old nemesis, Generalissimo Francisco Franco, in charge.

Among the gifts Mary brought back to Ann Arbor from the shower her friends hosted for her in Detroit was "a beautiful baby crib." As to the specifics of the baby who would sleep in the crib, she had no idea. "I don't know whether it will be blonde, brunette, girl, boy, whether it will look like Ace or myself, and as a matter of fact, we don't know for sure yet what it will be named."

Mary said she would send Phil's letter on to Elliott and recommend that he telephone Phil, since the long-distance charge for a call between them might be relatively cheap. "Elliott is still at Petersburg," she closed. "He is a first lieutenant in charge of a company (about 200 men) of Negro quartermaster salvage repair troops. . . . I think he feels pretty successful about the whole thing. The company will be used for overseas duty within the next couple of months or so, and then we'll be writing to an A.P.O. He may be here in time to see his offspring."

DAY BY DAY, Elliott's pride in his company grew. It was a good-looking outfit, he thought. The soldiers wore their uniforms sharply and tossed the smartest salutes in the camp. "To tell a tale out of school, we are already looked upon in Camp Lee as a clannish outfit," he confided to Mary in a March 1 letter. "My men stick together. There are very few men left, although there are still a few, who are bucking for 'out' and they are in very bad standing with the others." His unit was in such good shape that the next day the group commander announced that all the salvage repair units on the post would be inspected—except the 4482nd.

A report from one of his noncom leaders on the complicated subject of race pleased Elliott even more, he told Mary. "Staff Sergeant Anderson, platoon sergeant of the 2nd platoon, told me one day last week that despite the strict discipline and control our noncoms exercise they are the only group of noncoms in camp who are not called 'Toms' by the men. You know as well as I, of course, what the meaning of the term is; and you therefore know how I felt when I heard it. For it is indisputable proof that our program and plan and effort is taking hold, that our noncoms are beginning to exercise leadership in its proper meaning, and that the men are beginning to develop a group spirit that could come only from deep conviction that they are getting a square shake."

Life became an anxious waiting game: waiting to ship overseas, waiting to hear baby news from Ann Arbor. March 22 was a lovely night at Camp Lee, "warm and breezy, with the pungent odor of the pines." Early the next morning, Elliott was told that his mother-in-law, Grace Cummins, was on the line. Mary had given birth to a son. "Now that it has happened, I'm completely at a loss as to what to say," he wrote to her that night. "My first concern and greatest worry of course is about you; and you have no idea with what relief and joy I heard your mother's assurance that you were very well, recuperating nicely, and feel no ill-effects. When your mother called me this morning, I was stunned, surprised and bewildered but of course it was not long before I was filled with joy and pride and a deep love for you and our son. The connection was pretty bad, so I had a hard time hearing what she had to say. By dint of loud shouting, however, I managed to get all the sweet details. I was passing out cigars today with my chest stuck way out."

A few days later Elliott received orders to travel to Washington for a conference. He flew up and back the same day. The call to port was expected soon; the company's advance representative was already in Seattle preparing. The Tenth Army was landing on Okinawa, and Elliott's company would soon follow. "My guess is that we are going to hook up with the Tenth, which is now 325 miles from Tokyo and follow it into Tokyo, possibly via China, or possibly directly to Japan." Then word came that they were to wait again, for another few weeks. The delay had to do with shipping schedules to Okinawa. Elliott was frustrated but took advantage of the situation to get permission for a quick trip up to Ann Arbor to see his wife and baby son, James Elliott Maraniss. He flew Eastern Airlines from Richmond through Washington to Detroit, leaving at 4:30 on Saturday morning and returning at 5:15 Sunday afternoon.

Back at Camp Lee, Elliott was effusive. "I can't remember spending a more satisfying two days than those two with you and Jimmy," he wrote Mary. "On the surface they didn't seem much different than many another weekend. But there was a great qualitative difference in mood, emotion, and thought that sharply set it off from other leaves we've spent together. In the first place, there was the successful accomplishment of the audacious scheme of travel itself. It really was quite a trek, and ranks with the job we pulled off getting you and Margie to New

Orleans. I was taking quite a chance, and had my neck stuck out a mile, but it was a calculated risk with the odds in my favor, and I have never been one to shrink from taking calculated risks, especially when there were more important stakes involved. Most of the officers here were quite amazed at my 'daring,' and were frankly surprised that it worked out so smoothly. Then the visit itself. Darling, we've got a wonderful little baby. He looks good to me, every bit of him, and I'm proud as a peacock to be his father. He will never be a stranger to me, no matter how long I am away."

The call came the next day from the port of embarkation, the last and final word. They would leave Camp Lee in two weeks.

The day after that, April 12, Cpl. Henry Pohly heard the teletype bell go off in the camp's information office and ran over to see what news was breaking. It was 5:49 p.m. Soldiers were just leaving the chow line. President Roosevelt was dead.

"There is a deep unrelieved gloom in the barracks here tonight, as if every one of us has lost not only a leader but a close personal friend," Elliott wrote to Mary after hearing the news. "I don't feel like writing more tonight, so I'll close and go to bed. It seems the heart has been taken right out of me. O, my lord what a terrible thing has happened to us! Tomorrow evening at retreat my company will hold a brief memorial service, paying silent tribute to our fallen chief. I know that my men are going to be depressed and bewildered, and it will be my job to keep alive the hope in their hearts for victory and lasting peace. That hope will never leave my own heart, and I pledge now, to you and our son, that I will never falter and not give up for one minute my efforts to bring about that victory and peace."

16

Why I Fight

Saturday Night
April 14 1945

Dear Jimmie:

In another week or so I am going on a long journey to a strange land many thousands of miles away from you and Mother in Ann Arbor. The last time I saw you was last Sunday night when I flew home for my first visit with you and my last with Mother before leaving the country. You were two weeks old, a tiny infant lying in a crib. Your interests of course were quite simple. Most of the time you slept, on your tummy like your mother. When you were hungry you started to cry. Then you were fed and you went right back to sleep again. You were a healthy, happy, red-headed little baby, Jimmie, and I was mighty proud to be your Dad.

I would have liked nothing better than to have remained there with you and Mother, who is a wonderful woman whom I love deeply and tenderly. For many years we had been planning for your arrival. The three of us—and the brothers and sisters we hoped you would have—were going to have a happy time, filled with love for each other and our family and friends, and also filled with study and work and music and books and many of the other things that make people so glad to be alive.

You know of course that when you were born I was a soldier in our country's army. In fact I had been a soldier for many years before, ever since our nation was attacked back in 1941. As an enlisted man I had served overseas for some time in 1942. I came back to our country to attend an Officers' school. Now I am a first

lieutenant, and I am to go overseas again in command of a group
of Negro soldiers.

So it is going to be some time before I see you and Mother.
I have a hunch where I am going but I can't tell you just yet.
Naturally I don't know how long I will be gone, although it's a
pretty safe bet that I won't come back this time until the whole war
is over.

As you can see this "war" which I have been talking about is a
pretty important thing. It has separated me from you and Mother
at a time when I want to be with you most. It has already taken the
lives of many millions of people all over the world, including the
dads of many boys not much older than yourself. Many people all
over the world have been killed, murdered, starved and tortured
by our enemies in this war. Little Chinese boys of your age have
been bayoneted to death by the Japanese. Young women, as full of
life and love as your Mother, little girls as sweet and innocent as
your cousin Peggy, and older women as kind as your grandmother
have been murdered by the Germans. A few of those people were
Americans, but most of them were French or Russian or Polish or
Filipino or Czech. But they were all good people and they were all
our friends. We know they were our friends because it is only by
reason of their suffering that the Germans and the Japanese did
not kill American children, bomb American cities and land on
American soil.

Jimmie, you know that I love you and your Mother very much.
I wouldn't be a very good father, nor much of a man, if I didn't
stand up and fight against those Japs and Nazis. That is why I am
in the army and that is why I am going far away for a long time.
Your mother, who is not only very beautiful but also very brave
and very intelligent, understands all this. And I know that you will
understand too, Jimmie.

When I last saw you, it was very difficult for you to focus your
eyes. You probably didn't see very much. But in a little while you'll
be seeing all kinds of things that will make your eyes pop and your

head swim. And then you will understand another of the reasons
why I and your uncles Bob and Joe and John and Milty and many
millions of other Americans are fighting so hard in this war.
For you will see this great and beautiful country of ours and the
friendly, warm-hearted and hard-working people who live in it. I
have been in practically every corner of this big country, and it was
the hope of your mother and myself that you would get to see most
of it while you were young.

But even before you get to travel around very much you can
learn a great deal about our country. Right around home. Ann
Arbor is as beautiful a spot as you'll find in the world and it
symbolizes in itself and in the great university many of the most
cherished traditions of American life. Of course Ann Arbor will
always be a favorite spot for our family. Mother and I were married
there in 1939 when we were both students at the University of
Michigan. You were born there, at the University hospital, in
1945. And all of us spend many happy days there at grandpa and
grandma Cummins' house on Henry Street.

When Mother and I were students at the University we used to
walk through the streets of the town and we loved the big trees and
the green lawns and the flowers and the neat, well-built houses,
especially a little blue house on Stadium Boulevard. And we used to
say to each other how wonderful it would be if all the people in our
country could live in such clean and beautiful towns and in such
comfortable houses. For it was also in Ann Arbor, at the University,
that we started to learn a great many other things which we have
never forgotten and which have helped shape the course of our
lives. From our studies, our books, and our professors we learned
about the history of our country. The most important thing we
learned was that our country and our people became strong
because we loved liberty and freedom and fought and died for it.

Yes, Jimmie, for more than 200 years now, the American people
have been fighting for liberty every time it was threatened. They
have been ever-hopeful and ever-striving for a free land of free

citizens in a free world, in which every man could live in peace
with his family and friends & neighbors. They have sought to make
this a land of equal opportunity where men of all faiths and all
creeds and all colors could live in security and friendship, and by
their individual and collective efforts fulfill the great promise of
this nation. Some people have called this hope and this effort the
"American Dream." Well, I guess you could call it a dream, and I
can't think of a nobler one.

But the men who cherished this dream most dearly also worked
most diligently to make it come true. It was born in the hearts and
minds of the artisans of Boston, the pioneers of Virginia and the
farmers of Georgia, and it was given its most glorious expression
by Thomas Jefferson in the Declaration of Independence. It was
carried across the country in the wagons of pioneers who pushed
into Ohio and Michigan and Kansas and California and the
Northwest. It was preserved on the bloody battlefields of Vicksburg
and the Wilderness, and re-stated in simple majesty by Abraham
Lincoln at Gettysburg. It was immortalized in the lusty full-
throated songs of Walt Whitman. It was nourished and vitalized by
the freedom-loving millions who came from Europe to help build
our railroads, our cities, our industries. It lives today in the heart
of a Negro in Mississippi, an auto-worker in Detroit, a farmer in
Nebraska, a teacher in Massachusetts, a miner in Illinois, a student
in California, a President in Washington and soldiers, sailors, and
marines in Germany, Okinawa, the Philippines, Burma. It rides
over Tokyo in the nose of a B-29. It bounces along the roads of
Italy in a jeep. And Jimmie, it will cross the ocean with your Dad.

So you see, Jimmie, it is because I love you and Mother and my
country so much that I am leaving you all. I hope I have explained
to you why it is necessary.

This will be a wonderful land to live in when I come back. We
will have destroyed, for all time, the evil, criminal, war-makers of
Germany and Japan. We will have created an organization of all the
nations of the world that will be vigilant in preserving the peace.

And then you and Mother and I will take up our lives in a country dedicated to the task of making all of its people prosperous and secure and healthy and happy.

All my love
Dad

17

In the Blood

AS I READ MY FATHER'S WAR LETTERS, THERE WERE TIMES when I felt he had written them not just for my mother, or in one instance my older brother, but also for me. He wrote these letters before I was born, of course, and after finding their way to my mother in Detroit and Ann Arbor, they survived twelve moves over the following seventy years. I had had a vague idea they existed but had never looked at them until I started to plan the shape of this book. My sister Jean had them. I had sent them to her after my wife and I cleaned out my mother's apartment and storage bin at the senior living center in Madison where she lived the final year of her life, the lonely period when she was without Elliott, who died first, on May Day 2004, at age eighty-six.

A letter he wrote on April 15, 1945, the day after his good-bye letter to Jimmie, erased any lingering anxiety I had about telling his story. It was a letter that seemed to be talking to me directly over the years, newspaperman father to newspaperman son.

The weather was so bad last night, and there was so much to do around the company, that I just hung around the orderly room till about eleven o'clock. At about eight-thirty I had an irresistible feeling to sit down at a typewriter and write something. So I knocked off that letter to Jimmie in about thirty minutes just as if I were writing to make a nine o'clock deadline. It was a wonderful feeling to be sitting there and let the words and sentences and thoughts take shape. There is no other feeling like it in the world, and for me there is no greater happiness, no more satisfying activity. Whatever else I do in my life you can be sure that I will also write. When I come back to civilian life, I will most likely go back to newspaper work, and make that work my base of operations for whatever writing I do. From that I can branch off into other kinds of writing. But I will always do newspaper work also, for I love it, and it is in my blood.

Maybe you don't know it, but in addition to being a pretty good newspaper writer, I am also a pretty good all around newspaper man. I love everything connected with putting out a paper from gathering the news, writing it, editing it, printing it, and watching it roll off the presses. When I was on the *Daily* my best friends were the fellows in the composing room who used to say that I was born with a feeling for a well-laid out, well-edited, and well-printed paper. But enough of this boasting! Let's hope that I remember enough to be able to hold down a job!

Throughout my career, when people asked why I became a writer, I always had the same answer, but I never knew I was repeating the precise words of my father when I said, "I love it, and it is in my blood."

In one of his first war letters, back when he was a private at the air base in Trinidad, my father had told my mother that his daily letters would take the place of a journal. I don't believe in fate, but sometimes patterns emerge from the chaos of life that seem to have some larger purpose. The more I read the letters, the more I thought to myself: Why did he write them like a journal, and why did my mother keep them through their many moves over the years, until her dying day? Why, if not for me to find them and give him a voice again, to show the determination, romanticism, and patriotism of a man who once was called un-American?

18

The Power of America

THE LAST PARTY WAS UNDER WAY WHEN ELLIOTT EN-
tered the hall at half past eight on Tuesday night, April 24. It had started
as soon as the busload of young African American women arrived from
Richmond. The soldiers of the 4482nd knew it would be their final
dance at Camp Lee, and soon their dates knew it too, once Sergeant
Plinton announced it on the loudspeaker. Along with dancing, there
was a special buffet supper put on by company cooks.

The feeling in the room was warm and infectious, Elliott thought,
a distinctive camaraderie among his men. "Sgt. Reeves and his quintet
started singing at about 11:15 and from then until the dance broke up at
midnight, the girls were all but forgotten. All the men crowded around
the band-stand and joined in the singing. The whole room shook with
the echoes of their songs. When Sgt. Reeves started singing 'We're Shov-
ing Right Off,' they let out a howl and really let loose. Then T-4 Holden
took the mic and gave forth with 'Stardust.' He was terrific. Then Sgt.
Plinton put on a one-man show with the bass violin, the trumpet, the
saxophone and the piano. He brought the house down. The men sang
'Auld Lang Syne' about six times and shook hands all around. Then they
sang 'God Bless America.'"

Two days later, they shoved right off from Camp Lee, traveling
cross-country by train from Richmond to Columbus and Chicago, then
over the Plains through Council Bluffs and Omaha and on to Cheyenne
and Salt Lake City and Spokane and finally Seattle. The trip was long
and tedious but stirred Elliott nonetheless, reminding him of what he

first discovered when he hitchhiked from coast to coast before enrolling at Michigan in 1936: "the bigness and beauty of this land of ours."

The move toward action in the Pacific had been a long time coming, but now at last it had begun. Elliott's right hand was swollen from a last-day game of catch, but he was ready for this moment, and so, he thought, were his soldiers. "The battle is the payoff, it is rightly said," he wrote as the journey began. "But it is also true that when you reach the battlefield, it is too late to start learning what to do. Training is what makes the battle pay off for your side. And my men are well-trained." He claimed not to have given a second's thought to the danger he might face, not that he was any less afraid than anyone else, but because there was so much for him to do. As an officer, he had learned to send his thoughts outward to his troops rather than inward to himself.

In the final days before leaving Camp Lee, he had soaked up all the war news he could find. The *Times-Dispatch* had a long story from London and Moscow with accounts of the battle for Berlin. A radio report told him that Hitler had acknowledged the collapse of the German armies. "One of the most interesting developments of the past few days has been the first-hand experience of the Yank fighters with the evidence of Nazi barbarism," he said in a letter to Mary. "General Patton did a wise and sensible thing when he made the people of the Weimar come to the death pits of Bergen-Belsen and see for themselves the terrible deeds they permitted to be committed. And Gen. Eisenhower, in a typical Eisenhower move, also did a smart thing in inviting congressmen and editors to view the inhuman crimes of the Nazis." All of this, Elliott thought, would strengthen American resolve to work for a lasting world peace and finish the fight against the Japanese.

After four days in Seattle, Elliott and his soldiers boarded their troopship, the *Cape Canso*, on May 7. It carried 1,300 men, including various army outfits and a navy crew. There was only one all-Negro unit aboard: the 4482nd. On the third day out, Elliott got "sick as a dog from the choppy seas," but that discomfort faded, and he never suffered from seasickness again, which was lucky for him, because it turned out that their ship would be at sea an inordinately long time. He had time to organize bridge tournaments and cribbage contests and absorb the news from Europe and learn more about himself. He came to realize that despite his nervous habits—biting his nails, doodling, smoking—he was calm under most circumstances.

Every afternoon, after morning preparations, he conducted an hour-long orientation class to provide his men with a rudimentary understanding of the world to which they were heading. He led discussions on the people of the Philippines, Japanese militarism, the history of Japan, the progress of the war, and the life and customs of people in various Pacific islands, including the Marianas and the Ryukyu. Several nights a week, he left his quarters to take a shift with his men down in the hatch. "After the order is given to darken ship and clear the weather decks, all the men come down to the hatch," he wrote. "Some of them go right to bed. Others lie in their bunks reading. Still others gather in groups to shoot the breeze. And still others get involved in crap games and poker games. By this time the stakes in most of the games is pretty small. We haven't been paid in some time now."

He tried to consider the various needs and attitudes of the men, some thriving, some anxious. "Sgt. Plinton has already established himself as the most widely known person on board and is continuously paged over the loudspeaker system for one reason or another. Sgt. Anderson was chafing a bit at the lack of activity, and his constant hunger, so I solved both of his problems by putting him in charge of the detail that eats 3 meals a day. Some of the eighteen-year-olds have a natural, but not acute, case of homesickness. Young Leon Stanley looks like he's always about to bust out in tears. I've told the older men to lay off him." Stanley, a baby-faced eighteen-year-old from Baltimore, was the understudy to the company clerk. Among other duties, he sorted the mail, and he represented good luck to Elliott because when he approached it was often to bring a letter from Mary.

Their first stop was Oahu. The men went ashore with a liberty party as guests of the navy. Elliott had two beers and a Coca-Cola and took his first swim in the Pacific. He had grown up near the ocean, spent his adolescence on the beach at Coney Island, but had never experienced anything like this. "It was superb and satisfying, the clearest, loveliest water, a warm sun, a clean beach and cooling breeze." Only the fear of too much sun got him out of the surf.

A few days after the *Cape Canso* shoved off again, the ship's captain inspected the hatch where the men of the 4482nd were quartered. He complimented Elliott on the cleanliness of the hatch and the discipline of his troops. Elliott thought the remark was "especially significant" since his company was the only black unit aboard. The fact that his men were cohesive and disciplined did not surprise him, but given the racial attitudes of the time, he was always heartened when other white officers noticed this as well. "Many other officers, who have white units, have commented wonderingly on the fact that my men have been 'so well behaved' and such a 'soldierly-looking' unit." From the time they left Camp Lee, he had only one troublesome incident, when one of his men landed in the brig for wielding a knife during a craps game.

In early evening, after chow, hundreds of men from different units gathered on deck for impromptu entertainment. "Thus far a large share of it—far in excess of our proportionate number—has been supplied by the 4482," Elliott wrote as the ship sailed from Pearl Harbor to its next stop, in the Marshall Islands. "Our quintet, chorus, jive band (2 saxes, a trumpet, bass fiddle, and guitar) and our boxers have been in constant demand. Last night they all performed in 'Officers' Country' and brought the house down—especially Sgt. Willie Reeves' rendition of 'Who's Sorry Now?' and our band's playing of 'Keep Jumping'—a little-known but authentic piece of jazz written by Doc Wheeler. . . . Reeves has become the top single performer. He can never get away with less than three encores." The salvage and repair company also dominated shipboard boxing matches, which were arranged by one of Elliott's noncoms, Sgt. Clayburn, the motor sergeant, who fought as a welterweight in Washington, DC, under the name Tiger Nelson before joining the army.

Elliott often visited his boxers as they worked out on the ship's fan-tail, sparring a bit and skipping rope. Over a month's time, he estimated that he lost eight or nine pounds in this way. But then and always his favorite exercise was of the mind: reading. Every few days, he waited in line at the ship library to check out new books, and there seemed to be an ocean of time to read them. "From the time I went to college to the present I've never had the chance to read so continuously and with so much eagerness and pleasure. I must admit there is a good deal of the book worm in me."

Books about "American literature, American history, American life" most enthralled him. *The World of Washington Irving* by Van Wyck Brooks and *American Giant: Walt Whitman and His Times* by Frances Winwar were two of his favorites from the *Cape Canso* library. Of *American Giant* he wrote, "What I liked most about the book was the life-size portrait of Walt Whitman, the man, that emerges from it. And what a man he was! Poet, essayist, printer, reporter, patriot, nurse, and the friend of every living being on earth. Probably the most interesting chapters were those on his youth and young manhood, when he was a crusading editor of the *Brooklyn Eagle* and up to his neck in issues of the day. Miss Winwar very skillfully shows his political development and growth, from the time when he was a regular Democrat, a faithful follower of Tammany, to his split with them on the issue of the Wilmot Proviso which sought to exclude slavery from the territories won from Mexico, and right on through to his support of Fremont in '56 and of course Lincoln and the Republicans in '60." The book inspired Elliott to ask Mary if she could send him an edition of *Leaves of Grass*, the one edited and prefaced by Samuel Sillen, literary editor of *New Masses*, the Marxist magazine.

Days blurred as the *Cape Canso* sailed across the vast Pacific. He started keeping track by noting at the top of his letters not the date but how long they had been at sea. *Eighteenth day at sea. Twenty-first day at sea. 23rd day at sea.* "There have probably been transports in the Pacific that have been at sea longer than we have, but you'd have a hard time convincing anybody on this ship of that fact," he wrote one mid-June morning. "We might just as well be in the Navy. We speak the Navy lingo, do Navy details. I've got barnacles between the toes, seaweed in my hair, salt-water on my knees and bulkheads in my brain. A parrot on my shoulder, a tattooed arm and a beard on my chin are all that's lacking to complete my nautical ensemble. The Navy eats well all the time and has clean quarters to sleep in. Even so, I am now convinced that I am an Army man by conviction and preference, foxholes, C-rations, and mud notwithstanding."

Not that he had endured much hardship so far. His letters to Mary aboard ship at times vacillated between guilt about not carrying a heavier burden and despair that politics circumscribed his military duties. "No one knows better than I that the small inconveniences we have suffered are as nothing compared to the terrible ordeal of millions of peoples all over the world. Sometimes I feel that I should have done, or been in position to do, much more than I did. It was a bitter disappointment to me not to have gotten to Europe. I would have liked to have contributed to the defeat of the Nazis. In a general way, I suppose we have all achieved that historic task. . . . But none in so great measure as the infantrymen of the First, the 45th, the 1st Armored, the 82nd Airborne, and the scores of other divisions which fought the greatest campaign in the history of our nation."

With the European campaign now over, the War Department in Washington had turned its attention to an invasion of Japan. One reason the *Cape Canso* was kept at sea so long, with stops at Eniwetok in the Marshall Islands and Ulithi in the Caroline Islands, was due to uncertainty about where the soldiers aboard would be most needed. At anchorage in Ulithi on June 23, Elliott still did not know the answer. "For my part, I hope to hell it's Japan under General Stilwell," he wrote to Mary. "The road to Tokyo is the most direct route back to you in Michigan."

When the *Cape Canso* pulled anchor from Ulithi, their destination was finally made known to the troops aboard. They quickly transformed the news into a parody inspired by the Rodgers and Hammerstein musical *Oklahoma!* that had opened on Broadway in 1943.

Everything's up-to-date in Okinawa
They've gone about as far as they can go.

And

Ooooooooooh-key-na-wa, where the Japs lay dead upon the beach.

"The first ditty, a parody of the Kansas City song, was supposed to be ironic, expressive of our belief that in going to Okinawa we were getting about as far away from up-to-date civilization as we could possibly go," Elliott reported to Mary. "Our minds and imaginations were filled with visions of deadly snakes (the Army handbook on the island was so detailed on this subject that nearly all of us were more afraid of the snakes than the Japs), of typhoons, and jungles and insects, wild animals, of mud and dirt and disease."

When the island came into sight, the lightheartedness stopped, replaced by "grimness and silent determination."

They reached Okinawa on July 2, and after disembarking, Elliott was too busy to write for the first time since he enlisted at Christmastime 1941. He went silent for three weeks, the period before the War Department officially declared the island secure. Sixteen hours after they landed, the 4482nd had set up its mobile trailers and was fully operational, repairing boots, trousers, socks, field jackets, raincoats, shirts, caps, breeches, shelter halves, barracks bags, leggings, haversacks, canteens, electrical equipment, jeeps and other vehicles. On the Fourth of July they played a critical role helping the 11th Airborne Division before its planes arrived on the island in preparation for an invasion of Japan. For that work alone, Elliott received a letter of commendation from the division commander. The fiercest fighting had been over before his troops arrived, with more than 161,000 American and Japanese casualties during three months of combat so intense and bloody that it became known as the "Typhoon of Steel." But danger remained. "We saw plenty of fireworks here from the first day we arrived," Elliott wrote when he finally found time. "What with air raids nearly every night, kamikaze suicide planes, snipers, bypassed Jap detachments." As it turned out, "the Japs were more dangerous than the snakes, for while we never saw a single snake, we saw plenty of Japs, dead and alive."

At their camp on the island, they were 725 miles from Hiroshima and 551 miles from Nagasaki when the two Japanese cities and their civilians were devastated by atomic bombs. A few days later, when Japan surrendered, the night sky over Okinawa crackled with celebratory fireworks. "We heard the news at 0800 this morning on the radio from

San Francisco," Elliott wrote to Mary. "My first thoughts were of you sweetheart. I was trying to visualize the scene at 1402 Henry when Bob Trout or Bill Henry came on the air with the announcement of the surrender. And in my mind's eye I visualized the reactions and feelings of all the peoples of the world and the realization sunk in at long last, after the bitterest, costliest, and bloodiest war in the history of mankind, the world was at peace."

Two weeks later, on V-J day, he took part in an army baseball game against a marine regiment also stationed on Okinawa, losing 4 to 1, then hurried back to quarters in time to hear the broadcast of the official surrender ceremony aboard the USS *Missouri*. Elliott never thought much of Gen. Douglas MacArthur, but praised him for his performance that day. "I am somewhat skeptical when it comes to pomp and ceremony, but I think this whole surrender operation was very wisely handled and all the planning that went into it to make it dramatic and symbolic was justified," Elliott wrote. "It was truly an epochal event closing the most destructive era in the whole of human history and opening what surely must become a new age of peace and progress. The most moving and remarkable single moment about the whole ceremony was the short speech that General MacArthur made after the President spoke from Washington. . . . MacArthur has always been something of an aloof and enigmatic figure. When he began to speak I was prepared to hear some bombastic banalities. Instead, his voice came through clear, strong, and restrained, and his message was a model of sincere emotion, clarity, and showed a strength of purpose and conviction that rang true. He was truly 'a son of the American people,' expressing their thoughts and emotions."

Son of the American people. That is how Elliott thought of himself as well. He had a Whitmanesque love of the land and its people, and now that combined with more traditional expressions of patriotism, including admiration for the American military and its leaders. "After nearly four years in the service, I understand why the army life has always had a certain attraction and fascination for a certain type of man, and not all of those Regular Army men are lacking in imagination, initiative, and energy, either, as so many people think. The proof of that lies in the fact that our Regular Army produced a man the caliber of Dwight Eisenhower, certainly one of the greatest men in our nation's history. I've met many an old soldier whose pride in organization and country, uncompromising sense of duty, and whose natural, easy and friendly way of dealing with other men could well be emulated."

THE LETTERS MY mother wrote to my father during the war had vanished by the time I became interested in this story. For years they were stashed in Dad's olive-green army trunk in the attic of our house in Madison. My sisters read them at one point, and Jean later remembered that they "were full of news about family and friends" but also included vivid reports on Mom's dreams, often nightmares that reflected her sensitivity to violence and her fears for her husband and about the war. I never saw the letters, so reading only my father's responses was like listening to one end of a telephone conversation. One of the responses he wrote from Okinawa drew my attention. He was trying to answer her apparent concern that he sounded "complacent about the post-war world and was just looking toward security, job, home."

One way to read this is that she thought he was not being political enough, too bourgeois, that he had fallen into the rut of accepting the status quo. They were in dramatically different circumstances, even as they both worked in the war effort. He had spent virtually every hour of the day for four years with soldiers, talking soldier talk, thinking like a soldier. Every soldier thought about home, peace, security, job. Until my older brother was born, my mother had worked in the defense industry, but in her free time she had been consumed by leftist politics. Bereniece Baldwin would later testify that she encountered my mother in the offices of the Young Communist League on Broadway near Grand Circus Park sometime in 1944. By Baldwin's account, my mother went by the name Mary Morrison then, which is possible; she might have used a pseudonym, though no one in the family ever mentioned it later.

But there was more to it than politics. If my mother was more ideological than my father, her beliefs were shaped by a deep moralistic streak, a characteristic that drew on her midwestern roots and the rec-

titude of a disciplined father born in a lean-to in the rolling hills of
Kansas. I was very close to my mother and loved her deeply. She was
intelligent and forgiving. We had an unspoken bond of empathy. But I
also saw the sharp edge of her moralistic streak, which had little to do
with normal sins. If you did some trivial thing wrong, that would not
bother her much. But if she sensed that you thought you were better
than anyone else, or enjoying life too much while others were suffering,
or placing too much emphasis on material things or conventional notions of success, she would let you know it. I never got a letter from her,
but I got the message.

My father was more social and fluid. He was open to the world, with
all its contradictions. He understood his own flaws and accepted them
in others. He was more of a romantic than a moralist. And he was also
a survivor, adapting to his surroundings. A tinge of the Marrano heritage, perhaps. In any case, he certainly got my mother's message. "Do
you think I won't fight—or don't expect to have to fight—and work for
the things I want for myself, my family, and the nation?" he responded.
"Simply because I enumerated those things—job, home, peace, etc.—
as the elements of the kind of postwar world in which I want to live
doesn't necessarily mean that I expect to find it that way ready-made. If
I did expect that I wouldn't be complacent; I'd be stupid and ignorant.
I have known for a good many years now that nothing comes about in
this world without effort, struggle, work, sweat, blood."

ON THE MORNING of September 4, Elliott learned that all censorship regulations had been removed from mail leaving Okinawa and he
was able to tell Mary what he could not reveal before. He and his troops
would soon be going to Korea as part of the XXIV Corps of the Tenth
Army. The company was scheduled to depart with the second echelon
near the end of the month, but Elliott was planning to leave within a
week or ten days, taking Sergeant Henderson along with him, to arrange
for housing and an operations area. He thought it was an honor that his
unit was chosen. "The other 5 salvage repair companies in the Tenth
Army will sweat it out here or some other island," he wrote. "We are

the only Salv Rep Co going. The order which directed us to go stated: 'The units chosen for this operation have maintained a high standard of efficiency and have proven to the satisfaction of the Commanding General that they will be worthy of the high honor accorded them to help restore Korea to the list of free, independent nations, as provided by the Yalta agreement.' It was signed by 'Vinegar Joe' (Stilwell) himself."

Elliott was in the middle of a gin rummy game with Tom Meisner, the other lieutenant in the company, on the Saturday night of September 15 when a jeep pulled up in front of their tent and a messenger piled out with the orders: he and Sergeant Henderson were to leave that night by a ship known as an LST (Landing Ship, Tank), which was waiting and would leave as soon as they arrived at the loading beach. "Things began to fly fast and furious then as we completed our packing, loaded our stuff in a jeep and scrambled down to the beach in a driving, blinding thunderstorm," Elliott recounted. "All the way down, I kept yelling above the din of the storm and the jeep motor at Meisner, trying to tell him about a score of things he should check and watch while he was in temporary control of the company. It was a wild ride, all right, but as things turned out it was calm and peaceful compared with what was in store for us."

When they arrived at the loading point, Purple Beach #1, on the western coast of Okinawa, they realized they were in a classic military hurry-up-and-wait situation as the beachmaster struggled to bring order to the mass chaos of stalled jeeps, mud, darkness, and confusion. An hour before midnight, after sitting in their uncovered jeep for several hours, they received the signal to drive up the ramp and park with other vehicles on the lower tank deck. It was too late, and there was too much confusion, to make sleeping arrangements, so Elliott and his sergeant sat in the jeep the rest of the night and tried to sleep there. At 4:30 the next morning, the ship weighed anchor and set off into a choppy, waving sea.

Elliott recorded the scene in a letter to Mary as though he were keeping a journal. He explained that the LST was a vessel designed and built for an amphibious war. It was the largest of many different types of landing craft and ships the navy designed to land men and supplies directly on beachheads without a dock or pier. It was 220 feet long and about 50 feet wide, with two main cargo decks to carry tanks and other vehicles. LST 718, the one they were on, was packed on both decks with trucks, jeeps, and trailers, but no tanks. It was so crowded on board that it was hard to move without bumping into someone or something.

"On Sunday morning, Sgt. Henderson and I crawled out of our jeep, wet, cold and woozy, and climbed up to the upper deck to have a look around and to make some inquiries about sleeping and eating facilities. A chief boatman's mate gave us the dope and also apprised us of the obvious fact that we were heading for a storm. Before we could give way to the sickening feelings that were taking control of our bodies, we pitched in with the crew and other Army troops to lash and chain down all the vehicles on both decks. It was hard, slow, and difficult work, but at least the effort and the concentration prevented us from getting very sick."

By Sunday noon the storm had turned into a full-fledged typhoon. Typhoon Ida.

"Our little ship kicked and bucked and heaved and tossed and soon everybody, including the Navy men, were heaving and tossing too, overboard. Actually, we were in much graver physical danger than I ever suspected. It turned out that the Naval officers on board were seriously afraid that the ship might crack in two. It has happened to many a ship in these very waters, including much larger ones than this. We were all too miserable with our own personal troubles to worry much about the hazards of the sea."

Elliott did not hold down a meal on Sunday and lost the first two meals Monday. He might not have been the sickest man aboard, but he had never felt lousier. He managed to hold down Monday night's chow, and by Tuesday morning he was better. They had passed the peak of the storm by then. The waters were choppy, but smoother sailing appeared ahead. By Tuesday night they had passed from the East China Sea into the Yellow Sea. "The stars were twinkling in the sky that night and from all over the ship wretched creatures crept forth for a breath of fresh air," Elliott wrote. The voyage was supposed to take four days, but they hardly moved the first two rough days at sea and needed six before reaching the harbor at Inchon on the west coast of Korea. The bay was cluttered with ships from the U.S. fleet amid hundreds of junks, sampans, and fishing craft. In their little boats, Koreans grinned and waved at the arriving ship as they moved past.

Elliott grinned and waved back. He was overcome by a sense of fulfillment, invigorated by the realization that his experience with the 4482nd had been invaluable. During his time in the Pacific, he picked up a case of amoebic dysentery that would recur throughout his life, but also something far more important. "I didn't put in all this work and sweat and energy into the company without getting anything back," he wrote. "What I got back—in addition to the priceless respect and confidence and friendship of my men, and even in addition to the personal satisfaction of successfully accomplishing a mission—was a renewed and strengthened belief that the power of America lies in its people. I learned that I was one of them. I learned again that to be a leader of men a person must be trustworthy, strong, determined and above all else, selfless. It was that, more than anything else, which finally knocked the anomalies out of my thinking, actions, and character. For over ten months now, I have been strictly on the spot. One false move, one phony trick, and this company would have slipped out of control, irretrievably. I've learned that you get only in proportion to what you give. To this company, I've given everything in me, and I've gotten more out of it than I have from anything I've ever done. For the rest of my life, I intend to keep on 'giving out' with everything in me, for the things I believe and the people I love."

PART THREE

Trials and Tribulations

19

The Virginian

ON THE THIRD FRIDAY OF MARCH 1946, FRANK S. TAVEN-
ner Jr. boarded a flight from Washington to San Francisco, the first leg
of a journey that would take him across the Pacific to Tokyo. He had
fought as an infantry officer in France during World War I, the war that
was supposed to end all wars, and now he was seeking punishment for
leaders of an aggressor nation that had attacked America during World
War II. On leave from his post as U.S. attorney for the western district
of Virginia, he was bound for a temporary assignment as a prosecutor
at the International Military Tribunal for the Far East, more commonly
known as the Tokyo War Crimes Tribunal. At age fifty, bespectacled,
jowly, and pear-shaped in his three-piece suits, he was an unprepossess-
ing southern gentleman with a soft drawl, sharp mind, and composed
manner who was born into politics but had never held elective office,
despite family connections and deep ties to a powerful political machine. The courtroom was his domain.

This was six years before Tavenner interrogated my father and challenged his loyalty to America, but my father would have approved of the
Virginian's mission to Tokyo. If an invasion of Japan had been necessary
to end the war, putting the lives of untold thousands of American soldiers at risk, Lieutenant Maraniss and his salvage and repair company
would have been part of it. My father had seen and heard enough on
Okinawa to be repelled by the Japanese way of war; in an uncharacter-
istically harsh assessment, he had even written in a letter to my mother,
"The samurai of Japan are as cruel, ruthless, unprincipled a group of

men as ever trod the earth. I have no more feeling toward them than I do toward a poisonous snake or rat."

Not long into Tavenner's flight west from Washington on that March day, he looked out the window to the countryside below and caught glimpses of his home turf. Front Royal, Strasburg, Woodstock. Then Kern's Gap in North Mountain came into view, and through it he could just see the apple orchards that had been operated by the Tavenner family since the turn of the century. He was overwhelmed, he wrote in a letter home soon after, "by the beauty of the Blue Ridge and the Shenandoah Valley."

The transpacific flight from San Francisco to Tokyo was less familiar, but remarkable in its own way. As the only passenger on a military cargo plane, he flew as "freight" along with the other cargo: crates of smallpox serum packed in dry ice. "It seems that it took a smallpox epidemic to get me through," he joked in a letter he sent back to the U.S. attorney's office after the plane made a fuel stop in Honolulu. In its Socials and Clubs notices a few days later, the *Woodstock Herald* reported that Judge Frank S. Tavenner Sr. had received a cablegram from his son announcing his safe arrival in Tokyo. He and the serum got there at the peak of the smallpox outbreak, with 1,405 new patients—feverish, vomiting, hideously pocked—seeking treatment that week, most of them in the metropolitan regions of Osaka, Kobe, and Tokyo.

Even before Tavenner reached Japan, he had undertaken a research assignment delegated to him by Joseph B. Keenan, chief of counsel for the U.S. delegation. Keenan had been director of the Criminal Division at the Justice Department, where criminals he had prosecuted included the American gangsters Machine Gun Kelly and Ma Barker. Now he and his staff were pursuing criminals of a different sort: the leaders of Japan's war machine, led by Hideki Tojo, the former prime minister and general of the Imperial Army who had ordered the attack on Pearl Harbor. Keenan wanted Tavenner to establish that even before hostilities began the Japanese had entered into secret pacts with Hitler's Nazi regime on how they would conduct warfare against the United States and the Soviet Union. As it turned out, Tavenner's role became much larger. Only weeks after he arrived, Keenan fell ill and departed for Washington, leaving Tavenner in charge as acting chief counsel.

The tribunal followed the model of the Nuremberg Trials of high-ranking Nazi officials in Germany. Douglas MacArthur, as Supreme Commander for the Allied Powers during the postwar occupation of Japan, appointed a panel of twelve judges: two from the U.S., one from the Soviet Union, and nine from other Allied nations. The prosecution teams were also international, led by the U.S. and including lawyers from the Soviet Union, Great Britain, France, Canada, Australia, New Zealand, India, the Netherlands, and the Philippines. They were to make the cases against twenty-eight Japanese defendants, including nine high-ranking civilian officials and Tojo and most of his general staff. Notably not charged were Emperor Hirohito and other members of the imperial family. This controversial omission was said to be a matter of practical politics; it was believed that the transformation of postwar Japan would be easier with Hirohito's symbolic endorsement.

Documents detailing Tavenner's actions in Tokyo, later archived at the Arthur J. Morris Law Library at the University of Virginia, reveal how he faced one difficulty after another, from internal jealousies and disagreements within the American delegation to problems involving simultaneous translations (and transcript translations) and headaches dealing with his Soviet counterpart. One of his first decisions involved whether and how to explain the absence of Keenan, his boss. According to an internal memo, Tavenner was called by a captain in the tribunal's public relations office and told that the Associated Press was ready to run a story revealing Keenan's sudden and unexpected departure for the States. The captain told Tavenner that he had prepared a press release "denying the correctness of the news item." Tavenner figured he had three choices: approve the press release; ignore it, which would mean it would still go out; or tell the press office not to deny Keenan's departure. The best and proper course, he decided, was to tell the truth. "I knew you wanted no announcement made," he wrote to Keenan, "but the announcement was nevertheless going to be made, and I was of the opinion that any other action on my part would aggravate the situation rather than help it."

On May 1, shortly before the arraignments and opening of the trials, Tavenner held a press conference for the international press corps. He was asked why Japanese lawyers had not been allowed to meet with defendants at Sugamo Prison in Tokyo. That was a matter beyond the control of the prosecution team, Tavenner said, adding that the prosecutors had decided that no more interrogations should be undertaken at the prison until the matter of defense access was resolved. Another questioner brought up a rumor spreading across Tokyo, that a dance hall had been built in the court building and that court members were partying and eating delicious food while the defendants were waiting to see if they would be sentenced to death. This rumor spawned a phrase to describe it: "the Dance of Death." The questioner posited that this contrast between doomed men and carefree, well-fed judges "would have a very bad effect on the Japanese people." What did Tavenner think? "My personal view is the same as yours," he said, "that it would be a very bad thing should such a thing exist, but I am confident that it is a product of a very vivid imagination, to say the least."

But it was carried in a "first-class" Japanese newspaper, the questioner pointed out.

"That is rather in the nature of a scurrilous statement," Tavenner said. "It seems to me that it should be checked before publication." He did not point out what he soon complained about privately: that conditions at the Matsui House, where he and the American tribunal employees were quartered, became so dire at one point that there was concern their Japanese staff could not be fed due to a lack of food.

When questioned as to why Emperor Hirohito was not included in the indictments, Tavenner nimbly provided a nonanswer: "It is presumed that those charged with the preparation of the indictments were satisfied in their own minds that they were preparing a proper indictment."

The trials began in early May and lasted for nearly two years, until late April 1948. Tavenner was there from the opening statement to the final summation, though there were many temptations for him to return to Virginia. He was married and had two children, and though his wife, Sarah, visited him in Tokyo, she was more often back home. He was encouraged to run for Congress from Virginia's Seventh District when that seat became open in 1946, but he told friends in Woodstock that his duties in Tokyo meant that "under no circumstances" could he accept the nomination. The Southern Railway System offered him a lucrative job as counsel later that same year, but he also turned that down. The one job he would have taken was on the Court of Appeals of Virginia, when there was a vacancy, but although he gained permission from the Justice Department to pursue it, the appointment never came. All the while he was in Japan, Virginia was never far from his mind. He held on to the vision he had glimpsed out the window on the first leg of the flight to Tokyo, when he caught a faint faraway view of Kern's Gap and the Tavenner orchards below.

THE TAVENNER NAME was well known in Woodstock and its environs for influence and apples, which makes sense since the two were synonymous in the Shenandoah Valley. Another large apple operation out there, in the fields near Winchester thirty miles to the north, was run by the family of Harry Flood Byrd, whose political machine controlled state politics for much of the twentieth century. Byrd got his political start by succeeding Tavenner Sr. in the Virginia Senate from the Tenth District, then rose to become governor for four years and a U.S. senator for thirty more. He also owned the major newspaper in the Shenandoah, the *Winchester Star*. He and Tavenner Sr. were friendly competitors in the apple industry and allies in the political realm as conservative southern Democrats who adhered to the racial biases and traditions of the Old South while pursuing their own entrepreneurial agendas.

How appropriate that the apple would emerge in this search to understand the forces that intersected in Room 740 and the question of what it means to be American. The home territory of the future HUAC chief counsel was apple territory in a state—and nation—rich in apple history. The settlers at Jamestown brought the first apple seeds to North America in 1607, and by the end of that century there were orchards with as many as 2,500 apple trees in some parts of the commonwealth. By the time Woodstock was chartered in 1761, apples were emerging as a staple of the American diet, and for generations thereafter commercial orchards became ever more lucrative. "The orchards of Virginia are today worth more than the gold mines of other sections," the *Shenandoah Herald* proclaimed in 1905, the same year that a pomologist at the U.S. Department of Agriculture listed seventeen thousand different apple varieties, of different colors, shapes, and sizes.

The apple holds a special place in mythology, its evocations as contradictory as America itself. Emerson called the apple "the American fruit," even though it, like almost everything else American, came from somewhere else. The apple symbolized both the domestic and the wild, the innocent and the fallen, the vibrancy of the New World and the hackneyed clichés of shirtsleeve patriotism. *As American as apple pie.* Johnny Appleseed spreading apple trees through the heartland. *An apple a day keeps the doctor away. The apple doesn't fall far from the tree. How do you like them apples?* Henry David Thoreau, the national contrarian, disdained cultivated varieties and yearned for apples "sour enough to set a squirrel's teeth on edge and make a jay scream." *There's a rotten apple in every bunch.* Which leads to the most famous apple of all, that forbidden fruit in the Garden of Eden. Did Eve, at the urging of Satan disguised as a snake, bite into an apple? Scholars say it more likely would have been a fig, but John Milton used the word "apple" twice in *Paradise Lost,* and the apple appears in modern portrayals of the Bible's foundation story of human sin.

Few apple orchards in the valley were worth more than the Tavenner family's vast nurseries of Winesap and Ben Davis varieties, described by the *Herald* as "among the finest placed upon the market." When Tavenner Sr. was in the Virginia Senate, his key accomplishment also served his private interests as an orchardist, along with those of the Byrd empire. He was chief sponsor of legislation to help protect apple growers by mandating the barely compensated or uncompensated destruction of fungus-infected cedar trees in proximity to apple orchards. The Cedar Rust Law, as it was called, was bitterly contested by cedar grove owners, and whenever the cases reached court, Tavenner was the counsel for the apple growers. His son inherited the apple orchards, as he did so much else.

Born in 1895, Frank Jr. followed closely in the footsteps of Judge Tavenner, attending Roanoke College and Princeton University and attaining his law degree from Virginia. The family name was prominent enough that his daily doings might be recorded in the local newspapers from Woodstock to Winchester to Harrisonburg. Here was young Frank returning home from school for the Thanksgiving holiday; there he was receiving treatment for a head wound suffered in a college football game; now he was lettering as a captain on the Cavaliers baseball team; now he was volunteering for military service when the U.S. entered World War I.

His army unit was the 1st Pioneer Infantry, a regiment composed of "men experienced in life in the open" who performed construction and engineering tasks and cleared roads and paths in the vanguard of troop movements to follow. The 1st Pioneers left the dock in Hoboken, New Jersey, and rounded the Statue of Liberty on July 8, 1918, sailing across the Atlantic in a convoy that included the ships *America, LaFrance, Agamemnon,* and *Mount Vernon.* They disembarked at Brest ten days later. Tavenner was a first lieutenant and commanded his own company. In France they saw action in three decisive battles on the Western Front between late July and Armistice Day. Nothing quiet about any of them— the Aisne-Marne offensive, Oise-Aisne offensive, and Meuse-Argonne offensive. When the fighting was over, Tavenner's unit went to Germany for several months to hold the ancient Ehrenbreitstein Fortress on a mountaintop high above the east bank of the Rhine across from the town of Koblenz, where on Christmas Eve three thousand men filled the snowy parade grounds below a giant fir tree glistening with colored lights.

Home in Virginia between world wars, Tavenner furthered the family traditions in apple orchard cultivation, law, and Democratic Party politics. He proved better at the first two than the last. In 1932 he tried to secure the Democratic nomination for Congress in his district but lost out to another member of the Byrd machine, Absalom Willis Robertson (the father of evangelist Pat Robertson). Six years later Byrd and his Virginia Senate colleague, Carter Glass, tried to get Tavenner appointed to a judgeship on the U.S. District Court, but that effort was foiled by President Roosevelt, who was feuding with them over their opposition to New Deal policies. FDR called Glass "an unreconstructed rebel" and said he might just as soon consult with "Nancy Astor, the Duchess of Windsor . . . [or] a Virginia moonshiner" as with the state's two obstinate senators. Eighteen months later Tavenner was finally rewarded for his legal skills and political loyalty when he was appointed U.S. attorney in the western district of Virginia, a job he held until getting sent to Tokyo.

THE AMERICAN LAWYERS at Matsui House assumed that Keenan's departure from Tokyo would be brief, but he ended up being in the States nearly as often as in Japan for the duration of the tribunal proceedings.

On March 28, 1947, about a year after Tavenner arrived, he received a letter from Keenan explaining his situation. Writing from Washington, Keenan said that he had returned from the hospital only the day before "after undergoing a serious operation for which I had to prepare for many weeks preceding." Since his return to the States, he had been to three hospitals and was in no condition until after the operation to send any detailed instructions to the Tokyo staff. In his absence, there had been an internal dispute over assignments, but Keenan wanted to make it clear that he wanted Tavenner to be in charge of both preparation of the cases and the courtroom presentations. "Any long, protracted proceedings such as this trial, where men are away from home for a long period of time, are bound to bring about considerable differences of views and perhaps exhibitions of temperament," Keenan wrote. "I know, however, Frank, that you have excellent judgment and a fine sense of fairness and you have given so generously of your efforts at this trial that you are well equipped to make such decisions that are necessary." Which was a way of saying *Tavenner, you handle it.*

Along with negotiating his way through delicate staffing issues, Tavenner in Tokyo had his first interaction with Russians, an experience that in various ways might have influenced how he dealt later with the communist threat in the United States. Although the U.S. and Soviet

Union ostensibly were allies in the prosecution of the Japanese, their alliance was complicated by the onset of the cold war. It had been only a few weeks before Tavenner arrived in Japan that Winston Churchill delivered his Iron Curtain speech in Fulton, Missouri, warning of the totalitarian nature of the Soviet state and its controlling grip on Eastern Europe. During the war crime trials, Tavenner dealt often with his Soviet counterpart, Maj. Gen. A. N. Vasiliev. It was an uneasy relationship.

Vasiliev expressed unhappiness over the American reluctance to charge the Japanese with resorting to biological warfare in China. The Soviets said they had plenty of witnesses; Tavenner and the American attorneys thought the evidence was insufficient. Tavenner expressed concern about the Russian cross-examination of a crucial witness, Ryukichi Tanaka, a Japanese general who testified on both sides at the trials, three times for the prosecution and twice for the defense. Tanaka was so important, Tavenner told Vasiliev in a memo, that they had to be more careful in questioning him, and perhaps even "stop the cross and just rely on his affidavit so there are no holes the defense can pick at." Demonstrating his facility with diplomatic politesse, Tavenner concluded, "I have every confidence in your sagacious handling of the matter, but I am sure you will appreciate my concern over the turn the matter could take."

As the trials dragged on, interest in them dissipated back in the States. Tavenner was reminded of this in a letter he received from Samuel J. Pritchard, a banking official in Harrisonburg, Virginia. Pritchard's son, Cpl. B. W. Pritchard of the 770th Bombardment Squadron, on a B-29 bombing mission over Japan, had been shot down and captured in May 1945 and was executed by the Japanese that July, a month before their surrender. "I have followed all of the newspapers and magazines available trying to learn something of the prosecution of criminals in Japan for war crimes and I have found practically none," the elder Pritchard wrote. "I am afraid the press has lost some of its interest in this subject. However, I am interested beyond words and will have to appeal to you for information." He hoped Tavenner could tell him the names and addresses of the people responsible for the killing of his son and what penalties they would receive, and when. Tavenner made inquiries and told the father that, although this case and many others were being handled separately from the tribunal, he had heard that a trial involving his son's execution might begin in a few months. He also provided the father with a list of members of the B-29 crew, including two who were returned alive after the war.

Tavenner delivered the final summation at the tribunal on April 18, 1948. "These defendants were not mere automatons, they were no replaceable cogwheels in a machine, they were not playthings of fate caught in a maelstrom of destiny from which there was no extraction," he told the court. "These men were the brains of an empire. They were the leaders of the nation's destiny, a symbol of evil throughout the world. They made their choice; for this choice they must bear the guilt."

In the end, twenty-five defendants were convicted of war crimes. Of the other three, one was found insane and the other two had died in prison. Seven of the guilty, including Tojo, were sentenced to death.

Tavenner returned to Woodstock to practice law and run his apple orchards for a year. Then he was hired by Chairman John Stephens Wood to serve as chief counsel for the House Committee on Un-American Activities.

20

Foley Square

GEORGE CROCKETT SAT IN THE FEDERAL COURTHOUSE AT Foley Square in Lower Manhattan on the opening day of one of the seminal free speech trials of twentieth-century American history. This was in 1949, at 10:43 on the morning of January 17. The Detroit lawyer was there as a defense counsel representing Carl Winter, who also came from Detroit and was one of eleven leaders of the Communist Party USA charged with conspiring to advocate the violent overthrow of the government. What happened at the Foley Square trial in New York not only provided context for the hearings where Crockett defended my father three years later; it helped define the larger framework of the Red Scare.

The opening day scene crackled with tension. Thousands of protesters crowded into the nearby square, chanting and waving signs: "Hitler Began by Jailing Communists: Remember What Happened?" and "First Communists, Then Unions, Are You Next?" Inside the courthouse, Room No. 1 was brimming, half the seats taken by a press corps eager to chronicle this legal reckoning for men deemed to be enemies of the state. A phalanx of four hundred New York City policemen ringed the building inside and out. Federal judge Harold R. Medina wanted the police there for protection and to ensure there were no untoward incidents, but when Crockett first addressed the bench as part of a defense motion to have the officers removed, he said they represented an attempt at intimidation.

There was no difference, he argued, between the atmosphere surrounding this trial and the infamous Scottsboro trial of 1931, when nine young black men in Alabama were falsely accused of raping two white women. "I know exactly what happens when a trial is held under conditions resembling mob conditions," Crockett said. "I am convinced, and I think the court should be convinced, that a mob is no less a mob merely because it is clothed in uniform and has a pistol on the side."

The cops stayed, but the remark revealed Crockett on many levels. It set the tone for the audacious manner in which he would argue for the defense for the nine-month duration of the trial, and it also underscored the reason he took the case in the first place. To Crockett, in one way or another, it came back to the issue of race. He knew from the moment he decided to represent Winter that many people would think he was a communist, which he was not. While he understood that appearing sympathetic to communists could damage his reputation, he had never been overly concerned with his image or popularity. He thought there was a direct connection between the constitutional rights of free speech and the free association of American communists and African Americans, two outsider groups vulnerable to majority repression. He saw American communists consistently supporting the rights of black citizens at a time when many other groups would not, including the key role they played in defense of the Scottsboro Nine. On a personal level, he viewed his involvement in the Foley Square trial as an expression of freedom and possibility; at the time, there were few opportunities for black lawyers to work on national cases beyond the realm of racial discrimination. Even if he was invited onto the defense team largely because of his race, not despite it, he thought his participation would mark another step forward.

The case began with the indictment of the Communist Party leadership on July 20, 1948, by a grand jury in the southern district of New York on charges based on the Alien Registration Act of 1940. This law was commonly known as the Smith Act, in recognition of its sponsor, Virginia congressman Howard W. Smith, a conservative Democrat who opposed civil rights, organized labor, and much of the New Deal. Along with requiring all noncitizen adults to register with the federal government, the Smith Act also made it a crime to advocate the violent overthrow of the U.S. government through speech, publication, or association. It was the first American law since the Alien and Sedition Acts of 1798 to make the spreading of ideas a crime, regardless of whether action followed advocacy.

The first prosecution under the act came in 1941 and, among other things, revealed the situational hypocrisy of American communists. Leftist labor leaders in Teamsters Local 544 in Minneapolis were charged with advocating the overthrow of capitalism by force and violence if necessary. The communist hierarchy in the U.S. had no problems with this prosecution—heartily supported it, in fact—because the defendants were members of the Trotskyite Socialist Workers Party, who were Stalin's bitter enemies, and therefore theirs as well. It was only a year earlier that Trotsky had been assassinated, fatally attacked with an ice axe by one of Stalin's agents during his exile in Mexico. Other Smith Act trials came in 1942, against racist and anti-Semitic groups, and in 1944, against pro-fascists, but those efforts failed for reasons ranging from weak prosecution arguments to the death of a judge.

The Foley Square trial was the first time the Smith Act was used against the Communist Party. Dozens of Smith Act trials would follow over the next several years as local and state communist leaders were targeted around the country, one of the many manifestations of the Red Scare. Foley Square was in every respect a product of its time. President Truman, a Democrat, was seeking election when the indictments were handed down and did not want to appear soft on communism, a charge Republicans had been making with increasing political effectiveness since the onset of the cold war. The same grand jury that indicted the communist leaders had been hearing sensational testimony in a separate proceeding from a former Soviet spy, Elizabeth Bentley, who laid out in detail the inner workings of the CPUSA and the manipulative intentions of the totalitarian Soviet Union in its dealings with American leftists, whether they were willing conspirators or unwitting dupes.

Month by month as the Foley Square trial proceeded, the Red threat seemed more ominous. China went communist. The Soviets exploded a nuclear device. Alger Hiss was tried for perjury down the hall in the same federal building, charges that stemmed from his testimony at a HUAC hearing in Washington where Representative Richard Nixon had pressed him to deny that he had served as a Soviet contact during his years as a top diplomat in the State Department. The mood of the American public was hardening against *pinkos* and *commies* and *commie lovers*. It was in that heated atmosphere that Crockett took to the defense.

THE INDEPENDENT STREAK started with his surname. During slavery, the family name was the same as the Delaware slaveholders who owned them, Blodgett. With emancipation came a self-assigned new name, Crockett. George William Crockett Jr. was born in Jacksonville, Florida, in 1909. His namesake and father was a carpenter for the Atlantic Coast Line railroad, an ordained Baptist minister, and leader of the Black Elks of Florida. In personal characteristics, the son was more like his mother, Minnie Jenkins Crockett, a diminutive woman who wrote poetry, organized a preschool nursery, and was considered "strong-willed and pugnacious."

George was small in stature, eloquent in speech, and determined to follow his own path. He won a Kappa Alpha Psi scholarship to Morehouse College in Atlanta, where he gained recognition as an outstanding debater, was elected president of his class the first three years and student council president as a senior, wrote for the school newspaper, and served as a varsity cheerleader. When a Morehouse professor asked him what he wanted to be, he answered without hesitation, "A United States congressman." After graduating, he joined the Marine Cooks and Stewards Union and waited tables aboard ships sailing to South America and back. Then he left the Jim Crow–segregated South for the de facto segregated North as one of only two black students in a class of three hundred admitted to the University of Michigan Law School in 1931. He chose Michigan because tuition was $150 a year, compared to $500 a year at Harvard. Until his law school days in Ann Arbor, he had never been in a courtroom. Unless forced to, he explained, people of his color "didn't dare intrude in the white sanctuary of law."

Copies of the *Michigan Daily* during the three years Crockett was at law school there show that he was an active participant in student events. He was chairman of the Spring Parley in 1933 that focused on the topic "What is the purpose of education?" He led roundtable discussions among law students that year on the questions "Does the world want trained men?," "Is democracy dead?," and "Can there be a planned world society?" Also during that period, along with meeting his future wife, Ethelene Jones of Jackson, Michigan, Crockett befriended Willis Ward, a track and football star from Detroit who became the best-known African American at the university. One night in March 1934, Crockett and Ward visited nearby Ann Arbor High and led a symposium on "a critical survey of the problems confronting the Negro in the following fields: history, social progress, law, literature, public health, and education." Who attended that symposium is lost to history, but I would not be surprised if some members of the Cummins family were there. The siblings Bob, Barbara, Phil, and Mary, my uncles and aunt and mother, all attended Ann Arbor High and at an early age were interested in issues of racial justice.

The next fall, Ward experienced a sobering example of "problems confronting the Negro" in sports when the Michigan football team played a home game against Georgia Tech. The athletic director and coach at the school in Atlanta (only three miles from Morehouse, Crockett's alma mater) made it clear when the game was scheduled that the team would not take the field if Ward played. White Georgia Tech athletes were not allowed to compete against black athletes. The Michigan administration seemed willing to bow to this racist pressure, prompting a vociferous protest on campus, an early marker in the radicalization of the student body during that era.

There were petition drives, mass meetings, and an editorial in the *Daily* calling the Athletic Department either "astonishingly forgetful" for not realizing that it had an African American on its team or "extraordinarily stupid" for scheduling the game anyway and allowing Georgia Tech to dictate the terms. Bob Cummins and Arthur Miller were reporting for the *Daily* then, both covering and participating in the protests. Bob signed a petition along with 1,500 students and as a member of the leftist Vanguard Club was part of the Ward United Front Committee. Miller even tried to mediate the dispute by having one of his friends, a classmate from Arkansas, take him to a meeting with some of the Georgia Tech players. It did not go well, as Miller was told that they were inclined to kill Ward if he played. Ward's best friend on the team, the center, Jerry Ford, the future president, later said that he threatened to quit unless his teammate played, but relented after talking to his coach and stepfather. In the end Ward, who followed his friend Crockett's path to become a lawyer and judge, did not play, and carried a measure of disillusionment with him through the rest of his life.

When he finished law school, Crockett faced a dilemma: Where and how to practice his profession? He knew there would be some opportunities for a black lawyer in the South, representing only black clients, but after a brief return to Florida he determined that he did not want to remain in that suffocating atmosphere. He settled on West Virginia, a border state that seemed to have a growing black awareness and that was recommended by his father-in-law, who had once served as a minister there. He and Ethelene moved to Fairmont, a city along the Monongahela River in the coal country just below the Pennsylvania border. The University of Michigan loaned him $150 so that he could get there, open an office, and survive for a month. He found a mentor in U.S. Senator Matthew M. Neely, who had a law practice in Fairmont and had once been the city's mayor. Until Crockett reached West Virginia, he had considered himself a Lincoln Republican. Now he evolved into a New Deal Democrat. He also became a civil rights activist, on the local level as the president of the NAACP chapter, and on the national level as a founding member of the National Lawyers Guild, the first racially integrated bar association. With Senator Neely's help, he eventually made the move to a more influential setting than Fairmont, taking a job with the federal government in Washington.

In the first of many firsts, he became the first black staff lawyer at the U.S. Department of Labor, helping to pave the way for others. He specialized in employee lawsuits filed under the Fair Labor Standards Act. After rising to senior attorney status there, but hearing that he likely never would be promoted to chief of section because a black man could not oversee so many white lawyers, he switched to a job with more direct impact fighting institutional racism: as a hearing examiner for the

Fair Employment Practices Commission. One of his cases took him to Detroit to deal with the employment of blacks in the city's transportation agency, the Department of Street Railways, and on a train ride back to Washington he fell into a long conversation with a fellow passenger. The other man was white and surprised Crockett by showing great interest in his work dealing with discrimination in the workplace. When the conversation came around to racial difficulties in labor unions, his companion told him who he was: R. J. Thomas, president of the United Auto Workers. Thomas told Crockett how essential black workers had been in organizing at the Ford plant and how concerned he was about growing racial intolerance and tension in working-class Detroit. Racial animosity had spilled into violence during the race riots of 1943 and ensuing "hate strikes" by white defense plant workers who opposed the integration of their workplaces.

His chance encounter with Thomas on the train led to Crockett's return to Michigan to head the UAW's Fair Employment Practices Committee. He and Ethelene and their two children moved into a house on Detroit's West Side on a street named American.

While working for the UAW, Crockett also wrote columns for Detroit's black newspaper, the *Michigan Chronicle*. Two of his columns from 1945 show the contours of his political and sociological thinking. In an essay he wrote on March 17 he denounced the "separate but equal" status that whites imposed in the southern states with the acquiescence of some black leaders and instead championed a universal perspective. "For myself," he wrote, "I have never regarded race consciousness or race pride as a particular virtue, and I am hopeful that more and more Americans will become less and less race conscious. Hitler and his followers should be an example to these extreme race chauvinists. The sooner we begin to think, act, and react as Americans and not as hyphenated Americans, the sooner we shall find that common basis of understanding and partnership which is a prerequisite for America's race and color problem. The phrase 'our people' had no racial connotation for me. Indeed, all Americans, all humanity, constitute my people."

Four months later, in a column titled "Who Is a Red," his topic was communism and fear. The country was so gripped by a fear of communists, he wrote, that if they supported or opposed a measure, the safe course of action was to be on the other side. He considered the stigma foolish. "Why, for example, has this fear of being labelled a communist become such an obsession among liberal thinkers that we hesitate to purchase and openly read the communist paper as nonchalantly as we would read a Socialist paper or the *Detroit News*? Why do we steer clear of books by Karl Marx, or *The Communist Manifesto*, but have no qualms whatever about openly reading *Plato's Republic* or Henry George's *Progress and Poverty* or even the New Testament? The one contains about as much communist thinking as the other, except that we do not like to think of the Bible as containing communism—we prefer to say that it is social gospel or socialism." Crockett himself did not hesitate to purchase and openly read communist publications. Among the documents the FBI amassed as its agents investigated him during the Red Scare were receipts of $5.75 for six-month subscriptions to the *Daily Worker*.

The urgency with which anticommunist liberals sought to distance themselves from anything hinting of communism played out within the UAW, and eventually cost Crockett his job. The labor organization was caught in a power struggle between the center left and far left when Walter Reuther sought to clean the union of communists and communist sympathizers. Reuther came from a socialist family and had strong civil rights convictions, but he was a pragmatist who thought the only way the labor movement could flourish was to be strongly anticommunist. Crockett was in the middle for a few months, but ended up on the side that Reuther considered too radical, and when Reuther took full control of the union in 1947, Crockett left the UAW payroll and set up shop in the offices of leftist attorney Maurice Sugar in Cadillac Tower (first known as Barlum Tower) in downtown Detroit.

To understand the extent of de facto segregation in the northern city of Detroit then, consider: Crockett was the only black professional working in the forty-story building and one of the few in downtown Detroit. Any black clients who visited the tower had to ride the freight elevator with the black janitors. When Crockett and his white friend and future law partner, Ernie Goodman, went out to lunch together, they rarely received welcome service in nearby restaurants and often had to eat in the cafeteria of the predominantly black Lucy Thurman YWCA.

One night in the summer of 1948, after he had left his office at Cadillac Tower and returned to his home on American Street, Crockett took the call asking if he was interested in being a defense counsel in the Foley Square trial. His mentor, Maurice Sugar, had made the connection.

FORMALLY THE FOLEY Square case was *United States v. Dennis et al.* Eugene Dennis was general secretary of the CPUSA. One party member ranked above him in the leadership, William Z. Foster, but Foster was ill as the trial began and his case was separated from the others. Along with Dennis and Carl Winter, Crockett's client, the group included John Gates, a leader of the Young Communist League who had fought in Spain with my uncle in the International Brigade, and eight other members of the party's national board, including New York councilman Benjamin J. Davis Jr. and Henry Winston, both of whom were black. J. Edgar Hoover had wanted to put all fifty-five members of the party's national board on trial and was disappointed that a much smaller number had been indicted.

Although the same grand jury that handed down the indictments had heard testimony earlier concerning a Soviet spy network, none of the defendants was charged with espionage and no evidence was presented at the trial to connect them to spying. Thirteen FBI informants and ex-communists testified at the trial, but the prosecution presented no evidence showing any defendant directly planned or advocated the violent overthrow of the government. Most of the testimony was centered on the way the CPUSA reflexively responded to Soviet dictates and on the classic teachings of Marxist-Leninist thought and literature. The intent was to prove that anyone who spread these thoughts and books was inherently advocating revolution and that the Communist Party was a conspiracy not deserving of First Amendment rights. One thread of the prosecution's case involved what was called the Aesopian lexicon of American communists: communications through stories with a seemingly innocent but secretly sinister meaning understood by fellow travelers.

The language of Eugene Dennis was hardly innocent or indirect. One of the pamphlets introduced into evidence was a transcript of his 1946 address to the national committee of the Communist Party USA at its plenary meeting in New York, where he defended the expulsion of former party leader Earl Browder, who had dared to disagree with aspects of the party line as sent down from Moscow. Dennis called Browder "a notorious revisionist" who "deserted the ranks and the cause of communism and has become a servile champion of American monopoly capital." Then he quoted from a seminal communist text, the *History of CPSU* (Soviet Union), to explain why it was so essential for the party to eliminate dissent: "Opportunism in our midst is like an ulcer in a healthy organism and must not be tolerated. . . . Sceptics, opportunists, capitulators and traitors cannot be tolerated on the directing staff of the working class if, while it is carrying out a life and death struggle with the bourgeoisie, there are capitulators and traitors on its own staff."

This was the terminology of a cult, of blind true believers. Reverse the ideology and it would not differ much from the intolerant lexicon of Joe McCarthy.

Crockett had not read Marx and Lenin, or any of the foundational works of communism, until he signed up for the defense, whereupon he studied them intently. Reading those books, he said later, did not entice him to join the party. Nor did he find anything in them that made the prosecution's case; the government argument relied more on fear than reason, he thought. Crockett had a habit of conducting debates with himself, and he concluded this internal debate by deciding it was important to show his "defiance of the fear psychosis" that seemed pervasive in the country.

Judge Medina, a graduate of Princeton with a law degree from Columbia, had been appointed to the bench by President Truman only eighteen months earlier. Before that he practiced law and taught at his alma mater. Crockett, as the only black attorney on the defense team, sensed at first that Medina was subtly trying to separate him from the other lawyers. As Crockett later described it, Medina pulled him aside and confided that he was of Mexican heritage (his father was from Yucatán), had grown up in Brooklyn, and knew what discrimination was. Crockett responded to this, he recalled, by staring at the judge "with a deadpan expression until he felt uncomfortable." The relationship between the two men soured from there, reflecting the bitter atmosphere permeating the entire trial.

Crockett v. Medina, or *Medina v. Crockett*, was a play within the play. Who goaded whom more depended on one's perspective, but who suffered the consequences depended solely on who had the power. And Medina having the power, Crockett suffered the consequences.

Crockett to Medina at various points in the trial:

- "I think your honor that the defendants, as well as myself and other counsel, began this trial with certain illusions that have been shattered because of the prejudicial actions of the court."
- "I suggest that this latest ruling of the court merely confirms all of the prejudicial rulings that have been made in the course of this trial. I suggest that during the course of this trial it has actually been possible, and I have heard spectators making the court's rulings before the court himself made the ruling."
- "I have listened carefully to the proceedings during the whole time this was going on, and what surprises me, frankly, your honor, is the frequency with which Mr. McGohey [chief prosecutor John McGohey] will make an objection and the court will sustain the objection without asking Mr. McGohey to state the reasons for his objections or giving us an opportunity to suggest to the court the reasons why the objection should be overruled."

Medina saw the tactics of the defendants and the defense lawyers as having less to do with the merits of the case than with trying to disrupt the trial, offer political critiques, create havoc through "willful, deliberate and concerted delay," and perhaps force him to make a mistake that could help them on appeal. Four months in, Crockett became the first of the defense lawyers to be cited for contempt of court. While all the courtroom behavior of all the defendants and their counsels perturbed the judge, he seemed particularly critical of Crockett, often treating him with sarcasm bordering on condescension.

Medina to Crockett at various points:

- "Well, that is the most ridiculous thing I have ever heard, Mr. Crockett. I wish you wouldn't do that. There is just no sense in that at all."
- "Well, how any sane person can think otherwise is difficult for me to see."
- "Well, I am afraid that you understand things in a different sense from what they were said."
- "Well, that sounds crazy. You always seem to do that."
- "Oh my, Mr. Crockett. You have something to add?"
- "I wonder if it is possible for me to impress upon you . . . Now I beg of you try to absorb that thought."
- "Get down to business, Mr. Crockett."

The trial went on through the spring and summer and into fall, the atmosphere vacillating between tedium and tension. The battalion of police officers stood daily sentinel around Foley Square, and two officers were assigned to guard Judge Medina's home on East 75th Street near Madison Avenue, one arriving with Medina after the day's proceedings and staying until midnight, the other working from midnight until the judge left for Foley Square in the morning. In a letter to a sympathetic friend who had expressed concern about his well-being, Medina called the trial a "terrible experience," but said he was trying to keep himself in mental and physical trim. "Otherwise I should have folded up long before this. My regime is very strict. It involves massage treatments three times a week and the complete elimination of every sort of social activity even to the extent of eliminating all the members of the family except Eth [his wife]. I really am living like a hermit."

Every day for months, scores of letters arrived in Medina's mail, some from critics, but most offering support. His clerk stored them in brown cardboard files labeled "Commie Trial"—bulging containers that eventually were archived at the Mudd Manuscript Library at Princeton, Medina's alma mater.

Anonymous postcards:

"Thanks for a God-fearing judge!! Keep those Communists in jail forever!"

"We millions of Catholics are behind you! Good work! Keep it up—drive out all those Communists. They should be shot!!"

And hundreds more signed letters, many on the stationery of veterans groups. Typical was one from Leo B. Keltz, Welfare Officer for Father Stedman Post No. 846, Catholic War Veterans Inc., Chaplain for the Chaplains, Brooklyn, New York: "The members of our Post have been following with interest the trial of the Communists at which you are presiding. There are those among us who would prefer less lenient treatment for these enemies of our country. However, we feel confident that your patient forbearance will, in the end, result in a permanent setback for those who would destroy our institutions."

On September 20, after the prosecution had elicited the testimony of two black witnesses who accused the Communist Party of "using" and "exploiting the grievances" of Negroes, Crockett called to the stand a defense witness of world renown, Paul Robeson, whose life offered a kaleidoscopic image of what it meant to be American or un-American. Born in Princeton just before the start of the twentieth century, the son of a runaway slave, Robeson first achieved fame as an All-American football player at Rutgers, then as a dynamic actor and singer who strode the Broadway stage in *Othello*, *Porgy and Bess*, and *Showboat*, where his rendition of "Ol' Man River" transformed the song into a powerful evocation of the historic struggle of black men against white suppression.

In his rise to stardom, Robeson became disillusioned by the discrimination and segregation he encountered in America and turned to leftist politics. Year by year his admiration grew for the Communist Party, the anticolonial movement in Africa, and the Soviet Union, which he believed was on the side of civil rights and equality. He lived abroad for much of the 1930s, a period during which he made frequent visits to the Soviet Union and traveled to Spain to support and entertain the Americans in the Lincoln Brigade. In the cold war era, he became a target of various anticommunist agencies in the U.S. government. In 1949 he attended a Soviet-sponsored peace conference in Paris, where he said that another world war pitting the U.S. against the Soviet Union was not inevitable and that many black Americans hoped it would not occur. When the speech was interpreted by the American press as implying that black Americans would not fight in a war against the Soviets, editorials denounced him as a traitor. The controversy prompted the U.S. government to strip Robeson of his passport. It is also what prompted HUAC chairman John Stephens Wood to subpoena Jackie Robinson and other prominent black Americans to testify before his committee and denounce Robeson—testimony Wood later cited at the opening of the 1952 hearings in Room 740, where he encountered my father and uncle and George Crockett.

The anticommunist hostility toward Robeson was never stronger than during the period immediately before he took the stand at the Foley Square trial. Only weeks earlier, he had been the marquee name at two outdoor concerts outside Peekskill, New York, fifty miles north of Manhattan, sponsored by the Civil Rights Congress, a leftist organization pushing for racial equality that included many CP members, among them Benjamin Davis and Henry Winston, the trial's two black defendants. The first concert was aborted at the last minute; the second went on as scheduled. Both were marred by mob violence.

A few days before the first concert, scheduled for August 27, the *Peekskill Evening Star* ran an editorial lambasting Robeson for his communist sympathies and declaring that the concert should not only be shunned but met with protest. "Every ticket purchased for the Peekskill concert will drop nickels and dimes into the till basket of an Un-American political organization," the editorial said, predicting that the concert would "consist of an unsavory mixture of song and political talk by one who has described Russia as his 'second motherland' and who has avowed the greatest contempt for the democratic press. The time for tolerant silence that signifies approval is running out."

The local chapters of the VFW and American Legion responded by calling on all "loyal Americans" to make it clear that Robeson and his supporters were not welcome. That is an understatement of what happened. Before the concert was canceled an hour before it was to start, protesters attacked Robeson supporters with rocks and fists, and afterward chairs on the concert grounds were burned along with a Klan-style cross. At the second scheduled concert, held over Labor Day weekend at an abandoned golf course nearby, a few thousand people from New York labor unions, led by the leftist International Fur and Leather Workers Union, provided protection for the performers and concertgoers, and the concert went off without interruption. Folk singer Pete Seeger performed along with Robeson, who ended the afternoon with a stirring rendition of "Ol' Man River." But as Robeson and Seeger and their thousands of supporters departed, their car caravan was attacked by angry mobs lining both sides of the road. No "silence to signify approval," but instead a barrage of rocks, windshields broken, dozens wounded from shattered glass, doors dented, cars surrounded and jostled, some overturned. State troopers were there ostensibly to keep the peace, but most did nothing, and Robeson himself said a trooper approached his car and cursed as he clobbered the door with his club.

When word got out that Robeson would be called as a defense witness at the Foley Square trial, Medina was again besieged with letters. Wrote one admirer, "Anticipating that when Paul Robeson testifies he is going to be as impudent and nasty as possible, I hope you are going to dole out to him the same treatment that you have given others in your court who have been insolent and insulting. The nerve of Paul Robeson praising Russia as he does always with the worst comments for America.—why doesn't he stay in Russia?"

When Robeson did finally testify, or tried to, it could be argued that he was the least insolent person involved. He tried to answer questions from Crockett, but he did not get far with Judge Medina, who knew him from an earlier time; Medina had been Robeson's professor at Columbia Law School in the early 1920s. Crockett asked Robeson about his own history with racism and his connections to the men on trial, but invariably the questions elicited objections from the prosecution that were sustained by Medina in a pattern that went like this:

> Mr. Crockett: Have you ever shared the platform with Mr. Dennis at any public gathering?
> Mr. McGohey: Objection.
> The Court: Sustained.
> Mr. Crockett: Have you ever shared the platform with any of the other defendants at any public gathering?
> Mr. McGohey: Objection.
> The Court: Sustained.
> Mr. Crockett: I think you shared the platform with Mrs. Roosevelt, have you not?
> Mr. McGohey: Objection.
> The Court: Sustained.

Medina was especially critical of Crockett for mentioning the former First Lady, saying her connection to Robeson had nothing to do with the case. Soon after that, Crockett relented altogether. "In view of the court's ruling, I am convinced it will be impossible to bring before the court the testimony I had hoped," he said. Medina rebuked him, again, saying he never should have called Robeson to testify.

"May I—?" Robeson tried to interject.

Medina cut him off: "No, Mr. Robeson, I don't want to hear any statement from you. I can't find from anything in these questions that you have any knowledge of the facts that are relevant here in this case."

As he left the courtroom, Robeson complained about the way Medina treated him and also praised the Communist Party for playing "a magnificent role in fighting for the freedom of the American Negro."

Was he a communist? a reporter asked.

The question, Robeson responded, was not relevant.

CROCKETT CALLED HIS summation to the jury the highlight of his life. He said everything he had done before was in preparation for this opportunity to explain how much the Constitution meant to him—and how it applied to the eleven American communists put on trial for their beliefs.

In riding the subways in New York, Crockett told the jury, he noticed a sign that said, "Freedom is everybody's business." He thought it was the perfect motto to apply to the defense in this case. "Freedom is indivisible," he said. "We cannot deny freedom of speech to communists and at the same time preserve freedom for Jews and for Catholics and for Negroes or for persons of foreign ancestry. You cannot outlaw the Communist Party because of its political theories without creating a most dangerous precedent, a precedent that may in the future be used to outlaw a religious organization or the political organization or the inter-racial organization to which you or I might belong. Once we in America forget that freedom is everybody's business, once we accept the fascist theory that communists have no rights or that all communists should be sent to Russia or put in concentration camps, once we begin thinking and speaking in those terms we descend to the very depths of Hitlerism."

To defend the right of communists to speak or make known their beliefs did not mean that you had to agree with their views. "I have on numerous occasions in the past criticized communist views which I regard as contrary to my own views," he said. "Indeed, three months before I entered this case I publicly debated a political issue against Mr. Winter, my client. I have no objection to anyone criticizing communists or communism to their heart's content. As I read the Constitution, and especially its guarantee of freedom of speech, it is the privilege of every one of us to criticize not only the communists but any organization we please to criticize."

Crockett focused much of his summation on the connection between blacks and communists. He said that every time he heard the argument that communists were using or exploiting the grievances of blacks he "boiled with resentment" at the condescension behind that idea. "I resent anyone referring to the problems faced by Negroes in this country today as simply grievances, as though you stepped on someone's toe or refused him a drink of water. Is that all the significance the prosecution attaches to the denial to eight million Negroes of the right to vote simply because they happen to have black skin? Is it a 'grievance' to deny employment to Negro men and women or to Negro professional people in federal government or in state or city government? And yet you don't need evidence in this case to know that all this and more is being done, nor do we need to present more evidence in this case for you to know that the Communist Party's position is diametrically opposed to any such practice."

The case against the communists focused on the assumption that their teachings advocated force and violence, Crockett stated. "Let us look at this force and violence. There is a lot of evidence of force and violence in our country these days; but it is not force and violence emanating from the Communist Party. Force and violence takes the form . . . of force and violence against Negroes in the form of lynchings and other mob actions." One defense witness's testimony "regarding how the Communist Party concentrated the attention of the people of Chicago on the lynching of four Negroes in Monroe, Georgia, in 1946," along with Benjamin Davis's recounting of the role of the Communist Party in the defense of the Scottsboro Nine, Crockett argued, were indicative of a kind of force and violence that was "intended to overthrow constituted authority."

The Foley Square case, Crockett concluded, was "an attempt to illegalize the party that has fought against the whole system of force and violence practiced upon Negroes. This is an attempt to outlaw the party that leads the fight against those Jim Crow curtains in our railroad dining cars which set aside Negroes as untouchables. This is an attempt to outlaw the party that leads the fight against those who would confine Negro children to the tubercular slum areas of our city. This is an attempt to outlaw the party that leads the fight against those who would keep the Negro in its place." He hoped that attempt would not succeed, Crockett said, but if it did there would surely be another group to rise with the same mission. "And their voices will be heard."

OCTOBER 14, 11:24 that morning. The gray-haired bailiff issued the cry "All rise!" as Judge Medina emerged from his chambers, took his place in his high-backed chair framed by the American flag and the Great Seal of the United States, and instructed the clerk of the court to bring in the jury. Crockett sat with the defense team in front of the eleven defendants. Behind them stood a dozen deputy marshals. Led by Juror No. 8, the jury filtered in and sat down. They had deliberated for seven hours. None was smiling.

The clerk received permission from the judge to proceed and called the roll of jurors, then asked the foreman, Thelma Dial, the wife of a bandleader, whether a verdict had been reached. Dial rose, holding a document that recorded the verdict. Speaking softly, she said the jury found each of the defendants guilty. The charges called for maximum sentences of ten years in prison. After the jurors were polled individually, and the finding confirmed, Medina thanked them and dismissed them from the room. "Now I turn to some unfinished business," he said, asking the six defense lawyers to rise. Each of them was guilty too, he said. He found them guilty of contempt of court. He would have overlooked their actions if he thought they were taken in the "heat of controversy," but not long into the trial he concluded that the six had conspired in a "cold and calculating manner" to try to provoke incidents for a mistrial or impair the judge's health.

Crockett was sentenced to four months in prison. In a statement issued after his sentencing, he called it "a badge of honor."

21

Committee Men

DURING THE LONG AND CONTENTIOUS TRIAL OF THE eleven leading communists in the United States at the Foley Square Courthouse in 1949, John Stephens Wood was chairing congressional hearings on Capitol Hill and around the country to determine whether other citizens were sufficiently American or dangerously un-American.

In the historical context of the House Committee on Un-American Activities, Chairman Wood was regarded as a step up from the two virulently bigoted southern Democrats most associated with the committee in its earlier years. It was Martin Dies of Texas, the first and longest-serving chairman, who claimed there was insufficient evidence for his committee to investigate the Ku Klux Klan, which he described as "an old American institution." And it was John Rankin, a committee member from Mississippi, who referred to "niggers" and "kikes" on the House floor. When President Truman pressured congressional allies to yank Rankin off the committee by revising the rules, Rankin smeared the president as a Soviet tool, saying, "The word seems to have come down from Moscow."

Wood was less strident. As Walter Goodman described him in *The Committee*, his book on the panel, Wood surprised "friends and foes by being a gentlemanly hunter of communists. He was a conservative, but he was not a red neck; and he was by no means a showy or particularly forceful personality." The contrast was one of demeanor more than policy. His voting record was not much different from that of his Dixie colleagues, especially on civil rights and labor legislation.

Wood was one of 116 House members who voted against a 1949

measure prohibiting poll taxes in elections for federal offices, a bill that was strangled in the Senate, where segregationists controlled key committees. Imposed mostly in southern states, the poll tax was used specifically as a means of limiting the voting power of poor blacks. Wood had already established his credentials as a stalwart of the Jim Crow South by voting against bills denying federal school lunch assistance to institutions that discriminated against children based on race, creed, color, or national origin and against opening immigration quotas for Asian and Pacific peoples. He also had voted against legislation raising the minimum wage to seventy-five cents an hour, and in foreign affairs had taken a largely isolationist stance by opposing the Marshall Plan and military aid to the North Atlantic Treaty Organization, even though these efforts were intended to counteract the communist threat in Europe at the onset of the cold war. In opposing the Marshall Plan, Wood joined the side of the more vociferous Rankin, who said Americans should not put money into the "sinkhole of Europe" and called on "those lazy people in Europe to sober up." He also unwittingly sided in this case with Joseph Stalin, who feared that the Marshall Plan would weaken the Soviet position in Europe and became its loudest opponent.

The most publicized congressional controversy Wood became entangled in outside the committee involved a 1949 measure presented as a repeal of the Taft-Hartley Act, which had been enacted in 1947 to curtail the power of unions. This was in fact a phony repeal intended not to help unions but to further weaken them. An analysis of the new bill showed that of the twenty major provisions, it was tougher than Taft-Hartley in four key areas, with only insubstantial changes in the others. While Taft-Hartley allowed the use of court injunctions to prevent strikes, the so-called repeal bill permitted the general counsel of the National Labor Relations Board to seek an injunction even before complaints were issued. It was also tougher than Taft-Hartley in outlawing all existing and valid closed shop contracts and in making it easier for employers to fire workers for striking in violation of contracts or for engaging in subversive activities.

Wood's role was notable not because of the side he took but because he allowed himself to serve as a front for union-bashing Republicans. His name was on the bill as the main sponsor, even though he was not on the House Education and Labor Committee and his district in northern Georgia was not known as a hotbed of labor disputes, making his involvement seem peculiar to labor insiders in Washington. Columnist Peter Edson, writing for the Scripps-owned NEA news syndicate, was so curious that he approached Wood and asked, "Who wrote the Wood bill?"

Wood's first response was that it was not written by the Department of Labor. When Edson repeated the question, Wood said, "The bill was written in my office with the help of a few Republicans on the House Committee on Education and Labor." When Edson asked who, Wood replied, angrily, "It's none of your business," and walked away.

"Who wrote the Wood bill may not be the personal business of any reporter," Edson wrote. "But it most certainly is public business who writes these tricky pieces of legislation. And in the public interest, every reporter has the right to ask any question he chooses with the expectation of getting a civil answer. Congressman Wood's reluctance to come clean on this one may be due to several factors. One is that he wants all the credit for himself. The other is that he doesn't want it known how the bill was written, what deal it represents, or who supplied the brains."

Edson pursued all leads. He was a dogged reporter who three years later would break the story about a secret fund that Richard Nixon's business pals had set up to pay his office and travel expenses. That revelation led to Nixon's famous "Checkers" speech, during which the Republican nominee for vice president evoked the family dog named Checkers in a sentimental appeal to stay on the ticket as Dwight D. Eisenhower's running mate. In going after the Wood story, Edson tracked down William Ingles, who organized the Committee to Save Taft-Hartley. Ingles told him that he knew how the Wood bill was written, but that "Wood's unwillingness to discuss the subject seals the mouths of those who had anything to do with it." What Edson called "the frankest explanation of how the Wood bill came about" was from Pennsylvania congressman Samuel McConnell, ranking Republican on the Labor Committee. "It didn't take any brains to write the Wood bill and there is no mystery about it," McConnell told Edson. "I could have written the Wood bill myself. . . . Scissors and paste, not genius." The key to getting Wood's name on the bill, McConnell said, was simply that Wood was willing to lend his name. When the final wording was worked out, Wood was not even in the room.

Drew Pearson, author of the nationally syndicated Washington Merry-Go-Round column, also took an interest in the Wood bill and later wrote a column asserting that the Georgia congressman's behavior was affected by heavy drinking: "This was most important legislation. It affected scores of labor unions and millions of workmen. But when the time came for the final debate on the Wood bill, its author was so under the influence of liquor that ex-speaker Joe Martin and Congressman Charles Halleck of Indiana, two Republicans, substituted for him in arguing for his bill. When the final vote came, Wood managed to appear on the House floor to vote, though he could barely make it, and immediately thereafter retired to a couch in the Democratic cloakroom."

As Washington's most gossipy and feared insider columnist, Pearson demonstrated a disdain for HUAC in general and its chairmen in particular. His columns had helped lead to the indictment and eventual conviction of one of Wood's predecessors, John Parnell Thomas, a New Jersey Republican, who was involved in a long-running tax-avoidance kickback scheme with one of his aides. Thomas had taken the chairmanship of the committee away from Wood for the two years that Republicans controlled the House, in 1947 and 1948. It was in that window, in October 1947, that HUAC, with Thomas as chairman and Wood as the minority ranking member, subpoenaed what became known as the Hollywood Ten and cited them for contempt of Congress for refusing on First Amendment grounds to testify about their possible communist connections.

The best known of the ten Hollywood film professionals, all blacklisted from working in the industry, convicted, and imprisoned, was Dalton Trumbo, a novelist and future Academy Award winner, but the group also included Alvah Bessie, who fought in the Spanish Civil War alongside my uncle Bob Cummins and his Michigan classmates Elman Service and Ralph Neafus. Another of the Hollywood Ten was Ring Lardner Jr., the son of writer Ring Lardner and brother of James Lardner, who became close friends with Service while also fighting in Spain, where he was killed. When HUAC's Thomas went on trial for his congressional kickback scheme, he refused to testify against himself, citing the Fifth Amendment, the legal right that he and other congressmen denigrated when it was used by witnesses called before their committee. The balding, boastful Jersey pol, a former bond salesman, found himself locked up in the same federal prison as Ring Lardner Jr.

Chairman Wood provided more fodder for Pearson. In a column published on June 2, 1950, Pearson first described Wood as "a scholarly, dignified gentleman who looks the way you would expect a congressman to look," then drew the knife, claiming he had irrefutable evidence that "Mr. Wood has been acting the way a congressman should not." In that and several follow-up columns, Pearson reported that Wood's office collected a payoff fee from the family of a young constituent who suffered crippling injuries when struck by a U.S. Army truck. Wood got a special bill passed through Congress paying the family $10,000 in damages for the accident. But according to Pearson, who had a check stub, Wood's office collected a fee of $1,000 for the sort of constituent service that most congressmen performed routinely. Wood defended the action by saying the office assistant who charged the fee was also a lawyer back in his congressional district.

Pearson was not done. Two weeks later he reported that Chairman Wood had brought his family maid and her handyman husband to Washington and that to pay them he had placed the husband on the committee payroll as a janitor. "The peculiar thing is that financially Wood is well off," Pearson wrote. "As most congressmen go, he is affluent, and his wife is a member of one of the big textile families of north Georgia." The janitor was William Fowler, a black man who had worked in the Canton textile plant. Wood put him on the HUAC payroll when he took over the chairmanship in July 1945. Fowler's wife had worked at the Wood home for decades for room and board but no salary. Taken together with the constituent payoff, Pearson concluded, Wood presented himself as "a pillar of good Americanism and an example to the nation. The conclusion is inescapable that he isn't."

Wood responded by taking to the House floor, where he labeled Pearson a hypocrite on race. "In view of the many anguished wails which this man Pearson has mouthed about the benighted status of the Negro race in my state, as well as other southern states, his criticism of my action in giving this Georgia Negro a job, the duties of which he performed excellently, comes with poor grace." More than that, Wood said, shielding himself with the armor of his anticommunist agenda, Pearson's attacks on him personally and the committee he chaired made him an un-American subversive. "He has been the most effective weapon that the Stalinites have been able to use in America for the undermining of our whole constitutional system. To him there is nothing under the heavens that is sacred. He befouls and demeans everything he touches. He occupies the unique and unenviable position today of standing alone at the very pinnacle of all the slanderers and scandalmongers in all of American history."

Many politicians who had been subjected to Pearson's sharp pen likely cheered Wood on, including Joe McCarthy, who by 1950 had emerged as the most eager communist hunter on Capitol Hill. Before then, McCarthy had been a source for Pearson, providing him with dirt and gossip on congressional colleagues. But as McCarthy's charges about communists in the government grew more heated and reckless over the months since his February "I have here in my hand" speech in Wheeling, West Virginia, Pearson began writing critical columns about him. McCarthy then turned his sights on Pearson, asserting that Pearson had briefly employed an assistant with connections to a Soviet spy network, a claim that internal Soviet documents, unveiled decades later, showed to be true. A few weeks before Christmas 1950, during a spat at the Sulgrave Club near DuPont Circle in Washington, McCarthy did to Pearson what Wood was perhaps too gentlemanly to do: he gave him a punch to the jaw and a knee below the belt. The cloakroom melee was broken up by Nixon, who happened upon the scene. Biographer John A. Farrell recounted that Nixon said, "Let a Quaker stop this fight," as he pulled McCarthy away.

JOHN STEPHENS WOOD was a man of second chances, with Congress and with the committee. He served two separate stretches in the

House. The first had been brief, lasting only two terms, curtailed by the 1934 primary, when he was defeated by Frank Whelchel, a judge from Gainesville. Wood won the popular vote, but Georgia primaries then operated on a unit system somewhat comparable to the Electoral College for presidential elections. Each county was treated as a unit, and the candidate who won the most counties in the district was declared the winner. Whelchel won by carrying two more counties than Wood, one by only a few votes. That might seem undemocratic and un-American, but every aspect of Georgia voting then was undemocratic at a deeper level, when black citizens could not even participate in the White Primary. Wood went home to Canton and practiced law for a decade until Whelchel retired, then ran for his old seat in 1944 and won in a three-way primary, which in one-party Georgia meant he was back.

He returned to Washington, nearing age sixty, just in time to help resuscitate HUAC. It had been a temporary committee since its inception, but Wood voted with the majority to establish it as a permanent House body in 1945. By July of that year he had been made chairman in "Rankin's Coup," so called because when a northern Democrat stepped down from the chairmanship due to ill health, Rankin orchestrated a coalition of southern Democrats and conservative Republicans to put Wood, a fellow southerner, in charge. When the GOP gained control of the House in 1947, Wood was out of the chair for two years, before returning in 1949.

One of his first hires in his second ascension was a new chief counsel, Frank S. Tavenner, the Virginia lawyer, apple grower, beneficiary of the commonwealth's conservative Byrd machine, former federal prosecutor, and counsel at the Tokyo War Crimes Tribunal. Tavenner arrived with a reputation for being organized and imperturbable. One committee watcher, otherwise critical of HUAC, called him "perhaps the best-qualified and most dispassionate assistant it ever had."

When Tavenner took the job in May 1949, one of his first tasks was to examine how witnesses cited their Fifth Amendment rights against self-incrimination to avoid answering questions about their past. Committee members and staffers believed taking the Fifth was a dodge, that it implied guilt in fact if not in law. At Wood's direction, Tavenner tried to figure out ways the committee could hold witnesses in contempt for citing the Fifth as they were able to do for those, like the Hollywood Ten, who refused to testify by citing their First Amendment rights to free speech and association.

The merits of Fifth Amendment protections and what they meant became a debate topic for editorial boards around the nation. Among the more thoughtful perspectives came from the *Valparaiso Vidette-Messenger* in Indiana under the headline "Does Silence in the Face of an Accusation Indicate Guilt?" It was human nature to assume that it does, the editorial stated. "Probably human nature is only finding expression, then, when Congressman John S. Wood of Georgia, chairman of the House Committee on Un-American Activities, says that committee witnesses who refuse to say whether they are communists will be presumed to be such. This is the conclusion which most outside observers probably draw about any witness who refuses to answer the question, 'Are you now or were you ever a communist?' on the grounds of self-incrimination. As an individual conclusion it is a natural one. It is a conclusion which is not permitted in a court of law, however. The committee members are entitled to be human in their own thinking, but should be careful of the basis for public condemnation."

During Wood's brief first run as chairman, as America was adjusting to the postwar era, HUAC was relatively quiet, but the second go-round was different, as the committee went looking for un-Americans around the country. With investigators doing the groundwork and Tavenner preparing the questioning, the committee held 108 hearings that filled up thirty-five volumes of testimony during the Eighty-first Congress in 1949 and 1950, and picked up even more intensity during the following two years of the Eighty-second Congress, which was played out against the backdrop of American troops being killed by Korean and Chinese communist forces in the Korean War. During that time the committee also issued several substantial reports, including a study of Soviet espionage in the U.S. titled *The Shameful Years* and a voluminous *Guide to Subversive Organizations and Publications.*

The committee's work supplemented a network of federal programs designed to identify and track American communists and suspicious organizations. The FBI maintained a security index of individuals to be rounded up in case of a national emergency. Since President Truman signed Executive Order 9835 in March 1947, the Justice Department maintained its own list of subversive groups, a list that was often used to isolate political organizations. Americans who fought in the Spanish Civil War were targeted twice; both the Veterans of the Abraham Lincoln Brigade and one of its outgrowths, the Joint Anti-Fascist Refugee Committee, were labeled subversive. Among other things, the groups were required to register as foreign agents and submit membership lists to the government.

Truman's Executive Order also set in motion a requirement that all federal workers take loyalty oaths, with background checks for those suspected of having communist sympathies. Year by year thereafter, state and local governments and educational institutions added their own versions of loyalty oaths as the fear of communist subversion intensified. In Birmingham, Alabama, the town fathers ordered all communists to get out of town. In Jacksonville, Florida, it became a crime to confer with a Red or former Red. In part because of all that, but for a host of other reasons—disillusionment with the Soviet Union, the fighting in Korea, weariness, political transformation—the estimated number of CPUSA members diminished, by 1950 down to 31,609 out of a national population of slightly more than 150 million.

When Dies and Rankin were on the committee, many congressmen might rather have served anywhere else, but that changed once the bigoted rabble-rousers departed. The committee seemed less of an embarrassing backwater, and the fight against communism felt more relevant and politically prestigious. When an opening was created at the start of 1951, twenty Republican members of the House were considered for the post. It went to Charles E. Potter.

For Potter, it had been a long road back from the near-fatal injuries he suffered fighting against Nazi troops in France's Colmar Pocket. After a doctor at an army field hospital at Saint-Dié-des-Vosges removed his left leg at the hip bone and sawed off his right leg above the ankle, Potter had been evacuated on the U.S. Hospital Ship *Thistle*, a converted troop carrier, across the Atlantic to the port of Charleston,

South Carolina, and transported by train from there for recuperation at McCloskey General Hospital in Temple, Texas. Soon he was shipped up to Percy Jones General Hospital in Battle Creek, Michigan, where he underwent an orchidectomy to remove a damaged testicle and a more precise amputation, his right leg removed to within a few inches of the knee. The hospital in Battle Creek was overloaded with men suffering from grievous limb wounds. Among them were several who later made their way to Washington and called themselves the Percy Jones Alumni Club: Bob Dole of Kansas, Daniel Inouye of Hawaii, and Phil Hart of Michigan, a Democrat who thirteen years later effectively ended Potter's political career by defeating him in a U.S. Senate race.

Potter was fitted with an artificial left leg at Percy Jones and went home to Cheboygan on crutches, but his recovery was not over. Finding the most effective artificial right leg proved much more difficult, and for that he was sent to Walter Reed General Hospital in Washington, where he stayed for more than a year. While at Walter Reed, he began working as a vocational training rehabilitation adviser at the Department of Labor, helping state and local agencies respond to the needs of handicapped veterans and other disabled persons. He was still in the hospital in 1947 when he coauthored a booklet on the subject, *A Community Program for the Rehabilitation of the Severely Disabled*.

Two months later, with two artificial legs in place, Potter began his own program of a different sort. When the incumbent congressman in his Michigan district died, Potter resigned from his federal job and went home to run in the special election for the vacant House seat. He campaigned on an "Americanism" platform opposing communism and calling for better benefits for war veterans. Newspaper headlines called him the "legless GI." His campaign ads listed his honors: Silver Star, French Croix de Guerre, Purple Heart with two clusters, five major battle stars. His campaign slogan: "This man gave two legs for his country. Won't you give him one vote?"

Potter won the election in a landslide and returned to Washington. Leadership gave him an office in the Capitol Building to make it easier for him to reach the House floor. "There wasn't any use protesting that I could make better speed than many of them, even with my store-bought legs and canes," he once said. With his receding hairline cut into a curlicue businessman's mohawk, his translucent-framed glasses, and midwestern nasal drone, Potter came across as the quintessential Main Street Republican, cautious in foreign affairs but not isolationist, anti-union and pro-business, a habitual smoker and joiner if not the backroom sort. Along with Richard Nixon and Don Jackson from California and Michigan colleague Gerald Ford, he was a founding member of one of Capitol Hill's most exclusive informal political fraternities, the Chowder and Marching Club, composed of young Republican lawmakers who had served in the war. They started meeting at five on Wednesday afternoons to talk and drink and plot legislation protecting veterans and fighting communism, and on special occasions wore hale-fellow outfits of striped aprons and poufy chef's hats.

By the time Potter gained appointment to HUAC, Nixon had left the committee and entered the Senate, but his Chowder pal Jackson, a former marine, was a member, and together the two young Republicans pushed Chairman Wood to embark on a vigorous traveling show in pursuit of American communists. They gained notice for reopening the hearings in Hollywood in 1951 and pressuring dozens of actors, directors, and screenwriters in the film industry to name names. Friends turned on friends, reputations were ruined on both sides, squealers and subversives, blacklists were compiled, jobs lost. As Red Scare historian Victor Navasky notes, the entertainment industry "posed the smallest threat to the security of the republic—either in theory or fact, yet yielded the greatest per capita number of citizen informers." With every hearing, the committee gained status as American patriots.

It was typical of newspapers to promote the comings and goings of HUAC as if it were a visiting big league ball club. In California, "Anti-Subversives Will Dine Here Sept. 18," read a headline in the *Long Beach Press-Telegram*, boasting of a visit by Wood, Potter, Jackson, Tavenner, and company during a break in the second round of Hollywood hearings. The group was to be feted at a banquet in the Marine Room of the Wilton Hotel by chairmen of the local banks and fifty other prominent Long Beach businessmen. As a special tribute to Potter, arrangements were made for twenty patients from the local VA hospital to attend the banquet in wheelchairs.

Potter called his campaign against the "diabolical philosophy" of communism the "greatest fight" of his lifetime, exceeding even his horribly costly battle against the Germans. He expressed frustration whenever a witness invoked the Fifth Amendment. As far as he was concerned, anyone who refused to answer whether he was a communist "by his very refusal admits he is one." How any man or woman who loved this country could be a communist was beyond his understanding. It amazed him, he said, to discover that some of them came from "good American families."

A Good American Family

THE WINTER OF 1950, ONLY A FEW DAYS INTO THE NEW year, midpoint of the twentieth century. Our family assembles for a photograph on the front steps of the house on Henry Street in the Burns Park neighborhood of Ann Arbor. The house number, 1402, is visible above our heads, a number that to me evokes time, place, history, sensibility. I look at this photograph and think about Representative Potter's puzzlement that even people from "good American families" could be lured into something considered un-American.

The Cummins family is a good American family. Andrew and Grace Cummins are surrounded by their five children, four in-laws, and ten grandchildren. Grandfather Cummins stares straight into the camera from middle right, the erect and pensive civil engineer. I'm the infant, barely four months old, protected in a bonnet, cradled one-handed by my southpaw father, who stands in the upper left, dark hair, deep-set eyes, tan trench coat, collar up. My mother, blond, smiling, wholesome, is center stage, warmed in fur. My parents are eleven years into their marriage and have three kids, ages five and under. My big brother, Jim, and big sister, Jean, are in the middle of the little rascal scrum on the snowy walk. Jim poses openmouthed; Jean looks with concern toward a nearby drama as Grandmother Cummins bends to console an unhappy cousin.

Four of the men in the picture, my father and three uncles, served in World War II. Their wives worked on the home front. Only Uncle Phil, positioned next to my father in the back row, missed the war. His hospitalization for schizophrenia preceded it, and now, five years after its end, he is still living in a sanitarium in faraway Asheville, North Carolina. He must have come home for a holiday visit. My uncle Bob is in the back row, on the right, holding my cousin Sarah. His wife, Susan, is in the dark coat, head down, left hand to mouth, coughing. She would be dead from polio before year's end, leaving Bob a widower with two little girls.

All families are bent by burdens. The mental illness of Phil, the shocking death of Susan, various levels of depression in several relatives from grandfather on down—these wounds of life misshape ours. A. A. Cummins, born inside an earthen dugout cut into a hillside amid the wheat fields of north-central Kansas, has worked his way to success in his engineering business and drives a Cadillac, but his children and their spouses are not winning much bread. Their cars are run-down or borrowed or broken. They live in apartment flats and public housing and drink powdered milk and eat tongue and liver and chipped beef on toast.

Hard times, but not miserable. The Cummins clan in this 1950 photograph is not torn by irreparable jealousies or misunderstandings. The in-laws feel lucky to be in the family embrace. Their intelligence and good manners have not changed since the three oldest Cummins siblings were honored as Best Citizens in the Evansville schools in 1928. There are no financial cheats or backstabbers. No one has been in jail. Bob broke a federal law as an idealistic college graduate when he misstated his intentions on his passport and went off to fight in Spain, but he did it for noble reasons. The adults are imperfect but peaceful, free of bigotry, pained by the misfortune of others. They believe in the Golden Rule. The children feel different from their peers and cling to each other, bound by blood and circumstance.

It will be that way forever, just as it is that way in 1950, even as the Federal Bureau of Investigation shadows Bob and my father and confidential informants pass along their every move.

GO BACK THREE and a half years before the Henry Street family photograph, to May 14, 1946. It had been four months since Elliott received his honorable discharge from the army at Fort Sheridan, Illinois, having earned the rank of captain after four-plus years of service. In a letter from Korea, after the atomic bombs and the Japanese surrender and after determining that he could be a leader, Elliott promised that he would go all out for the rest of his life for the things he believed and the people he loved. Now he was in Detroit again, at work on this day in mid-May, picking up where he had left off after Pearl Harbor, an ace rewrite man at the *Detroit Times*.

He and Mary and Jimmy, their redheaded one-year-old, lived in a two-room apartment at 2023 Pingree Street. Apartment No. 23, on the third floor. The crib for Jimmy—"Squeezy," Mary called him—was in the dinette beside the kitchen. Mary was at home on that May afternoon, writing a letter to her brother at the mental hospital. "The main disadvantage is it leaves Jimmy with no yard or lawn of his own to play in, and I have to get up and down to take him outside," she wrote. "We're hoping that a friend of Elliott's on the *Times* may be able to get us in at Herman Gardens [a public housing project on Joy Road on Detroit's West Side]. That would be ideal. Elliott's job at the *Times* continues, though he doesn't like it because it's a Hearst paper and he works on the financial page. He's quite active in the Newspaper Guild here, which had needed transforming into a real CIO union." Squeezy, she said, kept them home more than ever, but he was certainly worth it. As a matter of fact, "bitten by the baby bug," they were expecting another child that fall, making the move to larger quarters more urgent.

They did get out of the house twice recently, Mary added. The previous Saturday, they went to see *Dark Is the Night*, a 1945 Soviet movie directed by the Anglo-Russian filmmaker Boris Barnet. She provided her brother with a capsule review: "It depicted the aid the Soviet people gave the Red Air Force and army despite German terror. Like all Soviet pictures I have seen, the sincerity and truthfulness of the acting makes up for the inferior film techniques—or rather equipment. I think the actual filming is much more effective than the average film." The day after watching the movie, they rode up to St. Clair Shores, "to the house of a fellow in my club. We roasted wienies, ate potato salad, etc. and had a pretty good time."

The wienie-roasting club she referred to was made up of commu-

nists. She had remained active in the Young Communist League during
the war, and Elliott joined her when he got home, as the group was
changing its name to American Youth for Democracy. The Detroit
chairman of AYD was her brother Bob. It was Elliott's choice to belong,
of course, and he was no innocent; he had been deep into radical politics at the University of Michigan long before she was, but after reading his letters from Camp Lee and aboard the *Cape Canso* and from
Okinawa and Korea, I wonder whether he might have gone in another
direction in the aftermath of the war had it not been for his devotion to
my mother. Maybe, maybe not. I say that without trying to criticize my
mother. He just loved her that much, and I understand why.

The Detroit Field Office of the FBI knew about the hot dog picnic.
They knew Elliott's every move. Special agents Watson, Lynch, Sullivan,
Fletcher, Kast, Cook, Coghlan, Paxton, Heystek, Hyble, Kraus, Rose, Anderson, and Stewart had been watching Elliott since his return, as they
would for the next six years, taking down addresses and license plate
numbers, snooping outside offices, snapping photos, checking signa-
tures, keeping notes, compiling lists, filing reports. They worked with
thirty-nine confidential informants and the Detroit police Red Squad
and other information gatherers who were identified in files by code as
T-1 through T-39. Elliott Maraniss was File No. 100-14520. *Character of
Case: Security Matter—C.* The *C* stood for "communist."

Following Elliott all of that first postwar May, the agents knew that
he attended the Michigan CP May Day celebration in the ballroom of
the Hotel Fort Wayne on Cass Avenue. An informant was there and reported that the guest speaker, Eugene Dennis, a member of the party's
national board, had spoken of the need to "liquefy existing injustices."
Such an explosive word, not quite as intimidating as "liquidate," but still
evoking violence. On May 17, three days after Mary wrote the letter to
her brother, an informant reported that Elliott had "offered his services"
to Billy Allan, the Detroit correspondent for the *Daily Worker* who intended to run for the Detroit City Council. A week later another informant saw Elliott working on a special edition of the *Daily Worker* that
promoted Allan's campaign. And on May 31 an FBI agent took note of
a brief article in a leftist labor pamphlet, *Wage Earner*, stating that El-

liott was at a meeting of a committee that talked about asking Marshall Field III, heir to the department store fortune, founder of what became the *Chicago Sun-Times*, and financial backer of Saul Alinsky, the radical organizer, to establish a liberal daily newspaper in Detroit.

Newspapering, the written word, framing a story or argument, laying out a page or pamphlet—that was what Elliott knew best, did best, and seemed to care about most. In June a confidential informant told FBI agents that local party leaders wanted Elliott to take over as chairman of a youth chapter, but he rebuffed them, saying he would be more valuable "in the journalistic field." In early August informants reported his presence at a meeting at the Twelve Horsemen Civic Center, a banquet hall at Erskine and John R Streets, where the subject again was launching a leftist newspaper, this time a weekly. By fall, plans for the paper were being finalized. It was to be called the *Michigan Herald* and would be published by the People's Educational and Publishing Association. Billy Allan and Hugo Beiswenger, a top CP official in Detroit, would be on the masthead. Subscription rates would be three dollars for a year, with an introductory rate of only one dollar for six months. Elliott would take a leave from the *Times* to help the launch. He would serve as chief rewrite man, in essence writing much of the copy, either without a byline or under someone else's byline, and do much of the editing, though he would not be responsible for assigning stories.

Volume 1, number 1, of the *Herald* came out on January 12, 1947. Beiswenger wrote a story criticizing Republican Kim Sigler, just sworn in as Michigan's new governor, for focusing his inaugural address on the dangers of communism, saying Sigler might better have talked about affordable housing. An editorial noted that Walter Reuther and other leading liberals, including Joseph Lash and Reinhold Niebuhr, had just founded Americans for Democratic Action as a means of countering communist influence on the left. The paper lamented what it called "red-baiting" by "those who claim to be part of the progressive camp." What America needed most was a united progressive coalition that included labor, farmers, blacks, women, veterans, the middle class, and young people, and "naturally, any such combination which is democratically organized will have communists in it."

The most compelling feature in that first edition was the unveiling of a sports column. "Forgive me if we bust a few buttons on our vest," the editor's note said. The columnist was Eddie Tolan, a world-renowned track star who had won gold medals in the 100-meter and 200-meter sprints at the 1932 Olympic Games in Los Angeles, where Damon Runyan called him the world's fastest human. Tolan, whose nickname was the Midnight Express, graduated from Cass Tech in Detroit and the University of Michigan, but his luck ran out almost immediately after his Olympic success, and by the time the *Herald* commissioned him as a columnist he had struggled through a dreary slog of low-paying jobs and had soured on the American Dream. In his inaugural column, he said he had become convinced that athletics revealed "the policy of a nation . . . towards a given people." In this case, black people.

It is common for athletes, politicians, and other celebrities to put their names on columns for which they offer general subjects and a few anecdotes but which they do not write. My father never told me that he ghostwrote Eddie Tolan's On the Mark column, but he never told me he did not. He never told me anything about the *Michigan Herald*. Safe to put it this way: Eddie Tolan seemed to write a lot like Elliott Maraniss, whose newspaper stories I read and studied over many decades. I could feel his presence in the sentences, whether he was being clear and analytical or sentimental and colloquial. Many of the columns focused on the racial pioneering of the first black player in organized baseball. The greatest sporting achievement of 1946, Tolan said in his first column, "belonged to Jackie Robinson, the second-sacker for the Montreal Royals of the International League. . . . It would not be stretching the point to say it was the most notable achievement of life in general in 1946."

The opening of the 1947 season marked the historic moment when Robinson, playing first base for the Brooklyn Dodgers, broke the color barrier in the major leagues. Tolan was there, and the story that he—and my father, I presume—put together afterward for the *Herald* began like this:

EBBETS FIELD, BROOKLYN, NY. APRIL 14—History was made here in old Ebbets Field today. It will al-

ways be one of the grandest memories of my life that I
was on the scene when Jackie Robinson took the field
with the Brooklyn Dodgers to become the first Negro
player in the major leagues.

Not only sports fans but every friend of democracy
in the United States felt that a great and significant
victory of the people was achieved when Jackie trotted
out to first sack today. He was greeted with a tremendous roar from the crowd which had come to see his
debut and to watch the Brooklyn Dodgers open the
season against the Boston Braves.

I was interested in watching the reaction to him
of his teammates and coaches. They paid no special
attention to him on the field, and treated him and accepted him as one of the team. Here's one example:
Ed Stanky, Brooklyn's peppery second baseman, on a
hard-hit ball down between second and first, seeing
that Jackie was in a better position to field the ball,
signaled for Robinson to take it, which he did easily.

Tolan met Robinson after the game, and his next column was about
that locker room interview: "When Jackie had finished his shower, he
pulled two chairs aside, and I interviewed him while he dressed. Jackie
said it felt great to be a Dodger. 'It is the greatest thrill of my life.' First
base was new to him, but he would adjust. His teammates were a great
bunch of guys. He said he felt loose, that [Roy] Campanella might join
him soon. He asked if I knew his brother, Mack Robinson, an Olympic
sprinter. I told him of the campaign of the *Michigan Herald* to break
down discrimination on the Tigers." (As it turned out, another eleven
seasons would go by before Ozzie Virgil broke the color line in Detroit.)
When Tolan left the stadium, he was swarmed by fans who mistook him
for the ballplayer.

Jackie Robinson was a significant figure in our family history. My
father had rooted for the Dodgers—*dem Bums!*—since childhood and
was proud that his team became the first in baseball to integrate. Al-

though he and my mother related few memories of their lives in Detroit in the years immediately after the war, one story they would tell us over and again was about when they drove from Detroit to Chicago to watch Robinson's Dodgers play for the first time against the Cubs, and how the sellout crowd included thousands of black citizens who had never before attended a major league game. The game was on Sunday, May 18. Jackie went hitless in four at-bats.

That same week, the *Herald* published a guest column by Coleman Young, five years before his contentious appearance in Room 740. He and Elliott would be represented then by the same lawyer, George Crockett, but their connection went back to this period in 1947, when Young was an organizer for the CIO and a national leader of black veterans disillusioned by the treatment they received after coming home. As the sympathetic white commander of a black company during the war, Elliott shared Young's perspective on the debilitating nature of race relations in America. In his guest column, Young announced a convention of black veterans to be held in New York at the end of May under the rallying cry "Veterans of the war for freedom have freedom yet to win." "Negro veterans should be able to walk without fear throughout the length and breadth of this great, dynamic country," Young wrote. "But a shadow falls over America. It is the shadow of Congress seeking to smash organized labor [a reference to the Taft-Hartley Act] and hysterically hunting progressives while turning its back on the Ku Klux Klan and other fascist groups."

The *Michigan Herald* lasted barely a year, publishing its final issue in February 1948. A remnant of it was folded into the *Daily Worker* and became known as the *Michigan Worker*. By then, an informant had advised the FBI that Elliott was a member of District 7, Communist Party USA, and had registration number 71945. This informant was Bereniece Baldwin. She reported to FBI agents that James E. Jackson, a high-ranking CP official, had told her that "Maraniss was very adept in popular newspaper journalism and would have specific duties in the field of general counter-propaganda." Much of that work involved supporting the newly formed Progressive Party and its presidential candidate that year, Henry Wallace, a former agriculture secretary in the Roosevelt administration who was challenging Truman from the left.

Baldwin was one of several confidential informants supplying information to the FBI about Elliott's comings and goings. She cited twenty instances where she saw him writing and editing for the *Michigan Herald* and then the *Michigan Worker*. It was during that period, she said, that he insisted on being called not by his name but only his nickname, Ace. Another informant, identified as T-9, reported in June 1948 that Elliott was seen participating in the first advanced class of the Michigan School of Social Science, operated by the party in a building on Michigan Avenue. The school had been classified as a communist organization under President Truman's Executive Order 9835. It was a sister school of the CP's leading educational institution in New York, the Jefferson School of Social Science, known as "the Jeff." According to the informant, the advanced class in Detroit "covered the teachings of Marx and Lenin by the following points: 1) The party as the vanguard of the working class. 2) The party as the organized detachment of the working class. 3) The party as the highest form of class organization of the proletariat. 4) The party as the instrument of the dictatorship of the proletariat. 5) Unity within the party."

Over the coming months, the FBI took note as Elliott moved his family from Herman Gardens to a small house at 7735 Beaverland; as he interviewed Henry Wallace when the Progressive Party candidate campaigned in Detroit; as he went to an anniversary party for the *Michigan Worker* at Schiller Hall; as he flew to Pittsburgh with Billy Allan; as he was seen "busily typing and receiving calls" at the Auto Section headquarters of the party on Grand River; as he took part in a party meeting at the Jewish Cultural Center where Saul Wellman, a Spanish Civil War veteran, emphasized the need to "raise the level of worker from trade union consciousness to class consciousness"; as he attended a rally where Maurice Sugar, the leftist lawyer and mentor to George Crockett, railed against the "unjust trial" taking place at the Foley Square Courthouse in Manhattan, where federal prosecutors were seeking to convict and imprison the top eleven leaders of the CP as conspirators advocating the violent overthrow of the government.

THE GOOD AMERICAN family was dealt another blow in early 1949. After seven lonely years at the sanitarium in Asheville, Phil Cummins was diagnosed by the staff doctors at Highland Hospital as deteriorating rather than improving, suffering from two different disorders. One disorder they called hebephrenia, characterized by delusions and inappropriate laughing; the other was obsessive-compulsive behavior. The doctors suggested to my grandparents that Phil might benefit from a prefrontal lobotomy. Dr. R. Burke Suitt, a brain surgeon at Duke, examined him and determined that rather than a lobotomy, a more effective operation would be a topectomy, involving the removal of "a small amount of tissue on either side of the front part of the brain surface." The operation was performed by Dr. J. Lawrence Pool at the Neurological Institute of Columbia-Presbyterian Medical Center in New York. It took three hours, and a week later Phil was back in Asheville, where doctors reported that his "repetitious and philosophical examination[s] of his own thoughts were definitely lessening."

Phil's siblings in Detroit were eager for news of his recovery. From her new house on Beaverland, my mother wrote a letter to her troubled brother on the afternoon of March 30. "We're hoping to hear from you soon to find out how you feel after your operation. Quite a bit of surgery!" She had two children at home with her: Jim had just turned four, and Jean was two and a half. I was on the way. "Has anyone told you that we are going to have another little baby in August? Does that seem rash? Three isn't that much more than two. And a little more fun sometimes. We haven't given it too much thought."

Phil's older brother soon followed with a letter of his own, reporting on his work and home life. Bob was watching the children, while Sue and Mary went shopping. One daughter, Rachel, was two, and the other, Sarah (Sally), was almost one. They finally got a car, an old Hudson club coupe. "I am still working at DeSoto," Bob wrote. "We have a new model, and I tighten the nuts which hold the tail lights on. There are ten to each car, and we run 464 cars a day—at least that is all we are supposed to do, but often there are more as a result of speed-up.

Speed-up is a big issue in the auto industry, and as you have probably read, the Ford workers are on strike in an attempt to stop it." Car sales were declining, Bob told his brother, meaning that he was likely to get laid off at some point soon.

My father's job at the *Times* also seemed uncertain. His active role in the Newspaper Guild put him at odds with management when he defended several union members who were laid off by the company, but his talents as a copy editor and rewrite man kept him in good stead with his immediate superiors. Although I often witnessed those considerable skills decades later, it is impossible for me to measure what he did at the Detroit paper in the late 1940s, since rewrite men left little or no forensic evidence of what they had taken as raw material and transformed into something clear and polished. But there is a story from those days at the *Times* that he loved to tell for the rest of his life, and that I never tired of hearing. It was about the day he channeled Louella Parsons.

Louella Parsons was a titan of Hollywood gossip. From her home base at Hearst's *Los Angeles Examiner*, her syndicated columns went out to six hundred newspapers and more than twenty million readers worldwide. She and Hedda Hopper, who wrote a gossip column for the *Los Angeles Times*, competed as the "Queens of Hollywood"—and they hated each other. So it was a major coup for Parsons when she won the favor of Rita Hayworth and gained exclusive rights to the glamorous movie star's May 1949 wedding to Prince Aly Khan, a wealthy Pakistani playboy of Persian royal descent. The wedding was to take place in Cannes in the south of France, where Aly Khan kept one of many homes. In the weeks leading up to the wedding, Parsons wrote a long series about Hayworth, and Hopper was so jealous that she suggested her nemesis was faking it and in fact would "not get within a mile of the wedding." As it turned out, Parsons did get into the wedding, but there was a hitch. The mayor of Cannes was a member of the Communist Party and demanded that the marriage ceremony take place not at Aly Khan's chateau but at City Hall. Parsons later noted that the mayor was the first communist she had ever talked with, but he let her use a phone after she greased his palm with a small bribe. She did not plan to file her story until after the reception back at the chateau. Alas, no one was allowed to use the phones there, and by the time Parsons concocted a trick to get one, it was approaching deadline back in the States for many evening papers like the *Detroit Times* that were hoping to splash her story on the front page. This is where my father takes up the story.

As he would tell it to his children and anyone who would listen decades later, the editors were gathered near the wire machine in the sixth-floor newsroom waiting anxiously for the Parsons file, but it was not coming. *Where the hell is she?* Finally, one of my father's bosses turned to him and shouted, "Elliott, you're Louella Parsons!" Dad dutifully gathered earlier stories about the famous couple and the scene in Cannes, sat down at his typewriter, and banged out what he imagined Parsons would be writing. This was an easy and enjoyable task for him; he had been rewriting reporters of various sorts for years. It was only as he was finishing the column that a subeditor announced that the Parsons dispatch was finally clickety-clacking on the wire. "The Arabian nights wedding of Rita Hayworth and Prince Aly Khan glittered to its storybook ending tonight."

"So, the editor grabs my copy and the Parsons copy," Dad would say, usually choking with laughter as he recounted the moment. "He looked at my copy. He looked at Louella's copy. He looked again at my column and looked again at hers." Dad would be pantomiming a sober-looking editor holding two pieces of paper, his eyes moving back and forth. "And then he said, 'Ah, hell. Elliott's is better'!"

Of that, I have no doubt.

That summer, a few weeks before I was born, my father returned to Coney Island for a vacation, taking along Jimmy, Jeannie, and Peggy, the daughter of Aunt Barbara and the oldest of the cousins. My mother, more than eight months pregnant with me, stayed home. In a letter to Phil, she reported that my father and his young charges "had a wonderful time, despite the polio epidemic, which kept them off the beach most of the time." The abundant praise my father got from sympathetic mothers, she added dryly, "was more than enough to make up for his difficulties."

I came along on August 6. "Hi Phil," my mother wrote the next day. "I'm in a hospital bed writing out announcements, watching women go

home with their babies and hearing funny stories about how women having babies acted under ether. "The baby is fine, very cute. He looks a little
like you, but no one else that we can think of. Doesn't do much but sleep
& eat. I'll take him home in 2 days, and then Elliott and I will be home
alone with him." My older siblings must have been sent off to Ann Arbor.
But my father was not exactly on paternity leave. He was a busy man, at
the *Times* and elsewhere. Five days later, an informant told the FBI that
Elliott Maraniss planned to write a story for the *Michigan Worker* about
"the so-called inhuman treatment of Henry Winston," one of the defendants in the Foley Square trial taking place then in the New York courtroom of Judge Harold Medina. Later that month, before I was a month
old, my father was seen attending a banquet at the Jewish Cultural Center
honoring Winston and his Foley Square codefendants, and a few weeks
after that he composed a leaflet in support of another of those defendants, Carl Winter of Detroit, who was represented by George Crockett.

My father was at work on Labor Day but found time to write a letter to his parents back in Coney Island. He described how my sister
Jeannie would slip into my room when I was sleeping and make just
enough noise to wake me up, then come running out yelling, "Davey's
awake, mommy, can I go in and see him?" He said that Jeannie was
"the smartest little girl we know" and that Jimmy had "an intelligence
and maturity that sometimes surprises us. He knows *everything* that is
going on and asks questions about everything." That is the big brother
I would come to know. Many decades later he would tell me that one
of the things he knew was going on—and that he would ask questions
about—involved our father's visits to the *Michigan Worker*. Dad would
take him to the office sometimes, he said, and Billy Allan was a frequent
visitor to our house.

THE YEAR 1950 began with that photograph of the Cummins family
posing on the steps of 1402 Henry Street. Things went downhill from
there.

In February, Joe McCarthy delivered the speech in West Virginia that
came to define the era. "I have here in my hand," he said. A list of names:

205 names of known Communist Party members who worked for the Department of State. This was not the first time McCarthy had done this, it was a variation on a theme he tried out in Kenosha, Wisconsin, a few months earlier, but now he was determined to stake his political rise to his anticommunist fervor, using a mix of truth, sloppiness, and exaggeration. As decryptions of secret Soviet documents later showed, the Soviets did in truth have a network of agents and helpers inside the government, and the Truman administration had been less than vigorous in dealing with the infiltration. But in spreading his message, McCarthy was less interested in being precise and correct than dramatic and bellicose. Within two months his name would be attached to a campaign that overwhelmed whatever truth there was behind his efforts; the word "McCarthyism" was first used in a Herblock cartoon in the *Washington Post* that March depicting a Republican elephant being pushed by senators to balance on a wobbly tower built from buckets of tar.

The House committee had been ferreting out citizens they considered un-American for more than a decade by then, but McCarthy made more noise. Then came the war in Korea, starting late that June, with Americans fighting and dying against communists on the other side of the world, and branding a scarlet letter on the forehead of anyone associated with the American version of the party became a matter of patriotic duty. One month after the war started, the gathering storm had direct and physical consequences for my uncle Bob. "CHRYSLER WORKERS THROW OUT PRO-RED" was the headline over an AP brief: "An employee, thrown out of Chrysler's DeSoto plant by fellow workers yesterday, did not return to his job today. The employee, Robert A. Cummins, was accused by his fellow workers of distributing pro-communist literature. Police identified Cummins as chairman of the Michigan branch of Youth for Democracy. If Cummins returned, workers declared yesterday, they would strike." The FBI recorded the action in a file that later went to HUAC investigators: "July 25, 1950. On this date Robert Cummins was 'walked out' of the DeSoto plant by his fellow workers, due to his Communist Party beliefs, which he was expressing in the plant to his fellow workers."

Bob had predicted in an earlier letter to his brother that he might soon be out of work at DeSoto, but this was not the way he thought it would happen. He told family members later that the experience complicated his notions about the American working class, disabusing him of proletariat romanticism. Now he was out of work, with a family of four to feed, and much worse was yet to come.

Susan, Bob's wife, had been one of three Goodman sisters. One, Barbara, died of ulcerative colitis in 1944, when Susan was working in Detroit and Bob was serving with the Army Air Corps in England. Now, only weeks after Bob was thrown out of the DeSoto plant, came news that Susan's other sister, Peggy, had committed suicide in Philadelphia. And in the final week of September 1950, Susan was struck with poliomyelitis, one of thirty-three thousand Americans who came down with polio that year. The Salk vaccine would not be available for another three years. Nine days after falling ill, Susan died. Her oldest daughter, my cousin Rachel Cummins, would speculate decades later that her mother's sister's suicide left Susan "pretty depressed, maybe guilty, and vulnerable." Susan also smoked and was very thin. Her body worn down and defenseless, she died three days before her thirty-second birthday, leaving Bob alone with his two "little ragamuffins."

"I don't know if anyone wrote you the sad news," Bob wrote to Phil later that month. "Susan died October 5 of polio. Rachel and Sally are staying with mother in Ann Arbor. Perhaps we will move in with John and Barbara if I can find a place large enough to hold us all. Now the future seems bleak in many ways, but I am still an optimist and have confidence in the future." For the rest of the letter, Bob did something that became a family trait passed down through the generations. He turned to sports and the arts as a means of easing his pain, blocking out, surviving.

"Say, do you get television down there? Maybe you saw the Notre Dame–Michigan State game yesterday? I saw it with Bob Purdy at his father's house, where there is a big 19-inch set. It was the best game I ever saw on television, or perhaps any other way. Elliott and I saw a pro game a few weeks ago. Detroit Lions vs. Los Angeles Rams. (They're playing again today, but out in L.A.) That was a good game, too. 30–28 was the score." That game was on October 15, ten days after Susan died.

That same week, Bob also took his niece Peggy to see the Ballet Russe. The themes, he told Phil, were on a childish level, "but the dancing was very good."

By early 1951, Bob and his girls were sharing a house with his twin sister, Barbara, and her husband, John, and daughter, Peggy, at 3026 Pingree Street in Detroit. Rachel, who was four, would remember that time as being "very dark." Her father was at a loss, she said, and "didn't know how to take care of us." The extended family was their lifeline: Barbara took them to a day care center, cousin Peggy was a responsible ten-year-old, Grandmother Cummins was within reach in Ann Arbor, and the Maraniss family lived nearby in Detroit. In Peggy's memory, the Pingree Street house was big and dark. Soon after the two families moved in, she noticed a cache of empty soda bottles in the garage, and for months this became her source of income. She would sneak into the garage and surreptitiously smuggle a six-pack of bottles to the corner grocery, trading them in for pocket cash, with which she would buy chocolate drops and sticky paper candy. The return racket came to an end one day when her mother accompanied her to the store and the proprietor ratted her out, bewildering her mother with a query about why the girl came in bottle-less.

Peggy had one other strong memory from that period, a more frightening one. It was of her uncle Bob telling her that some bad men in dark suits might come to the house, and when and if they did, under no circumstances was she to open the door to them.

On the afternoon of May 12, Bob was at home, listening to a ball game on the radio. His girls were in Ann Arbor with their grandmother. In a letter to Phil, Bob confessed that he was jobless again. "I have been working selling paint around the state, but have given it up because the job is too lonesome. I didn't do a bad job as a salesman. Monday, I'm going out to get some other job. I've seen several Tigers games so far this year. They looked pretty bad to begin with, but some of them are doing better now. No pennant in sight, however."

Again, the obsession with baseball. No matter what else was going on in their lives, Bob and Elliott could fall back on baseball. The national pastime, invented in America and claimed by some as a symbol of Americanism. Baseball, hot dogs, and apple pie. Eddie Stanky, the Dodger who played second base when Jackie Robinson broke in at first base, once said the Russians could never master baseball because it was a game of free people that required sportsmanship and teamwork, attributes the Soviets lacked. Herman Welker, a Republican senator from Idaho, seconded that opinion by claiming that he "never saw a ballplayer who was a communist." The American Legion embraced baseball and started sponsoring youth leagues in the early 1950s as a means of combating communism by teaching young men love of country, selflessness, and good citizenship. But all of this was mythology; baseball had nothing to do with ideology. Geography mattered. Hometown mattered. Nicknames mattered. Loyalty mattered. Pleasure mattered. Numbers mattered. Rooting for something that in a sense didn't matter mattered. But a certain definition of Americanism did not matter at all.

There were few places my father and uncle Bob would rather be than a ballpark, and if they could not get to a game they loved listening to it on the radio, and if they missed the broadcast they loved to read the box scores and talk baseball. If Dad came home with mustard on his shirt, Mom knew that he had slipped off to a Tigers game. Two of the most cherished stories our father told us involved baseball and decisive home runs that went against his teams. One was of him sitting in the outfield bleachers at Briggs Stadium when the Tigers were playing the Boston Red Sox and leading by a few runs as Ted Williams came to the plate with the bases loaded. "Walk him! Walk him!" Elliott yelled, even though that meant walking in a run. The Tigers ignored his advice and pitched to Williams, who smacked the ball into my father's section, and the Red Sox had four runs and the ball game. *They shoulda walked him.* The other baseball story involved the decisive playoff game between Dad's beloved Dodgers and the New York Giants at the end of the 1951 season. As we heard the story, he was listening to the game on the radio with all of us in the room, and probably Bob and his family too, and when the Giants' Bobby Thomson hit the three-run homer off Ralph Branca to win the game and the pennant, Dad reacted to the "Shot Heard 'Round the World" by swearing and throwing crackers across the room. Another version of that story was that he was holding me at the time and was so upset he dropped me. I prefer the version with the crackers.

BEAVERLAND. ALL I remember is the name. To me, it didn't mean a street or a house, but a mystical place, like Disneyland, but for beavers. How could a name so funny connote anything sinister? I was too young for anything to be deposited in my long-term memory bank, perhaps luckily. It was when we lived on Beaverland that I had my first traumatic asthma attack, after being exposed to some sheep wool at a fair. And it was on Beaverland, as my brother often told the story, where I rode my tricycle into the street. There was a screech of tires, Jimmy ran home screaming, "Davey got hit by a car!," and my father—who was supposed to be watching the kids—came dashing out in a panic. It turned out the car had stopped just in time. It was also when we lived on Beaverland that my brother and sister first walked to school. They went to Ann Arbor Trail elementary, modern and new, and were precocious students then and for the rest of their student days, wherever we were, however uncertain our existence. And it was while we lived on Beaverland that I appeared in the FBI's file on Elliott Maraniss for the one and only time.

> The following description of the Subject was obtained from Confidential Informant Detroit T-1:
> Race: White
> Sex: Male
> Age: 34
> Born: February 23, 1918 at Boston, Massachusetts
> Height: 5'10"
> Weight: 180
> Build: Heavy
> Complexion: Very dark
> Hair: Black, bushy
> Eyes: Brown

Features: Flat, heavy face
Marital status: Married
Wife: Mary Jane Maraniss
Children: Jimmy Maraniss, age 6;
Jean Maraniss, age 4;
David Maraniss, age 1½
Occupation: Newspaperman

MARY HAD THREE small children and a husband who was gone much of the time doing one job or another, so it was no surprise that she expressed joy one morning in the spring of 1951 when even a hospital operation brought her a bit of relief, an escape from the everyday routine of Beaverland. "It's sometime in the post-breakfast morning, and I'm in the hospital for a little rest," she reported to Phil. "Yesterday I had a cyst taken out from the base of my spine. The anesthesia was good and the operation short, so now I can settle down and have a little vacation here. The hospitals are quite crowded, though. The three kids are with Mother. Jimmy had his tonsils out, squeaky voice, Jeannie is quite the bossy type right now and has a memory like an elephant. . . . Davey is little and tough and part of anything the family is doing. He'll always have a smile for you, and has two front teeth both showing like Bugs Bunny."

There was a fifty-nine-day bus and streetcar strike in Detroit that spring and early summer. Bob decided to go to school to learn how to become a television repairman while also finding a part-time job selling paint at Montgomery Ward on Thursday and Friday nights and all day Saturday. Elliott worked the early shift at the newspaper. Based on the FBI reports, he was busy most nights, attending leftist functions and organizing for the Progressive Party. Since the establishment of the Subversive Activities Control Board in 1950, he had turned to the Progressive Party as the vehicle for expressing his political beliefs. This was to some extent a means of going underground. Communist organizations and known communists were required to register with the government, and more party members were being prosecuted on

Smith Act charges in the aftermath of the Foley Square trial. The essence of the civil liberties debate among American intellectuals then was whether the CPUSA represented heresy or conspiracy. If it was heresy, it was protected by the First Amendment; if it was a conspiracy, it was not. The legal reasoning used against communists followed a formula devised by Learned Hand, a widely respected federal judge and judicial philosopher, who said the government could curtail free speech on the basis of the gravity of the evil discounted by its improbability. The worse the evil and the greater the probability, the more free speech could be curtailed.

In midsummer, on July 22, FBI Informant T-6 reported that Elliott attended the annual Civil Rights Congress picnic at Welcome Park at 15½ Mile Road and Livernois. The main speaker was George Crockett, who, according to the informant, "warned those in attendance about talking to FBI agents or signing any statements."

Two days later informant Bereniece Baldwin told her FBI handler that Ace Maraniss was at a meeting of personnel of the *Michigan Worker*, where he was singled out as "the nucleus" of the paper. In October she reported that Ace was receiving compliments in the office for his work. In late November, Informant T-22, working for the Detroit Police Department Red Squad, reported that a car belonging to Elliott and Mary Maraniss was "seen in the immediate vicinity of the Jewish Cultural Center on three different occasions when the Michigan Freedom of the Press Club held their cultural festival." The informant said the club was a communist front.

Over the holiday season, many members of the family gathered again with Andrew and Grace Cummins at 1402 Henry Street. By early January, investigators for the House Committee on un-American Activities were in Detroit doing legwork in preparation for the hearings. One day that month, a man in a dark suit rang the front bell at 3026 Pingree Street. Reflexively, ten-year-old Peggy answered the door. She had forgotten her uncle's instructions. The well-dressed stranger was there to deliver a subpoena to Robert Cummins, summoned by HUAC to appear as a witness. Several weeks later, that same man in a dark suit entered the marble and granite atrium of the Times Square Building downtown and rode the walnut-paneled elevators up to the sixth-floor newsroom. In his coat pocket he carried a subpoena instructing Elliott Maraniss to appear before the committee at 10:00 on the morning of March 12 in Room 740.

23

March 12, 1952

THE WEATHER IN DETROIT WAS CLEAR AND DRY, WITH A
high sky. The attention of the American press was elsewhere, mostly in
New Hampshire, where, the night before, Dwight D. Eisenhower, the
war hero, had defeated Robert Taft, the Ohio senator, in the Republican
presidential primary. Ike won without campaigning; he was in Europe,
working as supreme commander of the North Atlantic Treaty Organization. In the Democratic primary, President Harry Truman was defeated by Estes Kefauver, the mob-fighting senator from Tennessee. It
was the political beginning for Eisenhower; the beginning of the end
for Truman. The Korean War was in its twenty-first month, with fifteen
more to go.

In Room 740 of the Federal Building in downtown Detroit, it was
the final day of hearings before the House Committee on Un-American
Activities packed up and returned to Washington. My father was called
fifth to last.

Testimony of Elliott Maraniss, Accompanied
by His Counsel, George W. Crockett

Mr. Tavenner: Mr. Elliott Maraniss.
Mr. Wood: Will you raise your right hand [to] be sworn, please?
    You do solemnly swear that the evidence you give this
    subcommittee will be the truth, and nothing but the truth, so
    help you God?
Mr. Maraniss: I do.

Mr. Tavenner: What is your name, please, sir?

Mr. Maraniss: My name is Elliott Maraniss.

Mr. Tavenner: Are you represented by counsel?

Mr. Maraniss: Yes, sir. Mr. Crockett is my counsel.

Mr. Tavenner: And Mr. Crockett is accompanying you?

Mr. Maraniss: (No response.)

Mr. Tavenner: He is sitting beside you? I want the record merely to show he is here.

Mr. Crockett: My name is George W. Crockett, offices located in the Cadillac Tower, Detroit, Michigan.

Mr. Tavenner: When and where were you born, please, sir?

Mr. Maraniss: I was born in Boston, Massachusetts, in February of 1918.

Mr. Tavenner: Do you now live in Detroit?

Mr. Maraniss: Yes, I do.

Mr. Tavenner: How long have you lived in Detroit?

Mr. Maraniss: I have been a resident of Michigan since 1936 when I entered the University of Michigan. I have been a resident of Detroit since 1941.

Mr. Tavenner: How have you been employed since 1941?

Mr. Maraniss: In June of 1941 I was employed at the *Detroit Times*. I am a newspaperman. I was employed at the *Detroit Times* from June until about the fourteenth or fifteenth of December 1941, when I enlisted in the Army of the United States and served in the Army of the United States until January of 1946, when I was discharged, honorably discharged, as a captain in the Army of the United States.

Upon my discharge, I returned to my employment as a newspaperman on the *Detroit Times*, and was continuously employed at the *Detroit Times* until February 29, 1952, on which date I received a subpoena from your committee, and was summarily fired from my job.

Mr. Tavenner: What was the nature of your employment with the newspaper?

Mr. Maraniss: I am classified as a copy reader on the *Detroit Times*.

Mr. Tavenner: Mr. Maraniss, the committee, in the course of its investigation, obtained information that on January 24 or 25, 1948, the Communist Party held a State conference at 2934 Yemans Hall, and that you were present as a delegate to the conference. Is that correct?

Mr. Maraniss: Upon advice of my counsel, I invoke the privileges under the Fifth Amendment of the Constitution which was written into the Constitution to prevent forced confessions.

Mr. Tavenner: You stated that your employment had been practically continuous with the *Detroit Times* since you came here in 1941 with the exception of the period of your service, which was military service, which was rather extensive.

Mr. Maraniss: That is correct.

Mr. Tavenner: During the period of time when you were employed here in Detroit, were you employed by any other newspaper or publication?

Mr. Crockett: On the basis of my recollection of the testimony—

Mr. Wood: Mr. Crockett, will you please conform to the rule and confer with your client in an undertone?

Mr. Maraniss: My counsel advises me to invoke my privileges under the Fifth Amendment and refuse to answer that question.

Mr. Wood: Do you do that under the advice of counsel?

Mr. Maraniss: I do.

Mr. Tavenner: Have you written articles for the *Michigan Worker* under the name of Oscar Williams?

Mr. Crockett: May I ask, Mr. Counsel, if the *Michigan Worker* has been listed as a subversive publication by your committee?

Mr. Tavenner: No.

Mr. Crockett: It has not been?

Mr. Wood: And neither has the witness.

Mr. Crockett: I didn't inquire about the witness, Mr. Chairman. I only inquired about the publication.

Mr. Wood: The question was asked as to what he did, not what the publication did.

Mr. Crockett: I only asked the question as a basis for advice to my client.

Mr. Maraniss: I invoke my privilege under the Fifth Amendment and refuse to answer that question.

Mr. Tavenner: In spite of the answer as to the citation of the publication?

Mr. Crockett: I think, Mr. Counsel, that the record here at this hearing indicates that the *Michigan Worker* has been labeled as the Michigan edition of the *Daily Worker*. Am I right?

Mr. Tavenner: I wouldn't attempt to recite the evidence on that.

Mr. Crockett: Very well.

Mr. Tavenner: Your answer is still that you refuse to answer the question?

Mr. Maraniss: I have given my answer.

Mr. Tavenner: Have you used the name of Oscar Williams in writing, or have you used that name in any other way?

Mr. Maraniss: I invoke my privilege under the Fifth Amendment.

Mr. Wood: Well, do you answer then, or not?

Mr. Maraniss: And I refuse to answer the question.

Mr. Tavenner: Have you at any time been a member of the professional section of the Communist Party of Detroit?

Mr. Maraniss: I invoke my privilege under the Fifth Amendment and refuse to answer that question.

 I wish to make a statement, however, about my views on un-American activities, if the counsel and Mr. Wood would permit.

Mr. Wood: After you answer the questions. If you answer them, we will be glad to have your explanation of anything you want to make, after you answer the questions.

Mr. Maraniss: Isn't the purpose of this inquiry to discover the thinking of people on what constitutes un-American activities, and what activities—

Mr. Wood: The purpose of this investigation at the moment is to determine first of all what your position is with reference to membership in the Communist Party, which you have refused to enlighten us about. I call your attention to the fact that you sought, at the outset of your testimony, to leave an inference that you had been deprived of your position with the paper here because of the fact that you had been subpoenaed by this committee.

Mr. Maraniss: That is no inference. That is a fact.

Mr. Wood: If that is true, we are offering you the best opportunity I know of for you to convince your employers—your previous employers or anybody else, for that matter, that if the committee had subpoenaed you for the purpose of identifying you as a member of the Communist Party and you are not, in fact, so a member, to so state.

Mr. Maraniss: Mr. Wood, you are not offering me any opportunity, as I see it. You have subpoenaed me and compelled me to come here and answer questions about my political beliefs.

Mr. Wood: Well, you were subpoenaed. That is true. But now you have been asked the question which you have declined to answer.

Mr. Crockett: Mr. Chairman, do I understand that you are penalizing this man because he relies on the Fifth Amendment, and, because of that, you refuse to let him make a statement?

Mr. Wood: If he isn't a member of the Communist Party, I am seeking to help him. If he is, I think the public is entitled to know it.

Mr. Crockett: The public isn't entitled to know anything that you may properly claim the privilege from disclosing under the Fifth Amendment.

Mr. Wood: I grant you the right to claim immunity under the Fifth Amendment.

Mr. Maraniss: Mr. Chairman, may I read you the constitution about eligibility in the union to which I belong, the union of newspapermen. Under Section 1: "Guild memberships shall be open to every eligible person without discrimination or penalty, nor shall any member be barred from membership or

penalized by reason of age, sex, race, national origin, religious
or political submission, or anything he writes for publication."

I believe that is an unassailable guaranty of freedom of
speech and freedom of expression for a newspaperman,
and right to indulge in any political activity without fear of
penalization.

Mr. Jackson: What is that from?

Mr. Maraniss: That is from my constitution of the American
Newspaper Guild, CIO, of which I am a member.

Mr. Jackson: Did you point that out to the board of the CIO
Newspaper Guild?

Mr. Maraniss: I certainly did. I pointed it out to my boss, too.

Mr. Jackson: Then that is the forum before which you should bring
the bylaws and your constitution, not this committee.

Mr. Maraniss: This is a question of the rights of newspapermen to
engage in political activity, freely, to hold opinions and beliefs
without being subject to penalization, or being forced to enter
into forced confessions before a group like this.

Mr. Tavenner: Do you take the position that the Communist Party
is not a conspiracy?

Mr. Maraniss: I rely upon the Fifth Amendment's guaranty and
refuse to answer that question.

Mr. Tavenner: Do you consider that the Communist Party is
nothing more than a political party?

Mr. Maraniss: I again rely on my constitutional privileges and
refuse to answer that question.

Mr. Tavenner: If it is nothing more than a political party, we are
wasting a lot of time.

Mr. Wood: Any further questions?

Mr. Tavenner: On the very day that you say you received a
subpoena, did you learn that Mrs. Toby Baldwin testified
before this committee and identified you as having been a
member of the Communist Party?

Mr. Maraniss: I rely upon my constitutional privileges under the
Fifth Amendment and refuse to answer that question.

Mr. Tavenner: Didn't you learn that on the day you were
    subpoenaed, Mrs. Baldwin testified before this committee?

Mr. Maraniss: Yes, I learned that.

Mr. Tavenner: Do you still state, in the light of that information
    that you were discharged from your position because of being
    subpoenaed, or was it because of the testimony that was given
    here before this committee?

Mr. Maraniss: If I had never been subpoenaed, I would never have
    been forced to answer that question—I mean the fact would
    never have made any difference, and I wouldn't have ever been
    discharged.

    However, Mr. Tavenner, it is my belief that back in—I
    believe that the management of the *Detroit Times* has been
    looking for a chance to fire me since 1947—because at that
    time, there was a discharge of about 12 employees of the
    Detroit Times for reason of economy, and I was one of the
    members of the Newspaper Guild who was trying to get the
    union and the men there to get the reinstatement of those
    men, and many of them were reinstated, and I think they have
    had it in for me ever since.

Mr. Tavenner: Were you discharged after the testimony of Mrs.
    Baldwin, or before her testimony?

Mr. Maraniss: I was discharged after her testimony.

Mr. Tavenner: Was her testimony with regard to you true or false?

Mr. Maraniss: I invoke my privileges under the Fifth Amendment
    and refuse to answer that question.

Mr. Tavenner: I have no further questions.

Mr. Maraniss: May I read the statement now, Mr. Wood?

    (Wood checks to see if other congressmen have questions.)

Mr. Wood: We don't permit statements. If you have one written
    there, we shall be glad to have it filed with the clerk.

    (Whereupon the statement of Mr. Maraniss was filed.)

Mr. Jackson: I have a question, Mr. Chairman. Mr. Maraniss, you
    were discharged a captain from the armed services, is that
    correct?

Mr. Maraniss: That is right.

Mr. Jackson: Do you hold a commission in the Reserve at the present time?

Mr. Maraniss: No. I do not.

Mr. Jackson: That is all.

Mr. Wood: The witness is excused.

24

The Whole Pattern of a Life

Statement of Elliott Maraniss

In the 34 years of my life, in war and peace, I have been a loyal, law-abiding citizen of the United States.

One week after this nation was attacked at Pearl Harbor in 1941, I enlisted as a private in the Army of the United States and served for more than four years, climaxed by the campaign in Okinawa. I was honorably discharged in January 1946, with the rank of captain.

Upon my discharge I returned to my job as a newspaperman with the *Detroit Times*.

I am a homeowner, taxpayer, and parent, father of two boys and a girl.

I was taught as a child and in school that the highest responsibility of citizenship is to defend the principles of the U.S. Constitution and to do my part in securing for the American people the blessings of peace, economic well-being, and freedom.

I have tried to do just that to the very best of my ability.

And for doing just that—and nothing more—I have been summarily discharged from my job. I have been blacklisted in the newspaper business after 12 years in which my competency and objectivity have never once been questioned.

I must sell my home, uproot my family and upset the tranquility and security of my three small children in the happy, formative years of their childhood.

But I would rather have my children miss a meal or two now than have them grow up in the gruesome, fear-ridden future for America projected by the members of the House Committee on Un-American Activities.

I don't like to talk about these personal things. But my Americanism has been questioned and to properly measure a man's Americanism you must know the whole pattern of a life.

I feel that nobody has the right to question my Americanism—least of all a committee which itself has been called subversive, un-American and anti-labor by the CIO, of which I am a member, by President Roosevelt and by responsible organizations representing many millions of Americans.

I view this committee's attempt to muzzle me and drive me off my job as a direct attack on freedom of the press and the right of newspapermen to participate freely in the political life of the country without fear of reprisal.

The U.S. Constitution and its Bill of Rights are not simply musty documents in a library. They have meaning only if they are used.

To betray and subvert the Bill of Rights is the most un-American act any man or committee can do: for that document was brought into being and maintained throughout our history by men who gave their lives and their blood.

Every newspaperman knows that history is not a printed page. It is the passion and striving, the struggling and endurance of men and women. These qualities that went into the making of our nation can be discarded only at great peril to ourselves and our children.

From the time of Peter Zenger, the colonial printer who defied the British crown's effort to impose censorship in the American colonies, right down to the present, newspapermen have zealously defended the freedom of the press.

For the First Amendment is not only a guarantee of free speech and a free press: it is also an indispensable part of self-government.

That's what makes this committee so dangerous. Ostensibly designed to protect the government against overthrow by force and violence, it proceeds by force, terror and threats to overthrow the rights of the American people.

A witness has no rights whatever. He is denied the elementary due processes of law. He has no opportunity to confront his accuser, to cross examine witnesses, to call witnesses in his own behalf or even to make a statement.

The committee is so poisoned with bigotry and malice that it is hard indeed to believe that it is indeed a committee of the Congress of the United States. It more resembles a session of the Spanish Inquisition or the witch-hunting trials in Salem in the late Seventeenth Century. If anyone believes this comparison far-fetched, read these words of Cotton Mather instructing the judges in the technique of extracting confessions from suspected witches:

"Now first a credible confession of the guilty wretches is one of the most hopeful ways at coming at them. I am far from urging the un-English method of torture . . . but whatever hath a tendency to put the witches into confusion is likely to bring them into confession. Here cross and swift questions have their use!"

Under this technique, as Supreme Court Justice Black has observed, many confessed; some were burned; all were innocent.

It was precisely to combat this technique, to rule it out forever from American life, that the Fifth Amendment was written into our Bill of Rights.

This committee reflects no credit on American institutions or ideas.

Its attempt to enforce conformity of political or economic thought is a long step toward dictatorship that holds the greatest danger to the entire American people.

In this country we have never acquiesced in the proposition that persons could be punished for their beliefs.

Back in Jefferson's time, when the Alien and Sedition laws were passed, countless newspapermen and editors were indicted, and many sent to jail for their fight together with Jefferson to restore the Bill of Rights. In their number Matthew Lyon, John C. Ogden, David Brown, William Duane, James Thomas Callendar, Jedediah Peck, Charles Holt and Thomas Adams.

These men never stopped fighting. They forced the repeal of the repressive legislation and set the nation on the high road of its future development.

I am supremely confident that the same spirit that motivated those men in the brave days of our past still lives in the American people.

I am confident that the people of Detroit will reject this committee's effort to subvert the U.S. Constitution.

I am confident that the American people will not allow our traditions and freedom to be transformed in the image of fascism nor allow our cities and millions of our people to be destroyed in the hellish fires of atomic war.

ELLIOTT MARANISS

25

Witches or Traitors

DURING THE STRETCH IN LATE FEBRUARY AND EARLY March 1952 when Chairman Wood's committee brought Elliott Maraniss and Bob Cummins into Room 740 to question their loyalty to America, Arthur Miller started to think about writing a new play that evoked what he saw as the fear and irrationality of the moment. This was more than an abstract issue for Miller. An earlier play, *Death of a Salesman*, for which he won the Pulitzer Prize for Drama in 1949, had just moved from the Broadway stage into movie theaters—and into a new round of controversy.

The film, starring Fredric March as Willy Loman, the tragic salesman, was being picketed and boycotted at theaters on Long Island and in Washington by members of the American Legion, who charged that the playwright and his story were both un-American, Miller for his past connections to communists and the story for its bleak portrayal of Loman as a victim of the capitalist system. Columbia Pictures, the studio producing the film, seemed afraid of the public reaction even before the movie was released and tried to soften the message by combining it with a ten-minute short titled *Career of a Salesman* that presented a rosier portrayal of the sales business. The short was finally pulled after Miller loudly objected. "Why the hell did you make the picture if you're so ashamed of it?" he asked. But both episodes only strengthened his determination to find a dramatic story that would illuminate the era.

It was at the University of Michigan, in an American history course, that Miller first studied the witchcraft trials that enflamed Salem, Massachusetts, in 1692. More recently, the story came back to him when he read *The Devil in Massachusetts* by Marion Starkey. His first impression was that Salem was trapped in "the long-dead past" and too centered on "inexplicable mystifications" to resonate in the present. "My own rationality was too strong, I thought, to really allow me to capture the wildly irrational outbreak," he explained later in *Timebends*, his autobiography. "A drama cannot merely describe an emotion, it has to become that emotion."

Then, slowly, he started to see connections between what happened in Salem and what the House Committee on Un-American Activities was doing in Washington and at hearings around the country. "The main point of the hearings, precisely as in seventeenth century Salem, was that the accused make public confession, damn his confederates as well as the Devil master, and guarantee his sterling new allegiance by breaking disgusting old vows—whereupon he was let loose to rejoin the society of extremely decent people. In other words, the same spiritual nugget lay folded within both procedures—an act of contrition done not in solemn privacy but out in the public air."

Miller decided to drive to Salem to see what he could find. As it happened, he stopped on the way to visit Elia Kazan, a close friend and theater-world associate who had directed two of Miller's plays, *All My Sons* and *Death of a Salesman*, on Broadway. Kazan had been called before HUAC in January and was questioned about his association with the Communist Party from 1934 to 1936 as a member of the Group Theatre. Born in Turkey in 1909, Kazan had immigrated to the United States as a child and was educated at Williams College, where he became disillusioned with America's privileged elite and receptive to communism as an alternative. But that was in the past, an affiliation long since rejected.

When the committee first called Kazan, he had refused to cooperate, but he could not live with that decision. Seeking to cleanse himself and clear his conscience, he agreed to appear before HUAC in executive session and name friends and associates who had been in the party with him. He wanted to talk to Miller about why he had changed his mind. Miller thought Kazan was seeking his blessing, confirmation that he was responding appropriately. He admired Kazan as a director of genius, but now he heard Kazan implying that his career would have been threatened had he not chosen to confess to the committee. At first Miller felt sadness, then a troubling sense of estrangement at the realization that his dear friend might have named *him* if they had been involved in the party at the same time and place, which they were not. Along with those reactions, Miller was overtaken by rage at the government for putting people in this situation. "Who or what was now safer because this man in his human weakness had been forced to humiliate himself?" Miller thought. "What truth had been enhanced by all this anguish?"

As Miller was leaving, Kazan's wife, Molly, came out to the car and started to defend her husband. Miller told her that he was on his way to Salem, to which she replied with dismay, "You're not going to equate witches with this!"

ONE IMAGINED, ONE real. There were no witches in Salem in the seventeenth century. But there were communists in America in the twentieth century. Was it reasonable to call the inquisitions led by John Stephens Wood and his congressional colleagues witch hunts, evoking Salem, where nineteen supposed witches were hanged in a bout of mass hysteria? If so, should one differentiate between people who were inaccurately accused of being communists and suffered through guilt by association and those, like my father and uncle, who had belonged to the party? Real or imagined, was being a communist the equivalent of being a witch? Those questions ran through my mind as I studied the transcript of my father's appearance before the committee and the statement he had written but was not allowed to read into his testimony.

In that statement, my father made a direct comparison to the Spanish Inquisition, during which the fidelity to Christianity of converted Jews like the Marranos and others was tested and an auto-da-fé was required—an act of faith involving contrition and penance—followed by punishment, which often meant burning at the stake. He also likened his situation to the witch hunts of colonial Massachusetts and urged anyone who "believes this comparison far-fetched" to consider a quote from Cotton Mather, the influential Puritan minister in Boston whose writings and sermons on satanic witchcraft laid the religious foundations for the Salem trials. Mather did not recommend torture to extract confessions, but other methods such as "cross and swift questions" to confuse the witches and get them to break. My father believed the Fifth Amendment, the right that he invoked during his testimony time and again, was written into the Bill of Rights "precisely to combat this technique, to rule it out forever from American life," even if the committee took it as a de facto confession of guilt.

I also considered his testimony and statement in the context of Judge Learned Hand's axiom on the curtailment of freedom of speech: "the gravity of the evil discounted by its improbability." Did my father's political beliefs and the likelihood they could lead to evil actions make it legitimate for the government to limit his First Amendment rights?

If my father had invoked only the First Amendment—freedom of speech and assembly, freedom of the press—the committee could have cited him for contempt of Congress, as it had the Hollywood Ten five years earlier. The Fifth Amendment was the only legal way for him to defy the committee's efforts to get him to confess and then, having done so, to name names, which he was determined not to do. But throughout his testimony and his statement, he made clear that he considered the committee's subpoena an abridgement of his First Amendment rights. "I view this committee's attempt to muzzle me and drive me off my job as a direct attack on freedom of the press and the right of newspapermen to participate freely in the political life of the country without fear of reprisal."

Along with the Bill of Rights, he thought, he should be protected by the constitution of the CIO's Newspaper Guild, part of which he read into the record during his testimony: that no guild member should be barred or penalized because of "political submission, or anything he writes for publication." He reinforced this idea with a recounting of the history of newspapermen standing up against authority to express their political opinions freely, from the time of Peter Zenger, a fearless printer in New York City who published articles critical of the colonial governor in the 1730s and was charged with libel and imprisoned for months before a jury found him not guilty. My father knew that history well, was proud of the tradition of press independence, and often talked to me about it in later years. He saw himself in that tradition, and by the time I knew him as a crusading newspaperman in Madison, I saw him that way as well. But I also thought there was a hole in his statement as it related to his situation in 1952. In my own career as a journalist, I would have been fired if it had been found out that I was surreptitiously doing political work elsewhere, and justifiably so. Whether it was for Democrats or Republicans, fascists or communists, was not the issue; it was against my newspaper's ethics for that sort of participation. Voting, yes. Expressing informed opinions, of course. A secret second newspaper life, no.

But that is an issue entirely apart from the purpose of the Detroit hearings, something solely between the *Detroit Times*, the Newspaper Guild, and my father. It had no direct correlation to the question of whether he should be forced to testify about his political beliefs, which is the only reason the *Times* found out about his other activities and the reason he was fired. He had broken no laws. He had served his country at a time of war. He had paid his taxes. He had a family and a job and a home. He had followed all the guideposts on the way to the American Dream. The FBI and its thirty-nine informants never reported a single instance when he advocated the violent overthrow of the U.S. government or much of anything beyond the fact that he wrote and edited for a communist newspaper and on behalf of leftist causes. He might have been, as he later said, stubborn in his ignorance about the horrors of the Soviet Union, but what was the gravity of his evil and its likelihood to cause harm?

THIS WAS MILLER'S first time in Salem. He knew it only from history books and was jolted by the reality of its modern dreariness in contrast with his mind's image of "an old wooden village." The past, again, seemed remote, if not irrelevant. At the courthouse, he asked the clerk for the village records of 1692. He combed through "the usual debris a town leaves behind it for the legal record" until he came across the transcripts of the witchcraft trials. He found them in a neat stack, all typed out by writers employed by the Works Progress Administration in the 1930s. It was that era's form of digitization, making the documents more accessible, and it proved to be an inspiration for Miller, giving him a sense of the vocabulary and rhythms of that long-ago time. He spent three weeks in Salem, reading the transcripts and other accounts of the trials, including Charles Upham's 1896 two-volume set, *Salem Witchcraft.*

Miller wrote in a trained cursive hand, neat and legible. He plotted out in notebooks the play that would become *The Crucible.* The first was a Pen-Tab composition book of ninety-two pages. In it, he tried out various titles that eventually were rejected—*If We Could Speak, Inside and Outside, The Reserved Crime*—and tested dialogue and jotted down thoughts and themes. On one page he wrote, "VERY IMPORTANT— To say 'There are no witches' is to invite charge of trying to conceal the conspiracy and to discredit the highest authorities who alone can save the community!"

THE MORNING AFTER Elliott was interrogated by the highest authorities, the *Free Press* ran a photograph on its front page summing up two weeks of testimony in Room 740. There were no people in the picture. Instead there was a close-up of an old satchel, with the caption "The hearings are over and back to Washington goes this briefcase stuffed with testimony taken by its owner, Frank S. Tavenner, chief counsel for the House Un-American Activities Committee. When it first appeared, it contained the secret testimony that stripped the veil from Detroit's communists."

The intent here was symbolic. Evil exposed, secrets revealed, names named, right prevailing, communists on the run, work done. The hearings had personal consequences for Elliott and Bob and others, yet they were essentially ceremonial performances. A few acts of repentance and contrition, more acts of blaming and shaming for the world to see, the curtain closing with the committee saving the community.

The real-life drama in Detroit took place at a time when Washington had aligned with the film industry to spread the message of the evils of communism to larger audiences. After the Hollywood Ten hearings in 1947, when Nixon was still on HUAC, he had called on the major studios to start making "pro-American" movies, and in response came *The Red Menace* in 1949, *I Was a Communist for the FBI* in 1951, and dozens of others, including two now in production: *My Son John* and *Big Jim McLain*. That last film, meant to glorify the communist-hunting House committee, was the creation of John Wayne, the actor, and his producer partner, Robert Fellows.

In the week between HUAC's two visits to Detroit, Donald Jackson, the congressman from California who had replaced Nixon on the committee, met with Wayne and Fellows to discuss the picture they were making for Warner Bros. about a committee investigator who goes to Honolulu to root out communists despoiling the tropical paradise. The plot was based in part on an article by Richard English titled "We Almost Lost Hawaii to the Reds" that ran in the *Saturday Evening Post*. William Wheeler, HUAC's lead investigator, was consulted for many of the details. The role of Big Jim McLain seemed made for Big John Wayne, one of the leading anticommunists in Hollywood and a major-domo in the Motion Picture Alliance for the Preservation of American Ideals. Wayne often played rough-hewn cowboys and rugged individualists, and for this movie he could maintain that character as a committee investigator instead of a sheriff, chasing commies instead of Indians or outlaws.

The committee was involved at every step of the movie-making process. In a follow-up letter to Jackson a few weeks after their first meeting, Fellows described the plot, said he would soon send along the screenplay, and asked the committee to keep mum about story details out of fear that opponents would cause trouble when the filming started if they knew the subject matter. "Because of this, we have announced the picture as an adventure story of a cowboy who goes to Honolulu to raise cattle," Fellows wrote.

The shoot began in April, and within a month Fellows wrote to Tavenner that he had shown "5 reels of a rough version to Mr. J. L. Warner last night at the Warner Studio." The Hawaii scenes would not be wrapped until June 5, Fellows noted, but Warner, after viewing the first reels, seemed "unusually enthusiastic about this picture both from an entertainment standpoint and its content on the American scene." Fellows enclosed the script for Tavenner to examine and sought permission to incorporate photos and newsreels of the committee into the movie to lend it authenticity. When Fellows visited Washington in June, Tavenner gave him notes on the script, but Fellows misplaced them and had to write a follow-up letter after he returned to Los Angeles, asking about the committee counsel's main suggestion, "something about communists being traitors."

"The note that I prepared was designed to be a statement made by the narrator at the place where he is describing Jim McLain and what Jim McLain stands for," Tavenner responded. "My thought was that Jim McLain could, at the appropriate place, make this statement: *He believed, as everyone should, that any person who has been an active communist since 1945 is a traitor to his country.* Best of luck, Tavenner."

Fellows took the advice, and turned it up a notch. In the opening scene, Chairman Wood and members of the committee are seen at work in their hearing room in Washington. "The Battle Hymn of the Republic" plays in the background as the narrator intones, "We, the citizens of the United States of America, owe these, our elected representatives, a great debt. Undaunted by the vicious campaign of slander launched against them as a whole and as individuals, they staunchly continue their investigation, pursuing their stated belief that anyone who continued to be a communist after 1945 is guilty of high treason."

That settled it, the movie wanted America to believe. Any attacks on members of the committee were slander. Anyone named by the committee, including Elliott, was a traitor. They were subhuman, just like the commies Big Jim hunted down in Honolulu. Brenda Murphy, analyzing the movie in *Congressional Theatre*, her book on dramatizations of the McCarthy era, wrote, "It also conveyed a vivid subtext that stigmatized communists as breeders of disease and insanity, instigators of disaster, insidiously deceptive co-workers and neighbors, hypocritical rich men who manipulate and exploit the working man only until they can take over the world—then liquidate. It appealed to America's self-satisfaction on the one hand and its deepest fears on the other."

In early July, Fellows wrote Tavenner to tell him the movie was done and to thank the committee for its cooperation. "The film turned out well and I think you will be pleased with the results." He enclosed stills for the committee's use. "If you or Judge Wood would like extra copies of any still, I will be glad to make them for you or send negatives." At the end of July, Wood was the guest of honor at a special showing at the Warner Bros. projection room in Atlanta. A few weeks later, the first public preview of *Big Jim McLain* was held at the Warner Theatre in Huntington Park, California. Viewers were given cards to offer their critiques. The reviews were mixed:

> The best anti-communist picture I have ever seen—a fine patriotic entertainment.
> Good for every American no matter what age.
> I think a different title would be better.
> Still better as a cowboy.
> More production companies in Hollywood should bring more of this to the screen.
> This is the kind of picture people want to see.
> Good in spots, except for the too, too obvious propaganda and I am NOT a Commie.
> One wonders about the future of this country when this sort of tripe passes for Americanism.

Witches or traitors. John Wayne's *Big Jim McLain* was a limited commercial success, costing less than a million dollars and earning almost three times that amount; then it disappeared, a period piece more interesting for its travelogue snippets of exotic Hawaii than for its sensationalized message.

Arthur Miller's *The Crucible* became an American classic.

— PART FOUR —

Five Years

26

American Wanderers

BY THE SUMMER OF 1952, WE WERE OUT OF DETROIT, SEEK-ing shelter in New York. My father had gone ahead, scrambling to find a job as a reporter on the *Daily Compass*, a liberal newspaper that had inherited some of its staff and much of its politics from the defunct evening paper *PM*. The rest of us followed once my older brother and sister finished the school year at Ann Arbor Trail. We left friends, relatives, and furniture behind and migrated east, our mother driving. She took the northern route through Canada, and somewhere in Ontario she struck a boy whose bicycle had scooted in front of our car. I was almost three, and I think that was one of my first memories, but I can't be sure. Sometimes you hear stories about childhood events so often you think you remember them. My vague memory was of landing on the floor between the front seat and the glove compartment, and that the boy died. But that was wrong; he didn't die, no more than I died when I rode my bicycle into the street on Beaverland and Jim ran home saying that I had. The boy wasn't even seriously hurt, but it rattled Mom very much even though it was not her fault. That is all according to Jean, who was almost six and whose memory I trust.

There is a photograph taken of the five of us soon after we rejoined Dad in the big city. We are posing at the stern of a ferry carrying visitors to the Statue of Liberty out in New York Harbor. The black-and-white picture is framed so perfectly it looks like a postcard. Mom is smiling, her arms gently touching Jeannie, whose auburn hair is in pigtails. Dad is next to her, his left arm drooped protectively over redheaded Jimmy. I am tucked in the middle front, wearing shorts and goofy striped socks, blinking in the sunlight. On the back rail to our side is a white life buoy marked "STATUE OF LIBERTY N.Y.," and looming behind that is the real thing, Miss Liberty rising high with her crown and her torch.

No photo could have had more levels of meaning for our family. The Statue of Liberty is an American totem my parents deeply believed in, even now that they had been identified by a congressional committee as un-American, or perhaps more now than ever. My father's parents were among the multitude of Eastern European immigrants who were welcomed symbolically by the torch, Joe at age two from Odessa, Ida as a teenager from Latvia. My father had spent much of his youth only twenty miles away, in the new American stew of Brooklyn. The Statue of Liberty represented the best of the American story he was taught at Abraham Lincoln High School, an expansive generosity evoked by Emerson and Whitman. The inclusiveness of "The New Colossus," Emma Lazarus's memorial poem on the base of the statue, powerfully evokes the idealized humanism that inspired both of my parents in their politics. The words and phrases seemed to speak to them. *Sea-washed, sunset gates. Mother of Exiles. Mild eyes. Tired. Poor. Yearning to breathe free. Wretched refuse. Homeless. Tempest-tossed. Golden door.*

Any American who belonged to the Communist Party after World War II should be considered a traitor, proclaimed Frank Tavenner. That was the message he wanted John Wayne to convey in his movie role as Big Jim McLain, the commie hunter working for the committee. But my parents' politics and their blindness to the horrors of the Soviet Union did not diminish their patriotism; it defined them less than the photo of the family posing in Lady Liberty's benevolent shadow. They were no innocents, but nor did the fact that they had been communists make them traitors. They never betrayed America and loved it no less than the officials who rendered judgment on them in Room 740 of the Federal Building in Detroit. They were dissenters who believed the nation had not lived up to its founding ideals in terms of race and equality, largely because of the reactionary attitudes of self-righteous attackers on the American right. In response, they latched on to a false promise and for too long blinded themselves to the repressive totalitarian reality of communism in the Soviet Union. And now they were paying the price.

It had been two and a half years since the entire Cummins clan assembled for a photograph on the front steps of 1402 Henry Street in Ann Arbor: the grandparents, their five children, four in-laws, and ten grandchildren. The good American family. Andrew and Grace, the patriarch and matriarch, had more to worry about now than ever. One of their sons, Phil, was still suffering at the mental hospital in North Carolina. Bob, their oldest son, was not only a widower with two young girls, but faced bleak job prospects after being named at the HUAC hearings and called to testify. Now Elliott, their son-in-law, was in a similar position, uprooted from Michigan. But among Elliott's many qualities, one of the strongest was his survival instinct, and he brought his family to New York with a will to survive.

We moved into the small apartment of our Brooklyn grandparents, Poppy and Bubby. Tight quarters for seven people, including three rambunctious children, but Coney Island was a children's paradise. "We kids spent all day and part of the night playing in the streets," Jean recalled. "We played with hard pink rubber balls, jacks. There were gangs of kids from all over, so it was easy to fit in. Trucks used to come around with a Tilt-a-Whirl on the back, and there were street-cleaning trucks that spewed refreshing water." The boardwalk. Splinters. Foot-burning sand. The sting of ocean salt. People everywhere. Kids everywhere. Baby boom. Before white flight. Rooming houses, bathhouses. Avenues with enchanting names: Surf, Mermaid, Neptune. The joyous crunch of a Nathan's Famous hot dog. Chocolate soda. Bagels. Salami. Dad would eat anything, but Jim and Jean avoided the gefilte fish and chopped liver. When summer ended, they attended P.S. 188 on Mermaid Avenue. Jim skipped a grade and went into third. Jean took an aptitude test that placed her in an advanced class for first grade. She remembered "a lot of crowding and congestion" in the school and "filling little booklets with pennies and dimes" and needing milk money.

THE *DAILY COMPASS*, a morning tabloid with a circulation of only thirty thousand, was barely two years old when Elliott arrived, but there was a sense of desperation to the place already. It inherited one star,

I. F. Stone, the iconoclastic columnist, but few thought it could last.
The city editor, Tom O'Connor, had been called before HUAC that May
and had refused to name names. Two months later, on July 24, O'Connor dropped dead in the office while watching the Democratic National
Convention on television.

At least here, unlike at the *Detroit Times*, Elliott could report stories and write them under his own byline. His most dramatic assignment involved a mysterious murder in New York that seemed to lead
back to the underworld henchmen of Rafael Trujillo, the dictator of the
Dominican Republic. The victim was Andres F. Requena, a Dominican
native who edited *Patria*, an anti-Trujillo newspaper in New York. On
October 2, Requena was shot and killed in the hallway of a tenement
house in Manhattan. It so happened that only hours earlier he had delivered a sensational story to his printer charging that Trujillo's general
counsel in New York had threatened his life.

"This newspaper has learned how Requena was lured to his death
last week in the dark hallway of a tenement at 243 Madison on the
Lower East Side," Elliott wrote in a front-page article. "The bait was a
stunningly beautiful woman." He also reported that a close friend of
Requena's, Pedro A. Bobadilla, then a civilian employee of the U.S. Navy
in San Juan, Puerto Rico, had received a death threat four days later,
warning that he would be next. An article by Bobadilla critical of Trujillo had been published recently in Requena's newspaper, and according to Elliott's account, Bobadilla had received the death threat from
Trujillo's assassins in Puerto Rico.

In follow-up stories, my father acquired and summarized a copy of
the article Requena had dropped off at his printer's before his murder,
and he updated the police investigation several times. The Trujillo story
became part of our family lore, not so much for the articles my father
wrote but for a story that he told about it afterward. We all heard variations of it over the years. He said he was getting on an elevator one day
during the time he was covering the Requena murder and a woman got
on, a Trujillo relative, perhaps his sister; she stood next to him and told
him that he was a good reporter and it would be a shame if anything
happened to him. "I remember Dad being proud of this, not scared at

all," my brother recalled. *A shame if anything happened to him*—but of course, short of death, something already had.

The *Daily Compass* folded on November 4. It was in hock so deep they had to sell the presses and fixtures to pay the mortgage. The next day was Election Day, Eisenhower versus Adlai Stevenson. Decades later my father confessed that he had voted for Eisenhower. After reading the letters he wrote home from the war, many of which extolled Ike's virtues, that no longer surprised me.

Our family was cut adrift again, and soon we moved from one set of grandparents to the other, from Coney Island to Ann Arbor, up the steps and into 1402 Henry Street. Again, a tight fit, Jean recalled, "but not quite as tight." As soon as we got there, Mom enrolled Jean and Jim at Burns Park Elementary, their third school in six months. Jim's teacher had once taught our aunt Jean, Mom's younger sister, "and remembered her and loved her," Jim recalled. Jim loved the Wolverines football team. His favorite player was Tony Branoff, a running back. The Burns Park neighborhood was comfortably middle class, and so was the school, but it was not a happy time for Jean. "I had to catch up in school since I don't think I learned anything at P.S. 188," she recalled. And after experiencing the big-city life, Ann Arbor seemed too tame and predictable for her. On top of that, it all seemed so temporary, a way station until our jobless father found somewhere else to work.

GEORGE CROCKETT WAS out of prison. Six months earlier, on April 24, he and the other four lawyers who had been cited for contempt of court in the Foley Square trial surrendered to authorities at the same courthouse in Lower Manhattan after their appeals had been exhausted. On the final appeal, their convictions had been upheld by the Supreme Court on a 5 to 3 vote, with Justices William O. Douglas, Hugo Black, and Felix Frankfurter dissenting. The liberal Douglas and conservative Frankfurter wrote, "One who reads the record of this case will have difficulty determining whether members of the bar conspired to drive a judge from the bench or whether the judge used the authority of the bench to whipsaw the lawyers, to taunt and tempt them, and to create for himself the role of the persecuted." In the majority opinion, Justice Robert H. Jackson said that the court would defend the vigorous advocacy of trial lawyers but would not "equate contempt with courage, or insults with independence."

On the day of reckoning, Crockett and the other sentenced lawyers asked the U.S. marshal not to put them in handcuffs as they were being taken from the courthouse to a federal detention center on West Street. The request was ignored. Crockett, the only African American in the group, asked to be sent to a penitentiary in the North, but that request too was denied, and he was sent to the Federal Correctional Institution in Ashland, Kentucky, a segregated facility. But his resolve was strengthened behind bars, he said; the four months there were not wasted.

"I actually felt relieved when I realized that I could withstand the worst that the establishment could dish out in the way of punishment," he said later. "And my fellow prisoners in that segregated prison treated me with special care. I was somewhat of a hero to them and their understanding of my efforts was an unexpected bright spot." He had always considered himself a champion of the underdog, and the prison experience only confirmed that position. From then on, he understood the reality behind telling clients that they would be spending months or years in jail.

Soon after Crockett was released from Ashland, the Civil Rights Congress and the Michigan Committee for Protection of the Foreign Born hosted a welcome home party for him at the Jewish Cultural Center in Detroit. He was greeted by more than three hundred friends and admirers who gave him a long and loud standing ovation. But his difficulties were far from over. The Michigan Bar began disciplinary proceedings against him for unprofessional conduct, leading to a public reprimand, and the FBI continued watching his every move, taking note even when Helen Winter, the wife of his Foley Square client, Carl Winter, "kissed George Crockett" at the homecoming banquet. He came to think of himself as even more of an outsider. He thought his phones were tapped, that his neighbors looked at him differently and would not mind if the Crockett family lived elsewhere than on American Street. There were times when he would be walking down

Woodward Avenue downtown and see approaching from the other direction someone he knew, who ignored him or veered left or right to avoid him.

One place he felt comfortable was at work, as a partner now in one of the few interracial law firms in the country, Goodman, Crockett, Eden and Robb. His law partner, Ernie Goodman, had essentially picked up where Crockett left off, defending more members of the CPUSA against Smith Act charges. When the Supreme Court upheld the first Smith Act convictions, prosecutors around the country were encouraged to bring more cases against Communist Party leaders, and one of the first of many such cases was in Michigan. The Michigan Six, as they became known, were indicted a few weeks after Crockett returned to Detroit. They included Helen Winter; Billy Allan, the *Daily Worker* journalist; and Saul Wellman, a local CPUSA official, who had fought twice against fascism, first in the Spanish Civil War with the International Brigade and then with the U.S. Army, where he was in the Battle of the Bulge. Goodman represented all three.

The government case against the Michigan Six would rely in part on the testimony of Bereniece Baldwin. After coming in from the cold to testify in February and March, Baldwin had been hot on the banquet and hearings circuits. She testified before a Detroit grand jury and at a HUAC hearing in Cleveland and was the guest of honor at a state convention of nurses in Grand Rapids and a homeowner association banquet in the Burbank neighborhood. On the same week that Crockett was incarcerated in Kentucky, she was honored with a testimonial dinner at the Veterans Memorial Building sponsored by the American Legion. FBI director J. Edgar Hoover was invited but did not attend, but the hall was filled with local politicians, business leaders, and members of civic and fraternal groups who felt that "Mrs. Baldwin's devotion to her country merits recognition." The main speaker was Representative Charles E. Potter, who had just formally entered the race for Michigan's open U.S. Senate seat. Potter won that election on the day after Elliott lost his job in New York. He took office in the first month of 1953.

WITH THE NEW year came the Broadway premiere of *The Crucible* at the Martin Beck Theatre on January 22, 1953. It starred Arthur Kennedy as John Proctor, the flawed but heroic protagonist who goes to the gallows rather than confess to false accusations; Madeleine Sherwood as Abigail Williams, the manipulative young maid who spreads malicious gossip to start the witch hunt frenzy in Salem as a means of protecting herself; and E. G. Marshall as Reverend Hale, the tortured minister who moves from righteousness to doubt. Although it would win the Tony for best play of the year, the audience reaction at first was mixed, as were reviews from critics. Arthur Miller himself thought the production was too austere, but he also worried it came at the wrong time, "when the gale from the Right was blowing at its fullest fury."

There was something beneath the rise of McCarthyism, Miller later wrote, that seemed "much more weird and mysterious." The reactionary campaign had created "not only a terror, but a new subjective reality, a veritable mystique which was gradually assuming even a holy resonance. . . . There was a new religiosity in the air, not merely the kind expressed by the spurt in church construction and church attendance, but an official piety which my reading of American history could not reconcile with the free-wheeling iconoclasm of the country's past."

A few months later, *Holiday* magazine sent Miller to his alma mater to chronicle the atmosphere at Michigan during the Red Scare and compare it to his days there in the 1930s. A member of the student council told him that many of her classmates thought she must be a communist for living in a cooperative rooming house instead of a dormitory. Miller's favorite old English professor, now a dean, lamented that the FBI was asking students and teachers to inform on one another. Members of the school's Socialist Club said they no longer came to meetings by car because an agent would be lingering outside the meeting place taking down license plate numbers. Then Miller paid a visit to his old haunt, the *Michigan Daily*.

The newspaper office seemed diminished from its former self, he thought. In his years there, it was a messy, loud, disputatious, crowded, energized place overflowing with talented writers elbowing each other for top spots on the masthead. "But now the building seemed deserted at two in the afternoon, and I soon learned that the paper, incredibly, was forced to advertise for applicants to the staff." Miller decided to examine issues of the paper from his student days. While leafing through the "musty pages," he was approached by a student who said he had recently written a four-part series on communists on campus that exposed a few student radicals. Nearby sat a middle-aged man who was taking notes while studying recent editions of the *Daily*. It turned out this man was from the state police; he was looking for any mentions of leftists whose names would go into a master file of people to watch for un-American activities.

OUR FAMILY MOVED again, this time from Ann Arbor to Cleveland, where my father landed a job on the copydesk of the *Cleveland Plain Dealer*. We stayed at first in a small apartment in the suburb of Parma. On February 18, 1953, my mother put a pot of pea soup on the stove and wrote a letter to her brother at the sanitarium. "We gave away most of our furniture in Detroit, and we're stuck here with no comfortable and cozy living room furniture to sit on. Sitting at the kitchen table at least keeps us from falling asleep when we're reading, and I've read more books since I've been here than I did all summer." Two of us were at the table keeping her company, she wrote. "Davey is drawing a 3-year-old's conception of a map, which includes China, Ann Arbor, Detroit, Parma, and Texas all in one picture. I guess he included Texas because that's the cowboy state. Jeannie is reading a comic book. Jimmy is on his way out with some kid he met at the bus stop here. Jim and Jean go by bus to the Pearl Road school here in Parma from 8:30 to 3." It was their fourth school in less than a year.

My uncle Phil kept the letter, and it was saved with the family archives by my aunt Jean, who passed her boxes along to one of my cousins, Mary Higgins. When I visited my cousin and found the letter more than sixty years later, my rendering of a map of the world was still there. I have no idea about China, but my mother was probably right about why Texas made the map. I thought of myself as a cowboy then and did a little "cowboy dance" to please the adults, where I shifted from leg to leg and shook my hands at my side and blurted out, "Get along, little dogies." Hopalong Cassidy was my favorite, not Roy Rogers or Gene Autry. No white hat for Hopalong; he dressed all in black.

As soon as Mom could arrange it, we moved into a house nearby at a new 1950s-style development called Snow Village. With all the instability in our lives, she thought it was important that we have a home of our own, wherever we went from there. "Mary thought it would make the children feel more settled," my father later wrote in a tribute to her. All the moving was taking a toll on my big brother. Jim started feigning illness to stay home from school, and it reached the point where Mom took him to a psychiatrist, who told her not to worry, that he was just a perfectionist. He had already skipped a grade and was so smart the teachers would pass him even if he had too many absences. He read the *World Book Encyclopedia* from Volume A to Volume W–Z and never fell behind in his schoolwork. "Teachers would admonish the other students for not doing as well as the new kid," he recalled. "Surprisingly, this did not make me unpopular. I never felt disliked." He won a prize at school for a poster he made to advertise a school bond issue. It was of a stork with the message "Get Ready for Us." "Us" being the baby boom generation flooding into the public schools. Jeannie rarely if ever missed a day of school and was delighted by the move to Snow Village. "I remember looking at our new house while it was under construction. It was great to have my own room when we finally moved in. Mom did a little painting and sewing to fix the place up. I think we were planning to stay there. At least that was my impression. Jimmy and I took piano lessons in Cleveland, and we often went to a swimming hole in Berea."

The simple pleasures of the 1950s: The family went to the cinema to see *Brigadoon* and *Seven Brides for Seven Brothers*. On our black-and-white television, we watched Sid Caesar and Jackie Gleason, Ed Sullivan and Steve Allen, and the crowning of Queen Elizabeth. Life seemed placid, but the world was churning. In swift succession after we arrived in Cleveland, Joseph Stalin died, Julius and Ethel Rosenberg were executed, the Korean War ended, and the Detroit communists known as the Michigan Six were convicted on Smith Act charges. When the judge offered to send them to Russia instead of prison, they refused and were sentenced to four to five years behind bars.

My own strongest early memories began around that time at Snow Village. Some memories were traumatic, but most were warm. I remember my asthma getting worse and a doctor sticking two rows of tiny needles in my forearm for allergy tests. I was okay during the day but often spent hours wheezing and struggling to breathe at night. I also remember the apple trees blossoming in a huge field across Snow Road, and men flying model aircraft in the field, and getting my first set of little rubbery bowlegged cowboys and Indians with horses to fit them on. At a nearby pond we collected tadpoles in jars. The father of one of our Snow Village friends took us to what we called "the cliffs," high above a railroad track; our dad did not want us to go but came along once and twisted his ankle on the rocks.

We made it through 1953 and much of 1954 without upheaval. We were a family of baseball lovers, and now our new team was the best around: the 1954 Indians. Mom and Jeannie went to see them play at cavernous Municipal Stadium on Ladies Day. We listened to them on the radio all summer long. Al Rosen, the hard-hitting Jewish third baseman. Larry Doby, the pathbreaking Jackie Robinson of the American League, in center field. Al Smith, another black ballplayer, usually next to Doby in left. Bobby Avila, the little second baseman from Mexico. And that world-class rotation of Bob Feller, Early Wynn, Bob Lemon, and Mike (Big Bear) Garcia. A team that won 111 games and took down the Yankees, the pinstriped establishment, the team we hated more than anything in the world. When the Indians clinched the pennant, Dad took us to the airport to greet the players returning from a road trip. I got Al Smith's autograph. Jim got Al Rosen's. Then we watched Willie Mays make the most famous catch in baseball history as the Giants swept four straight in the World Series.

The good American family leading the good postwar American life. Or so it seemed. One day Jim was at the house of a friend named Tony, and Tony's mother told them that communists were reptiles. "I said to her that my mother was a communist," Jim said later. "Not that I was about to denounce Mom or anything, but I think I wanted to see what

Tony's mom would say. 'Oh no she isn't. Your mother isn't a communist.'" Jim said he could take this response one of three ways. "(a) Mom
didn't look or talk like anything but an all-American girl. Peaches and
cream. Very gentle and considerate in manner. Evansville, Indiana accent. Or (b) maybe Tony's mother didn't want to see herself as attacking
the family of her son's friend. Or (c) didn't want Tony to see her as a
venomous gossip. In any case, I could deal with it."

On our phonograph at home, Mom played a Paul Robeson album
as part of her daily rotation of music. "There's a Balm in Gilead." "Ol'
Man River." "It Ain't Necessarily So." We knew his songs by heart. Jim
grew to love-hate him. When Jim's teacher, Miss Baer, asked the class to
name some famous Negroes, Jim said Paul Robeson. "Paul Robeson is a
communist!" she replied.

Dad worked the late shift at the *Plain Dealer*, going into the office at
five in the afternoon and staying until two in the morning. He usually
stayed up for a few hours after that and slept until almost noon. An
old friend from his *Michigan Daily* days helped get him the job. He
loved newspapering—he was a natural at it—even if he thought less
of the newspaper itself. "Have you ever seen a copy of the Pee-Dee?" he
wrote in a letter. "It is Cleveland's most 'influential' paper—big, fat, and
rich—but frankly it is awfully stuffy. Typographically it is still in the
19th century; but since it has practically no competition it doesn't feel
compelled to change."

The FBI continued to follow him in Cleveland. His name was on
Washington's Security Index of suspected subversives. But special agents
and informants were coming up with nothing, according to their internal reports. On June 17, 1953, the Cleveland special agent in charge sent a
memorandum to Hoover's office regarding "Ace" Maraniss, marked "security matter": "Cleveland informants have recently been contacted concerning subject's presence with the Cleveland Division and they advised
that they do not know him. Inasmuch as there is no reported activity by
the subject within the Cleveland Division and the fact that informants
have not reported any activity concerning subject since his arrival from
the former office of origin, Detroit, this case is being placed in a closed
status pending receipt of information reflecting renewed activity."

There was no renewed activity. Sometimes Dad looked after us children while Mom worked part-time during the day in the book department at Higbee's department store in downtown Cleveland, where she made enough money to buy furniture for our new house and bring home a shelf of books that she could buy at a discount. But in early May 1954, after a witness at another HUAC hearing in Detroit identified Dad as having been a party member in 1947, the Cleveland office became interested again and sought permission to interview him. There was internal debate between Cleveland and Washington about what was called "the plan of approach"—how and where that should be done, and whether Mom should be interviewed also—but in the end Washington rejected the idea. The directions were to watch, but not interview. Through that summer and early fall, there were no reports of communist activity on the part of my parents.

Then our lives were disrupted once again. On October 21, Wright Bryan, the editor of the *Plain Dealer*, called Dad into his office and questioned him about his appearance before the committee in 1952. According to an FBI report based on confidential informants, "in the above conversation between Bryan and the subject, Maraniss denied that he is presently active in affairs of the Communist Party. According to T-3, Maraniss advised Bryan that his past Communist Party activities were well known and that he, Maraniss, invoked the Fifth Amendment before the House Committee because he did not wish to be an informer and a source of embarrassment to others." Bryan fired him on the spot.

As he had in Detroit, my father hoped that the Newspaper Guild would come to his defense. It did, to an extent, according to the FBI report: "A committee of the guild called on Mr. Wright Bryan concerning the matter. According to the informant, Bryan advised the committee that he would consider re-hiring Maraniss provided the latter would make a full disclosure of his Communist Party activities to the FBI. The Newspaper Guild Committee then relayed this information to the subject who stated that he did not want to talk with the FBI for fear of embarrassing other people." The guild committee then told my father that his only recourse was to submit to arbitration and testify under oath. He refused again, and the guild dropped its support. He was out of a job, and soon we were on the move again, back to Detroit before Christmas.

FOR MANY PEOPLE, Joe McCarthy is the first thing that comes to mind at any mention of anticommunism and the Red Scare hysteria of the 1950s. After all, they named the era after him. And McCarthy was the looming specter in our lives. My parents read about him and talked about him and watched him on television during the Army-McCarthy hearings in the spring of 1954 in the living room of our house at Snow Village in Cleveland. He had nothing to do with the House committee that had labeled my father un-American, yet he had everything to do with whipping up national hysteria. Dad and McCarthy were participants in the same larger national drama, but their paths never crossed. McCarthy played a dominant role, and my father was barely a bit player in a cast of many thousands—collateral damage.

Charles E. Potter, one of the congressmen in Room 740 on the day my father was called to testify, went on to have a much closer look at McCarthy. Potter used his role as an earnest anticommunist on HUAC and an endorsement from McCarthy as springboards for his election to the U.S. Senate. Once there he became a member of the Permanent Investigations Subcommittee of the Senate Committee on Government Operations, a normally backwater panel that McCarthy, as chairman, transformed into a personal commie-hunting fiefdom from which he could gain maximum publicity. Potter was one of four Republicans on the subcommittee in 1953, along with McCarthy, Everett Dirksen of Illinois, and Karl Mundt of South Dakota. The three Democrats were John L. McClellan of Arkansas, Henry Jackson of Washington, and Stuart Symington of Missouri. The subcommittee's chief counsel was a twenty-seven-year-old Columbia Law School graduate named Roy M. Cohn, as brash and breathless as his boss.

Many historians of the McCarthy era have pointed out astutely that the beginning of the end for McCarthy came when a fellow Republican was elected to the White House, and not just any Republican but a former army general and war hero. It was not that Eisenhower moved aggressively against McCarthy, at least not at first. He had refused to denounce McCarthy while campaigning in Wisconsin in 1952, and during his first year in office mostly tried to keep his distance from the senator. Nixon, his vice president, had made his reputation going after Alger Hiss and Reds in the federal workforce, taking on that role long before McCarthy, and appreciated how central the anticommunist issue was to his success and that of his party. Even more than Eisenhower, Nixon wanted to avoid clashes with McCarthy, but this was not easy. McCarthy became more and more unhinged without a Democratic bogeyman. Before Ike reached the White House, the Democrats had controlled the executive branch for two decades, which McCarthy had labeled "twenty years of treason," and he was not ready to disembark from the treason train and stop his histrionics just because the Republicans controlled the White House and the Senate.

That is where Potter came into the picture. Like Eisenhower, and even more like Nixon, his old pal from the Chowder and Marching Club, Potter would rather have avoided any disputes between McCarthy and the Republican establishment, but at times that proved impossible. When McCarthy hired Joseph Brown Matthews as staff director, a disillusioned leftist who had become a strident right-winger, Potter joined with Democrats on the committee in voting for his removal after it was revealed Matthews had written an article titled "Reds and Our Churches" for *American Mercury* magazine, calling mainstream Protestant clergy the largest group of communist sympathizers in the nation.

McCarthy seemed intent on attacking revered American institutions—not only the churches but the military. In February 1954, after weeks of jabbing at the army, he ordered Brig. Gen. Ralph W. Zwicker, who had earned a Silver Star on Omaha Beach on D-Day, into the committee room to browbeat him for allowing the commissioning of a left-wing dentist. Here was the overreach that prompted Ralph Flanders, a moderate Republican senator from Vermont, to utter a line that came to define McCarthy's bullying tactics: "He emits war whoops. He goes forth to battle and proudly returns with the scalp of a pink Army dentist."

Eisenhower, who had devoted his life to the army, was infuriated by McCarthy's attacks, as were the military brass. This had become a war, and they soon found a vulnerable point of attack. The administration compiled a chronology that showed how Roy Cohn, abusing his status as committee counsel and McCarthy's right-hand man, sought to obtain preferential treatment for G. David Schine, Cohn's close friend and traveling companion, so that Schine could avoid being inducted into the army. The army gave a copy of the chronology to Potter, who shared it publicly on March 11, and things blew up from there. McCarthy responded the next day by saying that the army was trying to blackmail him because he was embarrassing the brass with his exposure of Reds in the military, but his bleating could not prevent the Senate subcommittee from taking the next step: starting hearings into the Schine affair, which became known as the Army-McCarthy hearings. "From his simple act and the selfish whim of two young men who seemed to be demonstrating a rare kind of irresponsibility, the entire country was swept into a tornado of emotional nonsense," Potter wrote later.

The Army-McCarthy hearings dominated daytime television from April through June, watched by millions of households, including ours. Since McCarthy and his top aide were being investigated, he stepped away from the chairman's seat during the hearings but stayed on the committee and took on the role of his own defense attorney, allowing himself cross-examination privileges that he had denied to all other witnesses. In the end, he did himself in, showing the country his hypocrisy, belligerence, and what army lawyer Joseph Welch, during their historic confrontation, called his "reckless cruelty" and lack of decency.

The hearings led to Cohn's firing and McCarthy's censure by his Senate colleagues. They also led to a transformation in the thinking of Senator Potter. Once, when he was a member of HUAC, he called his job rooting out un-Americans the most important fight of his life, more significant than the world war that had rendered him paraplegic. He had enthusiastically brought citizens like my father before the committee to challenge their patriotism and took full advantage of the anticommunist hysteria blowing across America to advance his political career. But eventually he reached a point of regret and wrote a book of repentance titled *Days of Shame*. In it, Potter described the Red-hunting phenomenon as "like a gigantic, tumultuous hurricane" that "dominated the thoughts and actions of the American people, disrupting their emotions, distorting their judgment. Sanity seemed to go in hiding, opinions whirled to the outer edges of human thought." He saw in McCarthy's supporters "a lineup of disgraceful racial bigots and American fascists." The wounded hero of World War II said he hated to admit it, but that group included many local branches of the American Legion and Veterans of Foreign Wars who were "noisy supporters of every irrational blast at Communism that McCarthy fired." One post of the VFW "made itself ridiculous by accusing the Girl Scouts of America of being a Communist front because it supported the United Nations."

There were sections in Potter's book that spoke directly to the sorts of things that happened to my father in Room 740. At one point he took issue with the role of HUAC altogether, saying that congressional committees should focus on the functioning of existing laws and whether there was a need for amendment or new legislation, and that it was "never intended that these legislative bodies should conduct quasi-trials with power of punishment." Where once he and Chairman Wood and Counsel Tavenner had declared that a witness invoking the Fifth Amendment was acknowledging guilt, he now wrote eloquently in the amendment's defense. "This protective shield given to a witness under the Fifth Amendment is written in the blood and lives of many people," Potter concluded. "But by distortion and abuse, the Fifth Amendment became a pair of dirty words."

These second thoughts were germinating in Potter's mind in the mid-1950s, though it would take another decade, when *Days of Shame* was published, for him to go public with them. In the mid-1950s, after the televised Army-McCarthy hearings and the senator from Wisconsin's censure, the fervor of the McCarthy era had diminished, but it was not yet gone. That would take a few years more.

JOHN STEPHENS WOOD had been home in Canton, Georgia, and largely out of sight for two years when President Eisenhower thrust him back into the news. On March 4, 1955, the former congressman was nominated by the White House for a seat on the Subversive Activities Control Board. This was the federal panel that served as another cog in the government's anticommunist machine, supplementing the work of the House and Senate committees and the FBI. It is where Bereniece Baldwin first came in from the cold in 1952 by testifying just days before she took a star role at the HUAC hearings in Detroit.

Wood had chosen not to run for reelection in 1952, in part due to his uncertain health. He had collapsed during an executive session of the committee that year and had to go home to Georgia to recuperate for a few weeks. He was tired and already past retirement age. Another election surely would have meant another pounding from his Washington nemesis, the columnist Drew Pearson, who for years had included Wood in his collection of nefarious pols in his Washington Merry-Go-Round. The SACB job seemed less taxing than being a congressman; it was only part-time, came with a $15,000 salary, and involved a subject with which he was familiar. If Ike knew little about Wood, there was one important connection: Wood was the uncle through marriage of Bobby Jones, the famed golfer and close golfing pal of the president. Ike stayed at Jones's private quarters, the Jones Cabin, during his frequent escapes from the White House for golfing vacations at the Augusta National Golf Club, and in return Eisenhower, an amateur artist, gave Jones a color portrait he had painted of the golfer in his prime.

The Wood nomination was referred to a subcommittee of the Senate Judiciary Committee. At first, it looked like a done deal. The subcommittee received a telegram from the current members of HUAC unanimously endorsing the former chairman of their committee. Wood's successor in the House, Phil Landrum, told the subcommittee that he had never known a public figure who, as a judge, lawyer, and congressman, had gone to greater lengths than Wood "to see that an individual received his rights." The Republican Party chairman in Georgia said that when he heard about Wood's nomination he paid a visit to Robert T. Jones Jr. and the immortal Bobby gave Wood "the highest recommendation that a man could give another man."

Then Pearson went to work. In two columns that May, he revived all the charges he had made against Wood a decade earlier, when Wood was first chairing HUAC. In one column he brought up the mysterious "payoff fee" that Wood's aide had received for getting damages from the federal government paid to a Georgia boy who had been struck by a U.S. Army truck, the sort of constituent work that is to be done for free. And he returned to the story of how Wood kept a family handyman on the committee payroll as a janitor.

Pearson's second column was intended to weaken Wood's reputation as an anticommunist. "The Democrats have had their noses so relentlessly rubbed in the charge of being soft to communism that it will be interesting to see what they do about Ike's recent error in the same direction," Pearson wrote. The gist of Pearson's story was that Wood as chairman of HUAC had backed away from investigating communist influence in Hollywood, and it was only when the Republicans briefly took control that the committee began hearings on the film industry. Pearson alluded to a mysterious middleman, a lawyer in Wood's Georgia district named Edgar Dunlap, who received a $25,000 fee from studio head Louis B. Mayer during the period Wood was chairman. When Pearson first interviewed Dunlap, whom he described as "a big, bluff, prosperous looking gentleman," Dunlap denied knowing Mayer "except to say that he met him casually on the MGM lot in 1946." When presented evidence of the $25,000 fee, Dunlap said it was to handle an interstate commerce problem with the shipment of horses. Pearson wondered why Mayer would turn to Dunlap for that rather than any of his "battery of high-priced lawyers in Washington," implying that the payment was to keep the committee at bay.

"Wood's appointment was so unusual that capital observers were flabbergasted at his appointment," Pearson concluded. "One explanation is that Wood is the uncle of Ike's golfing friend—Bobby Jones—which is a fact, though Jones has kept aloof from politics in the past."

Along with the attacks from Pearson in columns that always had more dots than lines connecting them, Wood's nomination became the subject of an intense letter-writing campaign from civil rights groups and leftist organizations. William Patterson of the Civil Rights Congress and Royal W. France of the Emergency Civil Liberties Committee testified in person against Wood, and Clarence Mitchell, Washington director of the NAACP, submitted a statement. They charged that Wood was a racist who had once been a member of the Ku Klux Klan. Wood appeared before the committee to defend himself against these charges, and at one point got into a revealing dialogue with Senator Thomas Hennings of Missouri.

Senator Hennings: In respect to the charge that you are a racist, Mr. Wood, I understand that you deny that and say that you never lost a Negro vote in your home town.

Mr. Wood: I stated it but in my last election they voted separately, and I carried every vote. Some of my best friends that I have are colored.

The senators seemed especially concerned with Wood's Klan involvement. It was in response to their questions that he said he was a joiner, had joined many organizations at the start of his career, and that as part of that effort he went to one Klan meeting and paid the fifteen-dollar initiation fee. But he insisted he had dropped out when he learned that he would have to wear a white hood and "administer such punishment" as Klan leaders required to people the Klan thought undesirable. "Count me out," Wood recalled saying, "and they kept my fifteen dollars."

The committee had difficulty figuring out what to do with the Wood nomination and eventually reached a decision by default. When Congress went into recess that August, the nomination was dropped. One story from his past never came up: his role as the wheelman in 1915 carrying the corpse of Atlanta industrialist Leo Frank to the undertaker after he was lynched at Frey's Gin near Marietta.

FRANK TAVENNER STILL maintained his rural domain of apple orchards in the Shenandoah Valley of Virginia during that period. A Virginia newspaper noted that "the man whose job when he is in Washington is to fight subversive activities" had found a new type of infestation closer to home. A parasite had threatened to destroy his crops, and

Tavenner came up with an effective if expensive new weapon to fight it: a helicopter. "Tavenner is the first to employ the helicopter method of spraying to rout the bug which causes the fruit to drop from the trees," the *Daily News-Record* reported. "The previous method was to use a tank sprayer, but the process was so slow there was a great loss of apples. The helicopter will be hovering over a tree and spray about 170 acres in about three hours."

Saving good apples, rooting out rotten ones: that is what Tavenner thought his life was all about. Apples, symbolic and real, connected his life in Washington to his life in Woodstock. But there was more to it than that, as I learned one December day when my exploration of what it meant to be American or un-American took me out on Interstate 66 from Washington to walk the streets of Woodstock, his hometown in the cradle of the valley.

The charter for Woodstock dates to 1761 and was sponsored in the House of Burgesses by none other than George Washington. That is about as old-school American as it can get. Its most famous citizen in the early years was John Peter Muhlenberg, a Protestant minister who was dispatched from Pennsylvania to serve a congregation in the little log church at the corner of Court and Main. Muhlenberg later became immortalized as a preacher-patriot, and there is a statue of him on the town square not far from what is considered the oldest courthouse west of the Blue Ridge Mountains. There are also statues of him in the U.S. Capitol Building and in a small park off Connecticut Avenue NW in Washington, but the one in Woodstock is the most stirring, capturing the mythmaking moment of this original American man.

The story later conveyed by Muhlenberg's descendants tells of a January Sunday in 1776 when he was in the middle of a sermon drawn from Ecclesiastes 3. Those unfamiliar with the Old Testament might know this as the scripture transformed by Pete Seeger into a folk song popularized by the Byrds in the 1960s as "Turn! Turn! Turn! (To Everything There Is a Season)." When Muhlenberg reached chapter 3, verse 8, about a time for war and a time for peace, he shed his clerical robe and strode from the pulpit in the uniform of a Continental Army colonel, marching out into the street to the pounding of war drums, ready to take on the Redcoats with his 8th Virginia Regiment. That seems the stuff to incite purple prose, and the poet Thomas Buchanan did not disappoint. American schoolchildren once memorized these lines from the fifth edition of *McGuffey's Reader*:

> *When suddenly his mantle wide*
> *His hands impatient flung aside*
> *And lo! He met their wandering eyes*
> *Complete in all a warrior's guise*

If Muhlenberg evoked the American patriotic myth at its creation, Tavenner devoted his life to protecting and perpetuating it nearly two centuries later in the middle decades of the twentieth century. And here it all connected in an unexpected way, from Muhlenberg to Tavenner to Seeger. Muhlenberg the soldier-preacher used Ecclesiastes 3 to march off to war. Seeger the folk singer reconfigured it as a hymn to peace (the key line in his version is "a time for peace, I swear it's not too late"). And Tavenner the lawyer brought Seeger into a hearing of the House Committee on Un-American activities to determine if his musical activities were sufficiently American.

The date was August 18, 1955. The place happened to be the same courthouse at Foley Square in Lower Manhattan where George Crockett was cited for contempt of court during the Smith Act trial of communist leaders. John Stephens Wood was long gone from the committee by then. The chairman was Francis E. Walter, a conservative, anti-immigration Democrat from Pennsylvania. But Tavenner ran the interrogation. Their opening exchange set the stage for all that was to come.

Mr. Tavenner: When and where were you born, Mr. Seeger?

Mr. Seeger: I was born in New York in 1919.

Mr. Tavenner: What is your profession or occupation?

Mr. Seeger: Well, I have worked at many things, and my main
      profession is a student of American folklore, and I make my
      living as a banjo picker—sort of damning, in some people's
      opinion.

Tavenner calmly and persistently tried to connect Seeger to specific concerts and actions that involved communists, and Seeger consistently refused to be pinned down or categorized or tainted by association, while never invoking his Fifth Amendment rights. He wanted to talk to the committee about the meaning of his songs. He said he would not answer any questions about his associations, or his philosophical or religious beliefs, or how he voted, calling them improper questions to ask any American.

In one exchange with Chairman Walter, Seeger said, "I feel that my whole life I have never done anything of a conspiratorial nature and I resent very much and very deeply the implication of being called before this Committee that in some way because my opinions may be different from yours . . . that I am any less of an American than anybody else. I love my country very deeply, sir."

"Why don't you make a little contribution toward preserving its institutions?" Walter asked.

"I feel that my whole life is a contribution," Seeger responded. "That is why I would like to tell you about it."

"I don't want to hear about it," Walter said.

Tavenner took over again from there. Did Seeger perform at a concert sponsored by the Communist Party on May Day? Did he sing at the Unity summer camp for socialist and communist youths at Wingdale Lodge in New York State? Did he first sing his song "If I Had a Hammer" at a fund-raiser for the Foley Square defendants at St. Nicholas Arena? Did he know about Elia Kazan's testimony that the Communist Party used entertainers for Communist Party functions, that it was all part of their propaganda effort?

"I have sung for Americans of every political persuasion, and I am proud that I never refuse to sing to an audience, no matter what religion or color of their skin, or situation in life," Seeger testified. "I have sung in hobo jungles, and I have sung for the Rockefellers, and I am proud that I have never refused to sing for anybody."

Turning to Chairman Walter, whose district included the coal mines of eastern Pennsylvania, Seeger added that his songs cut across social and cultural divides and spoke to basic humanity. "And that is why I would love to be able to tell you about these songs, because I feel that you would agree with me more, sir. I know many beautiful songs from your home county, Carbon and Monroe, and I hitchhiked through there and stayed in the homes of miners."

Tavenner did not like that answer. All he wanted to know was whether Seeger ever sang at functions of the Communist Party. The exchanges grew testier.

> Mr. Tavenner: I hand you a photograph which was taken of the May Day parade in New York City in 1952, which shows the front rank of a group of individuals, and one is in a uniform with military cap and insignia, and carrying a placard entitled CENSORED. Will you examine it please and state whether or not that is a photograph of you?
>
> Mr. Seeger: It is like Jesus Christ when asked by Pontius Pilate, "Are you king of the Jews?"
>
> Chairman Walter: Stop that!

The banjo-picker came out of the hearing unscathed, but not for long. The committee in due time cited him for contempt of Congress. He faced the possibility of time in jail before the conviction was overturned.

Pete Seeger was not quite up there with Paul Robeson or Beethoven in my mother's pantheon of musicians, but he seemed part of the same extended family. He and his fellow singers in the Weavers—Ronnie Gilbert, Lee Hays, and Fred Hellerman—had been active in the Henry Wallace presidential campaign in 1948, as had my parents, and were known for their embrace of songs from around the world about unions, working people, and justice. In 1949 Seeger and Robeson had performed at the concert to raise funds for the Civil Rights Congress and the Foley Square defendants near Peekskill, New York, where they were pelted with rocks and stones by an angry crowd of local citizens roiling with anticommunist fervor. Seeger had also recorded songs from the Spanish Civil War, including "Viva La Quince Brigada" and "Si Me Quieres Escribir," both of which had deep resonance in my family.

"Viva La Quince Brigada" means "Long live the 15th Brigade," or International Brigade, whose thousands of volunteers included Uncle Bob. "Si Me Quieres Escribir" is a song that reflects what Bob and his comrades in the Mackenzie-Papineau battalion experienced during the war. "If you want to write me, you know where I am posted": the lyrics evoke the battle of the Ebro River, the pontoon bridges across it, the enemy near Gandesa inviting soldiers to eat shrapnel shells and fragmentation grenades, the hatred for that son-of-a-bitch Francisco Franco ("que el hijo de puto Franco").

And the words echoed through the generations. At a Cummins family reunion in 2017, my brother, Jim, and cousin Peggy, both teachers of Spanish, sang "Si Me Quieres Escribir" with great feeling, just as Bob once had and just as Seeger had.

BY THE SUMMER of 1955 we had been back in Detroit for six months, and it felt like home, especially since we had a new little sister in the family. Her name was Wendy, born at Women's Hospital on June 27 while we other kids were shipped over to Ann Arbor to be with our grandparents and a crew of cousins. "They had a very hectic two weeks of it, but things are settling back to normal now," my mother wrote to her brother Phil in a letter in which she alerted him to "baby number 4." Wendy had red hair and blue eyes, and I felt especially proud of her name because I had suggested it. We had returned from Cleveland in time for me to go to school the previous spring semester at Angell Elementary, and there was a girl in my kindergarten class that I had a crush on whose name was Wendy. Dad always thought of my sister Wendy as the family's good luck charm, an omen of better times to come. She was far more than that, but it was one way for him to sustain his optimism through all his ordeals.

We spent that summer in a second-story flat at 9015 Dexter. The flat was long and dark, and to a boy of almost six it seemed the back windows looked out on hell while the view from the deck in front was of heaven. The phobia I have about rats started then, when I would look out a rear window at dusk and see a swirl of rats scurrying in and out of the garage. At least once a rat jumped out of a garbage can. There were rat holes in what passed for a backyard. As our father would say, it could have been worse—none of us got bit by a rat. The upper porch facing Dexter was our hangout. Mom was out there almost every day sunbathing Wendy, and Jim and Jean and I spent hours there observing the passing scene. In Detroit that meant one thing above all else: the newest models of cars from GM, Ford, Chrysler, Nash, and Studebaker. Before the summer was over, we could identify them all as they drove up and down the street below, from the two-tone DeSoto Fireflite and Plymouth Belvedere to my favorite, the Nash Metropolitan, a cute little pudge-on-wheels in pastel pink or blue-green that looked as if it had floated happily out of a Saturday-morning cartoon.

We were Detroiters. We swam at the Rouge Pool, took swimming lessons at the Fisher Y, drank Vernors ginger ale, rooted for the Tigers and Lions, shopped at Hudson's department store, watched *Lunch with Soupy Sales* on WXYZ-TV, rode the magical trains at the Detroit Zoo, and took the Bob-Lo boat out to the amusement park on the Ontario side of the Detroit River. Jim learned the leg-slapping rhythms of "Hambone" from his black friends. Jeannie heard "Shake, Rattle, and Roll" on the jukebox at a diner and was told by Peggy, the oldest and hippest of the cousins, that this was a new kind of music called "rock and roll."

Ann Arbor was only forty-two miles away, a soothing retreat where we enjoyed not only the uplift of a university town but also the wonders of a nearby farm that our Cummins grandparents owned. The black walnut trees at the edge of a deep woods enfolding a lily-padded pond with croaking frogs and dragonflies. The creaky old gray wooden barn stacked with hay, the arbor of seeded grapes, the patches of wild blackberries and cultivated rows of Kentucky Wonder beans, the ancient rock and the rolling hills out to the back acres. Our grandparents were planning a move from Henry Street to that farm when we returned to Detroit; the foundation of their new house would soon be laid, a modern split-level of redwood and cherry with a rear picture window overlooking a peach orchard. This house, with its sturdy foundation, represented the emotional foundation for our good American family, making everything feel stable despite tragedy, uncertainty, and upheaval.

Family was all around. Bob had remarried; Aunt Kay came from Ohio and loved books and sports and brought a sense of order. They still lived in the house on Pingree that Bob had once shared with his sister, Barbara Edmonds, but Barbara and her husband, John, had moved with their children, Peggy and Alan, out to the booming suburb of Warren, where they lived in a ranch house and both eventually found jobs as librarians. Phil was coming home at last; the new house on the farm would have a basement room just for him, down the hall from the freezer where Grandmother kept her prized black walnut cookies. Mom's younger sister, Jean, and her brood, the Chulaks, the largest and most rambunctious of the extended family, were on the move from one town to another in the Chicago area, where big Uncle Joe Chulak worked as a union organizer. Mom and Aunt Jean were close, and so were all the cousins, gathering whenever possible in Ann Arbor or one of their houses.

My father, the newspaperman born with ink in his blood, was out of the business for the first time in more than twenty years, going back to his high school days as sports editor of the *Lincoln Log*, with the exception of his stint in the army during World War II. He had been fired from two big-city dailies in Detroit and Cleveland after Bereniece Baldwin spoke his name in Room 740. He had no interest in returning to his past life in the communist orbit of the *Daily Worker*, and there was nowhere else in journalism for him to turn. The FBI made it clear that its agents would follow him wherever he went and whenever he applied for a job. They had let the *Cleveland Plain Dealer* know about his history, and he assumed they would do it again. He was on the blacklist. With a wife and four young children, he needed any job he could get, and he took one as a salesman for a company that provided wholesale picnic supplies, birthday party favors, safety programs, and advertising specialties and other items for trade unions and service organizations.

Organizational Services Inc. was run by Irving and Betty Richter, who had known our parents from the old days. Richter was a former communist, but there was more to him than that. He had studied economics in the early 1930s at the University of Wisconsin under the famed labor historian Selig Perlman, who was a progressive and sympathetic to the working class but not a radical or communist himself; in fact he argued that strong unions could be a bulwark against communism. In the circular nature of life, Richter went on to become an official with several New Deal projects, including the Works Progress Administration, then joined the United Auto Workers as its legislative lobbyist before losing that post when Walter Reuther, who agreed with Perlman, took over the union in 1947 and pushed out its communist and radical elements. The purge at the UAW included not only Richter but also lawyer Maurice Sugar and his disciple, George Crockett—so there, perhaps, was the connection to my father.

OSI was not a communist front; it was just what it appeared to be, a capitalist enterprise in the world of sales that specialized in unions. The company had a store on Grand River that we visited a few times. To a six-year-old, it felt like a five-and-dime, with kitchen gadgets and toys and balloons, though I don't remember seeing any slingshots or squirt guns. If my father was not quite a character out of an Arthur Miller play, if it would be unfair to compare him to Willy Loman, there is no doubt that he was unsuited for this job and unhappy in it. He took it to survive. "We sensed that the job was humiliating for Dad, although this remained unsaid," Jean recalled. "Cummins inhibitions, McCarthy-era discretion, and perhaps a family culture of tact that kept us from alluding to the situation."

Jean's assessment would apply to more than the sales job. The stress and psychological pain our parents felt during those years went largely unexpressed through seven moves, four kids, and the blacklist. The Cummins way, since my grandparents' childhood in Kansas, was to endure, neither boast nor complain too much, and Dad's way was to block out the uncomfortable as much as possible to keep going. We saw only a few outward signs of his inner turmoil. He smoked too much, and nervously, often putting out a cigarette and then plucking the butt out of the ashtray and relighting it, and he had what seemed to me to be a low rumbling murmur of nerves that sounded like a motor idling deep in his throat, a disconcerting noise I noticed especially when we were seated at the dinner table. We were by no means perfect kids, often teasing or defying our mother, and Dad tended to overreact when he came home and heard about it. Those were the few times I saw his anger, but it seemed just a show meant to demonstrate concern for his wife, who took up most of the child-rearing burden. Now and then he took off his belt and threatened to use it as a punishment strap, but he never caught me, or maybe never wanted to catch me.

The FBI visited the OSI office on what the Bureau called a "pretext" and determined that my father worked there. They had nothing more to say about it yet kept following his movements. They recorded our address on Dexter in their files, and when after several months we moved to a house on Cortland Avenue, less than a mile away but in a more middle-class neighborhood, they recorded that as well. "Elliott Maraniss resides at 4511 Cortland Ave., Detroit, and is employed by Organizational Services, Inc., 10200 Grand River Blvd, Detroit. Informant identified Subject as being active in Progressive Party of Michigan, 1949–1950. [Blank] advised that Subject was affiliated with *Michigan Herald* in 1947. Informants report no known recent CP or related activity on part of the Subject."

Buying the house was our mother's idea; when possible, she wanted us to have our own place rather than rent, wherever we lived, to make our lives feel less transient. And this was a real house, painted green, with two full floors, three bedrooms, and a yard covered with lilies of the valley. The major selling point was that it was a block from Winterhalter, one of the finest elementary schools in Detroit. The neighborhood was historically Jewish but in transition as more African Americans moved in; the school was integrated, though majority white. I went to first grade there, and even in that early grade we had homeroom and separate classes in civics, science, reading, art, music, and other subjects. Jeannie won a contest to take home a class snake, which she named Adlai, in honor of Adlai Stevenson, who was running for president again. Before the summer was out, the snake made its escape, slithering away, and soon enough Stevenson lost again to Eisenhower.

Jim was in another school, in junior high already. He knew things about the world that I felt I could never know, and, though it would not be true later, he was physically stronger than me and might have resented that my asthma kept him up at night and drew sympathy from our mother. Connected or not, I remember how he would pin me to the ground in the yard near the lilies of the valley and pretend he was a Nazi SS officer interrogating me. "Vcrc do you live!?" he would ask in a bad German accent, and when I answered he would execute a sharp left-right-left slap across my cheeks and shout, "Oh, you lie!"

This was just brothers at play, not exactly Frank Tavenner or Chairman Wood interrogating our father.

EVEN AS THE Red-hunting fervor ebbed, a variation of that boyhood slapping game was still being played by the House Committee on Un-American Activities. In June 1956, in what seemed like an effort to regain the spotlight, the committee turned its attention to Arthur Miller, who was everywhere in the news. Miller had traveled some distance from his days at Abraham Lincoln High and the University of Michigan, not only as a renowned playwright but as a celebrity. He was dating and about to marry the world's most lustrous movie star, Marilyn Monroe.

For their central case in a larger probe of the entertainment industry, committee investigators had spent six months digging into Miller's background. "The most important subject under investigation is Arthur Miller, the playwright," Donald T. Appell wrote to his colleague William Wheeler on January 13. Operating out of an office in Fullerton, California, Wheeler was the committee's West Coast gumshoe who had done much of the legwork for the Hollywood hearings. Appell, based in Washington, had already visited Michigan and New York to see what he could find on Miller and was disappointed at first that he had failed to round up cooperative witnesses, meaning no one would name Miller. "This necessitates full and complete investigation" of Miller as a hostile witness, he concluded.

Life imitating art imitating life: HUAC was writing its own version of *The Crucible*.

Wheeler wrote back that he had discussed Miller with the actor Lee J. Cobb but did not get much. "Mr. Cobb has advised that he only vaguely knew Miller, having met him during the rehearsals of the play

Death of a Salesman. Mr. Cobb stated that he does not know if Arthur Miller was ever a member of the CP. Also that conversations with Miller only related to the play and had no political overtones." Wheeler drilled deeper into the Hollywood network, but it was essentially a dry hole.

Appell had better success in New York. Working with confidential sources, he learned, among other things, that Miller had once applied for membership to the CP's Stuyvesant Club in New York and in 1947 had attended at least one meeting, and perhaps more, of party writers in Manhattan. Appell also unearthed evidence that Miller had offered scripts of his antiwar play *All My Sons* for sale to benefit the World Youth Festival held that year in Prague. The U.S. government considered the youth festival a communist-controlled event. In developing a chronology on Miller, Appell could link him to party involvement no later than 1947, nearly a decade earlier, but that was enough to try to call him before the committee. The assertion was that he had received passport number 54857 on May 1, 1947, by fraudulent means by claiming that he was not a member of any subversive organization.

On June 1, Appell sent Wheeler a package that included a subpoena he was directed to serve on Miller, along with instructions to travel to Nevada, to find the playwright. Miller was at Pyramid Lake outside Reno to obtain a quickie divorce from his first wife so that he could marry Monroe, a romance that prompted Director Hoover to denounce the actress as "the darling of the left-wing intelligentsia." It took Wheeler several days to find Miller in Reno, but he finally caught up with him on June 8 at a law office across the street from the Mapes Hotel. Miller had been tipped off that Wheeler was looking for him. The name, he noted later, rang a bell: "I had read about this diabolically clever investigator, who had had much success in bringing film people to see the light. I wanted to know what it felt like to be worked over by a talent like that." After handing Miller the subpoena, Wheeler chatted with him about the weather, then about his friend Lee J. Cobb, who had once played Willy Loman on Broadway but had also named names before the committee. When Wheeler said that perhaps Miller would like to talk to him again, Miller said he would not discuss any of his activities until he consulted his lawyers in New York. He told Wheeler that he had yet to file the divorce papers. Wheeler left without getting much but reported back to Appell that the conversation lasted for about a half hour and that Miller was "exceptionally friendly."

Miller's lawyers delayed his appearance before the committee until the divorce was finalized. On June 20, Miller's mother and wife-to-be accompanied him to Penn Station in New York, where he would catch the train to Washington. "All I could think of was the waste my trip implied. It was all for absolutely nothing, except that it would cost tens of thousands of dollars in legal fees," Miller later wrote. Monroe, he observed, was "trying gallantly not to seem unhappy," while his mother "actually succeeded in pretending nothing ominous was happening and talked about Marilyn's clothes." When he reached the platform stairway and turned around, the two women were arm in arm. That evening in Washington, he visited the home of his lawyer, Joseph Rauh, a noted civil liberties advocate. At one point Rauh excused himself to take a phone call. When he returned he said to Miller, "How would you like to *not* have to go into the hearing tomorrow?" Miller was puzzled. Rauh explained that he had been talking to an intermediary for the committee chairman, who said the hearing could be canceled "provided Marilyn agreed to be photographed shaking hands with him." Miller laughed it off.

The hearing room on Capitol Hill on June 21 was packed. I. F. Stone was there, along with scores of other reporters, including a contingent from the foreign press. This was not some unknown *Michigan Daily* alumnus like Bob Cummins or Elliott Maraniss being grilled; this was *the* Arthur Miller. Miller declared that he would willingly answer questions about his past activities but not those of others. He would not invoke the Fifth Amendment, but nor would he name names. The staffer handling the interrogation was Richard Arens, the committee secretary, whom Miller later described as "a short fellow with a shaved head and a square pug face, and he looked as though life had nastily disappointed him in every conceivable way." Arens, prepped for this task by Frank Tavenner, presented Miller with one document after another intended to show his communist or radical affiliations. If it was anything to do with Miller's past, he readily acknowledged it, sometimes saying "Yes" before Arens asked the question. "I remember feeling, as I glanced at one after another of the protests he handed me for identification, how fatuous it had all been," Miller wrote. "I remember thinking that my influence on my own history had been nil." Yes, he had once believed with passionate moral clarity that Marxism was the hope for mankind, but he had done so before understanding a different reality: the abject terror of a totalitarian Soviet regime that had murdered and starved millions of its own citizens. And he had never advocated the violent overthrow of the U.S. government.

Chairman Walter and the other congressmen sounded like small-minded theater operators who preferred happy musicals to sober dramas. They told Miller how much they wished he would write plays that glorified the American story, apparently not appreciating that he thought HUAC itself was a symbol of the nation's darker impulses. They questioned how he could claim to be a champion of freedom of speech and yet lambaste one of his fellow writers, Ezra Pound, for Pound's pro-fascist and anti-Semitic commentaries during World War II, as if, Miller said later, they expected a Jewish citizen to ignore the Holocaust.

Miller acknowledged to the committee that he had attended five or six meetings of Communist Party writers in Manhattan in 1947. He said that at those meetings he criticized and rejected the dictate that writers in their works should follow the party line. Arens then asked Miller to tell the committee who had been in the room when he entered those meetings, citing a specific writer. Miller did not want to answer. He felt the committee was "trying to break an implicit understanding among human beings that you don't use their names to bring trouble on them or cooperate in deforming the democratic doctrine of the sanctity of peaceful association." He asked the committee to suspend the question to a later time, and eventually left the hearing without answering. If he had invoked the Fifth Amendment, his refusal would have been legal. Refusing to name names on personal moral grounds placed him in contempt of Congress.

SOON AFTER THE school year started in September 1956, Dad was missing from our house on Cortland Avenue. He had gone ahead of the rest of us, again, to start yet another new job. The FBI agents knew all about it. Special Agent Clive G. Matthews went to Davenport, Iowa, and talked to Mrs. Lyle Gadient at the Davenport Credit Bureau, who told him she found notes in her files about Elliott Maraniss rooming at 1106 East Rusholme Street in Davenport and being employed at *Labor's Daily* in the neighboring suburb of Bettendorf. On that same day, Matthews contacted Mrs. Bertha Booth at the Rusholme Street address "under a suitable pretext" and learned the following: "For approximately two months . . . Elliott Maraniss occupied a rented room in her home at the above address, he obviously regarded such quarters as fairly temporary at the time he took them and retained them only long enough to find suitable quarters for his wife and family, with a view to moving them to the Davenport area from Detroit."

Our mother felt the weight of the move, as usual. We had little money, and Dad had upset her by investing a few thousand dollars in Organizational Services Inc. with funds he had borrowed from his mother in Coney Island. When he went in to tell the Richters that he was leaving for a new job, they persuaded him to let the company keep the money for a few more years, and it was only at Mom's insistence that he sheepishly returned to the OSI office and retrieved it. Mom was also the one stuck trying to sell the Cortland Avenue house less than a year after buying it. She said later, "The fairly well-off older woman who sold us the house—happily in the first place—now chided me, saying that she wouldn't have sold me the house if she had known I was going to sell it, to which I instantly and honestly replied that I wouldn't have bought it if I had known." The true source of the previous owner's ill temper was that we had sold the house to a black couple with two young sons, upsetting many white neighbors and leaving the inaccurate perception that we had bought and sold the house quickly as part of a blockbusting scheme perpetrated by bloodsucking real estate companies. Once the house was sold and we were ready to leave, Mom felt the weight had lifted. "It was a chance for Elliott to get back into newspaper work, which really was the most important thing to us both," she recalled. "It was a new beginning, in a new state, a new town."

We left Detroit around December 1, Mom and four children under age twelve. Jeannie didn't want to leave Detroit for a small town, Jim was sick of moving, Wendy was a baby, and I had no strong feelings either way. We traveled west across the bottom of Michigan by train, through Dearborn, Ann Arbor, Jackson, Battle Creek, and Kalamazoo, before dipping toward the Indiana line. Shards of memory stick in the brain for inexplicable reasons. I remember hearing at the stop in Niles that Floyd Patterson had won the heavyweight championship in a bout with Archie Moore. I felt crushed. Only seven years old, yet the ageless Archie somehow was my man. Once we reached Davenport, we reconnected with Dad and stayed downtown at the Hotel Blackhawk for a few nights. We had stopped at roadside motels before, but this was my first time in a multistory hotel with an elevator. We ate most of our meals nearby at Bishop's cafeteria, another exotic experience, before moving into a rented house on Grant Street in Bettendorf, a few blocks up the hill from the muddy Mississippi River.

If this was a new start for my father, it was a quixotic one. The newspaper he joined was the *Quint-City Labor's Daily*, the local version of the national *Labor's Daily* published by the International Typographical Union. "Quint" stood for the five tightly bunched cities of Davenport and Bettendorf in Iowa and Rock Island, Moline, and East Moline across the river in Illinois. The paper was a five-days-a-week morning daily that grew out of a strike by ITU local 107 against the *Daily Times* and *Morning Democrat* of Davenport, the *Rock Island Argus*, and the *Moline Daily Dispatch*. The strike began when the papers introduced a form of automation that allowed wire service copy to be set automatically without being touched by human Linotype operators. There were similar strikes during that era all around the country, early battles in a lopsided war between newspaper back shops and owners that would drag on for the next twenty-five years as advances made more and more jobs obsolete. But unions were still strong then, at their peak numerically, and the future is harder to see when people are fighting for their livelihoods.

By the time my father arrived in Bettendorf, the *Quint-City Labor's Daily* had become a sanctuary for a ragtag collection of iconoclasts, outsiders, and blacklisted leftists looking for a second chance. He fit in.

After spending nearly two years involuntarily away from the profession he loved, he was thirsting to get back into a newsroom. He heard about the job through old connections from his past life. In search of talent, the editor, Al Maund, contacted Carl Haessler, the founder of Federated Press, a leftist news service, who had heard about my father from his Detroit friends. Dad and Maund talked for an hour over the phone, feeling each other out, and when Maund said he could offer a salary of a hundred dollars a week, Dad was in. If this paper had uncertain prospects for survival, at least he would not have to worry about getting fired because of what had happened in front of the House Un-American Activities Committee. In this crowd, that would more likely be viewed as a badge of honor than a reason for dismissal. "I knew it was a shaky proposition, that it wasn't going to last very long, but I wanted to start fresh, shake the old place, pull up stakes," he told me later. "I just left. I didn't think I was deserting Detroit."

Alfred Maund was a maverick from New Orleans who had bounced around the South. He wrote editorials briefly for the *New Orleans Item*, worked at the *Louisville Courier-Journal* in Kentucky, and taught at Livingston State Teachers College, a white institution in the heart of Alabama's black belt. He had devoted his life to fighting southern racism and had joined with communists and socialists in that effort. Unlike my father, Maund did not think of himself as a professional newspaperman, but as a novelist. He had just completed the manuscript of his first novel, *The Big Boxcar*, when he and his wife, Dorothy, a social worker, and their twelve-year-old son, Steve, arrived in Bettendorf a few months before my father. It was their first time living in the North. *The Big Boxcar*, with its six vivid black characters, including a rape victim, a murderer, and a drug addict, riding the rails through Jim Crow Alabama, would receive positive reviews in the *New Yorker*, the *Saturday Evening Post*, and the *New York Times*, which described Maund's southern landscape as "a world of impoverishment, brutality, segregation, and sordidness, made the more compelling by reason of an occasional gesture of charity or protest by sympathetic whites." Jeannie read it later and was "quite excited about the racy language and sex."

The newspaper offices were in an old fire station—newsroom and advertising in front, divided by a rail, and printshop and press in back. In the division of labor within the newsroom, Maund wrote the editorials, worked with the ITU on financing the operation, and served as the public face of the newspaper, while my father ran the daily operation as a combination city editor, news editor, and one-man copydesk. He also wrote a sports column for the national edition of *Labor's Daily* under the pseudonym Jimmy Moran, and had two nicknames around the office: his old standby, Ace, and now also the Ol' Railbird, which he used when writing about horse racing, a subject about which he knew next to nothing.

My father's politics were still liberal—his sentiments then and always were with the underdog—but he had long since turned away from his past attachments to the Communist Party and viewed the Soviet Union, which had recently crushed a freedom movement in Hungary, as an oppressive force. He did not write about this directly, but it came out obliquely in a sports column about the violence of football, of all unlikely places. "A suffering world, grieving over man's inhumanity to man in Hungary," his column began, before working its way to arguing that the National Football League was rife with hypocrisy and violence.

The staff included Nigel Hampton, a jazz-loving hip southerner who had been Maund's student at Livingston; Guy Lewis, a lanky Iowan from Cedar Rapids who covered Davenport City Hall and cops and courts; and Eugene Feldman, a shy, bespectacled, lisping, young communist from Montgomery, Alabama, who subsisted on sardines and crackers in his darkened room and had been followed around the country by Red-seeking hounds from the American Legion. Along with covering news and features in the river towns, Hampton wrote a column called This I Can't Believe, a sarcastic take on Edward R. Murrow's CBS radio broadcast *This I Believe*. Feldman, along with working the switchboard, wrote a column called Fables and Foibles, gentle prose with about-town ruminations and fictional tales that often ended with the admonition "Feed the birds." Uncle Eugene, as we knew him, was very popular with old women readers who had no notion of his radical politics. Bob Meloon, a printer with a flair for page composition, worked with my father on the layouts, and the two also took turns writing a television column.

It did not take long for the reporters to learn why my father was called Ace. He performed with skill and professionalism every job he was assigned at the newspaper. While Maund described himself as having a "terrorist personality," meaning he cared more about making a point than being balanced, he thought Dad had an underlying decency that permeated his work. "Your father would show mercy," he once told me. But he was also no-nonsense, as Nigel Hampton quickly learned. "In my first week or so on the job I had written a news story that had a 'punch' ending," Hampton wrote in a letter to me decades later. "When the paper came out, my last few paragraphs were missing (filled by an ad, of course). I went to Elliott to complain, and without even looking up from some copy he was editing, he barked, 'No goddamn prima donnas on this newspaper!' Had it not been for your mother's warmth, I might never have got close enough to the crusty ol' Railbird to learn to love him."

Unable to afford the wire services for national and world news, the M and M boys, Maund and Maraniss, improvised. They started work around noon and lived close enough to the office to walk home for dinner, take notes while listening to the evening news on television and radio, and return to write up accounts of what they heard. My father, a fast if messy two-fingered typist, would also transcribe the evening broadcast of *Edward P. Morgan and the News* on the ABC radio network. Maund, with his southern connections, conscripted a civil rights activist in Montgomery to write about the bus boycott and its aftermath. The stories ran under the byline Shubel Morgan, which keen students of American racial history knew was the alias of abolitionist John Brown. They also published an edited version of the weekly radio address "Hello, Wisconsin" delivered by William T. Evjue, owner and publisher of the *Capital Times* in Madison. My father wrote a box next to each column describing Evjue as "a nationally known liberal newspaperman who wages a constant campaign against corruption in government and forces which threaten to undermine the inherent freedoms of the people."

They printed fifty thousand copies of the paper in the back room and charged five cents a copy, while also giving away bundles for free to railroad workers and porters to distribute up and down the lines all the way to St. Louis. The strike newspaper was popular with the railroad men, as the Maunds learned when they put their son, Steve, on the train for New Orleans to visit his grandparents at Christmastime. It was ferocious winter weather, and Dorothy Maund was worried about her boy traveling alone, but as soon as the conductors learned that he was the son of the editor of *Quint-City Labor's Daily* they treated him like family, handing him off by hand all the way south.

JEANNIE CONSIDERED BETTENDORF a backward move for everyone in the family but our father. "Our house was mean and cramped, there was no cultural life to speak of, [and the] schools were pretty bad," she recalled. "As always, we were good little stoics who never complained, but made the best of the meager opportunities on offer, such as a traveling carnival, a local cafeteria, a small library that seemed to carry nothing but Nancy Drew, of which Mom disapproved." There was also an Iowana Ice Cream dairy down the street, a good pizza place in Moline, and the riverbank as a playground, but not much else. The poverty was different from Detroit's, more southern and rural. A boy with a lame leg who lived in a trailer down by the river would stop by our house most mornings to walk Jeannie to Washington Elementary School. There was also a girl in her class who "always dressed in dungarees, with greasy, dirty hair." On the other side of town lived the golden girls and boys who had nice, modern ranch houses and new cars and better clothes. We were the outsiders and clung to each other. I spent a lot of time reading *Pogo* comic books. The Okefenokee Swamp full of talking critters seemed no more fantastic than anything else I had encountered in my young life. Albert Alligator was my favorite.

Our loneliness eased some in early 1957, when Uncle Bob and his wife, Kay, moved to Bettendorf with their daughters, Rachel and Sarah. Uncle Bob had been working as a television repairman in Detroit for the past few years and seized the chance to get back into newspapers when our father recommended him for an open reporting job. But not long after the Cummins family arrived and Bob started at the paper,

Maund announced to the staff that they were bleeding losses and had run out of money to continue as a daily. The ITU's national office in Indianapolis offered to give them $10,000 in seed money to turn the paper into a weekly, but Maund was ready to give up the project entirely. No one else was. That night Dad and the reporters took Maund out to a nightclub on the edge of town. "They buttered me up, buttered me up, buttered me up. And, of course, the buttering up didn't impress me one whit," Maund recalled. "It was the fact that I recognized that all these people were trying, had to, make a living. . . . I felt responsible, so I said okay."

The last edition of the daily came out on Friday, February 15. "So Long—For a While" was the headline in the box on the upper left of the front page. "With this issue the Quint-City edition of *Labor's Daily* is ending publication as a daily newspaper. But *Labor's Daily* is not dead." During the hiatus, Maund and my father studied the operations of successful weeklies in Oklahoma and suburban Chicago. They came away with plans to focus on feature stories, columns, occasional investigations, television listings, and inexpensive ad rates for local advertisers. The staff, including Dad and Uncle Bob, would double as advertising salesmen. Although this was meant to keep the paper alive and boost salaries at the same time (an extra fifteen dollars a week), Maund later called it "the worst idea in the history of journalism. It was like hitching thoroughbreds to plows." My brother, Jim, and Steve Maund were enlisted among the fleet of paperboys who distributed copies to households around the quint-cities and made a penny for every nickel they collected. A want ad seeking carriers said that boys could be eleven or older, but girls, according to Iowa law, had to be at least eighteen.

The first edition of the *Quint-City Special* came out on March 22. Among the few special moments in its existence was an investigative article by Bob Cummins about a subject close to his heart. His first wife had died of polio, and the deadly disease was still around in early 1957, though in the process of being eradicated due to lifesaving vaccines. The incidence of polio in America the previous year had been at the lowest level since 1947, but the largest national outbreak had been in the Midwest, and its epicenter was Chicago. With what was then known as the summer polio season approaching, Bob discovered that the Rock Island County Medical Society in Illinois had ignored an offer by the local polio chapter to provide $3,000 for an inoculation program. The medical society, he wrote, decided to turn down a program of mass injection in favor of individual shots through family physicians. In a companion editorial, Maund reported that neighboring clinics in Illinois and Iowa had set up public clinics and dispensed thousands of shots, in contrast to the Rock Island County Medical Society's selfish "determination to keep ironclad control over the Salk serum, administering it only on a paid, private-patient basis."

But the newspaper's end was near. Going from a daily to a weekly was a losing proposition. "Our funds shrank remorselessly," Maund recalled. "Finally I wrote a letter to [ITU president] Woodruff Randolph telling him of the attrition and didn't predict a turnaround—nor did I ask for more money." When my father saw the letter, he told Maund, "You are asking him to shut us down!" And that is what Randolph did. Maund said it came as a relief. "Everybody was so beat from their dual roles that there was no shock, no wrath, no grief. All our tears had been spent on the demise of the *Quint-City Labor's Daily*." The *Quint-City Special* was dead before Memorial Day.

THE MCCARTHY ERA had come to an end by then, at least the part that included Joe McCarthy himself. He had entered Bethesda Naval Hospital on April 28 for what his wife said was knee surgery, but in fact his liver had given out after a life of hard drinking, and he died at 6:02 p.m. on May 2.

There were never any witches, some said; others said that communists were witches. But in our cramped little house on Grant Street a few blocks up from the muddy Mississippi in a small town in Iowa, it was "Ding, dong, the Witch is dead!" McCarthy in the grave at age forty-eight. He'd gone where the goblins go, below, below, below.

Three days later, the same U.S. Senate that had censured him now allowed his flower-shrouded casket into the well of the Chamber, as members of the Washington tribe, love him or hate him, paid their respects. Vice President Nixon was there, along with Joe's consigliere, Roy Cohn, and the FBI's Hoover, and Senator Charles E. Potter, the former HUAC member. Then the casket was carried down the Capitol steps and driven to the airport for the flight back to Wisconsin, the state McCarthy had called home.

IOWA TURNED OUT to be a vital decompression chamber for men and families who had been submerged for years and might now rise to the surface. The Lerner newspapers in suburban Chicago offered jobs to Maund and my father, but they demurred, and instead helped land Bob a job there at the *Life of Niles Township*, covering Skokie, Morton Grove, Niles, and Lincolnwood. He and Kay had three daughters now and a fourth on the way. He left them behind briefly in Bettendorf and stayed in a small hotel in Skokie until they could all get settled. Maund took a job with the chemical workers union, where he continued writing novels. Guy Lewis caught on at a paper in Peoria; Nigel Hampton had been drafted into the army; and Eugene Feldman found a teaching job at a Jewish school in Chicago.

It had been five years since my father was identified as an un-American American in Room 740. Five years, five cities, four kids, eight homes, two papers that fired him, three papers that folded. Now, one more move. He wrote a letter to William T. Evjue, the publisher of the newspaper in Madison that for years had challenged McCarthy's Red-baiting—the *Capital Times*. The white-haired Norwegian progressive whose Hello, Wisconsin column ran in the *Quint-City Labor's Daily* called and invited my father up to Madison for an interview. He brought along Bob Meloon, the former printer who had been part of the ITU strike since its inception. The meeting at the newspaper office on South Carroll Street down the hill from the Wisconsin State Capitol was one my father would never forget. Copies of *Quint-City Labor's Daily* were spread across the old man's desk. The pages looked so clean, neatly laid out, the writing sharp, even the television page was clear and easy to read. Evjue turned to his city editor and asked, "Why can't we put out a paper like this?"—and our lives were changed forever.

My father was hired on the spot, at $114 a week. As usual, he went ahead, staying in an apartment until he found a house for the family. It was on Chandler Street in a good neighborhood near the Henry Vilas Park Zoo. My first concern was whether I would be eaten by a lion or tiger. But at least the FBI was no longer following us.

> To: Director, FBI
> From: SAC [Subversive Activities Control], Milwaukee
> Subject: Elliott Maraniss

> A review of the Milwaukee files shows that the Subject was last reported to be a member of the CP on 11/4/47. He was last reported to have attended a CP meeting on 2/8/52. The files do not contain any record of any activity on his part during the past 5 years. Since this case no longer fits the criteria required for the Security Index, Bureau authority is requested to cancel the SI card on the Subject. Elliott Maraniss is employed as a reporter for *The Capital Times*, a Madison, Wis., daily newspaper, which is considered unfriendly to the Bureau. For this reason, it is not recommended he be interviewed.

We drove north to Madison in our old two-tone brown and tan Chevy soon after the Fourth of July, arriving in time to root for our new National League baseball team, the Milwaukee Braves of Henry Aaron and Warren Spahn, as they played their way to a pennant and eventual World Series championship over the hated Yankees. McCarthy was dead. The Supreme Court had essentially overturned the Smith Act, ruling it was unconstitutional to bring charges against American citizens solely because of their political advocacy. The effects of HUAC were still felt by Arthur Miller, who was convicted on contempt of Congress charges for not naming names before the committee, but that conviction would soon be overturned on appeal. The world was opening anew. My father had survived, though not the nickname Ace. Madison reminded him of Ann Arbor, the Big Ten university town where he had met my mother in 1939 and they had dreamed together of filling a little blue house near the stadium with children and books and music. Now all that was possible. As he would say, it could be worse.

"Well, the wanderers are wandering again," my mother wrote in a letter to her brother Phil, apprising him of the move. The children seemed happy, she said, "but I think we would all be glad to settle down in Madison for a good long time."

We were, and we did.

Epilogue

Second Acts

MADISON IS WHERE ONE STORY ENDS AND ANOTHER BE-gins. The story that ends there is the one I set out to write, but the story that begins there lends meaning to what came before. In Madison we were finally able to come up for air and breathe free. Our parents had shaken off the chains of the past with their idealism and optimism intact. They had found their way to another chance and were determined to make the most of it. Their second act was an affirmation of the strength and resilience of a family—and of the American idea.

We moved one last time after our first year in Madison, but it was only five blocks away and only because our mother kept to her policy of buying a house whenever possible to provide a sense of stability to our family. This time she found a four-bedroom house on Regent Street on the western edge of the University of Wisconsin campus at the bottom of University Heights, an old neighborhood that evoked security and permanence. There was a creaky wooden porch swing in front and a pocket porch off the dining room where Dad and I could listen to Braves games on the radio. Our perimeter was bounded on one side by the limestone monolith of the UW Field House and the gridiron hulk of Camp Randall Stadium, and on the other side by the sturdy redbrick Tudor glory of Randall Elementary School and on up the hill four blocks to West High. Beyond that we were surrounded by water, three lakes that define the city. We quickly came to know all the public beaches, from Vilas to B. B. Clarke to the Willows, and though we were not particularly religious, Lake Wingra, Lake Monona, and Lake Mendota became our holy waters, protecting us from distant evil and baptizing us in our new lives.

If we had benefactors, they were the people at the *Capital Times*, especially old Bill Evjue, the white-haired publisher, friend and disciple of Fighting Bob LaFollette, the original progressive, and Miles McMillin, the square-jawed, gum-smacking, twinkle-eyed editorial editor. They all certainly knew about my father's history, but they never made a big deal of it. This was not a situation where he had to repent and genuflect and name names. Those days were over. They seemed to appreciate that he had learned from his past and that in any case he was a natural-born newspaperman who could bring a vital ink-in-his-blood ingenuity to their paper. While they were liberal capitalists with no love for communism, they had spent more than a decade fighting the inquisitions of Joe McCarthy and the House Un-American Activities Committee and considered those the greatest threats to American values. Many newspapers around the country had been intimidated by McCarthy, but the *Capital Times* stood out as his fearless home-state nemesis, attacking the hypocrisy of the self-righteous hyper-American long before he was exposed as a reckless zealot during the nationally televised Army-McCarthy hearings.

When my father, in his unread statement to HUAC in 1952, wrote about the importance of a press that was defiant and free, he could not know at the time that a model of what he had in mind was the paper that would hire him five years later. "Give the people the truth and the freedom to discuss it and all will go well." That was the motto of the feisty little afternoon paper. It was a lofty ideal that no one could reach; not the *Capital Times*, not the public, not the government—but a worthy principle nonetheless. On the Fourth of July 1951, during the heat of the McCarthy era eight months before my father's Americanism was challenged, the paper had put that public spirit to an extraordinary test. One of its young reporters, John Patrick Hunter, typed up the preamble to the Declaration of Independence and combined it with a petition listing six of the ten amendments to the Bill of Rights, along with the Fifteenth Amendment granting black men the right to vote. Then Hunter roamed Henry Vilas Park, stopping in at picnic celebrations to see if citizens would sign his petition. He gave the people the nation's foundational truth and it did not go well. Of the 112 people he asked to sign the petition, only one did. Twenty accused him of being a communist.

That experiment said more about the climate of fear in the early 1950s than about a university town known for its well-educated citizens. Madison by the time we arrived provided the setting my parents needed to survive and thrive. Like Ann Arbor, it was a forgiving and unpressurized midwestern haven that encouraged intelligence, nuance, and freedom of thought. The adage of the *Capital Times* echoed the university's defining credo, a declaration of academic freedom invoked in 1894 in defense of a professor's radical thinking: "Whatever may be the limitations which trammel inquiry elsewhere we believe the great state University of Wisconsin should ever encourage that continual and fearless sifting and winnowing by which alone the truth can be found."

A circle closes here, rounding back to the depiction of my father with which I started this book while considering the imperfect *S* in his statement to HUAC. His history shaped the public persona that emerged in Madison, but mostly in positive ways. It left him with a righteous anger that burned far below the surface and did not dominate his personality, which seemed remarkably free of bitterness. In Madison he was open to people of all ideologies unless he thought they were bullies, snobs, or demagogues who claimed to have all the answers and assumed an air of moral superiority. His politics changed, from radical to classic liberal, but not his values or belief in America—a generous spirit that he had carried with him since his days at Abraham Lincoln High and that he expressed so powerfully in his letters to my mother during the war. There was more to his philosophy than the expansive inclusiveness of Emerson and Whitman. He also had a sardonic, contrarian side, captured by his fondness for Mark Twain, H. L. Mencken, George Bernard Shaw, Gore Vidal, and William Hazlitt. And he often talked about the time early in his career at the Madison paper when he walked by Mr. Evjue's office and was awed to see three white-haired men talking and laughing: Evjue, Frank Lloyd Wright, and Carl Sandburg. The newspaperman, the architect, and the poet, singular, headstrong, iconoclastic representatives of the America my father loved.

As he rose from reporter to city editor to executive editor of the

Capital Times over a quarter-century in our adopted hometown, and for a time taught journalism as a lecturer at the university, he encouraged and trained scores of reporters who came into his orbit. His unwavering commitment to equality led him to bring the first black journalists onto the paper and to promote women, traditionally confined to the society pages, into important news reporting positions. His harrumphing "No goddamn prima donnas on this newspaper!" at Nigel Hampton during the Iowa days would have seemed familiar to anyone who ever worked for him. When my brother spent a college summer writing for the Madison paper, he recoiled at an assignment to interview the parents of a child killed by Winkie the elephant at the Vilas Park Zoo. "Dad, I can't do that!" he told our father, who responded by telling Jim he would be fired if he refused the order and then barked, "And don't call me Dad!" In the office he had the vocabulary and instincts of an old-school newspaperman, but this gruff demeanor was softened by his concern for people and his appreciation of the frailties of the human condition.

It is tempting to consider what-ifs as a way to assess the effects the Red Scare had on one man and his family. What if my father had not been followed for years by the FBI, and Bereniece Baldwin had not named him, and he had not been called to testify at the HUAC hearings, and he had not been fired by the *Detroit Times*?

The answers are necessarily unknowable, but I imagine they would be a mixed bag. From what I could determine, his disillusionment with communism began around the time he was called before the committee and was complete long before we reached Madison. But I doubt if we ever would have made it to Madison if not for the chain of events that began with the hearings in Detroit. That does not make what happened to our family any easier or justifiable. I'm not trying to play Professor Pangloss, presenting a "best of all possible worlds" take on misfortune. I see it as nothing more than an objective fact about unintended consequences. Although my father never particularly liked the Hearst newspaper chain, his abundant talents in the newsroom likely would have led him to an editing position at the *Detroit Times* or at another paper, perhaps even back at the *New York Times*, where he started his career as the student stringer on Coney Island. In any case, if he had stayed at

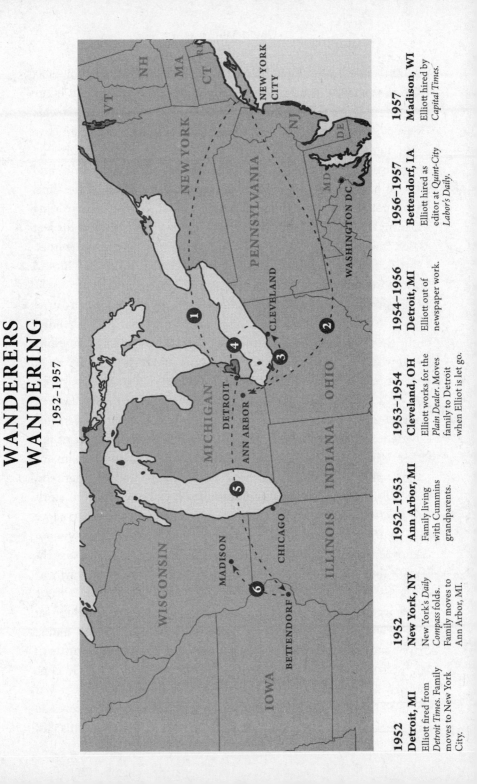

WANDERERS WANDERING

1952–1957

1952
Detroit, MI
Elliott fired from *Detroit Times*. Family moves to New York City.

1952
New York, NY
New York's *Daily Compass* folds. Family moves to Ann Arbor, MI.

1952–1953
Ann Arbor, MI
Family living with Cummins grandparents.

1953–1954
Cleveland, OH
Elliott works for the *Plain Dealer*. Moves family to Detroit when Elliott is let go.

1954–1956
Detroit, MI
Elliott out of newspaper work.

1956–1957
Bettendorf, IA
Elliott hired as editor at *Quint-City Labor's Daily*.

1957
Madison, WI
Elliott hired by *Capital Times*.

the *Detroit Times*, he would have been out of a job by the fall of 1960, when the paper folded. As his son, I am unavoidably biased, but in my own career I have worked for many first-rate editors at the *Washington Post*, and my father was as inspirational, levelheaded, and instinctive about a good story as any of them. While he took great pleasure in a journalistic fight for what he believed in, he also exuded a likability and sense of fairness. I was standing with my daughter, Sarah, at the time, so did not hear it, but family members recall a scene at her wedding when my father, at age eighty-four, was walking slowly toward his seat as Ben Bradlee, the legendary *Post* editor, announced in a stage whisper, "There's Elliott Maraniss, a great editor." Whatever compelled him to say it, it was true.

As good as Madison was for Dad, and for all of us, I see in retrospect ways that his life there was circumscribed by his past. Only a handful of the thousands of people he encountered in Madison knew anything about what had happened to him in Detroit, and even those few knew only the hazy outlines of the story. He would make clear his distaste for Joe McCarthy, Richard Nixon, and other politicians who staked their careers on Red-baiting, but he rarely if ever talked about his personal experience. As Jim told me when I started this book, that part of our father's history "was like another life, one that didn't belong to him any more at all," a dead letter that he wanted to keep dead. His desire to keep it dead meant that he could not fully express himself or his story. Late in life he began writing a memoir of sorts, but turned it into a love song to my mother, recounting her history and theirs together without acknowledging their involvement in the Communist Party and scratching out the only reference to the blacklist. I think I understand why he did this.

He wanted Madison and the world to see him and define him for who he was, who he had become, not who he once had been—and at that he succeeded. I took this Elliott for granted as I was growing up in Madison. Just as I had never deeply thought about what he had gone through in 1952 until I read his unread statement to HUAC, it was not until I undertook this book that I even considered the unexpressed anxiety he might have carried all those years in Madison that his past would be dredged up in public again and used to characterize him as something he was not.

LIFE UNFOLDS IN unexpected ways. Inside Room 740 of the federal courthouse in Detroit during those two weeks in 1952, the world was defined by judgments: who was American and who was un-American, who was good and who was bad, who was a patriot and who was a traitor. For the most part, when it comes to the people in this book, the judged and their defenders survived and went on to productive lives, while those who sat in judgment drifted into obscurity.

Coleman Young, who had turned the Detroit hearings on their end by attacking what he saw as the racist vocabulary and intentions of the committee, drew strength from the challenge to his Americanism and rode his popularity in the black community to the Michigan legislature and eventually to the mayor's office in Detroit, where the municipal building is now named in his honor. George Crockett overcame his imprisonment on contempt charges to become a judge in Detroit and later a congressman. Crockett had once called his contempt citation at the Foley Square trial a badge of honor, and for both him and Young, their tribulations during the Red Scare era, and the continued attacks on them by right-wing critics through the decades, seemed to enhance, not impair, their reputations among their constituents. While blacks were as patriotic as any other group, affinity with the Communist Party or leftist politics was not arbitrarily viewed as un-American by people who lived in a country that had brought their ancestors over as slaves and then denied them basic rights generation after generation. If there were a Mount Rushmore of American black leaders, it would include not only Martin Luther King Jr., who was wiretapped by the FBI and refused to disassociate himself from a few advisers who had Communist Party connections, but also W.E.B. Du Bois, who cofounded the NAACP, wrote one of the seminal works of American black existence, *The Souls of Black Folk*, was trailed by the FBI during the McCarthy era, and moved to Ghana and joined the Communist Party shortly before his death at age ninety-three in 1963.

John Stephens Wood stayed in Georgia after the Senate refused to confirm his appointment to the Subversive Activities Control Board in 1955. The former HUAC chairman lived out his years as a country lawyer, his health declining, his society wife still distant from him after her discovery that he was part Native American. He died at age eighty-three in 1968 in Marietta, only a few miles from the spot at Frey's Gin where more than a half-century earlier he had driven the car that carried the corpse of Leo Frank away from the lynching field.

Charles E. Potter, whose political rise in Washington was fueled by a Red-hunting posture he later came to regret, lasted only one term in the Senate. In 1958 he was defeated in his bid for reelection by Democrat Philip A. Hart, another veteran who had been wounded on D-Day and had recovered in the same Battle Creek hospital as Potter. Hart's political career was so distinguished that one of the senate office buildings on Capitol Hill is named in his honor. Potter became a lobbyist after his defeat, wrote *Days of Shame*, which deplored the excesses of the McCarthy era, retreated to a farm near Queenstown on Maryland's eastern shore, and died at the early age of sixty-three. His grave rests in Section 30 of Arlington National Cemetery.

Frank S. Tavenner Jr. stayed on as chief counsel for the committee for another twelve years, until he died of a heart attack at his home in Woodstock at age sixty-nine. In 1964, the year of his death, the committee was run by two southern segregationists, Chairman Edwin E. Willis of Louisiana and William M. Tuck of Virginia. Willis was among the leading opponents of the 1964 Civil Rights bill, and Tuck earlier had been a strong proponent of Virginia's massive resistance against public school integration, a movement led by Tavenner's first benefactor from the Shenandoah Valley, Senator Harry T. Byrd. In HUAC's annual report that year, Willis and Tuck took note of recent attempts to "destroy or curb" the committee and asserted that the effort had "Communists at its core." They also paid tribute to Tavenner, whose death came in late October as the report was being drafted, recognizing him for his service in World War I, for his role as acting counsel at the Tokyo War Crimes Tribunal, and "not only as a legal artisan of rare skills but also for the whole man who enjoyed them."

One winter afternoon more than a half-century later, I drove out to the Shenandoah Valley and along Main Street to the edge of Woodstock, turned right at Benchoff Drive, and headed up a hill before angling right again through the stone pillar entranceway into Massanutten Cemetery. As the biblical verse that became part of the folklore of this town says, to everything there is a season, and a time for every purpose under heaven. This was my time to confront Tavenner, or at least his gravestone. It would be a symbolic confrontation, a one-way conversation, me talking to a marble slab, cold and silent, but that seemed sufficient.

The winding paths of the old cemetery took me past markers for Painter and Pence, Hite and Hottel, Boyer and Bauserman and Burner, but after an hour of searching, still no Tavenner. I called the cemetery office, told a woman there the site I had been trying to locate, and minutes later she called back. You must have driven right by it, she said. According to her map, Tavenner would be on the right almost immediately after you entered the cemetery through the old stone archway off Benchoff Drive. I went to the spot she suggested. Didawick and Jones, but still no Tavenner. Then, below those, I noticed a row of headstones that seemed unmarked. I walked over and looked on the other side, and there it was, in the family plot, "FRANK S. TAVENNER JR."

It all seemed odd, unlikely, and unnerving. American as apple pie? Long ago this orchardist and inquisitor had challenged the Americanism of my father and unsettled my father's life, and my mother's life, and the lives of my brother and sisters and me. And now here lay his remains, buried in this craggy field in this remote valley, his headstone turned away from the road, away from all eyes, unlike all the others in the graveyard.

Bereniece Baldwin kept testifying at HUAC hearings and Smith Act trials into the late 1950s, then lived out the remainder of her long life in retirement and anonymity, dying in suburban Detroit in 1991 at age eighty-nine. She had three children and nine grandchildren. Her children—Burton, Violet, and Bill—are dead, and the grandchildren are of my generation, mostly in their sixties. The oldest, Susan Vella, is a retired nurse who lives in St. Clair Shores north of Detroit. She was an infant when HUAC held its hearings in Room 740 in 1952; her birth made it possible for the press to call Baldwin "the grandmother spy." When I interviewed her, I was struck by the points connecting our stories from different sides of the naming names divide. Both the Cummins family and her family carried burdens. One of Baldwin's sons, Burton, suffered a mental breakdown during World War II and lived with his mother or in a hospital for the rest of his life, not unlike my uncle Phil. "When I was in my thirties she told me one day, 'You know, your uncle Burton is schizo,'" Vella recalled. Baldwin's other son had polio as a child. Unlike my aunt Sue, Vella's uncle Bill did not die from polio, but one of his legs was malformed and he lost function in one of his arms.

Susan said that her grandmother's role as an FBI informant was never discussed in the family. She was extremely close to her grandmother and as a young adult talked to her "for hours at a time." But never a word about pretending to be a communist. Nor did Susan hear about it from her mother, Violet. She was an adult when she stumbled upon the truth. She and her younger brother, Michael Wiethoff, were rummaging through one of their mother's closets looking for old photos when they found a box of old newspaper clippings. "That's when we figured it out," she said. "I had no idea when I was a kid." Her first thought when she learned about her grandmother's past was about how daring and dangerous it must have been. "I'm surprised my grandmother didn't get killed," she said. "That was my first response. I couldn't believe it after I'd read all this stuff."

When Baldwin died, one of the speakers at her memorial service, the son of one of her close friends, made some oblique references to her secret past, telling stories of how she would slip into their house from a back alley to the rear door after parking a block away because of fears that she was being followed. But beyond that, all the grandchildren knew was what they read in those old clippings. In their family, unlike ours, politics was never discussed. The only time Susan heard her grandmother utter anything political was when she said she did not like Coleman Young. "But it's kind of funny, because the dad of my best friend when I was growing up worked as a policeman for Coleman Young when he was mayor, and he saw a different person, he really liked him. It all depends on your perspective, I guess." Michael described

"Grandma Baldwin" as a caring but strong-willed dynamo who drove around Detroit in a 1970 gold Pontiac Catalina, her head barely visible over the steering wheel, the dashboard darkened by smoke from a cigarette fire started by her schizophrenic son. Once, he recalled, he was in his work van with a colleague, driving down Eight Mile Road, when "this car comes flying out of a side street and cuts us off, and I had to sit there real quiet because it was my grandmother."

Near the end of my conversation with Susan Vella, she asked me about my father's experience as a witness called before the committee. I said that he never talked about it. "It's too bad," she said sympathetically. "And my grandmother didn't either. And what a history, eh? What a different era. So freaking bizarre."

LIKE HER FATHER, Andrew Cummins, before her, who had moved to Ann Arbor so that his children could get the best possible public education, my mother chose our neighborhood in Madison because of the excellent public schools nearby, Randall and West. Jim was class orator for his West High class of 1962, and Jean was one of two Wisconsin students selected in the first group of Presidential Scholars in 1964, an honor that took her to the White House to meet President Lyndon B. Johnson, and from there to Swarthmore. We were all warmed by Madison's embrace. As Dad had written in that hopeful letter to Jimmy soon after he was born, our house on Regent Street filled up with music and books. Our mother, who had sacrificed so much to keep the family afloat, went back to school and graduated Phi Beta Kappa from Wisconsin the same spring that Jim graduated from Harvard, then became a book editor at the University of Wisconsin Press. Her occasional depression was masked by her combination of gentleness and intellect. She sang in the choir at the Unitarian Church, played the piano and recorder, filled our house with the sounds of Beethoven, Mozart, Harry Belafonte, Miriam Makeba, Ella Fitzgerald, and Paul Robeson, studied Chinese, and constantly welcomed relatives and wayfaring friends for extended stays. She was the very definition of a bleeding-heart liberal, in the positive, not cynical, sense of the phrase. No one in Madison could have guessed that in her early adulthood she was known as Mary the Red.

Her brother Bob finally moved back to Ann Arbor. A writing career that began at the *Michigan Daily* ended with a twelve-year stint at the *Ann Arbor News*, where he worked as wire editor, feature writer, and higher education reporter, covering his alma mater. He and Kay raised five girls and infused them with their fascination with books and baseball. There was a time when the younger three, at their father's instruction, could recite the starting lineup for the Toledo Mud Hens, then a minor league farm club for his beloved Detroit Tigers. Those three daughters, Eileen, Laurel, and Sheila, knew very little about his past, unlike the older daughters, Rachel and Sarah, who had lost their mother to polio when they were very young.

At the *Ann Arbor News*, Bob developed a reputation for clever headline writing, which he compared to the right chess move. (He played chess by mail with expert players from around the world.) When he retired in 1978, the *News* published a feature story about his career without mentioning that he and Ralph Neafus and Elman Service had gone off to fight against fascism in Spain, and that Neafus had been killed by Franco's troops while he and Service survived, and that Service had gone on to become a world-class anthropologist even though both he and Bob had been investigated in their past. The focus in Bob's retirement story was on his love of newspapers and his reputation for being precise and fair. "While the papers are private businesses, they have a public responsibility," the story quoted him saying. "They must provide the readers with accurate, trustworthy information about what's going on in their community so those readers can form their own opinions on issues. Without good, conscientious newspapers, no democracy can survive."

Bob had long since become disillusioned by any ideology that tried to impose group thinking. In 1984 the extended Cummins family, by then more than fifty strong, held a reunion, the first of what would become an every-three-years tradition that continues today. Bob found the first site for it, a former WPA village near Fontana Dam in the Smoky Mountains that had been turned into a resort, but though he loved his family, something about the gatherings reminded him too much of a cult.

The organizer of the reunions was my mother's younger sister, Jean Chulak. One of many traditions at these gatherings was for Aunt Jean to give a lecture on the family genealogy and the newest connections she had found tracing the roots of the Cumminses and Devers and other mostly Scots-Irish ancestors as she visited courthouse archives in Ohio, Iowa, Kansas, Oklahoma, and Virginia. There were stories of success and failure and mobility, and it never occurred to me until I began this book that part of what Aunt Jean was doing, consciously or unconsciously, without ever saying so, was establishing the all-American bona fides of this family in which her brothers and sisters had once been called un-American. But her genealogical reports reinforced something even more important: the beneficent communal role that the Cummins family played in holding us all together.

Why it took my parents and uncle so long to reject the false promise of communism is a question my siblings and I have thought about but can only offer theories for, not certainties. A summation from Jean comes closest to capturing our conclusions: "Loyalty, friendship, pride, continuity with past beliefs, the fact that Russia had helped win the war and been our ally and was suddenly the enemy (talk about abrupt shifts), groupthink, confirmation bias, investment in a belief that they had sacrificed for (this applies to Bob especially), the persistence of colonialism, racial injustice and economic hardship even after the war, understanding that communists in Europe and other parts of the world were taken seriously and not considered weirdos, and maybe a feeling that they didn't really care that much about the U.S.S.R. but weren't going to attack it. The repressive atmosphere made it impossible for people to discuss their beliefs openly."

Jim and I both theorized that at the core of their reasoning was a profound dislike for right-wing anticommunists. "What they were sore about was the exploitation, the witch hunting, of right-wing politicians," Jim said in a note to me while reading the manuscript of this book. "And, of course, the threat to their, and everyone's constitutional rights. They thought they were more loyal to what they loved about

America, the real America. This is . . . not earth-shaking at this point, I don't think. Nobody but the crazies thinks anymore that internal security was ever threatened. And Dad was not about to inform on anyone. He used to say, 'Don't be a stool pigeon' to Jeannie and me if we would tell on each other."

That generation is gone now. After Bob died at home in August 1995 at seventy-nine, a comrade from his days in Spain was among the speakers at his memorial service. Mourners were encouraged to make contributions in his honor to the Veterans of the Abraham Lincoln Brigade.

My father died nine years later, in 2004, at eighty-six, and my mother in January 2006 at eighty-four. They are buried side by side along with Bob and Phil and Grace and Andrew and Barbara in a Cummins family plot at a cemetery on Whitmore Lake Road, in Ann Arbor, not far from where it all began at the University of Michigan. My father had become a permanent midwesterner.

There was a tragedy near the end of my parents' lives that cut deeper on a personal level than any of their political travails. It involved the youngest of their four children, Dad's good luck charm, the redhead who came along just as he was starting to turn his life around. Wendy, the most talented among us, a thrilling classical pianist trained at Wisconsin and Yale, as well as a wife and mother of two young sons, was killed in a car crash on an icy November Sunday in 1997 as she was driving from her home in Ithaca, New York, to Geneva to accompany a musician at Hobart College. Her loss created an ache for my parents that Dad's lifelong motto—"It could be worse"—could never soothe.

My research for this book took me back to Ann Arbor many times, and during one visit I went to my cousin Eileen's house to look through a box of artifacts from her father's life. There, alongside documents Bob kept from his time in Spain, was a letter that my brother sent him in 1981. Jim was a professor at Amherst then, where he taught Spanish and Spanish literature and would later teach a course on the Spanish Civil War. He was also intensely interested in labor history and the ideas and forces that drew young people in the 1930s and 1940s to the Communist Party. It was while reading about labor history that he first came upon a reference to the record of the 1952 HUAC hearings in Detroit, a discovery that inspired him to look for a transcript of the hearings, which he found in the Amherst College library.

Until then he did not know the full story. "I guess I don't need to tell you that I never knew that you and Elliott testified, or that Mary was also informed on. But there it was," Jim wrote in his letter to Bob. "You falsified a passport application [to go fight fascists in Spain]. And Elliott went and read the Guild Constitution to the committee, figuring I guess that they wouldn't let him enter any other kind of statement. It seems to me now, simplifying, that Elliott has more or less remained faithful to the civil libertarian doctrine he gave to the committee. . . . I don't know whether he ever was a revolutionary or whether he was on the liberal side of the popular front. I don't know how he, and you, felt sitting there before the committee. I can imagine. But you all were pretty articulate. I wonder endlessly about those things."

It took me another thirty-plus years to wonder what Jim was wondering. I lacked my brother's uncommon intellect and was absorbed with other things, but like so many stories that I've pursued over the decades, when I got to this one I felt that I was doing it with Jim and for him and Jean and Wendy and all of our family, my way of expressing gratitude. My parents were not perfect, but they created a good American family. They emerged from hard times bonded by love and open to the world. And though Jim never knew it, it was one small gesture of his that got me thinking in a way that led me down this road. It was in the summer of 2006 when we gathered at the cemetery in Ann Arbor for the first time after the ashes of our parents were buried together there. Jim insisted that our father's gravestone carry his nickname: Elliott (Ace) Maraniss. Why "Ace"? I knew that long ago some people called him that, but why put it on his grave marker? It took me all the way through the writing of this book to appreciate what that really signified, going back to the day in the late winter of 1952 when not just his name but his nickname was spoken in Room 740 of the Federal Building in Detroit.

Acknowledgments

Librarians and archivists are underrecognized angels for authors researching nonfiction books. This time, I am deeply indebted to these people and more: Mike Smith, Terrence McDonald, and Brian Williams at the Bentley Historical Library, and Karen Hutchens at the Hatcher Graduate Library at the University of Michigan. Katherine Mollan at the National Archives in Washington and Tim Nenninger at the National Archives at College Park, along with Mary Kay Schmidt, who expedited my FOIA request for FBI files. Matthew Boylan at the New York Public Library. Maira Liriano at the Schomburg Center for Research in Black Culture. Lynette Stout at the Georgia Historical Society. Luther Hanson at the Fort Lee Quartermaster Museum. Sarah J. Logue at the Seeley G. Mudd Manuscript Library at Princeton. Timothy Johnson and staff at the Tamiment Library at New York University. And William Fliss at Marquette University Special Collections.

Katherine Ward, one of my political biography students at Vanderbilt University, spent a summer as my research intern and could not have been more helpful finding people and information. Julie Tate and Margot Williams, among the world's most proficient researchers, also helped at key points along the way. Steve Oney's illuminating *And the Dead Shall Rise* was my bible for writing about the Leo Frank case and its connection to HUAC chairman John Stephens Wood, and he pointed me toward important files at the Georgia Historical Society. My longtime colleague and friend Glenn Frankel helped guide me through the Red Scare era, and I learned much from his book *High Noon*, an insightful study of Hollywood and HUAC. If there is an indispensable book on the interplay of witnesses and informants, it is Victor Navasky's *Naming Names*, which I turned to countless times. Robbie Cohen and his *When the Old Left Was Young* served the same role in my understanding of the student left of the 1930s. Alan Warren, with the look and sensibility of a modern-day Orwell, was an effervescent and encyclopedic guide through Spain as my wife and I traced my uncle's path in the Spanish Civil War. I am also indebted to Steve Fainaru and John U. Bacon.

Blaine Harden, Glenn Frankel, Pat Toomay, Mike Kail, Whitney Gould, and Michael Weisskopf were generous with their thoughts in reading the manuscript. At Vanderbilt, my teaching partners, Robert Barsky and Bruce Oppenheimer, were always supportive and insightful; thanks also to Dean John Geer, David Lewis, Alan Wiseman, and everyone in the Political Science Department. At the *Washington Post*, the anchor of my professional career for four decades, Marty Baron and Steven Ginsberg have helped me maintain the connection while I write books. I'm inspired by my writing pals Anne Hull, Rick Atkinson, and Paul Hendrickson. Thanks also to Bob Woodward and Elsa Walsh, Jim Warren and Cornelia Grumman, John Feinstein, Tom Kail, Andy Cohn and Kim Vergeront, Michael Feldman, Chip Brown, Neil Henry, Mark Schmitz's terrific crew at Zebradog, Michael and Beth Norman, and Ben and Judy Sidran.

This is my twelfth book with the incomparable Alice Mayhew at Simon & Schuster, and her unwavering belief in this story kept me going. Thanks also to her astute deputy, Stuart Roberts, as well as Carolyn Reidy, Jonathan Karp, Julia Prosser, Jackie Seow, Jonathan Evans, Amar Deol, and Richard Rhorer. Copyeditor Judith Hoover once again provided eagle-eyed care for my manuscript. Rafe Sagalyn, my literary agent, has also been with me through twelve books, helping me think my way through each of them, and for that I am deeply grateful, despite the fact that his Free Agents rotisserie baseball club has too often shellacked my Momen's Hombres.

At its core, this is a book about family, and in that realm I feel blessed. Cousins Eileen Thomas, Rachel Cummins, Mary Higgins, and Peggy Datz all provided papers and information that enriched this book. Thanks also for the support from Linda's side of the family—Dick and M. A. Porter, and Carol and Ty Garner—along with Gigi Kaeser and Michael Alexander, the spouses of my brother and sister. I've always been in awe of Jim and Jean, the smartest people I've ever known, and though their perspectives on our family unavoidably differ from mine in some respects, the meaning of our family history is deeply shared. The fact that they offered insight and information all along the way, and then gave careful readings of the manuscript at the end, means the world to me.

There is a point in the book where I write about being surprised to find a letter by my father in which he uses the exact phrase I've always used to explain my career, that writing is in my blood and I love it. I guess it is in the blood of my two wonderful children as well. Both Andrew and Sarah started down different paths and then came back to writing, continuing the tradition for another generation. As powerful as their writing is, I am more grateful for the larger loving "good American family" they have provided, Andrew with Alison and their kids, Eliza and Charlie, and Sarah with Tom and the redheads Heidi and Ava. Writing is in their blood, too. Linda is the center of everything in my life. From Ann Arbor to Detroit and from New York to Spain, she traced the arc of this book with me, taking pictures, combing through albums, books, and archives, making friends, reading first drafts. She is my Maria Penguina, as she called herself in Spain, my quirky saint, still and forever, amen.

Notes

The narrative of this book was constructed primarily from letters, papers, oral histories, and other documents from the following archival sources:

Abraham Lincoln Brigade Archive, Tamiment Library, New York University
Bentley Historical Library, University of Michigan, Ann Arbor
Capital Times (Madison, Wisconsin)
Cherokee County Historical Society, Canton, Georgia
Jean and Mary Chulak Family Papers, privately held
Robert Cummins and Eileen Thomas Family Papers, privately held
Detroit Free Press
Detroit News
Detroit Times
FBI File, George Crockett
FBI File, Elliott Maraniss
Georgia Historical Society, Savannah
Hatcher Graduate Library Special Collections, University of Michigan, Ann Arbor
Library of Congress Newspaper and Current Periodical Reading Room, Washington, DC
Maraniss Family Papers, privately held
Marquette University Special Collections
Maund Family Papers, privately held
Michigan Daily Digital Archives
Arthur J. Morris Law Library, University of Virginia
Seeley G. Mudd Manuscript Library, Princeton University
National Archives, College Park, Maryland
National Archives, Washington, DC
National Military Personnel Records, St. Louis, Missouri
New York Public Library
Quint-City Special (Bettendorf, Iowa)
Harry Ransom Center, University of Texas
Walter P. Reuther Library, Wayne State University
Schomburg Center for Research in Black Culture, New York Public Library

Sephardic Museum of Seville
Spanish Civil War Interpretation Center, Corbera
Spanish Civil War Interpretation Center, La Fatarella
U.S. Army Quartermaster Museum, Archives, Fort Lee, Virginia

Chapter 1: The Imperfect *S*

3 *My father . . . sat at the witness table*: Communism in the Detroit Area, Part 2, Mar. 10–12, 1952 (testimony of Elliott Maraniss), 3179–83.

4 *But the moment came alive to me*: The personal file of my father was in Series 3, Box 32, of the HUAC files at the National Archives. When I started researching this book, I knew from the transcript that he had written a statement but had no expectation that it was still around or that I could find it. Katherine Mollan, a dedicated government archivist, first told me the statement indeed existed.

4 *He was messy and noisy*: Although I sometimes saw my father working at the old *Capital Times* offices on S. Carroll Street in Madison, just off the Capital Square, my deepest memories are of him typing at our house on Regent Street, where he supplemented his salary from the paper by writing a state politics and farm policy column for an agricultural journal.

6 *the delight he took in teaching us silly tunes from his New York childhood*: Is it human nature that I can forget what I did yesterday yet remember most of the lyrics from a nonsensical song my father taught us when we were kids? "There was a little man and he had a little can and he tried to rush the growler / He went into a saloon on a Sunday afternoon and you should have heard the old man holler / No beer today, no beer today, no beer today is Sunday / No beer today, no beer today, you'll have to come around on Monday / For the only girl that he ever loved had a face like a horse and a buggy / She leaned against the middle of the lake, 'Oh, fireman, save my child' / But the child was bigger than the fireman / Go easy on the monkey wrench, your father was a nut."

7 *His favorite essayist was George Orwell*: My father's affinity for Orwell was mostly because of Orwell's clear-eyed view of the world, but it also had to do with writing style. Like Orwell, my father was allergic to pretentious writing and preferred simple Anglo-Saxon words to fancier ones with Latin roots.

9 *and dismissed as "premature anti-fascists"*: "Clarence Kailin: Premature Antifascist— and Proudly So," article on Lincoln Brigade survivor Clarence Kailin, John Nichols, *Capital Times*, Oct. 26, 2009.

10 *"I must sell my home"*: From Statement of Elliott Maraniss, Mar. 12, 1952. The entire statement is reproduced as chapter 24.

Chapter 2: In from the Cold

12 *Until the moment Bereniece Baldwin testified*: This account of Bereniece (Toby) Baldwin's testimony in Washington and Detroit—and her secret life before that— was drawn from Investigative Name file, Series 1, Baldwin, Bereniece, RG233, National Archives; transcript of Baldwin testimony before HUAC in Detroit, Feb.

29, 1952; along with interviews with her grandchildren Susan Vella and Michael Wiethoff and reports in the *Detroit Times, Detroit News, Detroit Free Press*, Associated Press, and United Press from Feb. 12 to Mar. 2, 1952.

16 *She was working for money*: Estimated payments to Baldwin in Babson et al., *The Color of Law*, 259–60.

16 *As Victor Navasky aptly described it*: Navasky, *Naming Names*, xxiii. "These people . . . contributed to the growing myth of the informer as folk hero—through the publication in newspapers and books, serialization on radio, on television, and in movies, of their tales."

17 *In the first weeks of 1952*: Account of Ford Motor Co. interaction with HUAC investigators drawn from Charles E. Potter Papers, Box 4, Miscellaneous re: Communist Party members in Michigan, Bentley Historical Library, John E. Bugas Memorandum for the File, Jan. 23, Jan. 28, Gordon L. Walker Memorandum for the File, Feb. 19, Feb. 22. It was Robert A. Caro, the prodigious biographer of LBJ, who once said his research motto was "Turn every page." Easier said than done, but I try to remind myself of that admonition every time I'm working an archive. In this case, I was looking for biographical material on Charles E. Potter, and at the end of a long day decided to look at one last folder, and there, unexpectedly, I found the Ford memos on HUAC.

Chapter 3: Outside the Gate

21 *Coney Island was a fantasyland*: Jeffrey Stanton, "Coney Island—Nickel Empire (1920's–1930's)," Westland Network, 1997, https://www.westland.net/coneyisland /articles/nickelempire.htm; Kurt Hollander, "Dreamland: Coney Island and the 20th Century Avant-Garde," *Brooklyn Rail*, Feb. 5, 2015, https://brooklynrail .org/2015/02/art/dreamland-coney-island-and-the-20th-century-avant-garde; Louis J. Parascandola and John Parascandola, eds., *A Coney Island Reader: Through Dizzy Gates of Illusion* (New York: Columbia University Press, 2014), 25; Federico García Lorca, "Landscape of a Vomiting Multitude," in *Poet in New York* (New York: Grove Atlantic, 2008).

22 *The living quarters were crowded and tense*: Elliott Maraniss (hereafter EM) letter to Mary Maraniss (MM), June 1945.

22 *The Boy Scouts kept him busy*: Description of EM's scouting days based on letter from Irving Schneider to David Maraniss (hereafter DM), Apr. 21, 1995; copies of Boy Scout Troop 162, *Barker*, Dec. 25, 1932; Mar. 31, 1933; Apr. 28, 1933; May 12, 1933; Nov. 24, 1933; Jan. 12, 1934; provided by Schneider. In his Personalities column of that last issue, EM wrote about fellow Scout Joe Rudolph: "The possessor of a husky, booming bass voice, Rudy amuses himself by imitating a conductor shouting out the stations. His short but muscular body serves him well in his favorite sport, wrestling. Before the amazed eyes of this scribbler, he proved that he could rip a telephone book in half, without breaking the binding."

23 *During a trip to Spain*: The Sephardic Museum in Seville was only two blocks from Las Casas de la Juderia, our hotel amid the winding, narrow streets of the Barrio de Santa Cruz, the old Jewish quarter of the Andalusian city. Ferrand Martínez, arch-

deacon of Écija, blamed the Jews for all misfortune and launched the first pogroms in March 1391 in Seville. By that summer it was estimated that 80 percent of the city's Jews were slaughtered.

24 *My family's branch of the Marranos:* U.S. Census data, Boston, 1900 and 1910. Maraniss Descendant Chart (compiled by Marjory Yamins Hyman, EM's cousin, one of his aunt Celia's children). According to these charts, Esocher and Fanny Spergol married in Russia circa 1885, and Esocher died in Palestine sometime between 1932 and 1935, while EM was in high school. As far as I can tell, my father never met his grandfather. He never talked about him.

25 *Herman . . . had a successful career:* Herman was the subject of a *Los Angeles Times* article on May 28, 1929, "Tin Pan Alley Denizens Live in Hollywood Now": "Tin Pan Alley, that small, and once-densely populated New York area where songwriters, publishers and pluggers went to gather, has 'gone Hollywood,' according to H. S. Maraniss, Victor Talking Machine Company official, now at the Ambassador Hotel. 'Tin Pan Alley has moved to Los Angeles since the advent of the talking picture,' Mr. Maraniss declared yesterday in explaining his presence here. 'For years the hundreds of song hits which my company recorded were creations of that famous area in New York. There we found the composers and publishers, and there, quite frequently, we found the singers. But all that has changed. Nowadays the Victor company looks to Southern California for many of its best recordings. Since motion pictures want theme songs and producers are paying so well for songs to fit in with their pictures, New York songwriters have come west and we have followed.'"

25 *Long after Joe was gone:* Irving Schneider letter to EM, Jan. 15, 1996.

27 *Abraham Lincoln High School was born of hope:* Description of Lincoln and EM's high school milieu drawn from Lincoln *Landmark* yearbooks, 1933–36, and *Cargoes,* the school's literary magazine, 1939, all retrieved from storage at the New York Public Library.

27 *the son of a wealthy manufacturer:* Description of Arthur Miller childhood drawn from the playwright's memoir, *Timebends;* also *Arthur Miller: Writer,* a documentary by his daughter, Rebecca Miller, aired on HBO spring 2018.

28 *Principal Mason was a liberal thinker:* Portrait of Gabriel R. Mason drawn from Lincoln *Landmark* yearbooks, 1933–36; also *Gabriel Blows His Horn,* his autobiography, and *Great American Liberals,* a text he edited.

29 *"Impious wretch":* Spinoza Quarterly, Spring 1933.

30 *"I rejoice that you do not go out into the world":* Lincoln *Landmark,* 1934.

31 *This is why, as Robbie Cohen:* Cohen, *When the Old Left Was Young,* 87.

31 *The strike started at eleven that morning:* Details of national student peace strike from Mary O'Flaherty, *Brooklyn Daily Eagle,* Apr. 12, 1935; also Cohen, *When the Old Left Was Young,* 86–97.

32 *In an oral history, Morton Jackson:* "Student Activism in the 1930s" segment on New Deal website of the Franklin and Eleanor Roosevelt Institute, 2000.

33 *The commencement ceremonies for Elliott's class:* Lincoln *Landmark,* 1936: "All the poorly paved roads in Brooklyn converged at the Academy of Music. Proud mamas

and doting papas swept regally into the auditorium. The usual hush fell as the band swung into the strain of the march of the graduates. Florence Epstein and Aaron Abramson, valedictorians, proclaimed eloquently to an audience convinced of their sincerity. Dr. Mason bid the graduates farewell and godspeed in a voice made halting by emotion."

Chapter 4: Red Menace

35 *"but this will be the public's first knowledge"*: *Detroit Free Press*, Feb. 25, 1952.

37 *Was America winning the cold war?*: Eddy Gilmore, Associated Press, Feb. 23, 1952.

38 *The first dispute in Detroit*: *Detroit Free Press, Detroit News, Detroit Times*, Feb. 26, 1952; Box 3, Charles E. Potter Papers, Bentley Historical Library.

38 *Estes Kefauver . . . came across as a southern . . . Jimmy Stewart*: Halberstam, *The Fifties*, 191.

39 *The FBI sent advance word*: *Detroit Free Press*, Feb. 25, 1952. The FBI informed Potter of the meeting and the protest plans, and Potter passed this along to the press.

40 *"There were approximately thirty-nine or forty persons"*: Detroit Red Squad Files, Crockett Files, Tamiment Library, New York University. The surveillance included a report on the protester who carried the placards back to his house after the demonstration ended at 1:35 that afternoon.

41 *When the hearing opened that afternoon*: Opening statement by Chairman Wood, *Communism in the Detroit Area*, HUAC transcript, Part 1, Feb. 25, 1952. His use of Jackie Robinson as a means of attacking Paul Robeson, and the relationship between Robinson and Robeson, was captured brilliantly in "What Paul Robeson Said," a *Smithsonian Magazine* article by Gilbert King, Sept. 13, 2011. King's concluding paragraph: "Toward the end of his life, Jackie Robinson had a chance to reflect on the incident and his invitation to testify before HUAC. He wrote in his autobiography, "'I would reject such an invitation if offered now. . . . I have grown wiser and closer to the painful truths about America's destructiveness. And I do have increased respect for Paul Robeson who, over the span of twenty years, sacrificed himself, his career, and the wealth and comfort he once enjoyed because, I believe, he was sincerely trying to help his people.'"

Chapter 5: Wheelman Wood

43 *John Stephens Wood . . . came from a very different place*: Biographical Dictionary of the United States Congress, 1774–1989; *New York Times* obituary, Sept. 14, 1968; *Washington Post* obituary, Sept. 14, 1968.

43 *For black Georgians, the reality*: Pauli Murray, *States' Laws on Race and Color* (Athens: University of Georgia Press, 2016); Edward A. Hatfield, "Segregation," *New Georgia Encyclopedia*, May 16, 2017, https://www.georgiaencyclopedia.org/articles /history-archaeology/segregation; "Examples of Jim Crow Law," *Jackson (TN) Sun*, special report, May 7, 2017. The Georgia state law for amateur baseball read, "It shall be unlawful for any amateur white baseball team to play baseball on any va-

cant lot or baseball diamond within two blocks of a playground devoted to the Negro race, and it shall be unlawful for any amateur colored baseball team to play baseball in any vacant lot or baseball diamond within two blocks of any playground devoted to the white race."

44 *He was one of fourteen children:* Biographical Directory of the United States Congress, *1774–1989* (Washington, DC: Government Printing Office); "Wood, John S.," *Facts on File,* The Truman Years, Arthur E. Scherr, U.S. House of Representatives Archive; *New York Times,* obituary, Sept. 14, 1968; *Washington Post,* obituary, Sept. 14, 1968; Rick Shockey, "The Controversial and Accomplished Life of Congressman John Stephens Wood," class paper, Kennesaw State University, Oct. 12, 2001.

44 *Newt Morris also came out of rural Cherokee County:* Depiction of Newt Morris before the Leo Frank case drawn from Newt Morris obituary, *Marietta (GA) Journal,* Sept. 22, 1946; Newt Morris File, Steve Oney Papers, Georgia Historical Society; *Atlanta Constitution* articles, Sept. 1–3, 1914.

45 *The victim was from Marietta and her name was Mary Phagan:* Account of the murder of Mary Phagan drawn from *Atlanta Journal* and *Atlanta Constitution* articles, Apr. 27–May 15, 1913; Oney, *And the Dead Shall Rise,* 3–17; *Leo Frank Appeal,* State of Georgia, 1918. Oney's meticulous and evocatively written book begins, "That morning, thirteen-year-old Mary Phagan, after eating a breakfast of cabbage and wheat biscuits, devoted herself to getting dressed."

46 *That conclusion was reinforced generations later:* Jerry Thompson and Robert Sherborne, "New Light Shed on Old Murder," *Tennessean,* Mar. 7, 1982; Wendell Rawls Jr., "After 69 Years of Silence, Lynching Victim Is Cleared," *New York Times,* Mar. 8, 1982. (Although Mann passed a lie detector test, as with most sensational murders, there are conspiracy theorists who assert that his confession to the reporters was a hoax.)

48 *Late on the night of August 16:* Account of Leo Frank's lynching and the involvement of Newt Morris and John S. Wood drawn from Oney, *And the Dead Shall Rise;* John Gollner interview, June 28, 2017; Herman Spence File, Oney Papers, Georgia Historical Society; Newt Morris File, Oney Papers, Georgia Historical Society; speech on Leo Frank case by Bill Kinney, associate editor, *Marietta Journal,* Oct. 7, 1992; *Atlanta Journal* and *Atlanta Constitution,* Aug. 16–20, 1915; Lynching Status Report, lynch party members or planners confirmed by Golmer Wilson, Oct. 2, 1990, Oney Papers, Georgia Historical Society. (There are eighteen names on the list, and No. 1 is Newt Morris.)

52 *Wood won a seat in the Georgia legislature:* Atlanta Constitution, June 8, 1918.

53 *So the joiner joined:* Wood's connection to the Ku Klux Klan came out decades later, during hearings conducted by a subcommittee of the Senate Judiciary Committee in June 1955 regarding his nomination to the Subversive Activities Control Board in 1955. The hearings transcript includes this explanation from Wood: "I think it might be interesting . . . to relate to you that back almost forty years ago, when I was a good deal younger than I am now, I was interested, beginning to be interested, in politics, and I was sort of a joiner. . . . I joined organizations like the Odd Fellows, the Improved Order of Red Men, the Junior Order of United American Mechanics,

and the Elks, the Masons, the Rotary, and the Shrine. Klanism in my state at the time was rather in the ascendancy."

53 *When Wood was first elected*: "Wood Will Represent an Isolated District," *New York Times*, Oct. 4, 1931.

54 *After a failed first marriage*: Wood's relationship by marriage to the prosperous Jones family and the famous golfer Bobby Jones drawn from interview with grandson John Gollner, June 27, 2017; "Personal Sketches and Family Accounts," *History of Cherokee County*, Cherokee County Historical Society.

55 *This was the* Hasty *case*: Associated Press wire stories, Nov. 22, Nov. 26, 1923; *New York Times*, Nov. 28, 1923. Not only did Wood promote his prosecution of this case in his defense before the Judiciary Committee, but years later a congressional colleague brought it up in a speech honoring Wood after his death, perpetuating the myth. The *New York Times* story reporting what actually happened began, "Marietta, Ga., Nov. 28—'All indictments against Keller Hasty, pitcher for the Philadelphia Americans [Athletics], and five others charged with flogging Mrs. Bertha Holcombe, a widow, and S. H. Morton, Smyrna, were dismissed here late today by Judge Blair, on motion of Solicitor General John S. Wood, after the acquittal of Parks G. Cook on a similar charge.'"

56 *There were secrets in the life of Chairman Wood*: Interview with John Gollner, June 28, 2017.

Chapter 6: "Negro, Not Niggra"

58 *the hearings in Room 740 took a dramatic turn*: Account of HUAC interaction with African American witnesses Edward N. Turner, Rev. Charles A. Hill, and labor organizer Coleman Young, along with George Crockett, the attorney for Hill and Young, drawn almost entirely from the transcript *Communism in the Detroit Area*, Part 1, Feb. 27, 28, 1952; also *Detroit Free Press, Detroit Times, Detroit News*, Feb. 27–29, 1952; and Studs Terkel, *American Dreams: Lost and Found* (New York: New Press, 2005). Coleman Young put Tavenner and the committee on the defensive from the beginning: "I can only state that in being interviewed and being asked questions, that I hope that I will be allowed to react fully to those questions, and not be expected to react only in such a manner that this committee may desire me. In other words, I might have answers you might not like. You called me here to testify; I am prepared to testify, but, I would like to know from you if I shall be allowed to respond to your questions fully and in my own way."

Chapter 7: A New World Coming

70 *The late-night hangout for students*: The tavern advertised regularly in the student newspaper. Another of the establishment's frequent ads in the 1930s featured a comic drawing of a tongue-out thirsty student in suit and tie with the caption, "Dry as Dust . . . Simply Must . . . come down to . . ."

70 *Once a year, on a Friday evening*: "To Those Who Have Not Understood," Stan

Swinton Papers, Box 4, Bentley Historical Library; aspects of Swinton's journalism career are in Boxes 1 and 2. He was always precocious, writing an autobiography as a sixteen-year-old high school senior that he titled "The World Goes Round and Round and I Come Out Where?" In Swinton's interview with Ho Chi Minh in 1949, Ho said that all the Americans he met in Vietnam were friendly to him.

72 *The Cummins family arose*: Late in life, Andrew Adair Cummins wrote an account of his family history. As an engineer, his writing was neat and legible, and his sentences were straightforward, often dry, but occasionally with a dry wit. Example: "My grandmother Cummins, whose maiden name was Harris, was a Hoosier. She was a slight woman and frail. When they were moving from Indiana to Iowa she was not feeling well and my grandfather took her to a doctor who told him he would do well to get her to Iowa alive. He must have been a poor diagnostician since she lived another 50 years."

74 *In one of their many stops*: Public Schools, Office of the Superintendent, Evansville, Indiana, letter to Mr. and Mrs. A. A. Cummins, July 12, 1928, Cummins Family Papers.

74 *Baseball was Bob's first love*: Bob Cummins letter to his father, Aug. 22, 1931, Cummins Family Papers. The seriousness with which Bob took his pretend career as a baseball scribe was demonstrated by the urging he gave his father at the letter's close: "P.S. Criticize."

75 *That passion for the national pastime*: Michigan Daily stories, Apr. 24, 26, May 22, June 1, Sept. 18, Oct. 20, 1934; Feb. 16, Mar. 22, 1935. In his Oct. 20 story about snow removal at Michigan Stadium he wrote, "When there is snow, 60 to 70 men are needed to clear the seats, others are needed to clear the aisles and runways. When the weather is threatening, 15 must spread the huge tarpaulin over the stadium turf."

76 *"In the thirties the building was home"*: Arthur Miller's depiction of the *Daily* in the 1930s drawn from *Timebends*, 94–99; *Holiday* magazine, Dec. 1953.

79 *Miller sat in the gallery*: Michigan Daily, May 24, 1935.

79 *Bob Cummins had become a prominent figure*: "National Student League to Hold First Meeting on May 1," *Michigan Daily*, Apr. 25, 1935.

80 *"We had been certain that if Franco"*: Miller, *Timebends*, 97–99.

81 *Miller was getting ready to stage his first student play*: Miller Papers, Hatcher Graduate Library. On Feb. 16, 1937, the *Daily* announced that Miller had received a $1,250 scholarship from the Bureau of New Plays for *They Too Arise*. Professor Erich Walter said the play "has unmistakable dramatic power—it is excellent theater. The authenticity of the experiences that gave birth to the play is the secret of the dramatic power."

82 *He found quarters at Wilma Nye's rooming house*: The addresses where EM lived are listed in his student file at the Bentley Historical Library. His landlady's name is listed in a background investigation conducted by U.S. Army Intelligence years later, when he applied for an officer training program during World War II.

83 *The drama that followed*: Michigan Daily, Apr. 29, 30, 1937.

83 *"It was the discovery of fascism"*: Melinda Burns, "Retired Professor Recounts War Experiences," *Santa Barbara News-Press*, July 26, 1987.

84 *"There was much for Bob to leave behind":* "To Those Who Have Not Understood," Swinton Papers, Box 4, Bentley Historical Library.

84 *Arthur Miller considered joining his pal Neafus:* Miller, *Timebends,* 294–98. Miller writes powerfully about the trip from Ann Arbor to New York with his friend, but in the book misspells his name as Neaphus.

85 *Robert Adair Cummins, age twenty, carried an American passport:* Cummins Family Papers; transcript of *Communism in the Detroit Area,* Part 1, Feb. 28, 1952.

Chapter 8: A Brief Spanish Inquisition

86 *Frank Tavenner, the chief inquisitor:* "Red Quizzer Mild Mannered but Hits Heart of Matter," *Detroit News,* Mar. 12, 1952.

86 *"He peers over the top of his glasses":* *Detroit News,* March 1, 1952.

87 *He said his last job had been selling paint:* All dialogue in this chapter from *Communism in the Detroit Area,* Part 1 (testimony of Robert Cummins), Feb. 28, 1952.

Chapter 9: The Runner

90 *the RMS* Aquitania *reached Cherbourg:* Robert Cummins File and Biografía de Militantes, Abraham Lincoln Brigade Archive (hereafter ALBA); Stan Swinton report home, July 7, 1938, Swinton Papers, Bentley Historical Library.

90 *on May 30, when the* Ciudad de Barcelona: Hochschild, *Spain in Our Hearts,* 236–37; Eby, *Comrades and Commissars,* 148–49; Carroll, *Odyssey,* 146.

91 *There were three passes through the Pyrenees:* Cummins's brief description from *Port Huron (MI) Times-Herald,* Apr. 5, 1939. The most evocative description of American volunteers crossing the mountains into Spain can be found in Alvah Bessie's *Men in Battle,* 18–27.

91 *"They went to Spain as political people":* "The Origins of a Crusade," in Carroll, *Odyssey,* 15–19.

93 *This battalion . . . was just being formed:* Account of Bob Cummins and his Michigan comrades at training camp taken from Cummins Family Papers; Neafus File, ALBA; Bessie, *Men in Battle,* 49–50; Eby, *Comrades and Commissars,* 162, 170, 245.

93 *The political commissar was Joe Dallet:* Depiction of Dallet drawn from Carroll, *Odyssey,* 37, 127; Eby, *Comrades and Commissars,* 235–50; letters from Dallet File, ALBA.

95 *Letters from Tarazona could not be sent by civilian mail:* Box 37, ALBA.

95 *"The staff planned to publish it":* Stan Swinton Papers, Box 4, Bentley Historical Library.

95 *Bob Cummins . . . was assigned as a runner:* Robert Cummins, "From Spain to Ann Arbor," *Michigan Daily,* Feb. 19, 1939.

95 *Service was assigned to drive a truck, and Neafus:* Service and Neafus files, ALBA; *Santa Barbara News-Press,* July 26, 1987.

95 *The Mac-Paps were deployed at last:* Description of Fuentes de Ebro fighting drawn from Cummins letter to *Michigan Daily,* Dec. 7, 1937; Neafus letters in Neafus File, ALBA; Carroll, *Odyssey,* 160–62; Eby, *Comrades and Commissars,* 248–57.

96 *My uncle, describing that period in an essay*: Robert Cummins, "From Spain to Ann Arbor," *Michigan Daily*, Feb. 19, 1939. This postwar story, written after the Americans had left Spain but before the war was over, was Bob's most detailed account of his experiences in Spain, though shaped by his desire to win support for the Loyalists even as their defeat was near, an outcome that already seemed clear to most observers.

98 *Their destination near Madrid was an expansive villa*: Bob Cummins, undated letter to A. A. Cummins, Cummins Family Papers. When I showed this letter to Alan Warren, a Spanish Civil War expert and our guide for several days in Spain, he immediately knew the location and took us there during our tour. The villa still stood, though now it was a rehabilitation center for drug addicts. Warren told me about Segundo the dwarf, and later sent a citation from a chapter by Scotsman Hugh Sloan in MacDougall, *Voices from the Spanish Civil War*, 213.

99 *Bob wrote a letter to Ed Magdol*: *Michigan Daily* account of undated letter published Dec. 7, 1937.

100 *With Christmas and the new year came new battles*: Scenes from fighting at Teruel drawn from Hochschild, *Spain in Our Hearts*, 267–80; Carroll, *Odyssey*, 166; Eby, *Comrades and Commissars*, 271–78. Bob Cummins later reported his relatively minor ear wound to his parents.

101 *On March 14 correspondent William P. Carney*: The story of the capture and disappearance of Ralph Neafus drawn from *New York Times*, Mar. 16–28, 1938; *Michigan Daily*, March 22, 25, 1938; Neafus File, Bentley Historical Library; *Detroit Free Press*, Mar. 24, 1938; Miller, *Timebends*, 317; Confidential U.S. State Department Files, 1938–44, Neafus, Ralph, Military Affairs Personnel—Enlistment, National Archives. Neafus's sisters kept wanting to believe that he was alive through the following fall and wrote letter after letter to various European embassies and officials at the State Department in Washington seeking more information. On Oct. 6, 1938, seven months after her brother's disappearance, Helen Neafus Tipton wrote to Secretary Cordell Hull, "My Dear Mr. Hull, I am in receipt of a letter from the Foreign Embassy in Saint Jean de-Luz, France. Mr. Bowers states that he is unable to locate my brother, Ralph Lawrence Neafus, in Franco's prison at Burgos—though he does not say where else Franco is holding American prisoners—only eighty at Burgos. Is there anything you can do now that the volunteers are being removed from Spain to quickly arrange a complete exchange of all American prisoners? Possibly by doing so all these prison camps can be emptied & my brother found."

106 *A sister of Grace Cummins*: *Michigan Daily*, Mar. 30, May 19, 1938.

106 *The International Brigade was in full retreat and disarray*: Bessie, *Men in Battle*, 93–127; Eby, *Comrades and Commissars*, 313–46. Eby relates the story of Bob Cummins getting lost and pretending to be a campesino on page 337, but his source notes do not denote whether he heard this from Cummins himself. Eby's daughters have his papers, but they are unprocessed and not open to research yet.

107 *Bob and Elman were among the Mac-Paps who regrouped*: Bessie, *Men in Battle*, 131–38; Jackson, *At the Margins of Mayhem*, 29–50; undated letter from Bob

Cummins in Cummins Family Papers. On May 12, 2017, Spanish Civil War guide Alan Warren took my wife and me to Marçà, a hilly village with narrow streets and old stone and cement houses. Warren held up a photograph of Mac-Paps marching down a village street as we looked beyond him to that same street. We also saw the soccer field where the troops played and the old stone theater where they held political meetings. The encampments were on the edge of town, where we saw the Mac-Paps' command post and the rock-ledged swimming hole where Bob and his comrades cooled down.

107 *A. A. Cummins sent letters to the Department of State*: The letters and replies were among the artifacts Bob Cummins stored in a cardboard box that was passed along to his daughter Eileen Thomas upon his death.

109 *The coda to White's story*: Carroll, *Odyssey*, 257. Carroll writes, "One day in the summer of 1945, White did not come to work at the VALB [Veterans of the Abraham Lincoln Brigade] office. A colleague found him dead in his bed. 'The pressure was too much for him,' said the person who identified his body. He left behind an envelope with cash for the Lincoln brigade and no note. The VALB announced that White died of a heart attack at the age of 42. Most veterans never learned the truth of his death. It was an embarrassment best concealed—a failure of the camaraderie for which the Lincolns were so famous."

110 *Lardner . . . had arrived in Spain in the company of Ernest Hemingway*: Account of Jim Lardner's arrival in Spain and friendship with Elman Service drawn from Lardner File, ALBA; Service File, ALBA; *Santa Barbara News-Press*, July 26, 1987.

112 *As a runner, Bob carried messages*: Letter from Bob Cummins, July 15, 1938, Cummins Family Papers.

113 *A few days later, Service and Lardner*: Wounds suffered by Elman Service and Jim Lardner documented in their ALBA files; *Santa Barbara News-Press*, July 26, 1987.

113 *Stan Swinton, now a rising junior*: Although it is unclear if they all were published, Swinton wrote several articles on his European tour that summer of 1938, along with letters he wrote home to his parents: Swinton Papers, Bentley Historical Library. Swinton ended one report from France with this telling summation: "Time passes and the world moves on, as the day nears when cognac will be exchanged for coffins and bread for bayonets, Europe prepares."

114 *Jim Lardner was out of the hospital by then*: Lardner's death drawn from Lardner File, ALBA; letters from Vincent Sheean and Elman Service to Lardner's mother, Tamiment Library.

115 *The logistics of leaving were complicated by the Soviets*: Account of withdrawal from Spain by the American soldiers drawn from *Michigan Daily*; Eby, *Comrades and Commissars*, 406–19; Carroll, *Odyssey*, 200–205; Hochschild, *Spain in Our Hearts*, 348–50; Cummins Family Papers; photographs of the men aboard the SS *Paris*, ALBA photo archives; *New York Times*, Dec. 16, 1938.

117 *Three weeks later in Ann Arbor*: *Michigan Daily*, Jan. 6–7, 1939. As my father always told the story, he first saw Bob Cummins's twin sister, Barbara, at the rally, and asked her to introduce him to her younger sister, Mary.

Chapter 10: Named

118 *There was only one witness all day:* Account of Bereniece Baldwin's appearance in Room 740 drawn from *Communism in the Detroit Area*, Part 1, 2926–58; Jim Maraniss recollection; *Detroit Times, Detroit News, Detroit Free-Press*, Mar. 1, 1952. In closing the hearings for the week, Chairman Wood said, "In extending these thanks, I wish to compliment the work of the press and radio that have covered these hearings. Their cooperation with the committee, their full and factual coverage of these proceedings, is deeply appreciated by the committee, and, I am sure, by the Michigan public."

Chapter 11: Ace and Mary

124 *Another memorable evening took place at Hagen's:* Swinton letter to Barnes Constable, May 2, 1952, Swinton Papers, Bentley Historical Library.

124 *The news of Elliott's ascension:* *Michigan Daily*, May 6, 1939; *Detroit Free Press*, May 7, 1939; *Brooklyn Eagle*, May 14, 1939.

125 *Mary thought Ace had "a certain magic":* She used those words during her brief eulogy for my father at his memorial service in 2004.

126 *After a day of voting on the 31st:* *Michigan Daily*, Apr. 1, 1939.

126 *Throughout her early life, Mary:* Maraniss Family Papers. At some point late in her life, my mother wrote a twenty-three-page account of her life, focused mostly on her childhood, typed and single-spaced. It wove details of her experiences through psychological ruminations about why she thought and acted as she did.

128 *An editorial in the* Daily: *Michigan Daily*, Apr. 29, 1937.

129 *His favorite teacher . . . Fred Cassidy:* Elliott Maraniss, "Cassidy Was Professor Who Opened the Minds of Students," *Capital Times*, June 24, 2000.

130 *The first front-page story Ace wrote:* *Michigan Daily*, Nov. 10, 1937. "That's the trouble with your writers," Ford told my father. "They only know how to write about their own backyards." The editorial on Republican presidential candidates ran in the *Daily* on Nov. 12, and the series on the TVA began on Nov. 20.

131 *"If Mr. Roosevelt could by some magic":* *Michigan Daily*, Mar. 13, 1938.

131 *People tend to see what they want to see:* *Michigan Daily*, Mar. 12, 1938.

133 *"The Spanish people may be fighting for the same principles":* *Michigan Daily*, Jan. 7, 1938.

133 *My father helped organize the letters:* Ralph Neafus Alumni File, Bentley Historical Library; *Michigan Daily*, March 17–30, 1938.

134 *Between his sophomore and junior years:* "War Department, Military Intelligence Service, To: Lt. Col. J. Edgar Hoover, Federal Bureau of Investigation, Subject: Elliott Maraniss, Interview with Mrs. A. C. Miller, landlady, Nov. 6, 1942," EM FBI file.

134 *Elliott paid his tuition and room and board:* Elliott Maraniss Alumni File, Bentley Historical Library; letters from EM to MM from aboard the *Cape Canso* on the way to Okinawa, June 22, 1945: "You know of course that in my first three years

at Michigan we used to correspond regularly. Perhaps some of her letters are still around, if you look farther in our desk drawer."

135 *This was captured first in a long essay*: *Michigan Daily*, July 3, 1938.

136 *What does it mean to love America?*: Elliott Maraniss, "Books: Adamic's America," *Michigan Daily*, July 14, 1938: "With a freshness and directness that are unique, a buoyancy, robustness and exuberance that are like some exhilarating blasts from Whitman, Adamic wades into America, trying to work out into a coherent organism the unchecked, unorganized, uncharted vitality of the contemporary scene."

137 *He saw Wolfe's hunger as his generation's hunger*: *Perspectives: University of Michigan Literary Magazine*, Oct. 30, 1938. EM also wrote of Wolfe, "Had Thomas Wolfe written and completed his saga of the search of the American man for the timeless values of democracy, he would probably have become one of our immortals in the same sense that Whitman is immortal."

137 *Elliott praised him as a believer in "the living law"*: *Michigan Daily*, Feb. 16, 1939.

138 *He did break out of the college market once*: *St. Louis Post-Dispatch*, Feb. 22, 1938.

138 *Elliott spent another summer in Michigan*: EM Alumni File, Bentley Historical Library; Military Intelligence Service memo, Nov. 6, 1942.

138 *Autumn was his favorite season*: EM letter to "Jimmie," Apr. 14, 1945.

140 *"Bitter mutual recriminations erupted"*: Hochschild, *Spain in Our Hearts*, 364.

140 *In a front-page editorial Elliott cowrote*: *Michigan Daily*, Sept. 26, 1939.

141 *The* Daily *soon started receiving angry letters*: *Michigan Daily*, Sept. 27, 28, 1939.

142 *"Time has apparently forgotten that the Daily"*: Morty Q., "Of All Things!," *Michigan Daily*, Oct. 6, 1939.

142 *In his editorials, Elliott argued that the Soviet goal was to buy time*: *Michigan Daily*, Nov. 10, 17, 1939. The give-and-take between Elliott and graduate student Robert Anderson was published on Dec. 6, 1939.

143 *Elliott and Mary were married on December 16, 1939*: From fragments of EM's unpublished ode to MM, Maraniss Family Papers; MM psychological history; Marley records, Bentley Historical Library. The Brinnin-inscribed copy of Blake poetry was a prized family possession.

144 *Mary was a delegate from Michigan*: *Michigan Daily*, Jan. 6, 19, 1940; Joseph P. Lash interview with Robert Cohen, Student Activism in the 30s; Cohen, *When the Old Left Was Young*, 295–98.

145 *In February, Elliott hitchhiked to Washington*: *Michigan Daily*, Feb. 18, 1940. He wrote, "The writer of this article was one of those thousands of young people who went to Washington. The Americans he met there were typical youngsters, who were wide-awake, who knew what they wanted, and who knew how to get it."

146 *"The best way to indicate the importance of this book"*: *Michigan Daily*, March 8, 1940.

147 *Something odd happened at the* Daily *offices*: "Morty Q." column, *Michigan Daily*, Jan. 5, 1940. In their sign-off that year, the 1940 editors wrote, "With this issue members of the senior staff disappear into the limbo of forgotten editors, and become just names among the thousands who have been associated with the *Daily* in the course of its 50 years of service to the University community."

Chapter 12: Fear and Loathing

149 *"The House Un-American Activities Committee has left town"*: Detroit Free-Press, Mar. 2, 1952.

149 *But Jim . . . knew what was going on*: Recollection of Jim Maraniss. Jim's full name is James Elliott Maraniss. He named his youngest son Elliott Maraniss, in honor of our father. When Dad was in his final days at a hospital in Milwaukee, Jim sat at his bedside and read him sections of *War and Peace.*

150 *There was more to come*: Detroit Free Press, Detroit News, Detroit Times, March 2–4, 1952. The inside pages of the newspapers were also filled with related stories. Page 4 of the *News* on March 4 had the headlines "Hunt for Red Suspect Ends: Former Secretary Subpoenaed for Quiz"; "Senators Ask School Red Investigation"; "Union Strikes Spread over Red Suspects"; and "Legion Aids Former Red Who Testified." That story began, "Detroit American Legionnaires will do their utmost to obtain new employment for Walter S. Dunn, County jail guard who resigned under pressure after revealing himself as a disillusioned ex-Communist and testifying against the party."

151 *Barnes Constable, a reporter at Elliott's collegiate newspaper*: Michigan Daily, Mar. 2, 1952. Constable was the student journalist who received a congratulatory note from Stan Swinton upon his appointment as a *Daily* editor, recalling the night Swinton and Maraniss received their appointments in 1939.

152 *Radio stations in Potter's constituency in northern Michigan carried his weekly broadcast*: Charles E. Potter Papers, Box 2, Bentley Historical Library.

152 *On the day the hearings resumed*: New York Times, Washington Post, Mar. 11, 1952.

153 *That night, two women arrived in Detroit*: Detroit News, Mar. 12, 1952.

153 *Joe Gollner was twenty-four when he died*: Daily Times (Salisbury, MD), Oct. 20, 1949; USS *Essex* website; Wicomico Civic Center memorial; USNA Virtual Memorial Hall; John Gollner recollection.

Chapter 13: Something in the Wind

157 *Elliott was stationed . . . in the British West Indies*: EM documents from National Personnel Records Center, Military Personnel Records; EM letter, June 4, 1942, Maraniss Family Papers.

158 *"It is a great comfort to know"*: EM letter to MM, June 7, 1942, Maraniss Family Papers.

160 *Elliott sensed that "something was in the wind"*: EM letter to MM, June 10, 1942, Maraniss Family Papers; letters from Portner, Wells, and George in EM's military personnel file, all written in late May 1942.

161 *The Military Intelligence Division of the War Department*: Depiction of investigation drawn from records of the military intelligence investigation of EM that were received in a batch of FBI papers after a Freedom of Information Act request. "REASON FOR INVESTIGATION: Elliott Maraniss, who has been stationed at Hq. Trinidad Center and Base Command, Trinidad, is being considered for employment in confidential work of said headquarters."

165 *This document was a lot for me to process*: Email correspondence with Morton Mintz, Aug. 15, 2017; interview with Mintz in Washington, DC, Feb. 21, 2018.

167 *"Soldier is no longer in this command"*: The Adjutant General's Office in the War Department wrote to Trinidad command regarding "Subject: Transfer of Potentially Subversive Personnel," but EM's commanding officer in Trinidad, who regarded him highly, merely noted that he was already in OCS school at Camp Lee and was not to be transferred.

168 *His first assignment . . . was close to home*: "Special Orders, No. 257, Headquarters, The Quartermaster School, Camp Lee, Va., Elliott Maraniss 0-1585810—QMC, Air Transport Comd, Romulus, Michigan; Subject: Commendation, To: Lt. Elliott Maraniss, Army Air Base, Romulus, Michigan."

168 *Again the military seemed at odds with itself*: On Mar. 12, 1943, Col. E. S. Wetzel, Air Corps, Military Personnel Division, wrote the memo seeking to keep EM at Romulus against the wishes of the Adjutant General's Office, which prevailed and shipped him off to West Texas.

169 *One of the stops Agent Maranda made*: Military intelligence investigation, Residence check, Mr. C. Lang, Gladstone Street, Detroit, EM FBI file.

169 *Bob had met Susan Goodman*: Correspondence with Rachel Cummins, Bob's oldest daughter.

170 *It was while Elliott and Mary were still in New York*: From Cummins Family Papers, later used in DM, "Uncle Phil's Brain," *Washington Post Magazine*, Oct. 27, 2002.

170 *Susan and her sister, Peggy, even sent off a telegram to Kenesaw Mountain Landis*: BA MSS67, Folder 8, National Baseball Hall of Fame.

171 *Mary was an outspoken activist in the campaign*: Account of MM working in the defense plant and being kept safe during the Detroit race riots drawn from Maraniss Family Papers, recollections of MM and EM, and EM's unpublished account of MM's life.

172 *Langston Hughes captured in verse*: Langston Hughes, "Beaumont to Detroit: 1943," in *The Collected Poems of Langston Hughes*, 281. Parts of this poem are etched in marble at an exhibit at the Smithsonian National Museum of African American History and Culture.

173 *Something was in the wind*: EM military personnel records, assignment to Camp Lee to begin training all-black salvage and repair company.

Chapter 14: Legless

174 *Charles Edward Potter, the future congressman*: Account of Charles E. Potter's battle experience and wounds suffered during battles in Belgium and France drawn from Charles E. Potter Papers, Boxes 1–3, Potter scrapbook, Bentley Historical Library; Battle of Hürtgen Forest, combat interview with "Lt. Charles E. Potter, lst Bn S-3, S-2 at Hürtgen Forest (The only officer left of the Bn staff)," interviewer, lst Lt. Harry G. Jackson; Rick Atkinson, *The Guns at Last Light* (New York: Picador, 2014), 254–317; Weaver, *Guard Wars*, 205. When Potter began his postwar political

career, his campaign materials emphasized his war heroism with a brochure titled "Charles E. Potter—Mr. American."

Chapter 15: Know Your Men

179 *First Lt. Elliott Maraniss was working late*: EM letter to MM, Feb. 1, 1945, Maraniss Family Papers.

179 *This discrimination had been reaffirmed*: Lee, *The Employment of Negro Troops*, 76. Ulysses Lee, the black army historian who wrote and edited the illuminating 738-page military history, noted that the White House claimed that this policy followed a meeting with top Negro leaders, but "the men who had attended the White House conference were especially annoyed by the implication that they had endorsed the announced policy."

180 *Camp Lee was "the most segregated"*: Jesse J. Johnson paper, Camp Lee Museum Archive. Thirty years later, Lieutenant Colonel Johnson, Ret., delivered a lecture at Fort Huachuca, Arizona, on the contribution and treatment of black soldiers during World War II and received a standing ovation.

182 *The 4482nd had been activated at Camp Lee six weeks earlier*: EM military records, "Efficiency Report, 2 Jan 45, Official Status of Officer, Salvage Officer, 4482nd, Officer joined unit 16 Dec. 44."

182 *At night he spent several hours in the orderly room*: EM letters to MM, Jan. 4, 10, 11, 15, 1945. From that last letter: "The fellow in the room next to mine has his radio on pretty loud, and so right now I am listening to Bob Trout's summary of the news: and very interesting news it is, too, what with the tremendous four-front offensive of the Soviet armies, the steady, southward advance of the Sixth Army from the Lingayen beachhead to Manila, and the squeezing of the Nazi bulge in Belgium."

183 *Tuesday nights were reserved for cadre school*: EM letter to MM, Jan. 19, 1945. "As you probably could imagine, one of the most important qualities of a non-com in a company like ours—with a technical mission in a military setting—is the ability to teach and instruct his men, by example, by demonstration, by conferences, lectures and every other way."

183 *"Know your men, and you will not only solve a lot of problems"*: EM letter to MM, Jan. 19, 1945.

184 *By the time Horkan took command*: Lee, *The Employment of Negro Troops*, 323–24; Horkan File, U.S. Army Quartermaster Museum, Archives. The installation changed its name from Camp Lee to Fort Lee after the war.

185 *Orrin C. Evans . . . praised Horkan for his innovations*: Lee, *The Employment of Negro Troops*, 76–77.

185 *The men in Elliott's company provided more than their share of talent*: Camp Lee *Traveler*, Jan. 16, 17, 24, 1945.

185 *One of the repeated themes in Elliott's letters home*: EM to MM, Jan. 20, 1945.

186 *"Of course, the really bad characters"*: EM to MM, Jan. 25, 1945.

187 *At seven on the morning of February 5*: EM letters to MM, Feb. 5–18, 1945; *Camp Lee Traveler* clippings; EM military personnel file. In his first letter from the field,

EM described the middle-of-the-night orders to relocate: "I had been expecting that they would throw the book at us—and I guess they will, all right. 'Shake-down' move is what they call this business of packing up and moving the very first night that you hit a bivouac area. Well, we made it all right, with a lot of work and sweat and cold toes and noses."

189 *"I just feel that I am doomed"*: Undated letter from Phil Cummins to his parents and family, Cummins Family Papers; DM, "Uncle Phil's Brain," *Washington Post Magazine*, Oct. 27, 2002.

189 *Mary told Phil that she had just returned from Detroit*: MM letter to Phil Cummins, Feb. 28, 1945.

189 *Purdy and his younger brother*: Account of Purdy brothers, Bob Cummins, and George Watt experiences in World War II drawn from Bob Cummins letter to Phil, Mar. 27, 1944, Cummins Family Papers; Honor States, honorstates.org; Fields of Honor database, https://www.fieldsofhonor-database.com/index.php/en/; Carroll, *Odyssey*, 250–64; Watt, *The Comet Connection*. In the prologue to his account of his daring rescue and escape, Watt wrote, "The volunteers of the Abraham Lincoln Brigade, with whom I served in the Spanish Civil War from 1937 to 1939, are also part of this story. They were the first Americans to take up arms against Hitler and Mussolini, who were supporting Franco. That war was the opening battle against Hitlerism and a dress rehearsal for World War II. Instead of welcoming our combat experience, we were considered 'premature anti-Fascists' and initially kept from going overseas. But a change in War Department policy in the spring of 1943 permitted Lincoln Brigade veterans to go into combat, making it possible for me to join the Bramwell crew. This is the memoir of one American's second chance at Hitler. The participants were many. I salute them all."

192 *Life became an anxious waiting game*: EM letter to MM, Mar. 22, 1945. On that breezy spring night, EM wrote to MM that "two items in the news seem to warrant special comment. I read them in the paper the same day: first, confirmation of Eisenhower's policy of using mixed companies of Negro and white volunteers in Europe. In fact, according to the story in the front page of Tuesday's *Detroit News*, those mixed companies have already been used and proven in battle. Secondly, and most contradictorily in the same Army, the case of the 4 Negro WACs at Fort Devens, Mass. Purely a miscarriage of justice and outrageous treatment by a colonel who should be court-martialed and dishonorably discharged from the Army." (The four black women were sentenced to a year's hard labor and dishonorably discharged from the army for refusing orders, arguing that they were assigned menial tasks not assigned to white WACs.)

193 *Back at Camp Lee, Elliott was effusive*: EM letter to MM, Apr. 9, 1945.

194 *The day after that, April 12*: EM letter to MM, Apr. 12, 1945; *Camp Lee Traveler*, Apr. 18, 1945: "The bulletin board roster told me I was CQ Thursday evening, an all-night trick," wrote S. Sgt. Jim Haughton. "I settled comfortably at the news desk, ready for a quiet night when suddenly the phone rang. The guttural voice on the other end was Henry Prohly, rotund and serious corporal in the I and E office. He spoke in an anguished and excited voice. 'The President. He's dead.'"

EM wrote a follow-up letter to MM the day after the announcement of Roosevelt's death: "I spoke to the men at reveille announcing the period of mourning and tried to relieve some of the tension and strain. It's funny, I can't recall exactly what I said, because it was completely extemporaneous. But when I finished the men stood silently in ranks without rushing to the mess hall, they crowded around me, asking questions and making statements to me. So I spoke to them again informally, for about ten minutes. What they wanted to know from me was this: Will we win the war, and will we have peace, and what will happen to us after the war?"

Chapter 16: Why I Fight

195 *Dear Jimmie*: Letter from EM to his infant son, Apr. 14, 1945. EM variously spelled the name as Jimmie or Jimmy. MM used only Jimmy. My brother can be a romantic about our family and the places of our lives, but he winces at certain types of predictable sentimentality. To him, this letter fell into that category. "Dad's letter to me is kind of painful to read," he wrote. "It's so unoriginal (and it reads like propaganda)."

Chapter 17: In the Blood

200 *The weather was so bad last night*: Letter from EM to MM, Apr. 15, 1945. EM was just at the early stages of an interrupted newspaper career when he wrote that letter, but it echoed through the decades when I read it more than seventy years later. It had a profound effect on me, somewhat like his statement with the imperfect *S*, but this time it thrilled me, with no pangs of regret.

Chapter 18: The Power of America

202 *The last party was under way*: EM letter to MM, Apr. 24, 1945. "Our party last night was quite a slam-bang success. When I got there at 8:30 it was already started—since the bus carrying the girls from Richmond had already arrived."

203 *"One of the most interesting developments of the past few days"*: EM letter to MM, Apr. 17, 1945.

203 *Elliott and his soldiers boarded their troopship, the* Cape Canso: Roland W. Charles, *Troopships of World War II* (Fort Eustis, VA: Army Transportation Association, 1947), 163: "Another C1A type vessel that went directly from the building yard to the conversion yard. She was converted at New York by Arthur Tickle Engineering Co., between 11 November 1943 and 17 February 1944. Following alteration the vessel went from New York to Hampton Roads, arriving there on 3 March 1944. Having transited the Panama Canal in late March, the ship reached Noumea in April and from there made several visits to Milne Bay and Oro Bay before going to Brisbane on 10 May. She returned to San Francisco in June and in mid-July left, via Heuneme and Honolulu, for Manus Island, Espiritu Santo, Noumea, and Havannah Pass. Return to San Francisco via Honolulu on 23 November. Next going

to San Diego, the CAPE CANSO sailed, two days before Christmas, for Honolulu, Eniwetok, and Saipan. She returned on 23 February to San Francisco. Following repairs, the ship next left (via Seattle), on May 7 for Pearl Harbor, Eniwetok, Ulithi and Okinawa." (That was the voyage that carried Elliott and his troops.)

203 *On the third day out, Elliott got "sick as a dog"*: EM letters to MM, May 10, 11, 1945.

204 *He tried to consider the various needs and attitudes of the men*: Undated letter, EM to MM, aboard the *Cape Canso*.

205 *He complimented Elliott on the cleanliness*: Undated letter, EM to MM, aboard the *Cape Canso*, approximate date determined by information in the letter. "I must admit with no little pride that my unit is a more cohesive, better disciplined and more military-looking and acting organization than a lot of the others I've seen here and at port."

206 *Books about "American literature"*: EM letter to MM, June 10, 1945 (thirty-fourth day at sea).

207 *"No one knows better than I"*: EM letter to MM, June 21, 1945. "Now with no false heroics, but no false apologies either, I am anxious to get on with the war against the Japanese: to destroy the last vestiges of the Axis war alliance, to finish the war and return home to you."

208 *"The first ditty, a parody"*: EM letter to MM, Aug. 17, 1945.

208 *"We heard the news at 0800"*: EM letter to MM, Aug. 15, 1945.

210 *He was trying to answer her apparent concern*: Undated letter, EM to MM, from Okinawa.

211 *On the morning of September 4*: EM letter to MM, Sept. 4, 1945. He signed off that letter, "JOIN THE ARMY AND SEE THE WORLD!"

212 *Elliott was in the middle of a gin rummy game*: Description of EM's experiences awaiting the LST and in the rough seas on the way to Korea from Sept. 19 letter to MM: "Somewhere on the Yellow Sea off the coast of Korea." He wrote a second letter on Sept. 22 at anchor in Jinsen Harbor summarizing what he had learned leading the company.

Chapter 19: The Virginian

217 *On the third Friday of March*: Description of Tavenner leaving Virginia and flying west to Tokyo drawn from Personal Papers of Frank S. Tavenner, and Official Records of the International Military Tribunal for the Far East, 1945–48; Tavenner file, Box 13, folder 1, University of Virginia (UVA) Law Library; "Woodstock Socials and Clubs," *Shenandoah Herald*, week of Mar. 15, 1946; "Serum Plane's Supercargo Is VA Attorney," *Washington Post*, Mar. 17, 1946.

218 *Even before Tavenner reached Japan*: Tokyo Wars Crimes Trial, Tavenner Papers, UVA Law School archive. The introduction to the trial papers: "Unlike the quick convening of Nuremberg, planning for the International Military Tribunal for the Far East (IMTFE) began with some delay under the State-War-Navy Coordinating Committee. Initially, multiple tribunals were envisioned, each focusing on a separate aspect: crimes against peace, war crimes, and crimes against humanity. The

Tokyo trial was supposed to focus predominantly on crimes against peace, known as Class A. [Instead, they were all combined in Tokyo.] An overt aim of the US planners of the tribunal was to create an educational moment for the world centering on the consequences of waging aggressive war."

219 *According to an internal memo*: June 10, 1946, letter, Tavenner File, UVA Law Library.

220 *On May 1 . . . Tavenner held a press conference*: Radiopress Special, "Complete Report of Press Conference by Hon. Frank S. Tavenner, May 1, 1945, 10:00 a.m.," Tavenner File, UVA Law Library.

221 *The Southern Railway System offered him a lucrative job*: Tavenner letter, Dec. 30, 1946, Tavenner File, UVA Law Library. "I do not feel that I can with propriety give consideration to the matter of employment."

221 *The Tavenner name was well known in Woodstock*: *Daily News Record*, Harrisonburg, Va., July 30, 1932; Tavenner File, UVA Law Library; *American Taitai: In Search of Beauty in the Mundane*, June 7, 2013, https://americantaitai.com/; Tim Hensley, "A Curious Tale: The Apple in North America," Brooklyn Botanic Garden, June 2, 2005, https://www.bbg.org/gardening/article/the_apple_in_north_america; William A. Fischel, "The Law and Economics of Cedar-Apple Rust," Dartmouth College, Apr. 23, 2004, https://www.dartmouth.edu/~wfischel/Papers/cedar%20rust%20Fischel%2028apr04.pdf; Nina Martyris, "'Paradise Lost': How the Apple Became the Forbidden Fruit," *Food for Thought*, NPR, Apr. 30, 2017, https://www.npr.org/sections/thesalt/2017/04/30/526069512/paradise-lost-how-the-apple-became-the-forbidden-fruit.

223 *His army unit was the 1st Pioneer Infantry*: *Daily News-Record*, Harrisonburg, Va., July 24, 1918; *Valley Boys in Action*, 382, Woodstock Public Library.

223 *He proved better at the first two than the last*: Associated Press, Feb. 8, 1939; stories of FDR's fight with the Virginia senators over judicial appointment carried in newspapers around the country that week.

224 *he received a letter from Keenan explaining his situation*: Tavenner Papers, UVA Law School.

224 *Tavenner in Tokyo had his first interaction with Russians*: Dec. 4, 1946, memo to Tavenner from Eugene D. Williams; May 22, 1947, memo, Tavenner to Vasiliev; Feb. 5, 1948, memo, Tavenner to Vasiliev, all in Tavenner Papers, UVA Law School.

225 *Pritchard's son, Cpl. B. W. Pritchard*: Letter to Tavenner, Aug. 21, 1947, Tavenner Papers, UVA Law School.

226 *Tavenner delivered the final summation*: Transcript, International Prosecution Section final summation, Apr. 18, 1948, Tavenner Papers, UVA Law School.

Chapter 20: Foley Square

227 *George Crockett sat in the federal courthouse*: Depiction of opening day of trial drawn from *New York Times*, Jan. 18, 1949; H. D. Quigg, United Press, Jan. 17, 1949; "Trial of Twelve Top Red Bosses in U.S. Opens: 400 Police Stand By in Court Area," Box 149, Folders 7, 10, 18, National Lawyers Guild Archive, Tamiment Library; Harold R. Medina Papers, Mudd Manuscript Library; Martelle, *The Fear Within*.

229 *The first prosecution under the act*: Michal R. Belknap, *American Political Trials* (Westport, CT: Praeger, 1994), and *Cold War Political Justice* (Westport, CT: Praeger, 1977); Michael Steven Smith, "About the Smith Act Trials," in *Encyclopedia of the American Left*, edited by Mary Jo Buhle, Paul Buhle, and Dan Georgakas (Oxford: Oxford University Press, 1998).

230 *The independent streak started with his surname*: Portrait of Crockett as a young man drawn from George Crockett Papers, Reuther Library; Wright, *The Making of a Champion*; Crockett Files, Tamiment Library; interview with Edward J. Littlejohn, retired Wayne State law professor and Crockett expert.

230 *Copies of the* Michigan Daily: *Michigan Daily* articles, July 16, 1932, Feb. 22, 1933, Oct. 6, 1933, Feb. 20, 1934, Mar. 17, 1934. The last item: "A Negro symposium led by Willis Ward '35 was held last night at Ann Arbor High. The question under discussion was 'A Critical Survey of the Problems Confronting the Negro' in the following fields: history, social progress, law, literature, public health and education. Those besides Ward who participated included George Crockett, James O. Slade, H. J. Harrison, Doxey A. Wilkerson, C. E. Boulware. The Bethel AME choir rendered several selections."

231 *There were petition drives, mass meetings*: *Michigan Daily* articles, Oct. 17–22, 1934; Stephen J. Nesbitt, "The Forgotten Man," *Michigan Daily*, Oct. 18, 2012; *Time*, Oct. 29, 1934; "Willis Ward, Gerald Ford, and Michigan Football's Darkest Day," *Detroit News*, Oct. 22, 2012; interview and material from Michigan historian John U. Bacon.

232 *When he finished law school*: Unpublished Crockett biography, Reuther Library; Crockett Papers, Tamiment Library.

233 *One of his cases took him to Detroit*: Depiction of Crockett working for UAW in Detroit drawn from Crockett column in *Michigan Chronicle*, "Labor Looks Ahead," June 16, 1945, George Crockett and Ernest Goodman files, Reuther Library; Wright, *The Making of a Champion*; *Detroit Free Press* profile, Jan. 12, 1975.

236 *The language of Eugene Dennis was hardly innocent or indirect*: Eugene Dennis, *What America Faces: The New War Danger and the Struggle for Peace, Democracy, and Economic Security* (Whitefish, MT: Literary Licensing, 2013). Text of Dennis's report to the plenary meeting of the National Committee of the Communist Party held in New York, Feb. 12, 1946. Subjects included "Strike Movement," "Truman Administration," "Struggle for Peace," "The '46 Elections and Third Party Question," "CP as Powerful Vanguard Party," and "Struggle against Browderism." Of former national leader Earl Browder, Dennis said, "Browderism is no longer current, a trend, in the communist party. Browder is an opponent, an enemy of our party. Browder has become what Lenin termed a social-chauvinist, a social imperialist. It is clear, comrades, that this meeting of our National Convention should and will expel this notorious revisionist who has deserted the ranks and the cause of communism and has become a servile champion of American monopoly capital."

236 *Crockett had not read Marx and Lenin*: "Freedom Is Everybody's Job!," George W. Crockett summation at Foley Square trial, published as pamphlet by National Non-Partisan Committee; also in trial transcripts of Medina Papers, Mudd Manuscript Library; Babson et al., *The Color of Law*, 192.

236 *Judge Medina, a graduate of Princeton:* Portrait of Judge Medina and account of back-and-forth between Medina and Crockett drawn from trial transcript, Medina Papers, Mudd Manuscript Library; "Hectic Trial Haunts Crockett's Bid for Bench," *Detroit News*, Oct. 10, 1966; Crockett FBI files, Tamiment Library; Crockett and Goodman Papers, Reuther Library.

238 *In a letter to a sympathetic friend:* Letter to George W. Alger, Esq., Park Avenue, New York, Mar. 14, 1949, Medina Papers, Mudd Manuscript Library: "In all the welter of thousands of letters, mostly cursing me out for not letting the defendants off or for not bearing down on them hard enough, and so forth, your affectionate letter came as a refreshing blast of fresh air."

239 *Paul Robeson, whose life offered a kaleidoscopic:* The most thorough biography is Martin Duberman's *Paul Robeson* (Knopf, 1989).

240 *The anticommunist hostility toward Robeson was never stronger:* Depiction of Peekskill riot and Robeson testimony at Foley Square trial drawn from Martin Duberman, *Paul Robeson* (New York: New Press, 1995), 365; "A Rough Sunday at Peekskill," *American Heritage Magazine*, Apr. 1976; *History Today* 62, no. 4 (Apr. 2012); Brave New Films, "Pete Seeger & Majora Carter," YouTube, https://www.youtube.com/watch?v=YjLdegTHIVA; trial transcript, Robeson testimony, Sept. 20, 1949, Medina Papers, Mudd Manuscript Library; Crockett Papers, Folder 6, Tamiment Library; *New York Times*, Sept. 21, 1949.

243 *In riding the subways in New York:* "Freedom Is Everybody's Job!" The National Non-Partisan Committee that published Crockett's summation to the jury featured Paul Robeson as a cochairman and novelist Howard Fast as treasurer. Other board members included the international president of the Farm Equipment Union, a cochair of the Republican Party in Columbia, South Carolina, and a judge from Sullivan, Indiana.

244 *The gray-haired bailiff issued the cry:* Medina Papers trial transcript, Mudd Manuscript Library; *New York Times*, *New York Herald Tribune*, Oct. 15, 1949; Crockett FBI file, Tamiment Library; George Crockett and Ernest Goodman Papers, Reuther Library.

Chapter 21: Committee Men

246 *Wood was less strident:* Walter Goodman, *The Committee: The Extraordinary Career of the House Committee on Un-American Activities* (New York: Farrar, Straus & Giroux, 1968), 173–74.

246 *Wood . . . voted against a 1949 measure prohibiting poll taxes:* Wood's congressional voting record is on www.govtrack.us.

247 *Wood's role was notable not because of the side he took:* The best coverage of Wood's role in the Taft-Hartley subterfuge was done by Peter Edson for the NEA news service, Apr. 29, May 5, 1949; also Drew Pearson, "Washington Merry-Go-Round," June 12, 1950.

250 *Pearson was not done:* Drew Pearson, "Washington Merry-Go-Round," June 20, 24, 1950.

250 *Wood responded by taking to the House floor:* "Rep. John S. Wood Answers Drew Pearson," Speech of Hon. John S. Wood of Georgia in the House of Representatives, *Congressional Record*, June 15, 1950.

251 *A few weeks before Christmas 1950:* Farrell, *Richard Nixon*, 163.

252 *When Tavenner took the job:* New York Times, obituary, Oct. 22, 1964.

253 *The merits of Fifth Amendment protections . . . became a debate topic:* Valparaiso (IN) *Vidette-Messenger*, Mar. 6, 1951.

254 *Truman's Executive Order also set in motion:* Responses to Red Scare drawn from Caute, *The Great Fear*; Morgan, *Reds*; Griffith, *The Politics of Fear*; Farrell, *Richard Nixon*.

254 *For Potter, it had been a long road back:* Potter's slow recovery from war wounds drawn from Charles E. Potter Papers, Boxes 1–2, Bentley Historical Library; information from the Hospital Admission Cards created by the Office of the Surgeon General, Department of the Army for Service, No. 01306316, World War II Military Records Group, National Archives. One campaign pamphlet quoted a magazine story on Potter: "There is something peculiarly American in the story of . . . Potter's personal victory over disaster. It is compounded of faith, optimism, ambition, risk-taking, and humor, and the steadfast support of his wife."

255 *Potter won the election in a landslide:* Potter election and appointment to HUAC drawn from *Escanaba (MI) Daily Press*, July–Nov. 1952; Charles E. Potter Papers, scrapbook, Bentley Historical Library. Several northern Michigan newspapers carried the headline "Legless Ex-GI Wins Election."

256 *It was typical of newspapers to promote the comings and goings of HUAC:* Long Beach *Press-Telegram*, Sept. 15, 1951.

Chapter 22: A Good American Family

260 *Go back three and a half years:* MM letter to Phil Cummins, May 14, 1946, Maraniss Family Papers.

262 *The Detroit Field Office of the FBI knew:* Account of FBI investigation from FBI files on EM, obtained by FOIA request through the U.S. National Archives and Records Administration, declassified and screened by Mary Kay Schmidt, June 17, 2015. The files came in two batches a year apart. The first batch was 69 pages. The second batch of 186 pages included the military intelligence report conducted during World War II.

264 *The most compelling feature in that first edition:* Michigan Herald, Jan. 12, Apr. 20, Apr. 27, 1947, Newspaper and Current Periodicals Reading Room, Library of Congress.

266 *the* Herald *published a guest column by Coleman Young:* Michigan Herald, May 11, 1947, Library of Congress.

266 *She reported to FBI agents that James E. Jackson:* EM FBI file. Jackson was a leading figure in the party in Detroit and New York City. Life circles around in strange ways. As I was writing this book, I became a patient of Mark D. Scarupa at the Institute for Asthma and Allergy in Chevy Chase, Maryland. During one visit to his

office, he asked me what my book was about, and I said HUAC and my father. He said that his grandfather had been hounded by Red hunters during that era. When I asked where, he said Detroit and New York. When I asked what his grandfather's name was, he said, "James E. Jackson." "James E. Jackson!" I exclaimed. "He's in my book." Scarupa is a world-class doctor. He remembered seeing Paul Robeson at his grandparents' house.

268 *The good American family was dealt another blow:* DM, "Uncle Phil's Brain," *Washington Post Magazine,* Oct. 27, 2002.

268 *Phil's siblings in Detroit were eager for news:* MM letter to Phil Cummins, Mar. 30, 1949; Bob Cummins letter to Phil Cummins, May 1949, Cummins Family Papers.

269 *But there is a story from those days:* EM recollection; Barbas, *The First Lady of Hollywood,* 282–88.

270 *I came along on August 6:* MM letter to Phil Cummins, Aug. 7, 1949, Cummins Family Papers. Two days earlier, MM had written another note to Phil: "I'm writing this note on the eve of someone's approaching birth. We're not sure of much about this person—name or sex. I hope I'll know by tomorrow. Maybe I'm being obscure, but the point is I'm sitting around biting my fingernails waiting for Maraniss child # 3."

271 *My father was at work on Labor Day:* Typed letter to Joe and Ida Maraniss, Sept. 5, 1949, Maraniss Family Papers.

272 *One month after the war started:* Associated Press, July 28, 1950. Bob's physical removal from the auto plant came on his birthday.

273 *Susan, Bob's wife:* Account of Sue's sickness and death from correspondence with Rachel Cummins, her daughter; also Bob Cummins letter to Phil Cummins, Oct. 27, 1950, Cummins Family Papers.

274 *Peggy had one other strong memory:* Interview with Peggy Datz, July 16, 2017.

276 *Bob confessed that he was jobless again:* Typed letter to Phil Cummins from Bob Cummins, May 12, 1951, Cummins Family Papers.

276 *The following description of the Subject:* EM FBI file, Mar. 3, 1951.

277 *Mary had three small children:* Letter from MM to Phil Cummins, Apr. 30, 1951.

278 *a man in a dark suit rang the front bell:* Interview with Peggy Datz, July 16, 2017.

Chapter 23: March 12, 1952

280 *The weather in Detroit:* Detroit Times, Mar. 12, 1952; *Detroit Free Press,* Mar. 13, 1952; *Detroit News,* Mar. 13, 1952.

280 *Testimony of Elliott Maraniss:* Communism in the Detroit Area, Part 2, Mar. 10, 11, 12, 1952, 3179–83. Fifteen witnesses were called on the last day of the hearings. EM was the eleventh witness to testify that day.

Chapter 24: The Whole Pattern of a Life

288 *Statement of Elliott Maraniss:* HUAC Investigative Name Files, Series 1, Box 32, National Archives. Along with the Mar. 12, 1952, statement, the file included a copy

of the subpoena served on EM on Feb. 29, 1952, and an abbreviated account of the FBI and Detroit Red Squad investigations of his comings and goings.

Chapter 25: Witches or Traitors

292 *"Why the hell did you make the picture"*: Miller, *Timebends*, 315–16. For an insightful examination of Miller's dispute with Columbia see "Arthur Miller vs. Columbia Pictures: The Strange Case of *Career of a Salesman*," Kevin Kerrane, *The Journal of American Culture*, Sept. 2004.

293 *His first impression was that Salem was trapped*: Account of Miller's first trip to Salem from Miller, "Journey to *The Crucible*," in *The Theater Essays of Arthur Miller*, 27–30, originally published in *New York Times*, Feb. 8, 1953; Miller, *Timebends*, 338–42.

294 *Real or imagined, was being a communist the equivalent*: Statement of EM, HUAC Investigative Name Files, National Archives.

295 *in the context of Judge Learned Hand's axiom*: Caute, *The Great Fear*, 148; "Gravity of the Evil Test," *First Amendment Encyclopedia*, https://mtsu.edu/first-amendment/article/963/gravity-of-the-evil-test. Hand's formula was his interpretation of an earlier judicial axiom constructed by U.S. Supreme Court justice Oliver Wendell Holmes Jr. in a 1919 case involving whether an antiwar activist had the First Amendment right to advocate draft resistance: "The question in every case is whether the words used are of such a nature as to create a clear and present danger that they will bring about the substantive evils that the United States Congress has the right to prevent. It is a case of proximity and degree."

295 *Along with the Bill of Rights*: Statement of EM, HUAC Investigative Names File.

296 *This was Miller's first time in Salem*: Miller, *The Theater Essays of Arthur Miller*, 27–30; Crucible Notebook, Arthur Miller Papers, Harry Ransom Center. In his notes to himself as he was plotting the play, Miller wrote, "It has got to be basically Proctor's story. The important thing—the process by which a man, feeling guilt for A, sees himself as guilty of B, and thus belies himself—accommodates his credo to believe in what he knows is not true." He also was thinking about the connection between the concepts of the devil and outsiderness. "[They] believed he (the devil) attacked to prevent Christianizing America—hence 'his woods' and 'his Indians.'"

297 *The morning after Elliott was interrogated*: Detroit Free Press, Mar. 13, 1952.

298 *That last film, meant to glorify*: Account of the making of *Big Jim McLain* and the interaction between producers John Wayne and Robert Fellows and HUAC counsel Tavenner and committee members Jackson and Wood drawn from Administrative Files for Frank Tavenner, HUAC, RG 233 LL Composite Box, National Archives; Murphy, *Congressional Theatre*, 75–86. Murphy wrote of the movie's close, "The last frame is an acknowledgment of HUAC's help: 'The incidents in this motion picture are based on the files of the Committee on Un-American Activities, House of Representatives, Congress of the United States. Names and places have been changed. We gratefully acknowledge the cooperation of this Committee.'"

Chapter 26: American Wanderers

303 *The rest of us followed*: Correspondence and conversations with Jean (Maraniss) Alexander and Jim Maraniss.

303 *There is a photograph taken of the five of us*: Maraniss family albums. A note on the back in MM's soothing cursive handwriting labels it summer 1952.

305 *We moved into the small apartment of our Brooklyn grandparents*: Correspondence and conversations with Jean (Maraniss) Alexander and Jim Maraniss. My strongest memories of Coney Island came later, when I was between ten and fourteen and we made annual pilgrimages east in our light green Rambler station wagon.

305 *The* Daily Compass, *a morning tabloid*: Copies of *Compass* in Maraniss Family Papers; EM's storytelling as recalled by my siblings and me.

307 *Our family was cut adrift again*: Correspondence with Jim Maraniss.

307 *George Crockett was out of prison*: Account of Crockett's imprisonment and experiences after his release drawn from FBI File, National Lawyers Guild, Crockett folders, Tamiment Library; "An Unofficial, Incomplete Biographical Sketch and a Few Personal Recollections of Congressman George W. Crockett, Jr., by his former law partner, Ernie Goodman," George Crockett and Ernest Goodman Papers, Reuther Library; *New York Times*, Apr. 24, 1952; Associated Press, Apr. 24, 1952; *Daily People's World*, Feb. 1952; Wright, *The Making of a Champion*; Babson et al., *The Color of Law*.

310 *With the new year came the Broadway premiere of* The Crucible: Miller, *The Portable Arthur Miller*, introduction to the original edition by Harold Clurman; Miller, *The Theater Essays of Arthur Miller*, 152–62, 171–74.

311 *Our family moved again*: Portrait of family life in Cleveland drawn from MM letter to Phil Cummins, Feb. 18, 1953.

312 *As soon as Mom could arrange it*: Portrait of family experiences in Cleveland drawn from EM unpublished story about MM, Maraniss Family Papers; Jean (Maraniss) Alexander correspondence; Jim Maraniss correspondence.

313 *We were a family of baseball lovers*: Like so many others of my generation, I wish I still had that Al Smith autograph, or any of the baseball cards I collected from age five to fifteen. I remember clearly one summer, when we were visiting our grandparents in Ann Arbor, walking home from the nearby grocery and opening a pack, and the first card was Jackie Robinson, who in our family was a deity (but so were Al Rosen and Ted Williams and a variety of other ballplayers, for different reasons). The Jackie card was one of those years that featured the ballplayers in lifelike miniature action paintings.

313 *One day Jim was at the house of a friend*: Jim Maraniss correspondence.

314 *"Have you ever seen a copy of the Pee-Dee?"*: EM letter to Phil Cummins, Feb. 18, 1953.

314 *The FBI continued to follow him in Cleveland*: EM FBI file, June 17, 1953.

315 *There was internal debate between Cleveland and Washington*: EM FBI file, Summary administrative page, Jan. 1, 1955: "By letter dated June 18, 1954, the Cleveland Office requested authority to interview the subject, ELLIOTT MARANISS. By

letter dated June 30, 1954, the Bureau requested that further consideration be given this matter and temporarily deferred authority to interview subject. By letter dated July 16, 1954, the Cleveland Office reiterated its request for authority to interview captioned subject. By letter dated July 28, 1954, the Bureau advised that a file review of the subject indicated the inadvisability of interviewing the subject at that time and authority for such interview was denied."

315 *Then our lives were disrupted once again*: EM FBI file. Summary of Elliott's firing and interaction with the Newspaper Guild: "Mr. Anthony S. Fernandez, a former Special Agent of the Bureau at Cleveland, Ohio. Fernandez orally furnished information to SA Robert S. Burgins, Jr. and stated that his information was received from a Confidential Source at the *Cleveland Plain Dealer*, whom he did not wish to identify."

316 *For many people, Joe McCarthy*: Depiction of Potter interaction with Joseph R. McCarthy and McCarthy's demise drawn primarily from *Days of Shame* (New York: Signet, 1971), Potter's retrospect book of regret; Farrell, *Nixon*; Morgan, *Reds*; Caute, *The Great Fear*; Griffith, *The Politics of Fear*; *Detroit Free Press*, Nov. 27, 1979; David Nevin, "An Insider's Memoir of a Sinister Era," *Life*, Oct. 1965.

319 *John Stephens Wood had been home in Canton*: Senate Transcripts, Wood nomination to SACB, from Mitchell F. Dolin, Covington and Burling, Oney Papers, Georgia Historical Society; Drew Pearson columns, May 18, 27, 1955; Wood Investigative File, HUAC Papers, National Archives; "Ex-Rep Wood Denies Ever Being in Klan," *Washington Post*, June 21, 1954; interview with John Gollner.

322 *Frank Tavenner still maintained his rural domain*: Account of John Peter Muhlenberg from Woodstock statue memorial; history of Shenandoah County papers at Woodstock Library.

324 *The date was August 18, 1955*: Transcript of HUAC hearing witness Pete Seeger, HUAC files, National Archives.

327 *By the summer of 1955 we had been back in Detroit*: Correspondence with Jean (Maraniss) Alexander and Jim Maraniss.

331 *The FBI visited the OSI office*: EM FBI file, Jan. 1956 summary.

332 *Even as the Red-hunting fervor ebbed*: Account of Arthur Miller and HUAC drawn from Arthur Miller Investigative Name File, HUAC Papers, 52, National Archives; Miller, *Timebends*, 389–94, 449–56. The Miller investigation came after the Youth Board of New York hired him to write the script for a film on juvenile delinquency. His hiring sparked protests by various conservative groups, including the Catholic War Veterans, and attracted the attention of HUAC investigators, who were looking for reasons to hold hearings on the theater world.

335 *Soon after the school year started*: Letter from MM to David Maraniss, July 8, 1991. At the time my mother wrote this letter, I was interested in writing a novel loosely based on our year in Iowa and was conducting research for that inept and aborted attempt at fiction.

337 *If this was a new start for my father, it was a quixotic one*: Account of EM and his colleagues at the *Quint-City Labor's Daily* and *Quint-City Special* drawn from lengthy interviews with Al Maund at his apartment in New Orleans, Sept. 24–25, 1986;

correspondence with Al Maund, Aug. 2, 30, 1986; correspondence with Dorothy Maund, Nov. 14, 1986; correspondence with Robert Meloon, Oct. 31, 1986; letter from EM to David Maraniss, Aug. 27, 1991; correspondence with Nigel Hampton, Nov. 4, 21, 1986; correspondence with and recollections of Jean (Maraniss) Alexander and Jim Maraniss; all copies of *Quint-City Labor's Daily* and *Quint-City Special* from Maund Family Papers.

345 *But at least the FBI was no longer following us*: EM FBI Papers, Oct. 17, 1958, summary report. The reports are so prosaic: "T-1 advised that Elliott Maraniss and his wife Mary Jane [she hated that middle name, and in fact had ditched it by then] and their four children had resided at 1443 Chandler Street in Madison for a little over a year until about the middle of September 1958, when they moved to another house on Regent Street in Madison. T-1 said that ELLIOTT MARANISS was employed as a reporter by the *Capital Times*, a Madison, Wisconsin, daily newspaper and he had evidently been quite successful in this position since he was assigned to the writing of feature stories and articles, on which his name appeared in the newspaper. T-1 advised that one of the assignments handled by ELLIOTT MARANISS was a series of articles on juvenile delinquency in the Madison area, and the informant said that Maraniss in this series, as well as in his other stories, appeared to be a competent reporter, who was objective and fair-minded in his attitude. . . . T-1 advised that no question had arisen concerning the loyalty of Mr. and Mrs. Maraniss since their arrival in Madison, and they appeared to be well regarded in the neighborhood in which they lived."

346 *"Well, the wanderers are wandering again"*: MM letter to Phil Cummins, June 22, 1957. Knowing her brother (and husband) loved sports, MM added, "You could say we're following the Big Ten championship, but I doubt if Wisconsin will make it next year. Or you could say we're doing personal research on the Midwest. In any case, we're heading for Madison."

Epilogue: Second Acts

348 *If we had benefactors*: William Evjue, born in 1882, was already a white-haired progressive legend when we reached Madison in 1957. He lived until 1970, but Miles McMillin, known as Mac, loomed larger during those years and was always supportive of our family. I know I would not have been hired by the *Trenton (NJ) Times* in 1977, when it was owned by the *Washington Post*, had Mac not written a winning letter about me to Richard Harwood, the *Post* editor who was brought up to Trenton to run that paper for a few years. I was covering Congress for the *Post* in 1982 when McMillin, suffering from terminal cancer, shot and killed himself and his wife, Elsie. Mac was retired by then, and he and Elsie were living at her family's Bay Pond estate near Lake Placid, New York. Her family happened to be the Rockefellers; she was the daughter of a grandson of the original William Rockefeller. Before marrying McMillin, Elsie had been married for a decade to William Proxmire, the Democratic senator from Wisconsin. I was in the well of the Senate at the U.S. Capitol talking to Proxmire the day the shootings happened.

350 *When my brother spent a college summer writing*: Jim Maraniss told this story at our father's memorial service. Horribly enough, there were at least two generations of Winkie the elephants who killed young children by slipping their trunks through the iron grills of the cage. Vilas no longer has elephants.

353 *For the most part . . . the judged and their defenders survived*: After retiring from the *Capital Times* in 1983, EM spent a few years in Milwaukee working as a senior adviser to Mayor Henry Meier and often accompanied Meier to U.S. Conference of Mayors conventions. Coleman Young was the mayor of Detroit during that period, and I can only wonder in retrospect whether he and EM ever met and acknowledged their past experiences in Room 740.

354 *John Stephens Wood stayed in Georgia*: *Atlanta Constitution*, Sept. 13, 1968; *Washington Post*, Sept. 14, 1968.

354 *Charles E. Potter . . . lasted only one term in the Senate*: *Washington Post*, Nov. 25, 1979; Potter, *Days of Shame.*

355 *One winter afternoon more than a half-century later*: Notes from reporting trip to Woodstock, Dec. 7, 2016. Among the many interesting things I learned during my time in Woodstock: (1) Fred Painter, who worked as a deputy sheriff there, wrote that during the Prohibition years his pay was based on the number of arrests and warrants served rather than a salary; (2) tobacco was the early money crop in Shenandoah County, and the pay for testifying in court was twenty-five pounds of tobacco in 1779; and (3) it was from the Old Shenandoah House that Gen. Philip Sheridan wrote his famous message back to Washington during the Civil War: "I have made the Shenandoah Valley of Virginia so bare that a crow flying over it would have to carry its knapsack."

355 *Bereniece Baldwin kept testifying*: Interviews with Susan Vella and Michael Wiethoff, Baldwin's grandchildren; Investigative Name Files, Bereniece Baldwin, HUAC Papers, National Archives; Babson et al., *The Color of Law*, 259–60; *Detroit Free Press*, Mar. 19, 1961.

358 *The focus in Bob's retirement story*: *Ann Arbor News*, July 29, 1978.

359 *Why it took my parents and uncle so long to reject*: Correspondence with Jean (Maraniss) Alexander and Jim Maraniss, Apr. 2018.

361 *Until then he did not know the full story*: Letter from Jim Maraniss to Bob Cummins, spring 1981. Although the letter is undated, Jim mentions that he is writing after a visit to San Antonio, where he participated in a symposium on Pedro Calderón de la Barca on the three hundredth anniversary of the Spanish playwright's death. Jim is a Calderón scholar.

361 *It was in the summer of 2006 when we gathered at the cemetery*: I wrote about the graveside ceremony in "Crossing the Water," an essay in *Into the Story* (New York: Simon & Schuster, 2010): "My parents left Wisconsin forever last Saturday morning at dawn. Their ashes were contained in two urns in the trunk of my car—my dad's made of solid wood, my mom's of intricate cloisonné. The August morning sky was high and cloudless, so soft and blue it hurt, like the sound of a melodious cello hurts. The world never seems more achingly fragile than on a late-summer day when you can sense something slipping away."

Selected Bibliography

Appleman, Roy E. *The War in the Pacific.* Washington, DC, Department of the Army, 1947.

Babson, Steve, Dave Riddle, and David Elsila. *The Color of Law.* Detroit, Wayne State Press, 2010.

Barbas, Samantha. *The First Lady of Hollywood.* Berkeley, University of California Press, 2005.

Bayley, Edwin R. *Joe McCarthy and the Press.* Madison, University of Wisconsin Press, 1981.

Beeching, William C. *Canadian Volunteers: Spain 1936–1939.* Regina, Saskatchewan, University of Regina Press, 1989.

Bernstein, Carl. *Loyalties.* New York, Simon and Schuster, 1989.

Bernstein, Walter. *Inside Out.* New York, Knopf, 1996.

Bessie, Alvah. *Men in Battle.* New York, Scribner's, 1939.

Brater, Enoch. *Arthur Miller.* New York, Thames and Hudson, 2005.

Carroll, Peter N. *The Odyssey of the Abraham Lincoln Brigade.* Stanford, CA, Stanford University Press, 1994.

Caute, David. *The Great Fear.* New York, Simon and Schuster, 1978.

Chambers, Whittaker. *Witness.* New York, Random House, 1952.

Cogley, John. *Report on Blacklisting.* New York, Fund for the Republic, 1956.

Cohen, Robert. *When the Old Left Was Young.* New York, Oxford University Press, 1993.

Communism in the Detroit Area, Hearings before the Committee on Un-American Activities, House of Representatives. 82nd Congress, 2nd Session. Parts 1–2. Washington, DC, Government Printing Office, 1952.

Cowley, Malcolm. *The Dream of the Golden Mountains.* New York, Viking Press, 1964.

Eatwell, Robert. *Fascism: A History.* London, Pimlico, 2003.

Eby, Cecil. *Comrades and Commissars.* University Park, Pennsylvania State University Press, 2007.

Farrell, John A. *Richard Nixon.* New York, Doubleday, 2017.

Frankel, Glenn. *High Noon.* New York, Bloomsbury USA, 2017.

Griffith, Robert. *The Politics of Fear.* Amherst, University of Massachusetts Press, 1970.

Halberstam, David. *The Fifties.* New York, Villard Books, 1993.

Hemingway, Ernest. *For Whom the Bell Tolls.* New York, Scribner, 1940.

Hernández, Miguel. *Poemas Sociales, de Guerra y de Muerte.* Madrid, Alianza Editorial, 1977.

Hoar, Victor. *The Mackenzie-Papineau Battalion.* Toronto, Copp Clark, 1969.

Hochschild, Adam. *Spain in Our Hearts.* Boston, Houghton Mifflin Harcourt, 2016.

Jackson, Angela. *At the Margins of Mayhem.* Pontypool, UK, Warren & Pell, 2008.

Kazan, Elia. *A Life.* New York, Knopf, 1988.

Klingaman, William K. *Encyclopedia of the McCarthy Era.* New York, Facts on File, 1996.

Kutler, Stanley. *The American Inquisition.* New York, Hill and Wang, 1982.

Lee, Ulysses. *The Employment of Negro Troops.* Washington, DC, Center of Military History, 1963.

Martelle, Scott. *The Fear Within.* Piscataway, NJ, Rutgers University Press, 2011.

Mason, Gabriel. *Gabriel Blows His Horn.* Philadelphia, Dorrance, 1972.

Mason, Gabriel, editor. *Great American Liberals.* New York, Starr King Press, 1956.

Miller, Arthur. *The Portable Arthur Miller.* New York, Viking Press, 1971.

Miller, Arthur. *The Theater Essays of Arthur Miller.* New York, Viking Press, 1978.

Miller, Arthur. *Timebends.* New York, Grove Press, 1987.

Miller, Edward G. *A Dark and Bloody Ground.* College Station, Texas A&M Press, 1994.

Morgan, Ted. *Reds.* New York, Random House, 2003.

Murphy, Brenda. *Congressional Theatre.* Cambridge, UK, Cambridge University Press, 1999.

Navasky, Victor S. *Naming Names.* New York, Hill and Wang, 1980.

Neugass, James. *War Is Beautiful.* New York, New Press, 2008.

Oney, Steve. *And the Dead Shall Rise.* New York, Vintage Books, 2003.

Orwell, George. *Homage to Catalonia.* London, Secker & Warburg, 1938.

Pearson, Drew. *Diaries: 1949–1959.* New York, Holt, Rinehart, 1974.

Roth, Norman. *Conversos, Inquisition, and the Expulsion of the Jews from Spain.* Madison, University of Wisconsin Press, 1995.

Watt, George. *The Comet Connection.* Lexington, University Press of Kentucky, 1990.

Weaver, Michael E. *Guard Wars.* Bloomington, Indiana University Press, 2010.

Wright, Nathan. *The Making of a Champion: George Crockett's Life Story.* New York, Black Media, Inc., unpublished manuscript.

Illustration Credits

Index

About the Author

David Maraniss is an associate editor at *The Washington Post* and a distinguished visiting professor at Vanderbilt University. He has won two Pulitzer Prizes for journalism and was a finalist three other times. Among his bestselling books are biographies of Bill Clinton, Barack Obama, Roberto Clemente, and Vince Lombardi, and a trilogy about the 1960s—*Rome 1960; Once in a Great City* (winner of the RFK Book Prize); and *They Marched into Sunlight* (winner of the J. Anthony Lukas Prize and Pulitzer Finalist in History). *A Good American Family* is his twelfth book.

"One of our most talented biographers and historians."

—*The New York Times*

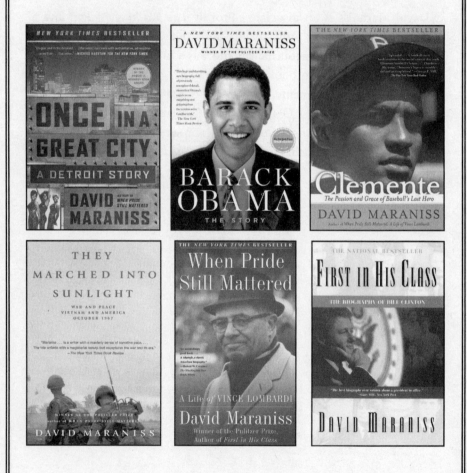